THE LAW OF DEPENDANTS' RELIEF IN CANADA

by

Cameron Harvey, Q.C.

CARSWELL
Thomson Professional Publishing

The publisher is not engaged in rendering legal, accounting or other professional advice. If legal advice or other expert assistance is required, the services of a competent professional should be sought. The analysis contained herein represents the opinions of the authors and should in no way be construed as being either official or unofficial policy of any governmental body.

This work reproduces official English language versions of federal statutes and/or regulations. As this material also exists in official French language form, the reader is advised that reference to the official French language version may be warranted in appropriate circumstances.

The paper used in this publication meets the minimum requirements of the American National Standard for Information Sciences—Permanence of Paper for Printed Library Materials, ANSI Z39.48-1984.

Canadian Cataloguing in Publication Data

Harvey, Cameron, 1939-
The law of dependants' relief in Canada

Includes bibliographical references and index.
ISBN 0-459-27075-3

1. Decendents' family maintenance – Canada. I. Title.

KE831.H37 1999 346.7105'2 C99-930758-4
KF778.H37 1999

CARSWELL
Thomson Professional Publishing

One Corporate Plaza, 2075 Kennedy Road, Scarborough, Ontario M1T 3V4
Customer Service:
Toronto: 1-416-609-3800
Elsewhere in Canada/U.S. 1-800-387-5164
Fax 1-416-298-5094

For Linda

Preface

When I commenced my law teaching career in 1966 there were very few books about Canadian law. Writers had a wide choice of virgin areas of the law. Now for almost every area of the law there is a book and, indeed, many more narrowly focused books within general areas of the law. Old growth areas are a rarity. Dependants' relief legislation is one such area. I am not forgetting Leopold Amighetti's *The Law of Dependants' Relief in British Columbia* (Toronto: Carswell, 1991). It is an excellent treatise on the law of British Columbia up to the time of its publication. However, its focus is the law of British Columbia and even for British Columbia it pre-dates the Supreme Court of Canada decision in *Tataryn v. Tataryn Estate*, which settled the long standing judicial debate in the courts of British Columbia concerning their primary jurisdiction under the *Wills Variation Act*. Aside from Amighetti's book, there are chapters in Feeney's *The Canadian Law of Wills, Probate*, 3rd ed., 1987; Macdonell, Sheard & Hull's *Probate Practice*, 4th ed., 1996; Holland Stalbecker-Pountney's *Co-Habitation: The Law in Canada*, 1990; several commentaries on Part V of the *Succession Law Reform Act* of Ontario listed in the bibliography (especially by Hoffstein, Hull, Oosterhoff, and Schnurr and Woodley), and the C.E.D. treatments.

This book attempts a treatment of the law in all of the Canadian provinces and territories. But, given the Amighetti treatise, which continues to be useful for many matters not affected by the *Tataryn* decision, this book, while dealing to a large extent with B.C. law and updating Amighetti, assumes that for a complete treatment of B.C. law readers will also canvass Amighetti. After the initial reference to Amighetti on p. 1 of the following text, reference is made to Amighetti simply as Amighetti. Similarly, *Probate Practice* by Macdonell, Sheard & Hull is cited simply by the authors' names.

I thank the Legal Research Institute of my Faculty of Law for its funding the helpful research assistance I received from Duncan Fraser and Tarya Harapiuk while they were law students. Also, I express my huge gratitude to Sue Law for her ever proficient word processing of the evolving text and footnotes. Finally, I am very grateful to Jane McDonald at Carswell for her encouragement and assistance and to her colleague Lorraine Aston for her editorial rescues.

Cameron Harvey
Professor,
Robson Hall
Faculty of Law
University of Manitoba,
October, 1998

Table of Contents

Alphabetical Table of Cases

Analytical Table of Cases

The following Table groups dependants' relief cases by province and territory. Two abbreviations are used. With British Columbia, "*Tataryn*" refers to *Tataryn v. Tataryn Estate*, [1994] 2 S.C.R. 807, the leading decision for the *Wills Variation Act*; with Ontario, "SLRA" refers to the *Succession Law Reform Act*, Part V, R.S.O. 1990, c. 488.

British Columbia Post-*Tataryn*

British Columbia Pre-*Tataryn*

Manitoba

New Brunswick

Newfoundland

Northwest Territories

Nova Scotia

Ontario (SLRA)

Ontario (Pre-SLRA)

Flannigan v. Ontario (Registrar of Motor Vehicles), [1950] O.W.N. 789 (Ont. Master) 169, 170, 171
Gold, Re (1975), 8 O.R. (2d) 694, 22 R.F.L. 280, 59 D.L.R. (3d) 58 (Ont. Surr. Ct.) 89, 91
Hannah, Re (1931), 39 O.W.N. 499 (Ont. C.A.) 201
Hull, Re, [1943] O.R. 778, [1944] 1 D.L.R. 14 (Ont. C.A.) 73, 74, 86, 87, 89, 157, 161, 232, 233
Hunt, Re, [1940] O.W.N. 408 (Ont. H.C.) 97
Jenkins, Re, [1955] O.W.N. 958 (Ont. Surr. Ct.), reversed [1956] O.W.N. 548, 3 D.L.R. (2d) 561 (Ont. C.A.) 95, 131
Jervas, Re (1953), [1954] O.W.N. 48 (Ont. C.A.) 86, 89
Jones, Re (1974), 6 O.R. (2d) 11, 19 R.F.L. 289, 51 D.L.R. (3d) 655 (Ont. H.C.) 49
Kerby, Re, [1949] O.W.N. 187 (Ont. Co. Ct.) 67
Knoll, Re, [1938] O.W.N. 282 (Ont. H.C.) 69
Laur, Re (1975), 7 O.R. (2d) 385, 21 R.F.L. 159, 55 D.L.R. (3d) 321 (Ont. Surr. Ct.) 48, 112
McCaffery, Re, [1931] O.R. 512, [1931] 4 D.L.R. 930 (Ont. C.A.) 3, 67, 68, 114, 183, 195, 199
Rankin, Re (1950), [1951] O.W.N. 121 (Ont. C.A.) 73
Rice, Re, [1952] O.W.N. 465 (Ont. H.C.) 199
Smith, Re, [1958] O.W.N. 415 (Ont. H.C.) 67, 68, 131
Soroka, Re (1975), 10 O.R. (2d) 638, 64 D.L.R. (3d) 234, 25 R.F.L. 169 (Ont. H.C.) 75, 85, 112, 116, 130, 160, 184
Stapleton, Re (1953), [1954] O.W.N. 132, [1954] 2 D.L.R. 107 (Ont. C.A.) 73
Stewart, Re, [1944] O.W.N. 380 (Ont. C.A.) 82-83, 85
Weir, Re (1962), [1963] 1 O.R. 53 (Ont. C.A.) 96
Winter, Re, [1954] O.W.N. 726, [1955] 1 D.L.R. 134 (Ont. H.C.) 69
Zajac v. Zwarycz, [1965] 1 O.R. 575, 49 D.L.R. (2d) 52 (Ont. C.A.) 75, 160

Prince Edward Island

Flood, Re (1978), 20 Nfld. & P.E.I.R. 448, 53 A.P.R. 448 (P.E.I. S.C.) . . . 42, 98, 116, 132
MacDonald v. MacKenzie Estate (1989), 64 D.L.R. (4th) 476, 36 E.T.R. 176, 78 Nfld. & P.E.I.R. 76, 244 A.P.R. 76 (P.E.I. T.D.) 50, 54, 89, 94, 157
Millar, Re (1976), 12 Nfld. & P.E.I.R. 440, 25 A.P.R. 440, 71 D.L.R. (3d) 120 (P.E.I. S.C.) 143
Sentner Estate, Re (1985), 54 Nfld. & P.E.I.R. 181, 160 A.P.R. 181, 24 E.T.R. 236 (P.E.I. S.C.), reversed (1986), 63 Nfld. & P.E.I.R. 151, 194 A.P.R. 151, 26 E.T.R. 69 (P.E.I. C.A.) 157, 177

Saskatchewan

Adams v. Irvine (1978), 4 R.F.L. (2d) 295 (Sask. Q.B.) 48, 74, 85, 112
Baker, Re (1919), [1920] 1 W.W.R. 259, 13 Sask. L.R. 109, 50 D.L.R. 422 (Sask. C.A.) 157
Bateman, Re (1965), 55 D.L.R. (2d) 763 (Sask. Q.B.) 130, 146, 154, 157, 188
Belaney v. Perrier, [1939] 3 W.W.R. 591, [1940] 1 D.L.R. 105 (Sask. K.B.) . . . 47, 112, 184
Berezowsky v. Berezowsky (1975), 23 R.F.L. 26 (Sask. Q.B.) 170
Berry, Re (1966), 58 W.W.R. 187 (Sask. Q.B.) 74, 130
Black v. Kronberger Estate (1989), 81 Sask. R. 106 (Sask. Q.B.), affirmed (1990), 83 Sask. R. 73 (Sask. C.A.) 48, 97, 116, 132, 154, 232

Yukon Territory

Non-Canadian

1

Introduction

Given the nature of this book, the historical evolution of dependants' relief legislation will not be treated in depth. For more on the historical evolution a good source with which to commence is Leopold Amighetti's, *The Law of Dependants' Relief in British Columbia.*[1] Suffice it to point out that New Zealand led the way in dependants' relief legislation, with its *Testator's Family Maintenance Act*, 1900,[2] and was followed by the Australian state of Victoria in 1906.[3] Alberta[4] and Saskatchewan,[5] in 1910, were the first Canadian provinces to enact such legislation. During the next sixty-four years the group gradually expanded to include all of the Australian states and Canadian provinces and the United Kingdom: Tasmania, 1912;[6] Queensland, 1914;[7] New South Wales, 1916;[8] South Australia, 1918;[9] Western Australia[10] and British Columbia, 1920;[11] Ontario[12] and the Capital[13] and Northern[14] Territories of Australia, 1929; the Uniform Law

---

1 (Toronto: Carswell, 1991) at 1-23 [hereinafter Amighetti]. See also Bale "Limitation on Testamentary Dispositions in Canada" (1964) 42 C.B.R. 367 and Feeney, T., *The Canadian Law of Wills Probate*, 3rd ed. (Toronto: Butterworths, 1987) at 257.

2 The *Testator's Family Maintenance Act*, S.N.Z. 1900, c. 20.

3 *Widows and Young Children Maintenance Act*, 1906.

4 The *Married Women's Relief Act*, S.A. 1910, c. 18 (2nd Sess.).

5 *Devolution of Estates Amendment Act*, S.S. 1910-11, c. 13.

6 The *Testator's Family Maintenance Act*, 1912, 3 Geo. V, No. 7.

7 The *Testator's Family Maintenance Act*, 1914, 5 Geo. V, No. 26.

8 *Testator's Family Maintenance & Guardianship Act*, S.N.S.W. 1916, No. 41.

9 *Testator's Family Maintenance Act*, 1918.

10 *Guardianship of Infants Act*, 1920, s. 11.

11 *Testator's Family Maintenance Act*, S.B.C. 1920, c. 94.

12 The *Dependants' Relief Act, 1929*, S.O. 1929, c. 47.

13 *Administration and Probate Ordinance*, 1929, No. 18, Part VII.

14 *Testator's Family Maintenance Ordinance*, 1929.

Conference of Canada, 1945;[15] Manitoba, 1946;[16] Nova Scotia, 1956;[17] New Brunswick, 1959;[18] Newfoundland[19] and the Yukon,[20] 1962; the Northwest Territories, 1971;[21] and finally Prince Edward Island, 1974.[22]

Dependants' relief legislation has changed over the years, at least in some jurisdictions. For instance, the initial Alberta and Saskatchewan legislation provided only for widows and only when a husband died testate; generally, the legislation has become more inclusive, both in terms of who can apply and the "estate" from which judicial awards can be made. While there is a substantial commonality in the legislation throughout the Commonwealth common law world, there are differences and therefore it is necessary to check the legislative context of an apparently helpful case.[23] Similarly, in *Currie v. Currie Estate*[24] Justice Bastarache advocated "reviewing old cases with a critical eye because of the need to adapt the exercise of judicial discretion to present social norms". It is important to be careful of dicta stating that despite differences in the wording of the primary jurisdiction sections, the jurisdiction of the courts in all places is the same.[25] One fundamental difference between the Acts of some places compared to others is whether the jurisdiction of the court is only to take care of the financial need of the applicant(s) or also to enforce either a moral claim of a dependant or a moral obligation on the deceased to give a fair share of the estate to immediate family members. All of the Acts create a discretionary jurisdiction in a court, rather than a proprietary right for the defined dependants in the deceased's estate and, subject to language of

---

15 The Testators Family Maintenance Act, Proceedings of the Twenty-Seventh Annual Meeting of the Conference of Commissioners on Uniformity of Legislation in Canada (Montreal, August 23-28, 1945) at 105-16. The 1974 Proceedings, (Minaki, Ontario, August 19-23) at 233, indicate that the 1945 Act was adopted, more or less, by B.C., Alta., Sask., Man., N.B., and N.S.; the 1945 Act was withdrawn in 1974 and not replaced.

16 The *Testator's Family Maintenance Act*, S.M. 1946, c. 64.

17 *Testators Family Maintenance Act*, S.N.S. 1956, c. 8.

18 *Testators Family Maintenance Act*, S.N.B. 1959, c. 14.

19 The *Family Relief Act, 1962*, S.N. 1962, c. 56.

20 *Dependants' Relief Ordinance, 1929*, O.Y.T. 1962 (1st Sess.), c. 9.

21 *Dependants Relief Act*, O.N.W.T. 1971 (2nd Sess.), c. 5.

22 *Testator's Dependants Relief Act*, S.P.E.I., 1974, c. 47.

23 *Meyer v. Capital Trust Corp.*, [1948] S.C.R. 329 (S.C.C.) at 331; *Gilles v. Althouse* (1975), [1976] 1 S.C.R. 353 (S.C.C.) at 359-60. Also Schnurr, B. Woodley, S. "Dependant Support Proceedings" (1995) 14 E.T.J. 159 at 167.

24 (1995), 166 N.B.R. (2d) 144 (N.B. C.A.) at paragraph 17.

25 *Shaw v. Regina (City)*, [1944] 1 W.W.R. 433 (Sask. C.A.) at 439, affirmed (1944), [1945] S.C.R. 42 (S.C.C.); *Re Lawther* (1947), 55 Man. R. 142 (Man. K.B.) at 149–151; *Re Willan Estate* (1951), 4 W.W.R. (N.S.) 114 (Alta. S.C.) at 127–28; *Re Maitland* (1954), 10 W.W.R. (N.S.) 673 (Alta. C.A.) at 667-78; *Re Cole* (1958), 40 M.P.R. 201 (N.S. T.D.) at 213; *Nelson v. Nelson* (1977), 17 N.B.R. (2d) 457 (N.B. C.A.) at paragraph 9.

Tataryn v. Tataryn Estate,[26] they do not impose any testamentary duty although they do restrict testamentary freedom.[27]

It has been said that as dependants' relief legislation infringes upon testamentary freedom it must be strictly construed[28] and that the courts will not readily change either the testamentary or, presumably, the intestate distribution of an estate.[29] On the other hand, this legislation has been described as remedial, deserving a liberal interpretation;[30]the willingness of the courts of some jurisdictions, including the Supreme Court of Canada,[31] to construe their jurisdiction as including the power to enforce either a moral obligation on spouses and parents to give a fair portion of their estate to their surviving spouse and children or a moral claim of a dependant suggests a remedial characterization; similarly, the willingness of some courts to anticipate subsequent statutory enlargements of the definitions of some dependants,[32] to allow spouses to apply notwithstanding that they have contracted out of that right, and to extend the application limitation period are indicative of a remedial, to-be-construed-liberally characterization.

The footnotes in the following chapters do not refer to the various provincial dependants' relief statutes by name; reference is only by an abbreviation of the province and section numbers and if to more than one Act then they are listed geographically west to east. Currently, the names of the Acts are: British Columbia *Wills Variation Act*,[33] Alberta *Family*

---

26 [1994] 2 S.C.R. 807 (S.C.C.), reconsideration refused (1994), 5 E.T.R. (2d) 210 (note) (S.C.C.).

27 *Re Willan Estate, supra* note 25 at 134; *Dower v. Alberta (Public Trustee)* (1962), 38 W.W.R. 129 (Alta. T.D.) at 135–37; *Hayzel v. Alberta (Public Trustee)* (1963), 44 W.W.R. 582 (Alta. T.D.) at 587; *Pauliuk v. Pauliuk* (1986), 48 Alta. L.R. (2d) 25 (Alta. Q.B.) at 29; *Golverk-Berger v. Berger Estate* (1986), 22 E.T.R. 195 (Ont. Surr. Ct.), amended (May 30, 1986), Doc. York 5345/80 (Ont. Surr. Ct.); *W. (D.J.) (Litigation Guardian of) v. W. (L.) Estate* (1994), 122 Sask. R. 299 (Sask. Q.B.) at paragraph 27, affirmed [1996] 2 W.W.R. 593, 137 Sask. R. 286, 107 W.A.C. 286 (Sask. C.A.).

28 For example, *Re McCaffery*, [1931] O.R. 512 (Ont. C.A.) at 517; *Re Willan Estate, supra* note 25 at 127 and 135-36.

29 *Beasley v. Willet* (1972), 4 N.B.R. (2d) 122 (N.B. Q.B.) at 126; *Re Hurley Estate* (1973), 8 N.B.R. (2d) 569 (N.B. Q.B.) at 575. Also see *infra*.

30 *Re Hourston*, [1919] 1 W.W.R. 521 (Alta. C.A.) at 522; *Barr v. Barr* (1971), 25 D.L.R. (3d) 401 (Man. C.A.) at 410; *Re Mannion* (1984), 45 O.R. (2d) 339 (Ont. C.A.) at 342; *Goldhar v. Goldhar* (1985), (*sub nom. Re Goldhar's Estate*) 21 E.T.R. 189 (Ont. Div. Ct.) at 194, reversed (April 8, 1986), Dubin J.A., Houlden J.A., Krever J.A. (Ont. C.A.).

31 *Tataryn v. Tataryn Estate, supra* note 26.

32 For instance, *Re Lawther*, [1947] 1 W.W.R. 577 (Man. K.B.) at 579; *Trainor v. Toronto General Trusts Corp.* (1953), 8 W.W.R. (N.S.) 465 (Man. C.A.) at 471; and *Re McAdam* (1925), 35 B.C.R. 547 (B.C. S.C.) at 549 regarding adopted children.

33 R.S.B.C. 1996, c. 490.

Relief Act,[34] Saskatchewan *Dependants' Relief Act, 1996*,[35] Manitoba *Dependants Relief Act*,[36] Ontario *Succession Law Reform Act* Part V,[37] New Brunswick *Provision for Dependants Act*,[38] Nova Scotia *Testators' Family Maintenance Act*,[39] Prince Edward Island *Dependants of a Deceased Person Relief Act*,[40] Newfoundland *Family Relief Act*,[41] Northwest Territories *Dependants Relief Act*,[42] Yukon Territory *Dependants Relief Act*.[43]

As is evident in the names of the current statutes and their predecessors in notes 11-22, the terms Testators and Dependants are variously spelled Testators, Testator's, Testators', Dependants, Dependant's, and Dependants'. I choose to use the word dependants' in phrases such as, dependants' relief legislation or dependants' relief proceeding.

34 R.S.A. 1980, c. F-2.
35 S.S. 1996, c. D-25.01.
36 S.M. 1989-90, c. 42; C.C.S.M., c. D37.
37 R.S.O. 1990, c. S.26.
38 R.S.N.B. 1973, c. P-22.3
39 R.S.N.S. 1989, c. 465.
40 R.S.P.E.I. 1988, c. D-7.
41 R.S.N. 1990, c. F-2.
42 R.S.N.W.T. 1988, c. D-4.
43 R.S.Y.T. 1990, c. 44.

2

The Primary Jurisdiction

1. BACKGROUND

Each of the provincial dependants' relief Acts contains a primary jurisdiction section, plus several supplementary jurisdiction sections. The primary jurisdiction section in the Ontario *Succession Law Reform Act*[1] reads:

> **Order for support**
> **58.** (1) Where a deceased, whether testate or intestate, has not made adequate provision for the proper support of his dependants or any of them, the court, on application, may order that such provision as it considers adequate be made out of the estate of the deceased for the proper support of the dependants or any of them.

The Alberta *Family Relief Act*,[2] New Brunswick *Provision for Dependants Act*,[3] Nova Scotia *Testators' Family Maintenance Act*,[4] Prince Edward Island *Dependants of a Deceased Person Relief Act*,[5] Newfoundland *Family Relief Act*,[6] the Northwest Territories *Dependants Relief Act*[7] and the Yukon Territory *Dependants Relief Act*[8] contain an identical or virtually identical section.

The primary jurisdiction section in the Saskatchewan *Dependants' Relief Act, 1996*[9] is a slight variation:

> **Maintenance order**
> **6.** (1) . . . if on an application the court is of the opinion that the deceased has disposed of real or personal property in a manner that reasonable provision

1 R.S.O. 1990, c. S. 26, Pt. V. [hereinafter Ontario Act].
2 R.S.A. 1980, c. F-2, s. 3(1) [hereinafter Alberta Act].
3 R.S.N.B. 1973, c. P-22.3, s. 2(1) [hereinafter New Brunswick Act].
4 R.S.N.S. 1989, c. 465, s. 3(1) [hereinafter Nova Scotia Act].
5 R.S.P.E.I. 1988, c. D-7, s. 2(1) [hereinafter Prince Edward Island Act].
6 R.S.N. 1990, c. F-2, s. 3(1) [hereinafter Newfoundland Act].
7 R.S.N.W.T. 1988, c. D-4, s. 2(1) [hereinafter Northwest Territories Act].
8 R.S.Y.T. 1990, c. 44, s. 2 [hereinafter Yukon Act].
9 S.S. 1996, c. D-25.01 [hereinafter Saskatchewan Act].

has not been made for the maintenance of the dependant to whom the application relates, the court may order that provision be made from the deceased's estate for maintenance of the dependant in an amount that the court considers reasonable.

The primary jurisdiction section in the British Columbia *Wills Variation Act*[10] reads:

Maintenance from estate

2. Despite any law or statute to the contrary, if a testator dies leaving a will that does not, in the court's opinion, make adequate provision for the proper maintenance and support of the testator's wife, husband or children, the court may, in its discretion, in an action by or on behalf of the wife, husband or children, order that the provision that it thinks adequate, just and equitable in the circumstances be made out of the testator's estate for the wife, husband or children.

The Manitoba *Dependants Relief Act*[11] contains a distinctive primary jurisdiction section:

Reasonable provision for dependant

2. (1) If it appears to the court that a dependant is in financial need, the court, on application by or on behalf of the dependant, may order that reasonable provision be made out of the estate of the deceased for the maintenance and support of the dependant.

Aside from an issue of whether an applicant qualifies as a dependant,[12] these sections create a two-step consideration for the court.[13] First, the court must determine whether the deceased, by will or by allowing the estate to be distributed on an intestacy, has made adequate or reasonable provision for the proper support or the maintenance (and support) of the applicant. If the answer is no, the second consideration is what order will be reasonable or adequate (just and equitable) for the proper support or maintenance of

10 R.S.B.C. 1996, c. 490 [hereinafter British Columbia Act].

11 S.M. 1989-90, c. 42; C.C.S.M., c. D37 [hereinafter Manitoba Act].

12 This issue arises respecting the legality of marriages, foreign divorces, and adoptions, and respecting co-habitees and illegitimate, *loco parentis*, step, and over-age children. It serves no purpose to list exemplary cases here; they can be found in Chapter 3, 7 *Stay of Distribution of the Estate* and 4, 2(b)(ii) *Nature*. The right of separated wives to apply has been confirmed in so many cases that it can no longer be made an issue.

13 *Re Willan Estate* (1951), 4 W.W.R. (N.S.) 114 (Alta. S.C.) at 135; *Shaw v. Regina (City)* (1943), [1944] 1 W.W.R. 433 (Sask. C.A.) at 438, affirmed (1944), [1945] S.C.R. 42, [1945] 1 D.L.R. 353 (S.C.C.); *Garrett v. Zwicker* (1976), 15 N.S.R. (2d) 118, (N.S. C.A.) at paragraphs 11, 35, 42; *Re Protopappas Estate* (1987), 25 E.T.R. 241 (Alta. Q.B.) at 249; *Tataryn v. Tataryn Estate*, [1994] 2 S.C.R. 807 (S.C.C.) at 814, reconsideration refused 5 E.T.R. (2d) 210 (note), [1994] 9 W.W.R. lxxiii, 95 B.C.L.R. (2d) xxxiii (S.C.C.). Also, Hull, R. and Hull, I. eds., *Macdonell, Sheard & Hull on Probate Practice*, 4th ed. (Toronto: Carswell, 1996) at 131-32 [hereinafter Macdonell, Sheard & Hull].

the applicant? Not so obvious, except respecting the Manitoba Act, is the purpose or purposes for which the legislatures have created this jurisdiction in the courts. Certainly, one purpose is to provide appropriately for the financial need and maintenance of statutorily defined dependants. There may be a second purpose, either to enforce a moral obligation of spouses and parents to give a fair share of their estates to the surviving spouse and issue, or to give effect to a moral claim which statutorily defined dependants may have upon the deceased's estate.

Up to the 1980s Canadian judges often referred to four cases, namely *Allardice v. Allardice*,[14] *Allen v. Manchester*,[15] *Bosch v. Perpetual Trust Co. Ltd.*,[16] and *Walker v. McDermott*.[17] Although these cases are not commonly cited or quoted currently, they continue to be of foundational importance. The *Allardice*, *Allen*, and *Bosch* cases were decided with respect to New Zealand and New South Wales statutes which provided:

> If any person dying . . . disposes . . . of his property . . . in such manner that the widow husband, or children . . . are left without adequate provision for their proper maintenance (and support) (education or advancement in life) . . . the Court may at its discretion and taking into consideration all the circumstances of the case . . . order that such provision . . . as the Court thinks fit shall be made out of the estate . . .

In *Allardice* Chief Justice Stout wrote:

> The question what principles the Court should follow is raised in this appeal . . . In my opinion these rules may be summarized as follows: 1, That the Act is something more than a statute to extend the provisions in the Destitute Persons Act; 2, that the Act is not a statute to empower the Court to make a new will for a testator; 3, that the Act allows the Court to alter a testator's disposition of his property only so far as it is necessary to provide for the proper maintenance and support of "wife, husband, or children" where adequate provision has not been made for their proper maintenance and support by the will of the testator; 4, that, in the case of a widow, at all events, if not in the case of a widower, the Court will make more ample provision than in the case of children, if the children are physically and mentally able to maintain and support themselves. . . .
>
> "Support," it has been held, at all events, in the case of a widow, does not mean merely having a supply of food and clothing. It means, it has been held, such kind of maintenance as the widow during the life of her husband has been accustomed to. The matter that should be considered, both as to widow and children, is how she or they have been maintained in the past. A child, for

14 The N.Z.C.A. decision (1910), 29 N.Z.L.R. 959 (New Zealand C.A.), affirmed [1911] A.C. 730 (New Zealand P.C.), not the subsequent J.C.P.C. decision.

15 [1922] N.Z.L.R. 218 (New Zealand S.C. In Banco).

16 [1938] A.C. 463 (South Wales P.C.).

17 (1930), [1931] S.C.R. 94 (S.C.C.).

> example, that has been living on a father's bounty could not be expected to begin the battle of life without means. A child, however, who had maintained her or himself, and had perhaps accumulated means, might well be expected to be able to fight the battle of life without any extraneous aid. But even in such a case, if the fight was a great struggle, and some aid might help, and the means of the testator were great, the Court might, in my opinion, properly give aid. The whole circumstances have to be considered. Even in many cases where the Court comes to a decision that the will is most unjust from a moral point of view, that is not enough to make the Court alter the testator's disposition of his property. The first inquiry in every case must be what is the need of maintenance and support; and the second, what property has the testator left.[18]

In the same case Justice Edwards wrote:

> I think that the duty of the Court . . . may be thus best expressed: It is the duty of the Court, so far as is possible, to place itself in all respects in the position of the testator, and to consider whether or not, having regard to all existing facts and surrounding circumstances, the testator has been guilty of a manifest breach of that moral duty which a just, but not a loving, husband or father owes towards his wife or towards his children, as the case may be. If the Court finds that the testator has been plainly guilty of a breach of such moral duty, then it is the duty of the Court to make such an order as appears to be sufficient, but no more than sufficient, to repair it. In the discharge of that duty the Court to make such an order as appears to be sufficient, but no more than sufficient, to repair it. In the discharge of that duty the Court should never lose sight of the fact that at best it can but very imperfectly place itself in the position of the testator, or appreciate the motives which have swayed him in the disposition of his property, or the justification which he may really have for what appears to be an unjust will.[19]

and finally Justice Cooper wrote:

> In *Plimmer v. Plimmer* in the Supreme Court, in a judgment which has not been reported, I stated what was, in my opinion, the principle upon which the Court should exercise its discretion in the case of a widow claiming against the estate of her husband . . . I said: What is an adequate provision for the wife of a testator is a question which depends: 1, upon the station in life of the parties; 2, upon the age, health, and general circumstances of the wife; 3, upon the means possessed by the testator at the time of his death; and 4, upon any property or means which the wife possesses in her own right. What would be an adequate provision for the wife of an artisan or a labouring man who died possessed of a comparatively small estate would be inadequate for the wife of a prosperous tradesman or a wealthy merchant or professional man. What would be an adequate provision for the wife of a man who died possessed of

---

18 *Supra* note 14 at 969-70.

19 *Ibid.* at 972-73.

> an estate of £20,000 would be inadequate for the wife of a millionaire. So also what might be considered sufficient for a woman in the prime of life, of robust health, and capable in mind and body might be insufficient for a woman of advanced years or in ill health.
>
> These observations, in my opinion, state a reasonable rule applicable to the claims of the widow of a testator. I think that the widow of a testator may stand in a different position to a widower or children of a testator. In the present case we have only to consider the position of the children. In my opinion it is impossible to lay down, except in very elastic terms, any general rule in such a case, for many factors have to be considered. The condition of life of the testator and the children, the sex, age, and health of the children, whether, if daughters, they are married, or, if sons, they are of sufficient health and strength to earn a reasonable maintenance for themselves or those dependent upon them in the condition of life in which they have been brought up, are necessary factors, as no doubt also to some extent is the value of the property left by the testator. But the Court has no jurisdiction to do more than to secure an adequate provision according to the condition in life of the children, measured to some extent by the estate left by their parent, and guarding also the interests of those who have an equal claim upon the particular testator but who have been provided for in the testator's will. I repeat that we have no power to recast the testator's will or to redress inequalities or fancied injustice, but only to secure a sufficient provision for the proper maintenance and support of those children of the testator who have been left by him without proper and adequate means of support. This general rule is, I think, the governing principle. Its application depends upon all the circumstances of each particular case.[20]

Bosch v. Perpetual Trust Co. had to do with the same New South Wales section. Lord Romer wrote:

> The first thing to be noticed is that the powers given to the Court only arise when any of the persons mentioned is left without adequate provision for his or her proper maintenance, which word will be used in this judgment where necessary as including education and advancement. The use of the word "proper" in this connection is of considerable importance. It connotes something different from the word "adequate." A small sum may be sufficient for the "adequate" maintenance of a child, for instance, but, having regard to the child's station in life and the fortune of his father, it may be wholly insufficient for his "proper" maintenance. So, too, a sum may be quite insufficient for the "adequate" maintenance of a child and yet may be sufficient for his maintenance on a scale that is "proper" in all the circumstances. A father with a large family and a small fortune can often only afford to leave each of his children a sum insufficient for his "adequate" maintenance. Nevertheless, such sum cannot be described as not providing for his "proper" maintenance taking into consideration "all the circumstances of the case" as the sub-section requires

20 *Ibid.* at 974-75.

shall be done. In the next place, it is to be observed that, when the condition precedent to the exercise of the powers given by the sub-section is shown to be fulfilled, those powers extend to making such provision as the Court thinks fit for "such" maintenance, that is to say, for proper maintenance. The task thus imposed upon the Court is obviously one of great difficulty. Upon what principles is the Court to act in determining what constitutes proper maintenance? This is a question that has been discussed in several cases to which their Lordships' attention has been directed. They are for the most part decisions of the New Zealand Courts. New South Wales is not the only State in Australia that has made statutory provisions of the nature now in question. Indeed, every state in Australia has done so. New Zealand appears to have been the pioneer. The provision now in force is contained in 33 of the *Family Protection Act, 1908*, and is in the same form for all practical purposes as the provision with which this appeal is concerned. The principal differences in language are that in the New Zealand Statute the words "maintenance and support" are used instead of "maintenance, education and advancement," and the Court is not in terms directed to take into consideration all the circumstances of the case, although such words would seem to be necessarily implied.

Of the cases cited their Lordships desire particularly to refer to *In re Allardice, Allardice v. Allardice* . . . [Lord Romer quoted from the reasons of Chief Justice Stout and continued].

With these observations of the Chief Justice their Lordships are in agreement. The amount to be provided is not to be measured solely by the need of maintenance. It would be so if the Court were concerned merely with adequacy. But the Court has to consider what is proper maintenance, and therefore the property left by the testator has to be taken into consideration. So, too, in the case of children, a material consideration is their age. If a son is of mature, or nearly mature, age, his needs both for the present and the future can be estimated without much difficulty. In the case, however, of a son of tender age, although his immediate needs can be readily ascertained, it is extraordinarily difficult even to guess what his needs may be in the future. Where, therefore, the testator's estate is a large one the Court will be justified in such a case in making provision to meet contingencies that might have to be disregarded where the estate is small. In the same case Edwards J. [pp. 972-3] expressed himself as follows (I): "It is the duty of the Court, so far as is possible, to place itself in all respects in the position of the testator, and to consider whether or not, having regard to all existing facts and surrounding circumstances, the testator has been guilty of a manifest breach of that moral duty which a just, but not a loving, husband or father owes towards his wife or towards his children, as the case may be. If the Court finds that the testator has been plainly guilty of a breach of such moral duty, then it is the duty of the Court to make such an order as appears to be sufficient, but no more than sufficient, to repair it."

Their Lordships agree that in every case the Court must place itself in the position of the testator and consider what he ought to have done in all the circumstances of the case, treating the testator for that purpose as a wise and just, rather than a fond and foolish, husband or father. This no doubt is what the learned judge meant by a just, but not a loving, husband or father. As was truly said by Salmond J. in *In re Allen* [1922 N.Z.L.R. 218, at 220]: "The Act is . . . designed to enforce the moral obligation of a testator to use his testamentary powers for the purpose of making proper and adequate provision after his death for the support of his wife and children, having regard to his means, to the means and deserts of the several claimants, and to the relative urgency of the various moral claims upon his bounty. The provision which the Court may properly make in default of testamentary provision is that which a just and wise father would have thought it his moral duty to make in the interests of his widow and children had he been fully aware of all the relevant circumstances."[21]

Were the judges in *Allardice*, *Allen*, and *Bosch* describing a jurisdiction limited to taking care of financial need and maintenance or a jurisdiction comprising a second purpose, either to enforce a moral obligation of spouses and parents to give a fair share of their assets to the surviving spouse and issue or to give effect to a moral claim a dependant may have, regardless of need? It is difficult to determine, certainly without considering the context of those judicial pronouncements including subsequent New Zealand and Australian cases, which the Canadian judges who cite and quote them never do. Even though Justice Edwards in *Allardice* wrote that the court is to consider "whether or not . . . the testator has been guilty of a manifest breach of that moral duty which a just, but not loving, husband or father owes towards his wife or towards his children," and Justice Salmond in *Allen* referred to the "moral obligation" and "moral duty" of a testator, and Lord Romer in *Bosch* wrote

> The amount to be provided is not to be measured solely by the need of maintenance. It would be so if the Court were concerned merely with adequacy. But the Court has to consider what is proper maintenance. . .

were these judges thinking in terms of a moral *duty* to give a fair share or, as Chief Justice MacKeigan put it in *Garrett v. Zwicker*, in terms of the moral *claim*, which a dependant may have, based, for instance, on a contribution made to the accumulation of the deceased's estate or to the deceased's welfare.[22]

Walker v. McDermott had to do with the British Columbia section, above. The testator left his $25,000.00 estate entirely to his wife. His daughter, who was in no current financial need, was not being supported by the testator, and prior to her marriage earned her own living as a stenographer. She made an application pursuant to what was then called the

---

21 *Supra* note 16 at 476-79.

22 See paragraph 36, quoted below in the text following note 103.

Testator's Family Maintenance Act. For the majority of the Supreme Court of Canada Justice Duff wrote:

> The provision which the court is authorized to make in the circumstances stated in the section, is, "such provision as the court thinks adequate, just and equitable." The conditions upon which this authority rests are that the person whose estate is in question has died leaving a will, and has not made, by that will, in the opinion of the judge, adequate provision for the "proper maintenance and support" of the wife, husband or children, as the case may be, on whose behalf the application is made.
>
> What constitutes "proper maintenance and support" is a question to be determined with reference to a variety of circumstances. It cannot be limited to the bare necessities of existence. For the purpose of arriving at a conclusion, the court on whom devolves the responsibility of giving effect to the statute, would naturally proceed from the point of view of the judicious father of a family seeking to discharge both his marital and his parental duty; and would of course (looking at the matter from that point of view), consider the situation of the child, wife or husband, and the standard of living to which, having regard to this and the other circumstances, reference ought to be had. If the court comes to the decision that adequate provision has not been made, then the court must consider what provision would be not only adequate, but just and equitable also; and in exercising its judgment upon this, the pecuniary magnitude of the estate, and the situation of others having claims upon the testator, must be taken into account.[23]

Certainly dependants' relief legislation exists to take care of the financial need and maintenance of statutorily defined dependants, and need and maintenance have always been considered to involve more than "the bare necessities of existence".[24] A second purpose came to the fore with the decision in *Walker v. McDermott*, namely the enforcement of a moral obligation of spouses and parents to give a fair share of their estates to the surviving spouse and issue. Remember, the applicant-daughter was not in need. Justice Duff for the majority wrote:

> The testator, no doubt, felt himself under great obligations to his wife, and justly so. But I can see nothing in all this to lead to the conclusion that the testator, if properly alive to his responsibilities, as father no less than as husband, ought to have felt himself under an obligation to hand over all his estate to his wife and leave his only child without provision.[25]

He did not base his decision on the possibility of future need, as had the court in *Allardice*. The Supreme Court of Canada restored the trial

23 *Supra* note 17 at 95-96.
24 *Supra* note 17 at 96.
25 *Supra* note 17 at 98.

judgment, which had ordered $6,000.00 of the estate to be set aside for the daughter, less $1,000.00 which her mother had given her voluntarily.

Justice Rinfret dissented and his dissent places the majority decision in bolder relief:

> ... I cannot construe the Act to mean that in every case where no provision is made, the section above quoted is mandatory and the court must make an order. In my judgment, the intention of the legislature was that the husband, the wife or the children should not be left without "proper maintenance and support," while the testator disposed of an estate sufficient to provide for it; and to that extent only, in order to carry out such intention, is the Court permitted to interfere with the liberty of any person to bequeath his property as he pleases.
>
> The first inquiry therefore must be whether, at the death of the testator, the petitioner lacked those means of maintenance and support which would be proper, having regard to her ordinary circumstances in life. For that purpose, the court should consider how she has been maintained in the past and what were, when the testator died, the means of support available to her.
>
> ...
>
> The petitioner never has been dependent on her father since she got her employment in the Bank of Montreal, in 1923, and certainly not since her marriage. She has never been since then and is not now in need of maintenance and support out of the estate and is adequately maintained and supported by her husband, who is a young man with a good income, a permanent employment, a reasonable opportunity of advancement and fully capable of supporting her in the future. In fact, from all appearances derived from the record, she lives now more comfortably than during the years prior to her marriage. She does not state that she is in need of maintenance, nor that her husband and herself are unable to meet their necessary household and incidental expenses of living. All she says is that they "are unable to save any money whatsoever." Even that is not borne out by the facts, since they own and maintain a Chevrolet motor car; and when the respondent made them a present of $1,000, they invested part of it in the purchase of Big Missouri stock and the appellant took a trip to Seattle, which cost her $100.
>
> The appellant complains that the judgment of the court of Appeal does "not take into account not only the chances of dismissal of the ordinary kind, but also the necessarily precarious business in which (the husband) is employed." These and other contingencies are possibilities in every case whatever. A young husband may die prematurely. A widow or a child now rich may lose everything through adverse circumstances. There would be no limit to considerations of that character, and it would mean that, unless provision such as is suggested by the appellant is made in every will, the latter should be recast and some order must be made in all cases. I would not think that, when considering the applicability of the statute, these possibilities should be taken into account. But suffice it to say that, in the present instance, the probabilities lead in a direction contrary to the contention and the claim of the appellant. It is much more likely than otherwise and much more in accordance

> with ordinary and reasonable expectation that the appellant's present condition will go on improving as years go by and, at all events, that both herself and her husband will be fully capable of maintaining themselves in the future.[26]

The only conclusion to be taken from the majority decision is that there is a moral duty upon testators to give a fair share of the estate to their statutorily defined dependants regardless of their need. Justice Fullagar in dissent in *Coates v. National Trustees Executors & Agency Co.*[27] correctly observed:

> The notion of a "moral duty" is found not in the statute, but in a gloss upon the statute.

In 1994 the Supreme Court of Canada decided *Tataryn v. Tataryn Estate*[28] respecting the *Wills Variation Act* of British Columbia. The Court spoke in terms of legal and moral obligations. Regarding the legal obligation of deceased spouses, in addition to British Columbia *Tataryn* is relevant only to Prince Edward Island and the two territories which, like British Columbia do not have matrimonial property legislation applicable to dissolution of marriage by death. Regarding the Court's view of moral obligation, courts in the other provinces and territories will want to consider carefully whether the Supreme Court's view is applicable to their legislation and how they have been applying it. Only the courts of Alberta have adopted *Tataryn*.

2. APPLICATION OF THE LEGISLATION

What has been the application of the legislation in the various provinces and territories?

(a) British Columbia

Despite the Supreme Court of Canada decision in *Walker v. McDermott* being an appeal from the British Columbia Court of Appeal, not all British Columbia judges subsequently agreed that their Act creates the moral duty jurisdiction upon which the *Walker* decision was apparently based. Leopold Amighetti has described adequately the divided record of the British Columbia decisions.[29] In 1994 the Supreme Court of Canada in

---

26 *Supra* note 17 at 99-101.

27 (1956), 95 C.L.R. 494 (Aus. H.C.) at 523.

28 *Supra* note 13.

29 Amighetti, L., *The Law of Dependants' Relief in British Columbia* (Toronto: Carswell, 1991) at 28-56 [hereinafter Amighetti]. Also Bale, G., "Re Osland, Testator's Family Maintenance in British Columbia—Fair Share or Equitable Maintenance and the Di-

Tataryn v. Tataryn Estate[30] clarified the British Columbia Act in favour of the Act having dual purposes.

In brief, Justice McLachlin for the Court said that the Wills Variation Act "confers a broad discretion on the court" and protects two interests, namely adequate, just, and equitable provision for a surviving spouse and child or children and testamentary autonomy, which must give way to the former. What is an adequate, just, and equitable provision is to be determined not solely by a need-maintenance approach, which the Court rejected in *Walker v. McDermott*, but by considering in turn the deceased's legal and moral obligations. Legal obligations are those which the statute and common law would have imposed during the deceased's lifetime had provision for the applicant arisen. Moral obligations are to be "found in society's reasonable expectations of what a judicious person would do in the circumstances having regard to contemporary community standards". Finally, a court should interfere with a will only to the extent necessary to fulfill the testator's legal and moral obligations. The more complete text of Justice McLachlin's reasons for the Court is:

> This case requires us to consider the principles to be applied to the British Columbia *Wills Variation Act* . . ..
>
> Discussion
>
> *The Language of the Act*
>
> The language of the *Wills Variation Act* is very broad. The court must determine whether the testator has made "adequate provision" for his spouse and children. If it concludes he or she has not, the court "may, in its discretion, . . . order . . . the provision that it thinks adequate, just and equitable in the circumstances".
>
> I do not interpret the section as imposing two different tests. The court must ask itself whether the will makes adequate provision and if not, order what is adequate, just and equitable. These are two sides of the same coin.
>
> The words "adequate, just and equitable" may be interpreted in different ways. At one end of the spectrum, they may be confined to what is "necessary" to keep the dependants off the welfare roles. At the other extreme, they may be interpreted as requiring the court to make an award consistent with the lifestyle and aspirations of the dependants. Again, they may be interpreted as confined to maintenance or they may be interpreted as capable of extending to fair property division. Complicating these questions are the issues of the weight to be placed on the "right" of the testator to dispose of his estates as he chooses—i.e., testamentary autonomy and the equities as between the

lemma Still Confronting the Courts by the Supreme Court of Canada Decision in *Walker v. McDermott*" (1977-78) 1 E.T.R. 129 and Bale, G., "Palm Tree Justice and Testator's Family Maintenance—The Continuing Saga of Confusion and Uncertainty in the B.C. Courts" (1987) 26 E.T.R. 295.

30 *Supra* note 13.

beneficiaries: spouses and children. Different courts, applying a variety of approaches to these questions, have, over time, arrived at different interpretations of the meaning of "adequate, just and equitable".

Whatever the answers to the specific questions, this much seems clear. The language of the Act confers a broad discretion on the court. The generosity of the language suggests that the legislature was attempting to craft a formula which would permit the courts to make orders which are just in the specific circumstances and in light of contemporary standards. This, combined with the rule that a statute is always speaking (*Interpretation Act*, R.S.B.C. 1979, c. 206, s. 7), means that the Act must be read in light of modern values and expectations. What was thought to be adequate, just and equitable in the 1920s may be quite different from what is considered adequate, just and equitable in the 1990s. This narrows the inquiry. Courts are not necessarily bound by the views and awards made in earlier times. The search is for contemporary justice.

The Interests Protected

The two interests protected by the Act are apparent. The main aim of the Act is adequate, just and equitable provision for the spouses and children of testators. The desire of the legislators who conceived and passed it was to "ameliorat[e] . . . social conditions within the Province". At a minimum this meant preventing those left behind from becoming a charge on the state. But the debates may also be seen as foreshadowing more modern concepts of equality. The Act was passed at a time when men held most property. It was passed, we are told, as "the direct result of lobbying by women's organizations with the final power given to them through women's enfranchisement in 1916". There is no reason to suppose that the concerns of the women's groups who fought for this reform were confined to keeping people off the state dole. It is equally reasonable to suppose that they were concerned that women and children receive an "adequate, just and equitable" share of the family wealth on the death of the person who held it, even in the absence of demonstrated need.

The other interest protected by the Act is testamentary autonomy. The Act did not remove the right of the legal owner of property to dispose of it upon death. Rather, it limited that right. The absolute testamentary autonomy of the 19th century was required to yield to the interests of spouses and children to the extent, and only to the extent, that this was necessary to provide the latter with what was "adequate, just and equitable in the circumstances." And if that testamentary autonomy must yield to what is "adequate, just and equitable", then the ultimate question is, what is "adequate, just and equitable" in the circumstances judged by contemporary standards. Once that is established, it cannot be cut down on the ground that the testator did not want to provide what is "adequate, just and equitable".

The Jurisprudence—Need or Something More?

The early cases equated what was "adequate, just and equitable in the circumstances" with what was required to support or "maintain" the spouse and children of the testator: *Re Livingston* (1922), 31 B.C.R. 468; *Re Hall* (1923), 33 B.C.R. 241; *Re Stigings* (1924), 34 B.C.R. 347; *Brighten v. Smith* (1926), 37 B.C.R. 518. As McPhillips J.A. put it in *Brighten v. Smith* (at p. 523):

> If . . . the husband or the wife should be in need, . . . the relationship that exists calls upon the husband or the wife to remember it and make provision, otherwise we should have the husband or the wife, . . . becoming a public charge upon the country.

This approach is consistent with the view of duties between husband and wife prevailing in the 1920s. For example, on marriage breakup the husband was generally required to support or "maintain" the wife and no more. She had no claim on his property. It is hardly surprising that the judges of the time interpreted the Act in terms of need or what was required to maintain the spouse.

This Court rejected the need-maintenance approach to the Act in *Walker v. McDermott*, [1931] S.C.R. 94. At issue was the right of an independent child to share in an estate which the testator had left entirely to his wife. This Court upheld the trial judge's decision to award the child $6,000 of the $25,000 estate, overruling the Court of Appeal's decision that all should go to the wife. Duff J. (as he then was), speaking for the majority, enunciated the following test (at p. 96):

> What constitutes "proper maintenance and support" is a question to be determined with reference to a variety of circumstances. It cannot be limited to the bare necessities of existence. For the purpose of arriving at a conclusion, the court on whom devolves the responsibility of giving effect to the statute, would naturally proceed from the point of view of the judicious father of a family seeking to discharge both his marital and his parental duty; and would of course (looking at the matter from that point of view), consider the situation of the child, wife or husband, and the standard of living to which, having regard to this and the other circumstances, reference ought to be had.

Walker v. McDermott may be seen as recognizing that the Act's ambit extended beyond need and maintenance. As Amighetti . . . puts it (at p. 36), "the award in *Walker v. McDermott* can be supported only on the basis that the court interpreted the Act as a vehicle for redistribution of the capital of the estate".

It may be noted that the need-maintenance rationale would not have permitted the court to recognize the claim of an independent adult child, as was done in *Walker v. McDermott*. The obvious question arose; if the British Columbia legislature had wished to confine the power of the court to order testamentary changes to need and maintenance, why had it not excluded adult independent children as was done, for example, in Alberta? This would have left the courts with three choices: (1) replace the need-maintenance test with a more generous test; (2) create two tests, need-maintenance for spouses and dependent children and something more generous for adult independent children; or (3) read the British Columbia Act as confined to spouses and dependent children. The fact that the Act lumped spouses and children together militated against the two-test approach, and the absence of words limiting claims to dependent children undercut the alternative of confining the Act to spouses and dependent children. Thus it is not surprising that the Court in *Walker v. McDermott* adopted a broader test, sometimes called the "moral duty" approach.

The decisions of lower courts after *Walker v. McDermott* follow two lines. The majority, in keeping with the philosophy of *Walker*, affirmed the principle that spouses and children were entitled to an equitable share of the estate even in the absence of need. "Moral duty" became the watchword . . ..

A second, weaker line of authorities followed the old view that the testator's wishes could be disturbed only on the basis of need . . . These authorities found a defender in Amighetti . . . In his view, the purpose of the Act was the modest one of preventing spouses and children from becoming charges on the state. It is essentially a welfare document. Subject to the obligation to care for the needs of his spouse and children, the testator's right to dispose of his property as he sees fit remains absolute. In Amighetti's view, this interpretation is mandated by the plain words and history of the Act. The early cases got it right when they confined the revisionary powers of the court to cases of need. *Walker v. McDermott*, on the other hand, erred in "attribut[ing] to the Act a meaning and a function clearly beyond that defined by the early British Columbia cases and the capabilities of the Act" (pp. 36-37).

It has been suggested that this Court ought to replace the "judicious father and husband" test it set out in *Walker v. McDermott* and return to the needs-based analysis which prevailed in the early years of the Act. With great respect to the arguments to the contrary, I am not persuaded that we should do so.

First, I cannot agree that the wording of the Act suggests a strict needs-based test. As noted above, the wording is broad and capable of embracing changing conceptions of what is "adequate, just and equitable". The Act does not mention need. Moreover, if need were the touchstone, the failure to exclude independent adult children from its ambit presents difficulty. Nor, as will be discussed in greater detail below, do the words of the statute suggest a test devoid of judicial discretion, as witnessed by the express references to "discretion" and what is "adequate, just and equitable <u>in the circumstances</u>" (emphasis added).

Nor can I agree that the history of the Act suggests that the only reason for its passage was to prevent persons becoming a charge on the state. While the Act certainly was intended to serve this minimum function, there is nothing to suggest that the women's groups who lobbied for it or the legislators who adopted it intended that it be confined to cases of need.

The remaining argument is that *Walker v. McDermott* extends the Act beyond its capabilities. Again with respect, I cannot agree. This argument is founded on the proposition that the *Walker* test introduces too much uncertainty into the law. Amighetti states (at p. 56):

> The final result, in any given case, is completely at the discretion of the presiding judge as he or she alone considers the facts and makes a judgement, doubtless influenced by his or her own perception of what is fair and right. We are thus regressing to the unacceptable "time when Equity was interpreted by the length of the 'Chancellor's foot' . . ."

This criticism is value-neutral. It does not support the adoption of a needs-maintenance approach. It merely suggests that there must be some yardstick, be it need or some other, by which courts might measure the terms "adequate, just and equitable". From time to time courts following *Walker v. McDermott* have attempted to suggest ways of rendering the task under the Act more predictable . . .

If the phrase "adequate, just and equitable" is viewed in light of current societal norms, much of the uncertainty disappears. Furthermore, two sorts of norms are available and both must be addressed. The first are the obligations which the law would impose on a person during his or her life were the question of provision for the claimant to arise. These might be described as legal obligations. The second type of norms are found in society's reasonable expectations of what a judicious person would do in the circumstances, by reference to contemporary community standards. These might be called moral obligations, following the language traditionally used by the courts. Together, these two norms provide a guide to what is "adequate, just and equitable" in the circumstances of the case.

The first consideration must be the testator's legal responsibilities during his or her lifetime. The desirability of symmetry between the rights which may be asserted against the testator before death and those which may be asserted against the estate after his death has been noted by the dissenting member of the British Columbia Law Reform Commission in its 1983 report on the Act, *Report on Statutory Succession Rights* (Report No. 70). Mr. Close argues (at p. 154):

> A person is under a legal duty to support his or her spouse and minor children. If this duty is not observed then it may be enforced through the courts. That a testator's estate should, therefore, be charged with a duty similar to that borne by the testator in his lifetime is not troublesome.

It follows that maintenance and property allocations which the law would support during the testator's lifetime should be reflected in the court's interpretation of what is "adequate, just and equitable in the circumstances" after the testator's death.

The legal obligations on a testator during his or her lifetime reflect a clear and unequivocal social expectation, expressed through society's elected representatives and the judicial doctrine of its courts. Where provision for a spouse is in issue, the testator's legal obligations while alive may be found in the *Divorce Act*, R.S.C. 1985, c. 3 (2nd Supp), family property legislation and the law of constructive trust: *Pettkus v. Becker*, [1980] 2 S.C.R. 834; *Sorochan v. Sorochan*, [1986] 2 S.C.R. 38; *Peter v. Beblow*, [1993] 1 S.C.R. 980. Maintenance and provision for basic needs may be sufficient to meet this legal obligation. On the other hand, they may not. Statute and case law accepts that, depending on the length of the relationship, the contribution of the claimant spouse and the desirability of independence, each spouse is entitled to a share of the estate. Spouses are regarded as partners. As L'Heureux-Dubé wrote in *Moge v. Moge*, [1992] 3 S.C.R. 813, at p. 849:

> . . . marriage is, among other things, an economic unit which generates financial benefits . . . The [Divorce] Act reflects the fact that in today's marital relationships, partners should expect and are entitled to share those financial benefits.

The legal obligation of a testator may also extend to dependent children. And in some cases, the principles of unjust enrichment may indicate a legal duty toward a grown, independent child by reason of the child's contribution to the estate. The legal obligations which society imposes on a testator during his lifetime are an important indication of the content of the legal obligation to provide "adequate, just and equitable" maintenance and support which is enforced after death.

For further guidance in determining what is "adequate, just and equitable", the court should next turn to the testator's moral duties toward spouse and children. It is to the determination of these moral duties that the concerns about uncertainty are usually addressed. There being no clear legal standard by which to judge moral duties, these obligations are admittedly more susceptible of being viewed differently by different people. Nevertheless, the uncertainty, even in this area, may not be so great as has been sometimes thought. For example, most people would agree that although the law may not require a supporting spouse to make provision for a dependent spouse after his death, a strong moral obligation to do so exists if the size of the estate permits. Similarly, most people would agree that an adult dependent child is entitled to such consideration as the size of the estate and the testator's other obligations may allow. While the moral claim of independent adult children may be more tenuous, a large body of case law exists suggesting that, if the size of the estate permits and in the absence of circumstances which negate the existence of such an obligation, some provision for such children should be made: . . .

How are conflicting claims to be balanced against each other? Where the estate permits, all should be met. Where priorities must be considered, it seems to me that claims which would have been recognized during the testator's life—i.e., claims based upon not only moral obligation but legal obligations—should generally take precedence over moral claims. As between moral claims, some may be stronger than others. It falls to the court to weigh the strength of each claim and assign to each its proper priority. In doing this, one should take into account the important changes consequent upon the death of the testator. There is no longer any need to provide for the deceased and

> reasonable expectations following upon death may not be the same as in the event of a separation during lifetime. A will may provide a framework for the protection of the beneficiaries and future generations and the carrying out of legitimate social purposes. Any moral duty should be assessed in the light of the deceased's legitimate concerns which, where the assets of the estate permit, may go beyond providing for the surviving spouse and children.
>
> I add this. In many cases, there will be a number of ways of dividing the assets which are adequate, just and equitable. In other words, there will be a wide range of options, any of which might be considered appropriate in the circumstances. Provided that the testator has chosen an option within this range, the will should not be disturbed. Only where the testator has chosen an option which falls below his or her obligations as defined by reference to legal and moral norms, should the court make an order which achieves the justice the testator failed to achieve. In the absence of other evidence a will should be seen as reflecting the means chosen by the testator to meet his legitimate concerns and provide for an ordered administration and distribution of his estate in the best interests of the persons and institutions closest to him. It is the exercise by the testator of his freedom to dispose of his property and is to be interfered with not lightly but only in so far as the statute requires.[31]

About *Tataryn* Leopold Amighetti wrote:

> Although impeccable in its result, the case does little to clear the uncertain path which the jurisprudence has created. Regrettably, it further obscures it. Rather than moving towards certainty and reduction of litigation, the legal analysis undertaken by the court and its rationale have done the exact opposite.[32]

Robert Freedman and Carolyn Berardino added:

> In *Tataryn*, the Supreme Court of Canada was given the opportunity to clarify the legal principles applicable to wills variation. While the court does set down a standard analytical approach to wills variation applications, closer examination reveals that the decision creates more problems than it resolves. Most importantly for the will writers, however, the *Tataryn* decision means that many more families will end up in court over whether a testator's last wishes will be varied by judicial order and, if so, how these wishes will be varied.[33]

Certainly, *Tataryn* has not stemmed the flow of British Columbia proceedings, which continue to total more than the proceedings in the rest of Canada combined. And certainly *Tataryn* has established a standard analytical approach which the courts of British Columbia are faithfully following. Since the *Tataryn* decision in July, 1994, there have been twenty

---

31 *Supra* note 13 at 814–824.

32 "Tataryn v. Tataryn" (1993) 14 E.T.J. 277 at 278.

33 "Tataryn v. Tataryn" (1995) 15 E.T.J. 6 at 7.

reported British Columbia cases involving decisions on the merits. In all but one of them[34] the courts applied *Tataryn*, often quoting from it extensively. Seven of those decisions had to do with actions commenced by a co-habiting spouse,[35] one by a separated spouse,[36] and twelve by independent children.[37]

In *Tataryn*, Justice McLachlin said that "in some cases, the principles of unjust enrichment may indicate a legal duty towards a grown, independent child by reason of the child's contribution to the estate". This argument was made and failed in three cases, but in each case the court decided that the evidence supported a moral obligation.[38] As for a parent's moral obligation to independent children, Justice McLachlin said:

> While the moral claim of independent adult children may be more tenuous [than that of a surviving spouse or a dependant child], a large body of case law exists suggesting that, if the size of the estate permits and in the absence

---

34 *Simkins v. Blumenthal* (1995), 9 E.T.R. (2d) 53 (B.C. S.C.) is the single case which ignored *Tataryn*, perhaps because the deceased died in 1990; perhaps the court overlooked the retrospectivity of common law decisions. Cf. *Tweedale v. Tweedale Estate* (1995), 1 B.C.L.R. (3d) 167 (B.C. C.A.) in which the Court of Appeal reviewed the trial judge's pre-*Tataryn* decision in terms of *Tataryn*. For a recent excellent treatment of the retrospectivity of common law decisions see *Edward v. Edward Estate* (1987), 57 Sask. R. 67 (Sask. C.A.) at paragraphs 16-33.

35 Successful: *Tweedale v. Tweedale Estate, ibid*; *Crerar v. Crerar Estate* (1997), 40 B.C.L.R. (3d) 274 (B.C. S.C.), varied (1998), 111 B.C.A.C. 194, 181 W.A.C. 194 (B.C. C.A.); *Glanville v. Glanville* (1997), 17 E.T.R. (2d) 181 (B.C. S.C.), additional reasons (July 3, 1997), Doc. New Westminster S0-32693 (B.C. S.C.), reversed in part (December 22, 1998), Doc. Vancouver CA023360 (B.C. C.A.). Unsuccessful: *Warwick (Guardian ad litem of) v. Warwick Estate* (1996), 11 E.T.R. (2d) 129 (B.C. S.C.); *Lobe v. Lobe Estate* (1997), 17 E.T.R. (2d) 275 (B.C. C.A.); *Howard v. Howard Estate* (1997), 32 B.C.L.R. (3d) 1 (B.C. C.A.).

36 *Holland v. Holland Estate* (1995), 9 E.T.R. (2d) 119 (B.C. S.C.), successful.

37 Successful: *Hammond v. Hammond* (1995), 7 B.C.L.R. (3d) 25 (B.C. S.C.); *Huang v. Chan* (1996), 11 E.T.R. (2d) 156 (B.C. S.C.); *Newstead v. Newstead Estate* (1996), 11 E.T.R. (2d) 236 (B.C. S.C.); *Williams v. Williams Estate* (1996), 11 E.T.R. (2d) 226 (B.C. S.C. [In Chambers]); *Mann v. Mann Estate* (1996), 13 E.T.R. (2d) 203 (B.C. S.C.), additional reasons at (February 14, 1997), Doc. Vancouver A942728 (B.C. S.C.); *Barnsley v. Barnsley* (1996), 28 B.C.L.R. (3d) 165 (B.C. S.C. [In Chambers]); *McRae v. Royal Trust Corp. of Canada* (1997), 16 E.T.R. (2d) 223 (B.C. S.C. [In Chambers]); *Crerar v. Crerar Estate, supra* note 35; *Pattie v. Standal Estate* (1997), 42 B.C.L.R. (3d) 211 (B.C. S.C.); *Willott v. Willott Estate* (1997), 42 B.C.L.R. (3d) 223 (B.C. S.C.). Unsuccessful: *Vielbig v. Waterland Estate* (1995), 1 B.C.L.R. (3d) 76 (B.C. C.A.); *Kelly v. Baker* (1996), 15 E.T.R. (2d) 219 (B.C. C.A.); *Chernecki v. Vangolen* (1996), 28 B.C.L.R. (3d) 33 (B.C. C.A.).

38 *Huang v. Chan, supra* note 37 at paragraphs 18-19; *McRae v. Royal Trust Corp. of Canada, supra* note 37 at paragraphs 52 and 54-55; *Crerar v. Crerar Estate, supra* note 35 at paragraphs 18-24; *Huang* and *Crerar* speak to contributions made by minor children to family enterprises.

> of circumstances which negate the existence of such an obligation, some provision for such children should be made. . .[39]

In *Hammond v. Hammond*[40] Justice Kirkpatrick added:

> . . . With respect to the moral obligations owed to the plaintiff, it is instructive to consider the following factors, as outlined by Amighetti in c. IV of his text. First, as provided for by the very words of s. 2(1) of the *Wills Variation Act*, the court must consider the "circumstances." In so doing, the court must consider the value of all assets or funds which pass by operation of law upon the testator's death . . .
>
> Secondly, the relative contributions of the beneficiaries are also an important consideration in the decision to vary. . . .
>
> Finally, by virtue of s. 2(3) of the Act, some consideration must also be given to the intent of the testator.

In *Newstead v. Newstead Estate*[41] Justice Boyd said:

> . . . Perhaps the best expression of a parent's moral obligations towards an adult child was articulated by Carrothers, J.A. in *Lukie v. Helgason* (1976), 1 B.C.L.R. 1 (C.A.), as follows:
>
>> I perceive in these cases a common principle, that the testator may (with immunity against the likelihood of a "proper maintenance and support" provision being imposed under the statute) by his will prefer one child or more over another or others, even to the exclusion of one or more of them, so long as he does not do so unjustly or in manifest breach of his paternal obligation or moral duty which, upon his death, might exist towards the child or children which by his will he treats sparingly or even spurns and disinherits. I further perceive in the fact patterns of these cases three distinct bases upon which this paternal obligation or moral duty after death is founded and what its nature is:
>>
>> 1. Where there is clear need on the part of the child, being more than basic necessities and in line with the accustomed standard of living of the child, the degree of which need varies inversely with the child's age at the testator's death and will be found in the independent adult child only in cases of illness, disability or ineptness on the child's part in fighting the battle of life.
>>
>> 2. Where there is an expectation on the part of the child to benefit from the estate, which comes from being accustomed to and dependent upon continued beneficence and support from the parent or a clear contribution on the part of the child to the testator's estate.
>>
>> 3. Where there is excess of affluence and abundance in the estate so that legitimate competing claims on the estate would not be materially affected by letting the rejected child or children have something.

---

39 *Supra* note 13 at 822–23.

40 *Supra* note 37 at paragraphs 27–28.

41 *Supra* note 37 at paragraph 55.

> Otherwise, there is no continuing parental obligation or moral duty to be breached. Clearly the parental obligation or moral duty does not arise solely from the paternity of the applicant.

A moral obligation argument based solely upon financial need failed in *Vielbig v. Waterland Estate*.[42] The bases of the moral obligations in the successful actions by independent children were contribution to the estate,[43] size of the estate,[44] fulfilment of testamentary intent,[45] need,[46] and an unfilled legal obligation of support during the applicant's minority.[47]

(b) Alberta

Justice Marshall in *Pauliuk v. Pauliuk*[48] described *Re Willan Estate*[49] as "a leading Alberta decision"; indeed it is the leading pre-*Tataryn* Alberta case. The wording of the Alberta Act's primary section, s. 3(1), has not been changed significantly since Justice Egbert wrote his reasons for judgment in *Re Willan Estate*, which are well worth reading in their entirety. He quoted the usual passages from *Allardice*, *Bosch*, and Duff's reasons in *Walker*. He noted the difference in the wording of the Alberta Act empowering "'such provision as [the court] deems adequate . . . for the proper maintenance and support' of . . ." and the British Columbia Act empowering "such provisions as the court thinks adequate, just and equitable"; he agreed with Justice Ford in *Re Gray Estate*[50] that, "despite the difference in the wording, the same interpretation should be given to the two Acts".[51]

Justice Egbert referred to and quoted from several other cases for specific points, as well as this general quote from *Shaw v. Regina (City)*:[52]

> Dependants' relief Acts mark a departure from the principle of freedom of testamentary disposition. . . . The task imposed upon the Courts by these enactments is one of great difficulty for there is cast upon them the duty of determining the moral obligations of the testator to his dependants and of

---

42 *Supra* note 37. Cf. *Newstead v. Newstead Estate*, *supra* note 37.

43 *Huang v. Chan*, *supra* note 37; *McRae v. Royal Trust Corp. of Canada*, *supra* note 37; *Crerar v. Crerar Estate*, *supra* note 35.

44 *Mann v. Mann Estate*, *supra* note 37.

45 *Hammond v. Hammond*, *supra* note 37; *Mann v. Mann Estate*, *supra* note 37; *Willott v. Willott Estate*, *supra* note 37; *Williams v. Williams Estate*, note 37.

46 *Newstead v. Newstead Estate*, *supra* note 37; *Barnsley v. Barnsley*, *supra* note 37.

47 *Pattie v. Standal Estate*, *supra* note 37 at paragraph 26.

48 (1986), 48 Alta. L.R. (2d) 25 (Alta. Q.B.) at 29.

49 (1951), 4 W.W.R. 114 (Alta. S.C.).

50 [1950] 2 W.W.R. 854 (Alta. S.C.) at 856.

51 *Supra* note 49 at 127; see also *Re Maitland* (1954), 10 W.W.R. (N.S.) 673 (Alta. C.A.) at 678.

52 [1944] 1 W.W.R. 433 (Sask. C.A.) at 438.

making such alterations in his will as will in the opinion of the Courts carry out such moral obligations.

Has the Supreme Court of Alberta defined for itself only a need-maintenance based jurisdiction or has it included in its *Family Relief Act* jurisdiction the enforcement of a moral obligation of spouses and parents to give a fair share of the estate to the surviving spouse and child or children? The quotes Justice Egbert made from *Allardice* and *Bosch* had to do with the court's jurisdiction to take care of financial need. He preceded his quote from Justice Duff's *Walker* reasons with ". . . the Supreme Court of Canada, in effect, without stating that it did so, adopted the principles laid down in *Allardice v. Allardice*".[53] He gave no indication that he considered the Supreme Court of Canada in *Walker* to have added a second purpose to the court's jurisdiction. Despite what might be the implication of the quote he made from the *Shaw* case, Justice Egbert specifically rejected the applicant's contention of entitlement to a substantial share of the estate based upon her intestate succession entitlement:

> This still leaves the matter of the lump sum awarded her by the will to be considered, and to be left intact, or cancelled or diminished or increased as I consider just and equitable for her proper maintenance and support. I gather from a perusal of the written agreement [sic], submitted by counsel for the applicant, that he believes that the applicant is entitled to a substantial portion of the corpus of the estate, and he urges that the discretion exercised by the court should be in the light of the general policy of the law as to what the applicant's proper share of the estate would be under the provisions of *The Intestate Succession Act*, RSA, 1942, ch. 211. This is a proposition to which I have already expressed my emphatic dissent and one which, so far as I can ascertain, has never found favour in any court in any jurisdiction where statutory provision is not made for such disposition, with the exception of the views expressed by O'Halloran, J.A. in *Barker v. Westminster Trust Co.*, [[1941] 3 W.W.R. 473, 614] views which have not been followed, even in his own province of British Columbia. I am afraid the applicant in this case has very much the same attitude as the applicant in *Shaw v. Regina, supra*—she has the erroneous idea firmly fixed in her mind that she is entitled to a share of the corpus of the estate which she will be able to dispose of by will; but the purpose of the Act is not to permit an applicant to build up an estate which she, in turn, may dispose of by will.[54]

His consideration of what he should order in her favour was made entirely upon a need-maintenance basis, bearing in mind *Allardice* and

53 *Re Willan Estate, supra* note 49 at 127.
54 *Supra* note 49 at 136-37.

Bosch. So, despite the reference and quote from *Walker v. McDermott, Re Willan Estate* stands for a jurisdiction limited to need-maintenance.[55]

In *Siegel v. Siegel Estate*[56] Justice Moreau came to a different conclusion from his analysis of several Alberta cases:

> [25] . . . In defining what is to be considered "adequate" for the "proper maintenance and support of the dependents", the Alberta courts have consistently rejected the approach which would see the spouse or dependent children maintained and no more, and which would leave them with no claim on the property of the deceased. . .

and therefore:

> [30] I am of the view that the principles in **Tataryn** do apply to applications under the **Family Relief Act**.

Earlier, in *Webb v. Webb Estate*[57] Judge Hembroff also embraced *Tataryn*, quoting with approval the paragraph in *Tataryn* in which Justice McLachlin describes the "two sorts of norms . . . [that] must be addressed".[58]

(c) Saskatchewan

The leading pre-*Tataryn* Saskatchewan case is *Shaw v. Regina (City)*.[59] Chief Justice Martin wrote:

> Dependants' relief Acts mark a departure from the principle of freedom of testamentary disposition . . . The task imposed upon the Courts by these enactments is one of great difficulty for there is cast upon them the duty of

---

55 See also a very similar decision, also need-maintenance based, *Re Maitland, supra* note 51. Other cases in which the court's primary jurisdiction is reviewed do not suggest other than a need-maintenance based jurisdiction: *Re Barclay* (1952), 5 W.W.R. (N.S.) 308 (Alta. S.C.); *Malychuk v. Malychuk* (1978), 6 Alta. L.R. (2d) 240 (Alta. T.D.); *Stepaniuk v. Koziol Estate* (1985), 60 A.R. 47 (Alta. Q.B.); *Re Protopappas Estate, supra* note 13. There are three cases, I think inconsequential, not clearly based upon need: *Re Magi*, [1935] 2 W.W.R. 422 (Alta. S.C.); *Jones v. Kline (Jones)*, [1938] 3 W.W.R. 65 (Alta. T.D.); *Re Mays*, [1943] 3 W.W.R. 479 (Alta. S.C.); there is also Chief Justice Milvain's statement in *Nickle v. Jones*, [1974] 3 W.W.R. 385 (Alta. S.C.) at 387 that he "found help" from several named cases, including *McCarvill v. Jones* (1961), 36 W.W.R. 337 (B.C. C.A.), affirmed [1962] S.C.R. 273 (S.C.C.) in which Chief Justice Des Brissay for the majority of the B.C.C.A. states at 341 that the purpose of the B.C. Act is not only to take care of need.

56 (1995), 177 A.R. 282 (Alta. Q.B.) at paragraphs 25 and 30. *Siegel* is one of two post-*Tataryn* Alberta cases.

57 (1995), 28 Alta. L.R. (3d) 110 (Alta. Surr. Ct.).

58 *Ibid.* at paragraph 51. Note Henderson, M., "Adequate Provision: Dividing the Family Pie" (1996) 21 L. Now No. 2 at 17.

59 *Supra* note 52. This case is incidentally dated by the subsequent change in the definition of "child" as a "dependant" and the repeal of s. 9(2); but, in terms of the discussion respecting s. 9(1) it remains valid.

determining the moral obligations of the testator to his dependants and of making such alterations in his will as will in the opinion of the Courts carry out such moral obligations. In all the statutes to which our attention has been called a condition precedent must be fulfilled before the Court can exercise the powers conferred upon it; in this province the Court must be of the opinion that the testator has not made "reasonable provision" for the maintenance of the dependants; in the *New Zealand Family Protection Act*, ch. 60 of the statutes of 1908, the language used is "adequate provision for the proper maintenance and support of the testator's wife, husband or children;" in the *Family Maintenance and Guardianship of Infants Act*, 1916, of New South Wales, "adequate provision for their maintenance, education or advancement in life;" and in the statute of the province of British Columbia . . . "adequate provision for the proper maintenance and support of the testator's wife, husband or children." Speaking generally I do not think that the differences in language used in describing "maintenance" can be said to make any difference in the construction to be placed upon the various statutes; "reasonable provision for maintenance" in my opinion means something adequate and proper under all the circumstances. Where the testator has a family and only a small estate he may not be able to provide any one of his dependants with adequate maintenance and at the same time the provision made for them may be reasonable and proper when all the circumstances including the size of his estate are considered. In the case of small estates where there are numerous persons having a claim upon the bounty of the testator and some dependant complains of unjust distribution, the duty of the court is to endeavour to see that the estate is justly divided among such persons after giving due consideration to the relative needs and deserts of the claimants. In the case, however, of a large estate where the applicant for relief complains that the testator out of his wealth has not made a provision reasonably sufficient for the maintenance of the dependant, the Court has placed upon it the duty of deciding to what extent a wealthy man should go in making provision for the maintenance of his dependants.

In this province the dependants who may apply for relief are the wife or husband of the testator, a child under the age of 21 years, and a child over that age who by reason of mental or physical disability is unable to earn a livelihood. In New Zealand, New South Wales and the province of British Columbia however the persons who may apply are the wife or husband and the children of the testator; there are no restrictions upon the children who may apply as to age, health or dependence on the testator.

Counsel for the appellants contended that, by reason of the limitations placed upon the dependants who may apply under the Saskatchewan Act, it is clear that the intention of the Legislature was to ensure provision of reasonable maintenance for those who were actually dependent upon the testator and in accordance with the well-established meaning of the word "maintenance," namely, "providing a person with the requisites of life." I do not think however that the limitation placed upon the children who may apply under the Saskatchewan statute should have any effect upon the principles to be applied in

> dealing with applications made by those who under the statute are entitled to apply. It surely cannot be argued that in a case such as the present, where the applicant is the widow of the testator (and there are no others having a moral claim upon him), the words "reasonable provision for maintenance" should be given a restricted meaning because of the fact that under the statute children only of two classes are entitled to the benefit of the Act.
>
> The principles to be applied in the construction of the British Columbia statute were set forth by the Supreme Court of Canada in *Walker v. McDermott*. . . .

Chief Justice Martin proceeded to quote the familiar passages from *Walker*, *Allardice*, *Allen,* and *Bosch,* and to make an award to the widow applicant upon a need-maintenance basis.[60]

There have been eight post-*Tataryn* Saskatchewan cases, *Wilson v. Kosok*,[61] *Ostrander v. Kimble Estate*,[62] *Paxman v. Saskatchewan (Public Trustee)*[63], *Sakundiak v. Sakundiak Estate,*[64] *Ford v. Bell Estate*,[65] *Surminsky (Litigation Guardian of) v. Ulmer Estate*,[66] *Nelson v. Stroshein Estate*,[67] and *Re Penner*.[68] Justice Klebuc dealt with *Tataryn* in *Ostrander* and his treatment has been followed in *Sakundiak* and *Nelson*. Justice Klebuc confirmed that cases subsequent to *Shaw*:

> . . . focused on the dependant's need for maintenance. . . . None considered a redistribution of the testator's assets based on the community's sense of fairness or by way of compensatory maintenance.[69]

Justice Klebuc proceeded to consider the relevance of *Tataryn* to the Saskatchewan Act. After summarising and quoting from the reasons of Justice McLachlin in *Tataryn* and Justice Moreau in *Siegel v. Siegel Estate*[70] in which the Alberta Court of Queen's Bench considered the relevance of *Tataryn* to the Alberta Act, Justice Klebuc continued:

---

60 Some subsequent cases, such as *Re Finnimore* (1956), 17 W.W.R. 668 (Sask. C.A.) at 674, and *Re Ducherer*, [1977] 6 W.W.R. 495 (Sask. Surr. Ct.) at 497, have emphasized a need based jurisdiction and expressly rejected a moral obligation jurisdiction.

61 (1996), 146 Sask. R. 105 (Sask. Q.B.).

62 (1996), 146 Sask. R. 64 (Sask. Q.B.).

63 (1996), 146 Sask. R. 312 (Sask. Q.B.). The court in line with the Shaw quote, in the text above, rejected the respondent's submission that because the applicant was not financially dependant on the deceased he was not qualified to apply. The court said in paragraph 15: "Although the applicant's capital and income are relevant, they are not solely determinative of the issue".

64 (1996), 149 Sask. R. 99 (Sask. Q.B.).

65 (1997), 154 Sask. R. 193 (Sask. Q.B.).

66 (1997), (*sub nom. Surminsky v. Ulmer Estate*) 159 Sask. R. 217 (Sask. Q.B.).

67 (1997), 161 Sask. R. 311 (Sask. Q.B.).

68 (1997), (*sub nom. Re Penner Estate*) 161 Sask. R. 317 (Sask. Q.B.).

69 *Supra* note 62 at paragraph 22.

70 *Supra* note 56.

[29] Is *Tataryn* applicable in Saskatchewan given the differences between the [Saskatchewan] Act and the Wills Variation Act [of British Columbia], and if so, to what extent? The first difference involves the definition of "dependant". Under the Wills Variation Act, adult children of a testator may claim an interest in the testator's estate while the [Saskatchewan] Act restricts such claims to children under the age of 18 and children more than 18 years of age, if by reason of mental or physical disability, they are unable to earn a livelihood. Madame Justice McLachlin noted the significance of this difference at p. 616 of *Tataryn*:

> "It may be noted that the need-maintenance rationale would not have permitted the court to recognize the claim of an independent adult child, as was done in *Walker v. McDermott*. The obvious question arose; if the British Columbia legislature had wished to confine the power of the court to order testamentary changes to need and maintenance, why had it not excluded adult independent children as was done, for example, in Alberta?"

[30] *Siegel* does not reconcile McLachlin, J.'s, interpretation of the Alberta legislation with the broader approach adopted in *Tataryn*; nor does it suggest that a testator's wealth be distributed according to community standards. To the contrary, it confirms that testamentary dispositions are not to be interfered with beyond what is required to maintain the claiming dependant at a reasonable standard.

[31] Secondly, the [Saskatchewan] Act uses the phrase "reasonable provision . . . for the maintenance of the dependant" while the Wills Variation Act employs the phrase "adequate provision for the proper maintenance and support . . ." Chief Justice Martin in Shaw concluded both phrases had the same operational effect in calculating the adequacy of a maintenance provision. *Siegel* and *Tataryn* extend a far broader meaning to the phrase "proper maintenance and support" than contemplated in *Shaw*.

[32] Upon taking into account the material differences between the [Saskatchewan] Act and the Wills Variation Act, and McLachlin, J.'s, interpretation of the differences between the Wills Variation Act and the Family Relief Act of Alberta, I conclude that the [Saskatchewan] Act contemplates a need maintenance approach. As a result the principles in *Tataryn*, while still applicable, must be applied with deference to the underlying legislative intent. Such deference will not materially affect the legal obligation norm described in *Tataryn* for nothing in the [Saskatchewan] Act militates against symmetry between a testator's inter vivos obligation and the post mortem legal obligations of her or his estate. Thus, the testator's inter vivos legal obligations apply in assessing the extent of the testator's obligations under the Act.

[33] While the moral duty norm in *Walker v. McDermott* has applied to the [Saskatchewan] Act since *Shaw*, it never received the broad interpretation extended to it in *Tataryn*. Rather, as previously noted, *Shaw* and later decisions limit the moral obligation of the judicious father to providing adequate

> maintenance without regard to the spousal compensation or equitable distributions. Their interpretation is consistent with a need maintenance approach and the narrower view of spousal maintenance taken prior to *Moge v. Moge* [1992] 3 S.C.R. 813; . . . In my view, *Moge* has materially extended the moral obligations of the judicious father referred to in *Walker v. McDermott* in addition to extending the legal obligation of spouses generally. Therefore, the moral duty norm currently is of greater significance in assessing the adequacy of a testamentary provision, and where the provision is found wanting, in awarding an appropriate allowance having regard to the size of the testator's estate, the dependant's contribution to the creation of the estate and the competing moral claims of others interested in the estate. In that context, reference to current community standards is not only appropriate but essential. Such broader application in my view does not allow for awards under the need maintenance approach of the [Saskatchewan] Act that deliberately facilitate the dependant accumulating an estate for the benefit of her or his beneficiaries at the expense of the testator's designated beneficiaries.
>
> [34] In summary, following *Tataryn* the phrase "reasonable provision" can no longer be defined as that "which would permit the dependant to maintain the standard of living enjoyed during the lifetime of the testator" as suggested in *Shaw*, *Murray* and *Serdula* but is to be determined having regard to the dependants and others within the context of a need maintenance approach and the provisions of s. 9 of the Act. A more generous award may result.

The applicant in *Ostrander* had lived in a "common law relationship" with the deceased for twelve years prior to his death. Justice Klebuc said:

> [37] To determine [the deceased's] . . . inter vivos and post mortem legal obligations to [the applicant] . . . the Act must be applied with regard to the Family Maintenance Act. . ., the law of constructive trusts, the principles of unjust enrichment and the legal principles applicable to spousal maintenance.[71]

(d) Manitoba

The former *Testator's Family Maintenance Act* contained a primary jurisdiction section like s. 58(1) of the Ontario Act, quoted at the beginning of this chapter. Over the years the courts implemented their jurisdiction not only to take care generously of financial need, but also to award a fair or at least a token share of, or to reward a moral claim to the deceased's estate. In 1990 The *Testator's Family Maintenance Act* was replaced by the *Dependants Relief Act*. The primary jurisdiction section of the current Act clearly stipulates that the court's jurisdiction is limited to taking care of financial need. The applicability of *Tataryn* should be limited to the Justice

---

71 *Supra* note 62 at pararaphs 29-34 and 37.

McLachlan's discussion of the legal obligations or responsibilities of a deceased during his or her lifetime, which are largely, if not entirely, fulfilled by Part IV of the *Marital Property Act*. There have been two reported cases decided pursuant to the current Act. In only one of them, *Hoeppner (Litigation Guardian of) v. Misiewicz Estate*,[72] might the court have considered the applicability of *Tataryn*; but it did not do so.

(e) Ontario[73]

Two points are evident from the reported reasons for judgments. First, the courts consider the current Act to be significantly different from its predecessor, the *Dependants' Relief Act*. Second, while moral or ethical considerations are not irrelevant, they are subsidiary to economic considerations. Ponder Judge Dymond, in *Re Davies*,[74] comparing the *Dependants' Relief Act* and the current legislation:

> . . . the class of person included as dependants has been widened and, in addition, the words "future maintenance" [in the primary jurisdiction section] have been replaced by the words "proper support" [in current s. 58] . . .
>
> The Legislature has also made other changes of importance in that the matters into which the Court is to inquire at the hearing under the S.L.R.A. have been made more explicit on the one hand and broader on the other hand because evidence as to the reasons of the deceased for dispositions made in his will may be heard. Thus one must tread carefully in so far as reliance upon previous case-law in this Province is concerned. It is my view that by the word "support" the Legislature has deliberately focused on a change from "maintenance". The word "support" does not appear in legislation from other jurisdictions but usually with the word "maintenance". The *Family Law Reform Act*, 1978 (Ont.), c. 2, it may be noted, has also gone away from the use of the words "maintenance" or "alimony".
>
> Some examination of dictionary definitions of the word "support" may be helpful . . . These definitions lead me to the conclusion that "support" as

72 (1995), 106 Man. R. (2d) 24 (Man. Q.B.).

73 See also Hull, R., "Support of Dependants under The Succession Law Reform Act" (1977-78) 1 E.T.R. 145; Hull, R. and Cullity, M., "The Succession Law Reform Act, 1977: An Overview" (1978) 4 E.T.Q. 366; Oosterhoff, A., "The Effect of Death on Familial Obligations" (1981) 23 R.F.L. (2d) 272 at 283-85; Bale, G., "Re Dentinger, Dependant's Relief Legislation and the Changed Emphasis Effected by Part V of The Succession Law Reform Act (Ontario)" (1982) 10 E.T.R. 7; Oosterhoff, A., "Re Mannion, Dependants' Support—New Principle Under the Succession Law Reform Act (Ontario)" (1982) 6 E.T.Q. 1; and Oosterhoff, A., "Some Aspects of Support of Dependants" (1982-83) 12 E.T.R. 197; Hoffstein, M., "Support of Dependants—Part V of The Succession Law Reform Act" (1986) 21 E.T.R. 23 at 37-38; Macdonell, Sheard & Hull, *supra* note 13 at 132-39; Schnurr, B. and Woodley, S., "Dependant Support Proceedings" (1995) 14 E.T.J. 159 at 167.

74 (1979), 27 O.R. (2d) 98 (Ont. Surr. Ct.) at 101–103.

used in the S.L.R.A., includes not only furnishing food and sustenance and supplying the necessaries of life, but also the secondary meaning of giving physical or moral support. While the Ontario cases under the *Dependants' Relief Act* extended the meaning of "adequate provision for the further maintenance of a dependant", to a determination of the question, "is the provision sufficient to enable the dependant to live neither luxuriously nor miserably, but decently and comfortably according to his or her station of life" (*Re Duranceau*, [1952] O.R. 584, . . . [headnote]), I am inclined to the view that the word "support" in the S.L.R.A. extends that meaning to include what might by some be considered as non-essentials or luxuries. For example, if a living husband has been accustomed to reading aloud to his wife whose sight had failed, it may well be that for her support, sufficient money should be provided to pay for a reader to substitute for that husband.

Consider Judge Carter in *Re Dentinger*:[75]

We now come to consider, having regard to all the circumstances I have set out above, whether the deceased made adequate provision for the applicant's proper support.

Those cases which deal with this question, and which have been decided since the passage of The Succession Law Reform Act . . . indicate a tendency to give a more generous meaning to "proper support" than that which had been given to "future maintenance" under The Dependant's Relief Act, R.S.O. 1970, c. 126, s. 2(1). Furthermore, the financial circumstance of the dependant is but one of the factors considered by the Courts, and the fact that a dependant has assets—sometimes substantial assets—is not necessarily a bar to a finding that a deceased had not made adequate provision for the proper support of such dependant.

In this regard it is interesting to note that the circumstances set out in the present legislation are [more lengthy] than those which had been set out in The Dependants' Relief Act, and that those now set out not only parallel those set out as matters to be considered in an application for support under s. 18 of The Family Law Reform Act, but also include some of the factors a Court would consider in making an unequal division of family assets under s. 4(4) of the latter Act, or in considering the contribution of a "former spouse" under s. 8 of the latter Act insofar as non-family assets are concerned. . . .

I am satisfied that if I were to exclude the considerations set out in s. 69(1)(a)(vi)(vii) and (viii) [now s. 62(1)(g) "the proximity and duration of the dependant's relationship with the deceased", (h) "the contributions made by the dependant to the deceased's welfare, including indirect and non-financial contributions", and (i) "the contributions made by the dependant to the acquisition, maintenance and improvement of the deceased's property or business"] of The Succession Law Reform Act from my mind, the other considerations of s. 69(1) would force me to the conclusion that the deceased, while not exactly generous towards the applicant, had made adequate provi-

75 (1981), 10 E.T.R. 6 (Ont. Surr. Ct.) at 27–29.

> sion for her support. When, however, I consider the circumstances set out in s. 69(1)(a)(vi) (vii) and (viii), and also note that I am concerned not with the adequacy of support only, but with the adequacy of *proper* support, I am satisfied that the deceased testator was "guilty of a manifest breach of that moral duty which a just, but not a loving, husband . . . owes towards his wife. . .". *Re: Allardice* . . .

Also consider Judge Carnwath, in *McSween v. McSween Estate*;[76]

> I return to the question posed at the beginning of the consideration of the various provisions of s. 62 of the Act: Did the deceased make adequate provision for the proper support of the two children of the applicant as of May 1, 1985, the date of the hearing? Having considered those paragraphs of s. 62 which I feel are applicable to the facts of this case, I must also consider the meaning to be applied to the words, "adequate provision for the proper support of the dependants" as set out in s. 58(1) of the Act. I note in passing, that s. 2 of the Dependants' Relief Act spoke of "adequate provision for the future maintenance" of dependants. The omission of the word "proper" suggests to me that cases decided prior to the introduction of the Succession Law Reform Act in Ontario would be of little assistance.
>
> The meaning of the words "proper support" is essential to the construction of s. 58(1) for until "proper support" is understood, "adequate provision" for each support cannot be quantified. No greater assistance can be found, as a point of departure, than the judgment of Lord Romer in Bosch v. Perpetual Trustee Co. . . .
>
> I accept Lord Romer's analysis of the difference between "proper" and "adequate" and adopt it for the purposes of this judgment.
>
> In the case of Re Davies . . . Dymond Surr. Ct. J. extensively canvassed the meaning of the word "support" . . .
>
> I concur with the conclusions reached by The Honourable Judge Dymond as to the meaning of support as contemplated by the Succession Law Reform Act.
>
> To what extent am I required by the provisions of Pt. V of the Succession Law Reform Act to consider any moral obligation on the part of the testator to his children as opposed to the demonstration of need on the part of such dependants? In provinces other than Ontario, under similar legislation, Judges have concluded that they are free to make provision for "proper support" even though the dependant or dependants in question have not established a demonstrated need for assistance. . . .
>
> My reading of Pt. V of the Act persuades me that, in Ontario, the primary consideration should be those matters enumerated in s. 62(1)(a) of the Act. Section 57(d) defines "dependant" as someone "to whom the deceased was providing support or was under a legal obligation to provide support immediately before his death". If one takes as an example a son of a testator over 18 years of age who was not receiving support from the testator immediately prior

76 (1985), 21 E.T.R. 195 (Ont. Surr. Ct.) at 208-13.

to his death that son would have no standing to obtain an order under Pt. V of the Act no matter how strong a moral duty might be found to exist on the part of the deceased father.

Secondly, s. 58(3) of the Act requires that the adequacy of provision for support shall be determined as of the date of the hearing of the application. I find it is of little assistance to speak of the deceased's moral obligation to his dependants at the time of the hearing when all sorts of factors affecting the need of the dependant may have arisen since the execution of the deceased's will, if such exists, or indeed since the date of death of the deceased.

Further confirmation that Pt. V of the Succession Law Reform Act should be construed with the need of the dependant in mind may be found in comparing its provisions with the support provisions of the Family Law Reform Act. The two acts are strikingly similar and the relief afforded by the Family Law Reform Act is clearly based solely on need.

I therefore conclude that in seeking the correct meaning to be ascribed to the words "proper support", in Ontario, under the Succession Law Reform Act, primary importance must be attached to the economic situation of the dependant at the time of the hearing as opposed to ethical or moral obligations to be imputed to the deceased at whatever point in time. That is not to say that the opening words of s. 62(1)(a) of the Act should be ignored; there is a requirement to "inquire into and consider all the circumstances of the application". I find, however, that in determining the adequacy of proper support as a prerequisite to the making of an order under s. 58(1) of the Act, that moral or ethical obligations on the part of the deceased are subsidiary to the primary consideration of the economic circumstances of all the parties who would be affected by any order made pursuant to s. 58.

For the preceding reasons, it may also be appropriate to re-examine a time-honoured precept, often quoted in dependant's relief legislation cases. The concept directs the Judge to "put himself in the place of the testator". . . .

. . . The mental exercise of placing oneself in the position of the testator seems designed to create, in the mind of the finder of fact, a proper appreciation of the moral and ethical obligations of the deceased. With respect to those who find otherwise, this approach offers little assistance to me, given my views that the primary consideration should be the economic situation at the time of the application.

This is doubly so because of the direction in s. 58(3) of the Act, requiring that the adequacy of provision for support shall be determined as of the date of the hearing of the application. Bearing in mind that the will may have been drafted several years before the death of the deceased, and that the application may be brought some time after the death of the deceased, it is of little help to me to "put myself in the position of the testator" at the time of the application, when every imaginable change in circumstance may have altered his disposing mind since the time of the drafting of the will. I prefer rather to assess the economic situation and, in so doing, follow the direction contained in s. 62(1) and consider all the circumstances of the application including those enumerated from (i) to (xvi) [now s. 62(1)(a)-(s)]. . . .

3. If adequate provision for proper support was not made, what is the order that should issue?

In the words of s. 58(1) "the Court . . . may order that such provision as it considers adequate" be made out of the estate of the deceased. What limit, if any, is there on the discretion of the Court? Having determined that a deceased has not made adequate provision for the proper support of the dependants, is the Court limited to awarding that amount of support which would, in effect, bring the disposition of the deceased up to that level of proper support (but no further) which would have persuaded the finder of fact that adequate provision had been made and that the Court therefore had no jurisdiction to grant the order contemplated? I think no. Section 58(1) provides that the Court may order such provision as "it considers adequate" (my emphasis). I find that once I am entitled to exercise my jurisdiction under the section, it is then open to me to exercise my discretion in an unfettered manner having regard only to those matters enumerated in s. 62(1)(a) of the Act. It seems apparent that a testator may make provision for a dependant in an amount less than that which the Court would have provided, but more than sufficient to constitute "adequate provision for the proper support of the dependant", in which case the Court cannot interfere, however, merely because a Court would not interfere if the testator left $50,000 to a dependant does not mean that the Court is limited to $50,000 where little or no provision is made, and the Court finds that adequate provision has not been made. In this latter case, the prerequisite to assuming jurisdiction has been met, and the Court is directed by the section to make such provision "as it considers adequate" and the discretion thereby granted in the legislation can only mean that the Court has a range within which to work in making the order.

In the exercise of the discretion granted by s. 58(1) of the Act, the Court should, of course, review and bear in mind all the circumstances of the application including those specific matters itemized from (i) to (xvi) as directed by s. 62(1) of the Act. In addition, there are all those contingencies found present in any situation where an attempt is made to forecast the future. . . .[77]

There have been nine post-*Tataryn* decisions, *Fune v. Hoy Estate,*[78] *Gaudet (Litigation Guardian of) v. Young Estate,*[79] *Gocsei v. Skublak*

---

77 Also, *Re Mannion* (1981), 39 O.R. (2d) 263 (Ont. Surr. Ct.) at 269–70, varied (1982), 39 O.R. (2d) 609 (Ont. Div. Ct.), affirmed (1984), 45 O.R. (2d) 339 (Ont. C.A.) at 342; *Fox v. Grass* (1986), 22 E.T.R. 318 (Ont. Surr. Ct.) at 320; *Swire v. Swire* (1986), 23 E.T.R. 246 (Ont. Surr. Ct.) at 262–63, affirmed (1987), 10 R.F.L. (3d) 399, 28 E.T.R. 206, 24 O.A.C. 147 (Ont. Div. Ct.); *Blago v. Aetna Life Insurance Co.* (1988), 30 E.T.R. 283 (Ont. Surr. Ct.) at 301–03.

78 (1995), 6 E.T.R. (2d) 91 (Ont. Gen. Div.).

79 (1995), 7 E.T.R. (2d) 146 (Ont. Gen. Div.).

Estate,[80] *Horodyski v. Tobin Estate*,[81] *Roussel v. Hill Estate*,[82] *Modopoulos v. Breen Estate*,[83] *Neumann (Next Friend of) v. Neumann Estate*,[84] *Obringer v. Kennedy Estate*,[85] and *Vernon v. Dieleman Estate*.[86] No reference to *Tataryn* was made in any of them. In only *Fune*, *Goudet*, *Modopoulos*, *Lister*, and *Vernon* was there a decision on the merits of the application in which *Tataryn* might have been considered. *Vernon* is the only Court of Appeal decision of the four cases; it involved a pre-*Tataryn* trial decision. Given that *Tataryn* states a common law gloss on a dependants' relief statute, given the retroactivity of common law judicial decisions, and given appellate jurisdiction of dependants' relief cases, the Court could have reconsidered the trial decision in terms of *Tataryn* if the Court thought that it was applicable.[87]

In only one case decided pursuant to the current Act, *Re Trenton*,[88] might it be said that a court made an award on a purely moral duty basis. The applicant's basic needs were met by a "disability pension and auxiliary benefits . . . [and] his standard of living [had] . . . likely improved"[89] since his father's death. The court awarded the applicant $500.00 per month to replace accommodation which he had been receiving free from his father but, which after his father's death, the son was able to provide for himself out of his pension income.

(f) New Brunswick

The primary jurisdiction section in the New Brunswick Act, s. 2(1), reads:

> Where a person dies . . . without making . . . adequate provision for the proper maintenance and support of the deceased's dependants . . . a judge . . . may . . . order that such provision as the judge considers adequate shall be made . . . for the proper maintenance and support of the dependants. . .

This section is practically identical to the comparable sections in the Alberta Act and the former *Testator's Family Maintenance Act* of Manitoba. The interpretation and application of those sections was markedly

80 (1995), 8 E.T.R. (2d) 201 (Ont. Gen. Div.).
81 (1996), 13 E.T.R. (2d) 305 (Ont. Gen. Div.).
82 (1996), 14 E.T.R. (2d) 111 (Ont. Gen. Div.).
83 (1996), 15 E.T.R. (2d) 128 (Ont. Gen. Div.).
84 (1996), 15 E.T.R. (2d) 159 (Ont. Gen. Div.), additional reasons at (June 13, 1996), Doc. Barrie G11103 (Ont. Gen. Div.).
85 (1996), 16 E.T.R. (2d) 27 (Ont. Gen. Div.).
86 (1997) 16 E.T.R. (2d) 68 (Ont. C.A.), varying (1992), 46 E.T.R. 242 (Ont. Gen. Div.).
87 See for ex., *Tweedale v. Tweedale Estate*, *supra* note 34.
88 (1987), 26 E.T.R. 209 (Ont. Surr. Ct.).
89 *Ibid.* at 222.

different. The courts of Alberta construed and applied their section as conferring a single need-maintenance based jurisdiction. The Manitoba courts gradually turned the *Testator's Family Maintenance Act* into a piece of forced heirship legislation for a surviving spouse and issue; if that Act were still in existence, the Manitoba courts would feel very comfortable with the *Tataryn* decision.

What has been the record of New Brunswick courts interpreting and applying their primary jurisdiction section? The New Brunswick decision to which reference is most often made in subsequent New Brunswick cases is *Beasley v. Willet.*[90] Justice Barry quoted Justice Stout in *Allardice* and Justice Duff in *Walker v. McDermott.* As well, he referred to *Re Hornett*[91] and *Re Schurman.*[92] In *Hornett* a daughter claimed an absolute right to a share of her mother's estate; the court disagreed, dismissing the application, given the very modest size of the estate, the *inter vivos* assistance given to the daughter by her mother, and the daughter's current assets and income. *Schurman* appears to have been a decision based upon both need and the moral entitlement to a fair share of the deceased's estate. Justice Barry in *Beasley* did not expressly indicate whether he considered the New Brunswick Act's primary jurisdiction section to encompass only one or two purposes. However, on the facts and given his case references, the award which he made can be described as taking care of need to some extent and giving the applicant a fair share of the estate, notwithstanding her estrangement from the deceased. Three of the four cases decided subsequently by Justice Barry were not need-maintenance based.[93]

In *Nelson v. Nelson*[94] Chief Justice Hughes, for the New Brunswick Court of Appeal, in his review of authorities concerning general principles referred to *Beasley* and included the usual quotes from *Bosch* and *Walker* and also, perhaps most importantly, the oft-quoted statement of Justice Dickson (as he then was) in *Barr v. Barr*:[95]

> The dominant theme running through the cases, and they are myriad, is one of ethics, even more than economics. Although the *Testators Family Maintenance Act* is couched in terms which at first impression appear to be pragmatic and economic, "adequate provision for . . . proper maintenance and support",

---

90 (1972), 4 N.B.R. (2d) 122 (N.B. Q.B.).

91 (1962), 33 D.L.R. (2d) 289 (B.C. S.C.).

92 (1965), 54 D.L.R. (2d) 77 (N.S. S.C.).

93 *Re Phillips* (1973), 8 N.B.R. (2d) 188 (N.B. Q.B.), *Davidson v. Allen* (1976), 14 N.B.R. (2d) 60 (N.B. S.C.) in which need does not appear to have been the driving force, and *Re Gamble* (1981), 33 N.B.R. (2d) 132 (N.B. Q.B.). The fourth case, *Nelson v. Nelson* (1977), 17 N.B.R. (2d) 457 (N.B. C.A.), seems to have been a need based dismissal of the application of a widow.

94 *Ibid.*

95 (1971), 25 D.L.R. (3d) 401 (Man. C.A.) at 410.

it soon becomes apparent on a review of the authorities that heavy emphasis is placed upon the moral aspects of the problem.

Although the court dismissed the widow's application on a lack of need basis, the quotation from *Barr* is an indication by the court that the New Brunswick Act is not solely need-maintenance based. In *Lynds v. Lynds*[96] Justice Hoyt for the court reiterated the *Barr* quote in his reasons; although again the court's decision might be described as need-maintenance based, there are several other New Brunswick awards which were not solely or at all need-maintenance based.[97]

Therefore, it is not surprising that the New Brunswick courts have embraced *Tataryn*, beginning with the trial court in *Currie v. Currie Estate*,[98] concerning the applications of a 60 year old daughter and a 62 year old son, neither of whom was impecunious, although their means were modest. Justice Athey said:

> [15] Legislation similar to the **Provision for Dependants Act** was recently considered by the Supreme Court of Canada in **Tataryn et al. v. Tataryn Estate**, . . . The court said that the legislation limits "the right of the legal owner of property to dispose of it upon death". A testator must fulfil his legal obligations to provide support to his dependants (as defined in the applicable statute) and to share his estate according to "family property legislation" and the principles of unjust enrichment. Testators also have "moral duties toward spouse and children . . . Any moral duty should be assessed in the light of the deceased's legitimate concerns, which, where the assets of the estate permit, may go beyond providing for the surviving spouse and children. Where the estate permits, all (conflicting claims) should be met."

Although the applicants had been estranged from their father for the last thirty years of his life, nonetheless Justice Athey held:

> [19] In my view Donald Currie had a moral obligation to make provision for. . . . his two children. . . . I am unable to attach sole responsibility for [the estrangement] to his children.

96 (1986), 73 N.B.R. (2d) 296 (N.B. C.A.); also *Rollins v. Beyea Estate* (1987), 81 N.B.R. (2d) 58 (N.B. Q.B.) and *Black v. Keith Estate* (1989), 96 N.B.R. (2d) 322 (N.B. Q.B.).

97 *Crilley v. Beckingham* (1986), 74 N.B.R. (2d) 91 (N.B. Q.B.); *Black v. Keith Estate, ibid*; *Hanselpacker (Litigation Guardian of) v. Hanselpacker Estate* (1993), (*sub nom. Hanselpacker v. Hanselpacker Estate*) 140 N.B.R. (2d) 1 (N.B. Q.B.). However, *Walsh v. Clifford* (1985), 68 N.B.R. (2d) 231 (N.B. Q.B.) and *Rollins v. Beyea Estate, ibid.* were unsuccessful applications by needy applicants who might have expected at least a modest award if the court considers its jurisdiction to include enforcement of a moral obligation to give a fair portion of one's estate to certain dependants.

98 (1994), 154 N.B.R. (2d) 200 (N.B. Q.B.) at pararaphs 15 and 19.

The Court of Appeal disagreed and dismissed the applications.[99] In so doing the Court quoted with approval Justice McLachlin in *Tataryn*:[100]

> "If the phrase 'adequate, just and equitable' is viewed in light of current societal norms, much of the uncertainty disappears. Furthermore, two sorts of norms are available and both must be addressed. The first are the obligations which the law would impose on a person during his or her life were the question of provision for the claimant to arise. These might be described as legal obligations. The second type of norms are found in society's reasonable expectations of what a judicious person would do in the circumstances, by reference to contemporary community standards. These might be called moral obligations, following the language traditionally used by the courts. Together, these two norms provide a guide to what is 'adequate, just and equitable' in the circumstances of the case."

In between the trial and appeal decisions in *Currie*, there were two other trial decisions, *Spinney v. Spinney Estate*[101] and *Robicheau v. McGibbon*,[102] both of which considered the applications, with reference to *Tataryn*, in terms of the deceased's legal and moral obligations to the applicants, who were adult non-needy children. In both cases the applicants were adult children to whom, as in *Currie*, the courts concluded the deceased owed no legal or moral obligations.

(g) Nova Scotia

The leading case is *Garrett v. Zwicker*.[103] The testator left his $40,000.00 estate to his second wife of a year and a half. An adult daughter, "not suffering from actual want but undoubtedly . . . in poor circumstances, with no security", applied successfully. The widow appealed. Chief Justice MacKeigan for the Court of Appeal in reviewing the court's jurisdiction said:

> 13 Our Act, like the similar Acts in most provinces, adopts the principles and most of the language of the New Zealand Family Protection Act of 1908, as do statutes in the Australian states. Canadian Courts have viewed with respect

---

99 (1995), 166 N.B.R. (2d)144 (N.B. C.A.) at 155-56.

100 *Supra* note 13 at 820-21.

101 (1995), 165 N.B.R. (2d) 69 (N.B. Q.B.).

102 (1995), 165 N.B.R. (2d) 255 (N.B. Q.B.).

103 *Supra* note 13 [hereinafter *Zwicker* or *Garrett v. Zwicker*]; note *Corkum v. Corkum* (1976), 18 N.S.R. (2d) 501 (N.S. C.A.) at paragraph 10 regarding the *Zwicker* case name. Chief Justice MacKeigan refers to the earlier Nova Scotia case of *Re Cole* (1958), 40 M.P.R. 201 (N.S. T.D.). Another significant earlier Nova Scotia case concerning general principles is *Spinney v. Royal Trust Co.* (1973), 9 N.S.R. (2d) 699 (N.S. T.D.); see also *Smith v. Hunter Estate* (1993), (*sub nom. Smith v. Hunter*) 126 N.S.R. (2d) 254 (N.S. S.C.) at paragraph 17.

Australasian decisions on the subject, especially those of New Zealand Courts (see, for example, the exhaustive reviews by Williams, C.J.K.B., in *Re Lawther* . . . by Egbert, J., in *In re Willan Estate* . . . and by Mannie Brown in "Dependents' Relief Acts", (1940) 18 Can. Bar Rev., pp. 261-291, (449-483). They have considered themselves bound by the judgments of the Privy Council in *Allardice v. Allardice* . . . (and, particularly, the New Zealand decisions therein approved) and in *Bosch v. Perpetual Trustee Co. Ltd.* . . . I have benefited especially from the thorough review of these cases by Chief Justice Ilsley in *Re Cole* (1958), 12 D.L.R. (2d) 406. All these cases explain what is involved in the basic concept of "adequate provision . . . for the proper maintenance and support" of a dependent. . . . [Chief Justice MacKeigan proceeded to make the usual quotes from *Allardice*, *Bosch*, and *Walker* and to review several Canadian cases; he continued:]

35 . . . The cases hereinbefore discussed have implicitly, and often explicitly, applied the classic statement of Chief Justice Stout in *Allardice v. Allardice* that:

> The first inquiry in every case must be what is the need of maintenance; and the second what property has the testator left.

The dependent claimant need not, however, show need in the sense of actual want in order to qualify for consideration under the Act, and need not show actual dependency upon the testator. The need is relative, relative to the extent of the estate and the strength of other claims. I agree, as did Dickson, J.A., in *Barr v. Barr* . . . (25 D.L.R. (3d) at p. 411), with Gresson, P., of the New Zealand Court of Appeal in *Re Harrison (Deceased), Thomson v. Harrison*, [1962] N.Z.L.R. at p. 13:

> It is rather unfortunate that there has crept into the cases over the years a disposition sometimes to consider first the 'need' of the applicant and then to turn to a consideration of the extent of the estate and other claims there might be upon the testator. These considerations do not admit of separate consideration; they are interrelated. The 'need' of an applicant, or rather his or her needs -- the plural form is I think preferable -- cannot be considered *in vacuo*. What has to be assessed are the merits of the claim having regard to the applicant's circumstances as at the date of the death of the testator; relations between the testator and the applicant in the past; and the extent of his estate and the strength of other claims.

36 To justify interference with a will a court must thus find a failure to provide "proper maintenance and support", *i.e.*, both a need for maintenance, relative to the size of the estate, and a moral claim, which maybe of varying strength.

37 All "dependents" of a testator do not necessarily have moral claims of equal strength. A testator is entitled, for example, to discriminate among his children, giving one more than another, for good reason or no apparent reason, so long as he commits no "manifest wrong" in failing to give one the minimum that is "proper maintenance and support" in the circumstances: see Bull, J.A.

in *Re Woods* (1965), 56 D.L.R. (2d) 369 (B.C.C.A.), at pp. 376-7, approved by Martland, J., in 1966, 59 D.L.R. (2d) at p. 362. On the other hand, I question whether today's moral and social standards permit a court to discriminate in favour of adult daughters and against adult sons to the extent the courts did in *Allardice v. Allardice*.

38 The legal and moral duty to support a wife, infant children or disabled adult children is obviously much stronger than the moral duty to give marginal support to a normal adult child, male or female. . . .

. . .

40 This necessary differentiation between types of dependents and the requirement to consider a claim in the light of other claims and the size of the estate were classically expressed by Fullagar, J., in *Re Sinnott*, [1948] V.L.R. 279, at pp. 280-1 (quoted by Dickson, J.A., in *Barr v. Barr* . . . at pp. 409-410, and described by Dixon, C.J., in *Pontifical Society for the Propagation of the Faith v. Scales* (1962), 107 C.L.R. 9, at p. 19, as "perhaps the soundest and most illuminating of all the discussions of the statutory provisions"):

> No special principle is to be applied in the case of an adult son. But the approach of the Court must be different. In the case of a widow or an infant child, the Court is dealing with one who is *prima facie* dependent on the testator and *prima facie* has a claim to be maintained and supported. But an adult son is, I think, *prima facie* able to "maintain and support" himself, and *some special need or some special claim must, generally speaking, be shown to justify intervention by the Court under the Act.* (It is perhaps necessary to add that in using the word 'adult' and the word 'infant' I am not thinking of a hard and fast boundary line fixed conclusively on the attainment of 21 years.)
>
> The discretion given by the Act is obviously intended to be very wide. *The size of the estate is always important, and there will commonly be needs and claims other than those of the applicant to be considered.* But it is always, I think, primarily a matter of estimating need and moral claim. Often need and moral claim will co-exist. Sometimes there may be a strong moral claim on the testator's consideration but no need. In such cases I think that, as a general rule, the Court should not interfere, though no rigid rule can be laid down. Sometimes the moral claim may be slight, and yet the need so dire that the Court will hold that a wise and just testator would have made some provision, or, in other words, that wisdom and justice can connote a degree of generosity without degenerating into fondness and foolishness. (Emphasis added)

41 After quoting the foregoing, Dickson, J.A., in *Barr v. Barr* at p. 410 pointed out that "the dominant theme running through the cases . . . is one of ethics, even more than economics" and "that heavy emphasis is placed upon the moral aspects of the problem". He went on:

> The Court was never intended to rewrite the will of a testator and in discharging its difficult task of correcting a breach of morality on a testator's part the Court must not, except in plain and definite cases, restrain a man's right to dispose of his estate as he pleases.[104]

Chief Justice MacKeigan for the Nova Scotia Court of Appeal re-iterated his *Zwicker* views in *Corkum v. Corkum*.[105] Although in both reasons for judgment Chief Justice MacKeigan used the terms "moral duty" and "moral claim", I think that what he had in mind was a jurisdiction which includes the satisfaction of moral *claims* rather than the enforcement of a moral *duty*.[106] This, perhaps subtle, distinction is significant; if the court's jurisdiction includes the enforcement of a moral duty, rather than ensuring the satisfaction of moral claims, the moral duty is easily extended to comprise a duty to give a fair portion of the estate to the surviving spouse and issue regardless of need and familial relationship. The essence of the jurisdiction conferred by the Nova Scotia Act is gleaned from paragraph 36 of Chief Justice MacKeigan's *Zwicker* reasons, above, and the second half of the second paragraph quoted in paragraph 40, above. This is a jurisdiction different from the moral duty approach mandated by the Supreme Court of Canada in *Tataryn*.

In the single Nova Scotia case since *Tataryn*, *Redmond v. Redmond Estate*,[107] the court awarded the residue of an estate to six adult children, relying on *Zwicker* and without referring to *Tataryn*.

(h) Prince Edward Island

There have been only four reported cases. Only one of these cases involved a decision by the Court of Appeal, which comprised a couple of paragraphs of reasons given orally with no discussion of the court's primary jurisdiction. The most substantial discussion is to be found in *Re Flood Estate*[108] in which Justice McQuaid described and quoted from *Allardice*, *Bosch*, and *Walker* as "the leading cases", and "found help" from several cases including *Garrett v. Zwicker*[109] and *Bennett v. Morrison*.[110] Justice McQuaid proceeded to analyse the facts exactly the way that Chief Justice MacKeigan for the Nova Scotia Court of Appeal would have done.

---

104 *Ibid.* at paragraphs 13, 35–38, 40, 41.

105 *Supra* note 103. See also *Bennett v. Morrison* (1976), 16 N.S.R. (2d) 476 (N.S. C.A.).

106 See also *Miller v. Rankin Estate* (1986), 72 N.S.R. (2d) 441 (N.S. T.D.) at paragraph 46.

107 (1996), 155 N.S.R. (2d) 61 (N.S. S.C. [In Chambers]).

108 (1978), 20 Nfld. & P.E.I.R. 448 (P.E.I. S.C.).

109 *Supra* note 13.

110 *Supra* note 105.

(i) Newfoundland

In none of the few reported cases is there any discussion of or reference to cases relied upon respecting the primary jurisdiction of the court. All of the successful cases involved needy widows.

(j) Northwest and Yukon Territories

There are no relevant reported cases.

3

Procedure

1. WHO CAN APPLY

None of the provincial Acts is truly a dependants' relief Act in the sense of providing simply that any person who was dependant upon the deceased is able to apply. All of the Acts provide a more or less limited definition of persons able to apply. Two of the Acts, the Manitoba Act[1] and the Ontario Act[2], contain distinctive requirements, which are worth particular note. Under the Manitoba Act several dependants must have been "substantially dependant on the deceased at the time of the deceased's death". The Ontario Act defines "dependant" in s. 57:

> **57.** In this Part, ...
>
> "dependant" means,
>
> (a) the spouse of the deceased,
> (b) a parent of the deceased,
> (c) a child of the deceased, or
> (d) a brother or sister of the deceased,
>
> to whom the deceased was providing support or was under a legal obligation to provide support immediately before his or her death;

There is some commentary about the last twenty-two words of the definition.[3]

---

1 *Dependants Relief Act*, S.M. 1989-90, c. 42; C.C.S.M., c. D37 [hereinafter Manitoba Act].

2 *Succession Law Reform Act*, R.S.O. 1990, c. S.26, Part V [hereinafter Ontario Act].

3 Bale, G., "Re Dentinger, Dependants' Relief Legislation and the Changed Emphasis Effected by Part V of The Succession Law Reform Act (Ontario)" (1982) 10 E.T.R. 7; Oosterhoff, A., "Re Mannion, Dependants' Support—New Principle Under the Succession Law Reform Act" (1982) 6 E.T.Q. 1 at 3; Oosterhoff, A., "Some Aspects of Support of Dependants" (1982-83) 12 E.T.R. 197 at 199; Hoffstein, M., "Support of Dependants—Part V of The Succession Law Reform Act" (1986) 21 E.T.R. 23 at 30–34; Youdan, T., "The Status of a Dependant under Part V of the Ontario Succession Law Reform Act" (1986) 21 E.T.R. 303; Hull, R. and Hull, I. eds., *Macdonell, Sheard & Hull on Probate Practice*, 4th ed. (Toronto: Carswell, 1996) at 127-30 [hereinafter Macdonell Sheard & Hull].

(a) Spouses

All of the dependant's relief statutes provide for an application to be made by a wife or husband,[4] widow or widower,[5] or spouse.[6] In the off-chance that a spouse's marital status to apply is challenged, less than strict proof of the applicant's marriage to the deceased was satisfactory for the Alberta Court of Appeal in *Tatko v. Liefke*. Justice Macdonald for the Court said:

> It is contended that the evidence [sic] on the trial was insufficient to establish the marriage of the plaintiff and Jacob Tatko. There is no doubt that on a criminal prosecution for bigamy very strict proof of the former marriage is required. But this rule has no application in a civil proceeding in which a deserted wife seeks to share in the estate of her deceased husband who, contrary to the ordinary dictates of humanity, has made no provision for her in his will. There is evidence by the plaintiff of the fact that a marriage ceremony took place in the Russian Orthodox Church which was the church she usually attended. She and Jacob Tatko were the participants in this ceremony. This was followed by cohabitation for a period of about 12 years, and three children were born to them. Under these circumstances, everything necessary for the validity of the marriage will be presumed. . . .[7]

Similarly, in *Gilbert v. Standard Trusts Co.*, when a second-wife-widow's status to apply was contested on the basis of the illegality of a foreign decree of divorce respecting the deceased's first marriage, the court said:

---

4 British Columbia *Wills Variation Act*, R.S.B.C. 1996, c. 490, s. 2 [hereinafter British Columbia Act]; Saskatchewan *Dependants' Relief Act*, S.S. 1996, c. D-25.01, s. 2(1) [hereinafter Saskatchewan Act]; New Brunswick *Provision for Dependants Act*, R.S.N.B. 1973, c. P-22.3, s. 1 [hereinafter New Brunswick Act].

5 Nova Scotia *Testators' Family Maintenance Act*, R.S.N.S. 1989, c. 465, s. 2(b) [hereinafter Nova Scotia Act]; Prince Edward Island *Dependants of a Deceased Person Relief Act*, R.S.P.E.I. 1988, c. D-7, s. 1(d)(i) [hereinafter Prince Edward Island Act]; Newfoundland *Family Relief Act*, R.S.N. 1990, c. F-2, s. 2(c) [hereinafter Newfoundland Act]; Yukon Territory *Dependants Relief Act*, R.S.Y.T. 1990, c. 44, s. 1 [hereinafter Yukon Act].

6 Alberta *Family Relief Act*, R.S.A. 1980, c. F-2, s. 1(d) [hereinafter Alberta Act]; Manitoba Act, s. 1; Ontario Act, s. 57; Northwest Territories *Dependants Relief Act*, R.S.N.W.T. 1988, c. D-4, s. 1 [hereinafter Northwest Territories Act].

7 [1946] 1 W.W.R. 497 (Alta. C.A.) at 498; also *Re Tero*, [1949] 2 W.W.R. 203 (B.C.C.A.) at 206 and *Re Quon* (1969), 4 D.L.R. (3d) 702 (Alta. Q.B.) provide worthwhile treatments of the validity of a foreign marriage. Cf. *Trainor v. Toronto General Trusts Corp.* (1953), 61 Man. R. 154 (Man. C.A.) at 160 and 165-168.

> This Court should not pronounce the [divorce] judgment of the [foreign] . . . court of no effect except upon the clearest possible proof that it was without jurisdiction.[8]

The definition of "dependant" in the Ontario Act includes:

> **57.** In this Part, . . .
>
> "dependant" means,
>
> (a) the spouse of the deceased . . .
> to whom the deceased was providing support or was under a legal obligation to provide support immediately before his or her death.

This definition includes a spouse who was co-habiting with the deceased spouse, since s. 30 of the *Family Law Act*[9] imposes an obligation on "[e]very spouse . . . to provide support . . . for the other spouse. . .".[10]

A separated spouse[11] and a divorced spouse, so long as the divorce has

---

8 [1928] 3 W.W.R. 111 (Alta. T.D.) at 114; *Edward v. Edward Estate* (1987), 57 Sask. R. 67 (Sask. C.A.) is another case in which the validity of a foreign divorce was an issue.

9 R.S.O. 1990, c. F.3.

10 See *Re Davies* (1979), 27 O.R. (2d) 98 (Ont. Surr. Ct.) at 103–04; *Re Cooper* (1980), 30 O.R. (2d) 113 (Ont. Div. Ct.) at 116–21; *Re Dentinger* (1981), 10 E.T.R. 6 (Ont. Surr. Ct.) at 15-16; commentary by Youdan, T., "The Status of a Dependant Under Part V of The Succession Law Reform Act" (1986) 21 E.T.R. 303; and Macdonell, Sheard and Hull, *supra* note 3 at 129-30; and *Modopoulos v. Breen Estate* (1996), 15 E.T.R. (2d) 128 (Ont. Gen. Div.) at 133–35. Note that the waiver contained in a pre-nuptial agreement has barred an application, *Frye v. Frye* (1992), 41 R.F.L. (3d) 145 (Ont. Gen. Div.), affirmed (1996), 23 R.F.L. (4th) 283 (Ont. C.A.); see the text at note 116, *infra*, this chapter.

11 *Re Magi Estate*, [1935] 2 W.W.R. 422 (Alta. S.C.); *Re Wilson*, [1937] 1 W.W.R. 161 (Alta. S.C.); *Re Gouge* (1938), 52 B.C.R. 544 (B.C. S.C.); *Peill v. Peill*, [1939] 2 W.W.R. 519 (Sask. K.B.); *Belaney v. Perrier*, [1939] 3 W.W.R. 591 (Sask. K.B.); *Re Thomson Estate*, [1942] 2 W.W.R. 46 (Sask. C.A.); *McNamara v. Hyde* (1943), 59 B.C.R. 70 (B.C. C.A.); *Re Mays*, [1943] 3 W.W.R. 479 (Alta. S.C.); *Plumb v. Royal Trust Co.*, [1943] 3 W.W.R. 513 (Alta. T.D.), affirmed (1944), [1950] 2 W.W.R. 334 (Alta. C.A.); *Re Blackwell*, [1948] O.R. 522 (Ont. C.A.); *Renwick v. Currie*, [1948] 2 W.W.R. 683 (Sask. C.A.); *Re Pemberton*, [1948] 2 W.W.R. 745 (Sask. K.B.); *Re Willan Estate*, [1951] 4 W.W.R. (N.S.) 114 (Alta. S.C.) at 131; *Re Maitland* (1954), 10 W.W.R. (N.S.) 673 (Alta. C.A.); *Pope v. Stevens* (1954), 63 Man. R. 162 (Man. C.A.); *Re Johnson* (1955), 17 W.W.R. 88 (Sask. Q.B.); *Re Edgelow* (1955), 18 W.W.R. 235 (B.C. S.C.); *Reinsch v. Crown Trust Co.* (1956), 19 W.W.R. 63 (Man. Q.B.); *Chernoff v. Chernoff* (1962), 33 D.L.R. (2d) 742 (Sask. C.A.); *Re Hawley* (1962), 38 W.W.R. 354 (Sask. Q.B.); *Re Gosse* (1963), 43 D.L.R. (2d) 664 (Nfld. T.D.); *Re Cassidy* (1965), 54 D.L.R. (2d) 329 (Sask. Q.B.); *Re Gilbert* (1965), 51 W.W.R. 701 (Sask. Q.B.); *Re Shirley Estate* (1965), 55 W.W.R. 56 (Sask. Q.B.); *Rill v. Miller* (1969), 9 D.L.R. (3d) 211 (Sask. C.A.); *Keane v. Keane* (1972), 7 N.B.R. (2d) 187 (N.B. Q.B.); *Re Nixey* (1972), 31 D.L.R. (3d) 597 (Man. Q.B.); *Spinney v. Royal Trust Co.* (1973), 9 N.S.R. (2d) 699 (N.S. T.D.); *Dmytriw v. Dmytriw* (1975), 22 R.F.L. 382 (Man. Q.B.);

not become final at the time of the deceased spouse's death,[12] are able to apply, except in some circumstances in Ontario.[13] In *Plumb v. Royal Trust Co.*,[14] which was an application by a separated wife, it was contended that, having failed to advance a claim for support against her husband during his lifetime, the applicant was estopped from applying for relief under the then *Widow's Relief Act* of Alberta. Justice Macdonald rejected this argument;

> The claim which plaintiff makes in this action is entirely different from any claim she might have made against her husband during his lifetime. It is a claim which she could not possibly assert until after the death of her husband and then only in the event of his leaving a will, under which she received less than if he had died intestate. There was no undue delay in instituting these proceedings and no representation either by word or conduct, on the part of the plaintiff, on which estoppel could be based.[15]

Respecting divorces which have been finalized, the legislation of Ontario enables divorced spouses to apply;[16] the constitutionality of this

---

Collard v. Collard (1976), 28 R.F.L. 252 (Sask. Surr. Ct.); *Adams v. Irvine* (1978), 4 R.F.L. (2d) 295 (Sask. Q.B.); *Sing v. Sing* (1977), 23 N.S.R. (2d) 251 (N.S. T.D.); *Re Kiel* (1979), 24 A.R. 469 (Alta. Q.B.); *Manson v. Shoaf*, [1980] 5 W.W.R. 106 (Sask. Surr. Ct.); *Adams v. Broughton* (1982), 45 Alta. L.R. 390 (Alta. Q.B.); *Jeffers v. Jeffers* (1982), 20 Sask. R. 52 (Sask. Q.B.); *Lampert v. Lampert* (1983), 45 A.R. 390 (Alta. Q.B.); *Peslari v. Pestruic* (1984), 33 Sask. R. 315 (Sask. Q.B.); *Niebergall v. Niebergall Estate* (1986), 53 Sask. R. 289 (Sask. Q.B.); *Chityala v. Chityala* (1986), 71 A.R. 200 (Alta. Q.B.); *Harry v. Harry Estate* (1988), 67 Sask. R. 279 (Sask. Surr. Ct.); *Black v. Kronberger Estate* (1989), 81 Sask. R. 106 (Sask. Q.B.), affirmed (1990), 83 Sask. R. 73 (Sask. C.A.); *Cummine v. Cummine Estate* (1991), 91 Sask. R. 304 (Sask. Q.B.); *Penteluk v. Penteluk Estate* (1991), 95 Sask. R. 128 (Sask. Surr. Ct.), varied (1992), 100 Sask. R. 178 (Sask. C.A.), leave to appeal refused (1992), 105 Sask. R. 79 (note) (S.C.C.); *Baker v. Baker Estate* (1992), 136 A.R. 94 (Alta. Q.B.) at paragraph 87, additional reasons at (1993), 138 A.R. 1 (Alta. Q.B.); in some of the cases the applications were not successful.

12 *Re Keroack* (1957), 65 Man. R. 96 (Man. Q.B.) at 102; *Re Laur* (1975), 7 O.R. (2d) 385 (Ont. Surr. Ct.); *Adams v. Irvine*, *supra* note 11; *Menrad v. Blowers* (1982), 137 D.L.R. (3d) 309 (Man. Q.B.); *Harry v. Harry Estate*, *supra* note 11.

13 See the text at notes 112-114, 116, *infra* this chapter.

14 *Supra* note 11 at 515.

15 Also *Re Tero*, *supra* note 7 at 207. In some of the other cases contained in note 11 the courts took no notice of the fact that the separated wife had not claimed support from the husband while he was alive.

16 Ontario Act, s. 57 definitions of "dependant" and "spouse"; *Re Tothivan* (1982), 36 O.R. (2d) 410 (Ont. Surr. Ct.) at 412-13; *Re Burke* (1983), 44 O.R. (2d) 335 (Ont. Surr. Ct.); *McMacken v. McMacken* (1984), 47 O.R. (2d) 701 (Ont. Div. Ct.). Note that a term contained in the minutes of a divorce settlement terminating maintenance payments in the year 1983 barred an application by the ex-spouse against the estate of her ex-husband who died in 1985, *Taylor v. Taylor Estate* (1985), 53 O.R. (2d) 174 (Ont. Surr. Ct.); also see the text at notes 112-114, 116, *infra* this chapter.

provision was unsuccessfully challenged.[17] The legislation of Prince Edward Island and the Yukon adds the requirement "who, for a period of at least three years immediately prior to the date of the death of the deceased, was dependant upon the deceased for maintenance and support". The Manitoba Act enables applications by

> **1.** In this Act, . . .
>
> "dependant" means . . .
>
> (c) a person of the opposite sex to the deceased not legally married to the deceased who . . .
>
> (iii) was being paid or entitled to be paid maintenance and support by the deceased under an agreement or a court order at the time of the deceased's death.

A surviving spouse who has obtained or submitted to a final decree of divorce in a foreign jurisdiction which is not recognized as valid is also able to apply.[18] However, in all of these situations the separation, or the initiation or participation in the divorce proceedings might be considered disentitling conduct. *Downton v. Royal Trust Co.*[19] concerned a first wife who submitted to a Nevada divorce proceeding, commenced by her husband, to "protect her existing benefits which were given as a result of her separation from her husband in Newfoundland".[20] On the same day that the Nevada decree was granted the husband married his second wife in Nevada. The Nevada "divorce decree was without effect in Newfoundland where the spouses were domiciled at the time it was sought and granted and where the deceased remained domiciled until his death".[21] Justice Laskin, for the Court, said:

> The controlling issue in this case is not the status of the applicant [first wife] as the deceased's lawful widow but rather whether, on the facts . . . , she is precluded from asserting that status to claim statutory relief, in modification of the deceased's will, out of his estate.[22]

---

17 *Re Burke*, *supra* note 16.
18 See for example *Jones v. Kline (Jones)*, [1938] 3 W.W.R. 65 (Alta. T.D.) at 73-76.
19 [1973] S.C.R. 437 (S.C.C.).
20 *Ibid.* at 453.
21 *Ibid.* at 443.
22 *Ibid.* at 440. See also *Re Jones* (1974), 6 O.R. (2d) 11 (Ont. H.C.).

Does a common law spouse or co-habitee qualify as a spouse, wife, or husband? The legislation of Saskatchewan,[23] Manitoba, Ontario,[24] New Brunswick, Prince Edward Island,[25] the Northwest Territories,[26] and the Yukon[27] defines dependant or spouse to include co-habitees for varying lengths of time or with whom deceased had or adopted a child,[28] and in some instances requiring the applicant co-habitees to have been financially dependant upon the deceased.[29] Absent such legislation, according to *Re O'Connell*[30] a common law spouse or cohabitee does not qualify. However, in *Armstrong v. McLaughlin Estate*[31] Justice Veit of the Alberta Supreme Court decided that the Court "has the jurisdiction to define 'spouse' as including someone other than a legal spouse".[32] She remitted the issue for trial; on appeal a "full trial" was ordered.[33]

The legislation of British Columbia treats common law spouses inconsistently. The *Wills Variation Act*[34] applies, as its name indicates, only if there is a valid will or to the part of the estate in connection with which a valid will exists. It provides for applications to be made by a "testator's wife, husband or children". Amighetti asserts that "[t]here is no question

23 *Ostrander v. Kimble Estate* (1996), 146 Sask. R. 64 (Sask. Q.B.); *Paxman v. Saskatchewan (Public Trustee)* (1996), 146 Sask. R. 312 (Sask. Q.B.); *Nelson v. Stroshein Estate* (1997), 161 Sask. R. 311 (Sask. Q.B.); note also *Cummine v. Cummine Estate*, *supra* note 11 at paragraph 9, an obiter comment about an applicant having had a relationship of some permanence, resulting in a child, but no co-habitation.

24 *Re Cooper*, *supra* note 10; *Re Geiger* (1982), 11 E.T.R. 152 (Ont. Surr. Ct.); *Gibbins v. Ontario (Public Trustee)* (1981), 26 R.F.L. (2d) 282 (Ont. H.C.); *Re Nalywayko* (1984), 17 E.T.R. 151 (Ont. Surr. Ct.); *Holland v. Clements Estate* (1991), 43 E.T.R. 299 (Ont. Gen. Div.); *Burnett v. Noble Estate* (1990), 72 O.R. (2d) 583 (Ont. Surr. Ct.); *Amatnieks v. Benkis Estate* (1992), 46 E.T.R. 204 (Ont. Gen. Div.), which is particularly interesting for its consideration of whether the applicant, who lived with the deceased for 21 years in a non-sexual relationship, could be said to have cohabited with the deceased; *McEachern v. Fry Estate* (1993) quoted in *Fitton v. Hewton Estate*, *infra* note 27 at paragraph 22; *Horodyski v. Tobin Estate* (1996), 13 E.T.R. (2d) 305 (Ont. Gen. Div.), similar to *Amatniecks*, *supra* in this note; *Obringer v. Kennedy Estate* (1996), 16 E.T.R. (2d) 27 (Ont. Gen. Div.) at 31–35; *Vernon v. Dieleman Estate* (1992), 46 E.T.R. 242 (Ont. Gen. Div.) varied (1997), 16 E.T.R. (2d) 68 (Ont. C.A.).

25 *MacDonald v. MacKenzie Estate* (1989), 78 Nfld. & P.E.I.R. 76 (P.E.I. T.D.).

26 *Raymond v. Public Trustee*, [1985] N.W.T.R. 304 (N.W.T. S.C.).

27 *Fitton v. Hewton Estate* (1997), 18 E.T.R. (2d) 57 (Y.T. C.A.).

28 The Northwest Territory Act includes a co-habitee who was "acting as a foster parent of the children of the deceased in the same household and who was dependant on the deceased for maintenance and support" (s. 1 "dependant" (f)).

29 For ex., the Yukon Act, s. 1(f) and in regard to this requirement see *Fitton v. Hewton Estate*, *supra* note 27 at 65-66.

30 (1979), 109 D.L.R. (3d) 584 (N.S. T.D.).

31 (1994), 150 A.R. 343 (Alta. Q.B.).

32 *Ibid.* at 350.

33 (1995), 178 A.R. 125 (Alta. C.A.).

34 R.S.B.C. 1996, c. 490.

that the terms 'wife' and 'husband' mean a relationship resulting from a lawful marriage only [and] . . . [t]he wording of the Act does not admit any other type of union or relationship".[35] By comparison, ss. 85 and 86 of the *Estate Administration Act*[36] give the court jurisdiction to make provision for common law spouses upon an intestacy.

Although common law spouses or spouses of invalid marriages may not be able to apply for relief, certainly courts have recognized their moral claim to whatever testamentary provision a partner has made for them.[37]

The eligibility of same sex cohabitees to apply has been raised in two cases. It remains to be considered on its merits. In *Modopoulos v. Breen Estate*[38] the court commented that "the applicant may well have a compelling argument on this point", but for lack of notice the court refused to deal with it and in any event the court dismissed the application on other grounds. In *Obringer v. Kennedy Estate*[39] the court held that before the applicant could raise the constitutional issue in support of the application the applicant had to prove that he was otherwise qualified to apply, which the applicant had failed to do.

In *Bailey v. Public Trustee*[40] the Court held that a surviving spouse who had remarried was nonetheless entitled to apply as "[t]he status of a wife is fixed by her position at the moment immediately before the death of the husband and that, being a wife then, she is a qualified applicant at any time subsequently".[41]

(b) Children

Of course, all of the dependants' relief Acts enable an application by a "child" of the deceased. Although the Saskatchewan, New Brunswick, Nova Scotia, and Newfoundland Acts specifically define child to include an adopted child, there is no need for such specific inclusion because there

---

35 Amighetti, L., *The Law of Dependants' Relief in British Columbia* (Toronto: Carswell, 1991) at 73 [hereinafter Amighetti].

36 R.S.B.C. 1996, c. 122. See also *Phipps v. Cartmill* (1980), 25 B.C.L.R. 222 (B.C. S.C.); *Godden v. Cookson* (1981), 34 B.C.L.R. 263 (B.C. S.C.); *Desjarlais v. MacDonell Estate*, [1988] 3 W.W.R. 534 (B.C. C.A.).

37 *Re Schurman* (1965), 54 D.L.R. (2d) 77 (N.S. S.C.); *Re Quon*, *supra* note 7; *Simmonds v. Rehn* (1969), 3 D.L.R. (3d) 565 (Man. Q.B.) at 571; *Menrad v. Blowers*, *supra* note 12 at 318; *Pauliuk v. Pauliuk* (1986), 48 Alta. L.R. (2d) 25 (Alta. Q.B.) at 30.

38 *Supra* note 10 at 133.

39 *Supra* note 24 at 35.

40 [1960] N.Z.L.R. 741 (N.Z. C.A.). Note the commentary of Oosterhoff, A., *Succession Law Reform in Ontario* (Toronto: Carswell, 1979) at 102-03.

41 *Ibid.* at 744. *Simkins v. Blumenthal* (1995), 9 E.T.R. (2d) 53 (B.C. S.C.) involved a remarried spouse; no issue was made of the fact.

is legislation for all of the provinces[42] like ss. 57 and 61 of the *Child and Family Services Act* of Manitoba:[43]

Adoption in another jurisdiction.

57. An adoption granted according to the law of any other province, territory of Canada or of any other state or country that is substantially similar in effect to an adoption under this Part shall be recognized in the province and shall have the same force and effect as if made under this Part.

Status of adopted child.
61. (1) For all purposes of the law of Manitoba, as of the date of the making of an adoption order,

(a) the adopted child becomes the child of the adopting parent and the adopting parent becomes the parent of the adopted child; and

(b) the adopted child ceases to be the child of the person who was his or her parent before the adoption order was made and that person ceases to be the parent of the adopted child,

as if the adopted child had been born to the adopting parent.

How relationships determined.
61. (2) The relationship to one another of all persons, including the adopted child, the adopting parent, the kindred of the adopting parent, the parent before the adoption order was made and the kindred of that former parent shall for all purposes be determined in accordance with subsection (1).

Reference in will or other document.
61. (3) In any will or other document made at any time before or after the day this section comes into force, and whether the maker of the will or document is alive on that day or not, a reference to a person or group or class of persons described in terms of relationship by blood or marriage to another person shall be deemed to refer to a person who comes within the description as a result of an adoption, unless the contrary is expressed.

Application of section.
61. (4) This section applies and shall be deemed always to have applied with respect to any adoption made under any Act heretofore in force, but not so as to affect,

---

42 *Adoption Act*, R.S.B.C. 1996, c. 5, s. 37, *Child Welfare Act*, S.A. 1984, c. C-8.1, ss. 65 and 65.1, *Adoption Act*, S.S. 1989-90, c. A–5.1, ss. 18 and 26, *Child and Family Services Act*, R.S.O. 1990, c. C.11, s. 158, *Family Services Act*, S.N.B. 1980, c. F-2.2, s. 85(1), *Children and Family Services Act*, S.N.S. 1990, c. 5, ss. 80 and 97, *Adoption Act*, R.S.P.E.I. 1988, c. A-4, s. 42, *Adoption of Children Act*, R.S.N. 1990, c. A-3, s. 20, *Child Welfare Act*, R.S.N.W.T. 1988, c. C-6, ss. 100-102, *Children's Act*, R.S.Y. 1986, c. 22, ss. 5 and 98.

43 S.M. 1985-86, c. 8; C.C.S.M., c. C80.

(a) any interest in property or right of the adopted child that has indefeasibly vested before the date of the making of an adoption order; and

(b) any interest in property or right that has indefeasibly vested before the day this section comes into force.

Exception where adoption by spouse.
61. (5) Where the adopting parent has a spouse who is a parent of the person to be adopted and that parent chooses not to apply for the adoption jointly with the adopting parent, the relationship of that parent and of his or her kindred with the adopted person shall continue and shall not be altered in any way by the order for adoption.

The burden of proving an effective adoption is upon the person asserting it.

The court in *Re McAdam*[44] acknowledged a tendency of courts to accept less than strict proof of adoptions.[45] The Northwest Territories Act uniquely provides:

3. In this Act,

"child" includes . . .

(b) a child who appears to the satisfaction of the Supreme Court in effect to have been adopted although there has not been compliance with the *Child Welfare Act*,

If an adoption is proved to the satisfaction of the court it is of no consequence that it occurred in another province, state, or country; in other words, foreign adoptions should be recognized.[46]

Absent legislation such as the definition of child in the Northwest Territories Act

1. In this Act,

"child" includes . . .

(a) . . . a stepchild,

---

44 (1925), 35 B.C.R. 547 (B.C. S.C.) at 549.

45 For ex, *Re Lawther*, [1947] 1 W.W.R. 577 (Man. K.B.) at 579; *Trainor v. Toronto General Trusts Corp.*, *supra* note 7, McPherson C.J.M. dissenting 163 and Adamson J.A. 173 in regard to one of the children. Cf. *Re Esplin*, [1946] 1 W.W.R. 679 (B.C. S.C.); *Kennedy v. McIntyre Estate* (1987), 47 Man. R. (2d) 16 (Man. Q.B.) at paragraphs 21-22; *Hutton v. Podgurski* (1989), 58 D.L.R. (4th) 637 (B.C. C.A.), additional reasons at (1989), 58 D.L.R. (4th) 637 at 641 (B.C. C.A.); *Hope v. Raeder Estate* (1994), 2 B.C.L.R. (3d) 58 (B.C. C.A.).

46 *Re McAdam*, *supra* note 44; *Re Ramsey* (1935), 50 B.C.R. 83 (B.C. S.C.).

> (b) a child who appears to the satisfaction of the Supreme Court in effect to have been adopted although there has not been compliance with the *Child Welfare Act*[47]

in the Manitoba Act

> **1.** In this Act,
>
> "child" includes . . .
>
> (b) a child to whom the deceased stood in loco parentis at the time of the deceased's death, except under an arrangement where the child is placed for valuable consideration in a foster home by a person having lawful custody

and in the Ontario Act

> **57.** In this Part,
>
> "child" means a child . . . and includes . . . a person whom the deceased has demonstrated a settled intention to treat as a child of his or her family, except under an arrangement where the child is placed for valuable consideration in a foster home by a person having lawful custody.[48]

courts have rejected applications by children to whom the deceased stood in *loco parentis*[49] and stepchildren.[50]

While adopted children can apply for relief from the estates of their adopting parents, can they also apply for relief from the estates of their natural parents other than a parent to whom s. 61(5) of the Manitoba *Child and Family Services Act*, above, applies? I think that the answer is no. However, the court in *Hart (Guardian ad litem of) v. Hart Estate*[51] came to the opposite conclusion. The case involved applications by the children of the deceased. Two of the children had been adopted by their mother's second husband following her divorce from the deceased. They were adopted by their then step-father "for the sake of appearances" after they began attending the same school as his children and using his surname. With

---

47 For ex., *Butt v. Chittock Estate* (1995), [1996] N.W.T.R. 104 (N.W.T. S.C.).

48 *Re Pflanzner* (1983), 15 E.T.R. 144 (Ont. Surr. Ct.) at 153.

49 *Re Buchanan Estate* (1975), 16 N.S.R. (2d) 262 (N.S. Co. Ct.); *Re Esplin, supra* note 45; *Kennedy v. McIntyre Estate, supra* note 45, superceded by the definition of child in the current *Dependants Relief Act* of Manitoba; *MacDonald v. MacKenzie Estate, supra* note 25 at paragraphs 26-29; *Hope v. Raeder Estate, supra*, note 45.

50 *Naples v. Martin Estate* (1986), 7 B.C.L.R. (2d) 134 (B.C. S.C.). Cf. *Re Pflanzner, supra* note 48, in which a step-child qualified pursuant to the Ontario *Succession Law Reform Act*, s. 57 definition of "child".

51 (1993), (*sub nom. Hart v. Hart Estate*) 124 N.S.R. (2d) 333 (N.S. S.C.).

reference to a Manitoba case, which has been eclipsed[52] by a s. 61 of the *Child and Family Services Act*, above, the court decided that s. 80(1) of the Nova Scotia *Children and Family Services Act* does not "preclude an adopted child seeking proper maintenance and support from his or her lawful lineal ancestor under the *Testator's Family Maintenance Act*". There is essentially no difference in the wording of s. 80(1) of the *Children and Family Services Act* of Nova Scotia from s. 61(1) of the Manitoba *Child and Family Services Act*, above, and the comparable legislation in the other provinces.

The Alberta, Nova Scotia,[53] and Northwest Territories Acts by defining child to include "a child born . . . outside marriage", "of which the testator is the natural parent" and "a natural child", respectively, enable applications by illegitimate children; such applications are enabled in other provinces by other legislation.[54] While it is easy to say that illegitimate children potentially qualify as dependants under all the Acts, proving parentage may not be so easy.[55] Court ordered blood tests have been an issue in a couple of cases.[56]

Except for in the British Columbia Act,[57] the definition of child in all the Canadian Acts includes with various wordings a child conceived before and born alive after the parent's death or a child of the deceased en ventre

---

52 *Huston v. Ash* (1984), 30 Man. R. (2d) 241 (Man. C.A.).

53 For ex., *Re Johnson* (1982), 52 N.S.R. (2d) 508 (N.S. T.D.).

54 *Charter of Rights Amendments Act 1985*, S.B.C. 1985, c. 68, ss. 80 and 119, which makes obsolete *Re Brosseau* (1974), 19 R.F.L. 255 (B.C. S.C.); *Children's Law Act*, S.S. 1990-91, c. C-8.1, ss. 40-41, which makes obsolete *Blair v. Fishleigh* (1950), 1 W.W.R. (N.S.) 20 (Sask. C.A.) and *Re Garajczki* (1960), 32 W.W.R. 145 (Sask. C.A.); *Family Maintenance Act*, R.S.M. 1987, c. F20; C.C.S.M., c. F20, ss. 17-18, which supercedes the concern of the court in *Pam v. Gale* (1949), 58 Man. R. 68 (Man. Referee), reversed [1950] 2 W.W.R. 802 (Man. K.B.); *Children's Law Reform Act*, R.S.O. 1990, c. C.12, ss. 1-2; *Family Services Act*, S.N.B. 1980, c. F-2.2, ss. 96-97; *Child Status Act*, R.S.P.E.I. 1988, c. C-6, ss. 1-2; *Children's Act*, R.S.Y. 1986, c. 22, ss. 5-6.

55 See for ex., *Cox v. Nova Scotia (Public Trustee)* (1983), 56 N.S.R. (2d) 657 (N.S. T.D.); *Re Ruby* (1983), 43 O.R. (2d) 277 (Ont. Surr. Ct.); *Re Anderson Estate* (1986), 76 N.S.R. (2d) 251 (N.S. T.D.); *Hafner v. Sarganis Estate* (1994), 95 B.C.L.R. (2d) 389 (B.C. S.C.); and also Hull, R., *Support of Dependants under the Succession Law Reform Act of Ontario* (Toronto: Carswell 1978) at 8-9. For a couple of cases decided pursuant to a now repealed section of the Saskatchewan Act respecting illegitimate children of a male testator see *Chickeness v. Shields* (1984), 32 Sask. R. 61 (Sask. Q.B.) and *Cook v. Hrychuk Estate* (1987), 63 Sask. R. 310 (Sask. Q.B.), varied (1989), 71 Sask R. 303 (Sask. C.A.).

56 *S.(D.M.) v. C.(J.) Estate* (1994), 6 E.T.R. (2d) 197 (B.C. S.C.) ordered DNA testing of two nephews of the deceased; *Roussel v. Hill Estate* (1996), 14 E.T.R. (2d) 111 (Ont. Gen. Div.) refused testing the deceased. Note also *Lee v. Lee Estate* (1993), 84 B.C.L.R. (2d) 341 (B.C. Master) at paragraphs 1-6.

57 But see Amighetti at 78-79.

sa mère at the time of the deceased's death. The various definitions are capable of being interpreted to include children born after a father's death and, in the rare situation, a child born after the mother's death.[58]

The Acts of Alberta, Saskatchewan, Manitoba, and Prince Edward Island distinguish between children under 18 years of age and older; the significant age in the Northwest Territories Act is 19 and in the Yukon Act it is 16. Children under the designated age are able to apply without qualification. Various qualifications are imposed for children of or over the designated age: "unable by reason of mental or physical disability to earn a livelihood", Alberta,[59] Prince Edward Island, Northwest Territories, and the Yukon; "who alleges or on whose behalf it is alleged that: (i) by reason of mental or physical disability he or she is unable to earn a livelihood; or (ii) that by reason of need or other circumstances he or she ought to receive a greater share of the estate . . .", Saskatchewan;[60] "who by reason of illness, disability or other cause was, at the time of the deceased's death, unable to withdraw from the charge of the deceased or to provide himself or herself with the necessaries of life or . . . who was substantially dependant on the deceased at the time of the deceased's death", Manitoba. The qualification in the Saskatchewan Act includes "who alleges . . . by reason of need or other circumstances he ought to receive a greater share of the estate. . .". This enabled an impoverished son living in Hungary to apply, who would not have been eligible to apply by the qualifying wording of the other Acts.[61]

All of the Acts expressly indicate that the determining date is the date of the deceased's death. Thus, in *Alberta (Public Trustee) v. Buchholz*[62] it was of no consequence that one of the applicant children attained the age of 18 subsequent to her father's death. Similarly, the court in *Hiebert v. Ward*,[63] with reference to *Re Brown*,[64] entertained the applications of

---

58 *In re Franks*, [1948] Ch. 62 (U.K. Ch.).

59 *Re Barclay* (1952), 5 W.W.R. (N.S.) 308 (Alta. S.C.); and *Re Bowers* (1955), 19 W.W.R. 241 (Alta. S.C.).

60 *McCaw v. McCaw* (1983), 29 Sask. R. 39 (Sask. Surr. Ct.). Regarding "being unable . . . to earn a livelihood", the court in *Re Taylor* (1960), 33 W.W.R. 699 (Sask. C.A.) held that a daughter, who deposed that she was "in a poor state of health and require[d] surgery" was only suffering a "temporary disability . . . not sufficient to qualify the applicant as a 'dependant'"; similarly, *Re DeRoche Estate* (1964), 51 W.W.R. 120 (Sask. Q.B.) at 123.

61 *Re Parkanski* (1966), 56 D.L.R. (2d) 475 (Sask. Q.B.). See also *McCaw v. McCaw*, *supra* note 60 at paragraphs 20-38.

62 (1980), 24 A.R. 287 (Alta. C.A.) at paragraph 28.

63 (1980), 3 Sask. R. 255 (Sask. Q.B.) at paragraphs 10-11.

64 (1969), 70 W.W.R. 543 (Sask. Q.B.).

over-age children on the basis that they were under-age on the date of the deceased's death.[65]

The Ontario Act limits applications by children but not by reference to age. The Act defines dependant in part as follows:

> **57.** In this Part, . . .
>
> "dependant" means,
>
> . . .
>
> (c) a child of the deceased,
>
> . . .
>
> to whom the deceased was providing support or was under a legal obligation to provide support immediately before his or her death.

The *Family Law Act*[66] provides:

> **31.** (1) Every parent has an obligation to provide support, in accordance with need, for his or her unmarried child who is a minor or is enrolled in a full time program of education, to the extent that the parent is capable of doing so.
>
> (2) The obligation under subsection (1) does not extend to a child who is sixteen years of age or older and has withdrawn from parental control.

In *Re Trenton*[67] the court held that a father was providing support to his 57 year old son by providing him with rent free accommodation.

(c) Grandchildren

The Manitoba, Ontario, Prince Edward Island, and the Yukon Acts make grandchildren eligible to apply, but in Manitoba only if the grandchild "was substantially dependant on the deceased at the time of the deceased's death" and in P.E.I. and the Yukon only if the grandchild "for a period of at least three years immediately prior to the date of the death of the deceased was dependent upon him for maintenance and support". In British Colum-

---

65 Cf. the earlier decision in *Re DeRoche Estate*, *supra* note 60 and the recent decision in *Wilson v. Kosok* (1996), 146 Sask. R. 105 (Sask. Q.B.) at paragraphs 16-17; note also *Re Bourne*, [1950] O.W.N. 807 (Ont. Surr. Ct.) decided at a time when the Ontario Act of the day required a child to be under the age of 16 or unable to earn a livelihood.

66 R.S.O. 1990, c. F.3.

67 (1987), 26 E.T.R. 209 (Ont. Surr. Ct.) at 219–21.

bia and Saskatchewan, the Acts of which are silent about grandchildren, the courts have rejected applications by or on behalf of grandchildren.[68]

Although grandchildren may not be able to apply, minor grandchildren are a circumstance which courts have taken into account on applications by children of the deceased[69] and which s. 62(1)(k) of the Ontario Act requires to be considered.

(d) Parents, Grandparents

The Manitoba, Ontario, Prince Edward Island, and Yukon Acts enable applications by parents and grandparents, who were dependent and in the Ontario Act "to whom the deceased . . . was under a legal obligation to provide support". The Ontario Act defines parent to include "a person who has demonstrated a settled intention to treat the deceased as a child of his or her family, except under an arrangement where the deceased was placed for valuable consideration in a foster home by a person having lawful custody".

The New Brunswick Act enables applications by needy parents who have cared for and provided support to the deceased child.

(e) Siblings

Dependant siblings are able to apply pursuant to the Manitoba and Ontario Acts.

(f) Representatives

All of the Acts, except the Ontario Act, provide for applications to be made "by or on behalf of" a dependant. Presumably, "on behalf of" contemplates the commencement of a proceeding by the personal representative of the deceased to accelerate the administration of the estate, by a parent or guardian on behalf of a minor, and by a committee or attorney

---

68 *George v. Else* (1958), 26 W.W.R. 229 (B.C. C.A.); *DeRoche Estate*, *supra* note 60 at 123.

69 *Re Jones* (1934), 49 B.C.R. 216 (B.C. S.C.) at 221; *Re Dickinson* (1944), 60 B.C.R. 214 (B.C. S.C.) at 217; *Re Cole* (1958), 40 M.P.R. 201 (N.S. T.D.) at 217–18; *Re Pfrimmer Estate* (1968), 66 W.W.R. 574 (Man. C.A.) at 575, leave to appeal refused (1968), 2 D.L.R. (3d) 720 (Man. C.A.); *Leard v. Maki* (1982), 36 B.C.L.R. 92 (B.C. S.C.) at 98; *Driscoll v. Driscoll Estate* (1988), 88 N.S.R. (2d) 1 (N.S. T.D.) at paragraph 94; *Kuhn v. Kuhn Estate* (1992), 112 N.S.R. (2d) 38 (N.S. T.D.) at paragraph 48. Cf. *Re DeRoche Estate*, *supra* note 60 at 123. Besides these cases, it is common for judges to mention in the description of an applicant's circumstances the existence of minor children of the applicant.

pursuant to an (enduring) power of attorney on behalf of an incapable dependant. The Ontario Act in s. 58(2) provides for applications to be made by a "dependant or the dependant's parent". The Alberta Act also provides:

> **13.** (2) An application may be made
>
> (a) by the trustee of the estate of a dependent adult on behalf of the dependant if the dependant is one for whose estate a trustee has been appointed by a court or designated by statute, and
>
> (b) by a parent or by a guardian appointed by a court or by the Public Trustee, on behalf of a dependant who is a minor.
>
> **14.** If it appears that at the date of the deceased's death the spouses were living together and
>
> (a) all the children of the deceased who at the date of the deceased's death were under the age of 18 years, and
>
> (b) all the children of 18 years of age or over who by reason of mental or physical disability were unable to earn a livelihood,
>
> were living with or being supported by the spouses or either of them, there is no obligation on the guardian, Public Trustee or other person representing a child who is a dependant under this Act to make an application on behalf of the child if the guardian, Public Trustee or other person is satisfied that the child is receiving adequate maintenance and support.

Surely, even apart from this express Alberta legislative enablement, the Public Trustee (or the Official Guardian or whatever that office is called in the other provinces) has a right to apply on behalf of a minor or otherwise incapable dependants.[70] One question is when is such an application appropriate?[71] This question has been considered in four cases respecting a surviving spouse and minor children when the deceased spouse's will gave all the deceased spouse's estate to the surviving spouse. The conundrum for the Public Trustee was nicely described by Justice Lieberman in *Alberta (Public Trustee) v. Buchholz*.[72] The trial court made an order in favour of the children, which was appealed by the Public Trustee, but not by the widow even though her counsel

> . . . made it abundantly clear that Mrs. Buchholz was offended by the intervention of a branch of governmental bureaucracy into the life of a warm, caring and happy family unit. This, it is suggested is particularly offensive

70 For ex., *Re Brousseau* (1952), 7 W.W.R. (N.S.) 262 (B.C. S.C.), at 264.

71 *Hayzel v. Alberta (Public Trustee)* (1963), 44 W.W.R. 582 (Alta. T.D.) the court held that, regarding a mentally incompetent child resident in Czechoslovakia, it was up to the appropriate public authority of Czechoslovakia, not the Public Trustee of Alberta, "to have vested in it the right to apply".

72 *Supra* note 62.

when there is no intimation that Mrs. Buchholz will do anything other than continue to provide a superior family environment, including ample maintenance and support for the dependent children. The evidence overwhelmingly suggests that she will do just that, and certainly that was the view of the testator. Counsel for the appellant agrees that in this case there is no basis for fearing that the dependent children will not have adequate maintenance and support, but he suggests that Mrs. Buchholz may fall prey to "unscrupulous confidence men" or to "suave Lochinvars", who will influence her to the extent that the dependent children will ultimately be deprived of adequate maintenance and support.

In essence counsel for the appellant is asking this court to treat this appeal as a "test case", so that in all estates where the will makes no provision for the maintenance and support of dependent children such maintenance and support should be ordered by the court if the Public Trustee, notwithstanding the provisions of [s. 14] of the Act, chooses to make an application for maintenance and support.

I am of the firm view that the circumstances of this case are not appropriate for setting any policy or precedent. I have come to this conclusion for the following amongst other reasons:

1. There has been no cross-appeal, and therefore no consideration has been given to [s. 14] of the Act. . .

2. The learned Chambers judge's exercise of discretion to make provision for the support and maintenance of the dependent children has not been challenged.

3. The fact that at the time of the application herein only two of the five children were found to be dependent. . .

I recognize that there is an increasing awareness of the rights of minors and of their need for legal representation in many areas, such as contests between husband and wife over custody. I am, however, cognizant of the deep resentment that people in our society feel towards governmental interference into essentially private family areas, particularly where all the evidence leads to only one conclusion, namely, that the children are being treated with love and understanding, that they are being brought up in an excellent environment, that their education is being encouraged and that there is ample provision for their maintenance and support.

The conflict that exists between society's concern for the welfare of dependent children and our traditional concept of the privacy and sanctity of the family unit and the right of one parent to depend upon the other to provide maintenance and support in all facets to their children was faced by Ford J., as he then was, in *Re Denton Estate,* [1950] 2 W.W.R. 848. In that case the testator died at age 41 leaving him surviving his widow and five infant children, the eldest of whom was 11 years of age. The testator's will was a simple one and was in his own handwriting. It read:

> I leave everything I own to my wife Elizabeth. She can act as trustee to see that the children get good and complete education out of my estate.

> Application was made by the Public Trustee under the then *Testators Family Maintenance Act*, . . . the relevant sections of which are similar to those sections of the *Family Relief Act* that come into play in this appeal. Ford, J., found that the five infant children were dependants within the meaning of the Act. He further held that the "maintenance and support" referred to in the Act was not limited to the age upon which a dependent child ceases to be dependent under the Act.

> With respect to the provision for adequate maintenance and support Ford, J., says this:

>> I was impressed with the evidence of the widow of the testator and I think that the confidence of the testator in her, as shown in the will itself, is to be considered in deciding whether or not adequate provision for the proper maintenance and support of the five infant children of the testator is provided for in the will. However, after giving the question some anxious thought, I have reached the conclusion that a sense of prudence must indicate that it does not ensure such adequate provision.

> The learned judge then ordered that the sum of $100,000 be held in trust for the benefit of the five infant children equally.[73]

In *Re Malat*,[74] the court dismissed an application by the Public Trustee to be appointed guardian of two minor children for the purpose of making an application on their behalf pursuant to the then *Testator's Family Maintenance Act* of British Columbia. Justice Meredith could have dismissed the application on a technical ground but he chose to say:

> In any event I do not think it has been shown, nor should it be assumed, that, even if proceedings under the Testator's Family Maintenance Act were to result in some special provision for the two children out of the estate, such provision would in net advance the welfare of the children. Proceedings under the Act would effectively pit the children against their mother, thrust upon the estate unwanted costs, occasion anxiety, pre-occupation and other strains on all sides, to say nothing of the risk of family discord. The possible disruption might well be much more harmful to the children than any benefit they might possibly receive from the estate

> I have not the slightest reason to suppose that Mrs. Malat will do other than the best for all her children during her lifetime. Nor should I speculate that she will do other than make adequate provision for her children out of what may remain of her assets, including those inherited from her husband, on her death.

---

73 *Ibid.* at paragraphs 26-28.

74 (August 18, 1975), Doc. Vancouver X8945/75 (B.C. S.C.).

> Accordingly, as I am inclined to the view that the order sought would detract from rather than advance the interest of the two children, the order is refused.[75]

Justice Hood came to a similar conclusion in *Cameron (Public Trustee of) v. Cameron Estate*,[76] which was appealed by the Public Trustee, but only in respect of the order of costs.[77] In *British Columbia (Public Trustee) v. Williams Estate*[78] the Public Trustee commenced an action on behalf of a severely mentally retarded son who had been given nothing by his mother's will. In the writ the Public Trustee was described as guardian *ad litem* of the son even though the Public Trustee had not been so appointed and had received no instructions to act on behalf of the son. The Public Trustee filed the writ to preserve the son's cause of action. The executors of the mother's estate sought to have the Public Trustee's action dismissed. On the basis of British Columbia's *Public Trustee Act* and the Court's Rule respecting guardians *ad litem*, the Court of Appeal decided:

> . . . where, as here, the Public Trustee becomes aware of a person under disability ordinarily resident outside the province for whom no person ordinarily resident within the province is prepared to act as guardian ad litem, it is appropriate for the Public Trustee to act as guardian ad litem in order to preserve a right of action which may accure to such person under disability.
>
> . . . the Public Trustee is authorized to act as guardian ad litem of a person under disability who resides outside the province, without being appointed by the court. I have concluded, contrary to the decision reached by the learned Chambers Judge, that the Public Trustee had authority to act in this case as guardian ad litem of Ronald Williams and to commence the action herein on his behalf without court approval.

The Alberta Act, s. 14, above, expressly makes it clear that there is no obligation on the Public Trustee to intervene on behalf of minor children in these circumstances. The cases indicate a similar judicial opinion.

(g) Other

The Ontario Act in s. 58(3) uniquely provides:

> (3) An application for an order for the support of a dependant may also be made by one of the following agencies:

---

75 Amighetti at 80-81.

76 (1991), (*sub nom. British Columbia (Public Trustee) v. Cameron Estate*) 58 B.C.L.R. (2d) 71 (B.C. S.C.).

77 (1991), (*sub nom. British Columbia (Public Trustee) v. Cameron Estate*) 58 B.C.L.R. (2d) 82 (B.C. C.A.).

78 (1991), 42 E.T.R. 44 (B.C. C.A.) at paragraphs 32-33.

(a) the Ministry of Community and Social Services in the name of the Minister;

(b) a municipal corporation, including a metropolitan, district or regional municipality, but not including an area municipality;

(c) a district welfare administration board under the *District Welfare Administration Boards Act*; or

(d) a band approved under section 15 of the *General Welfare Assistance Act*,

if the agency is providing or has provided a benefit under the *Family Benefits Act* or assistance under the *General Welfare Assistance Act* in respect of the dependant's support, or if an application for such a benefit or assistance has been made to the agency by or on behalf of the dependant.

This legislation allows applications to be made by agencies to recover the costs of providing support and maintenance to dependants. Similar legislation was proposed but eventually not enacted in Manitoba. The issue of whether such applications can be made within the general wording "on behalf of" a dependant has never been litigated.

2. BARS TO APPLYING?

(a) Lack of Need

Although lack of need may have been, in effect, a bar to applying pursuant to the former *Dependants Relief Act* of Ontario[79] and pursuant to one line of British Columbia cases, need is not a *sine qua non* under any of the Acts, except the Manitoba Act. Only under the Manitoba Act must an applicant have been truly dependant upon the deceased. In provinces other than Manitoba, while not a bar to an application, need is a very important factor.

(b) Death

Does the right to apply or to continue an application to an appellate conclusion survive the death of a dependant? In other words, can the personal representative of a dependant who survives a deceased spouse, co-habitee, parent, or child, as the case may be, commence or continue an application? The Nova Scotia Act uniquely provides:

17. The right to apply for an order for relief under this Act does not survive the death of a dependant.

---

79 *Re Cooper*, *supra* note 10 at 119.

The section does not speak to the continuation of a proceeding commenced before a dependant dies.

Justice Egbert dealt with the situation of a dependant who died before the application was heard in *Re McMaster*.[80] First, he decided that had the dependant been alive he would have awarded her a lump sum of $5,000.00. Then he proceeded:

> Assuming that the widow was entitled to relief in the amount and manner above indicated, what was the effect of her death before any application was made or any order given?
>
> Counsel for the plaintiffs contends that the widow's rights under the Act devolved upon her executors, who may still maintain the application for relief. He relies principally upon the judgment of O'Halloran, J.A. in *Barker v. Westminster Trust Co.* [1941] 3 WWR 473, 614, and that of the Ontario Court of Appeal in *Re McCaffery* [1931] OR 512. In the *Barker* case O'Halloran, J.A. was emphatically of the opinion that the petitioner husband's right under the B.C. *Testator's Family Maintenance Act*, RSBC, 1936, ch. 285, passed to his personal representative; that the maxim *actio personalis moritur cum persona* had no application as it is applicable only to actions in tort in which loss did not result to the estate, and to actions in contract founded on injury to the person or reputation only; that the petitioner's right was a vested statutory right to proper maintenance and support; and that a corresponding statutory duty lay upon the testator to provide such proper maintenance and support; and that any attempt to read into the statute an intent that it apply only to living persons was an attempt by misdirection to read the above maxim into the statute in a case where it was definitely excluded. O'Halloran, J.A. also referred to sec. 13 of the B.C. Act which provides that an application under the Act may be made by "an executor on behalf of any person entitled," [the current Act no longer so provides] which he interpreted as including the executor of a deceased dependant. The views of O'Halloran, J.A. seem to rest chiefly upon his belief that by the statute there is conferred on and vested in the dependant a statutory right, and imposed on the deceased a statutory duty to provide adequately proper maintenance and support. I gather that the learned judge had not had the advantage of reading the Privy Council judgment delivered by Viscount Cave, L.C. in *Dillon v. N.Z. Public Trustee* [1941] 3 WWR 865, [1941] AC 294, 110 LJPC 24, which was published at about the same time as the *Barker* judgment. In that case Viscount Simon pointed out that the New Zealand statute (similar to the Alberta statute) does not impose any duty on a testator to frame a will in any particular way and that a testator does not fail to observe any statutory duty by failing to make adequate provision for the proper support and maintenance of a dependant; that all the statute does is to confer on the court discretionary jurisdiction to amend the provisions of a will by ordering additional provision for dependants; that the willmaking power remains intact and no legal duty is offended against when

80 (1957), 21 W.W.R. 603 (Alta. S.C).

adequate provision is not made. With respect, it seems to me that this judgment is an effectual answer to the main reason for judgment of O'Halloran, J.A. As to his reason based on sec. 13 of the B.C. statute, I would point out that the similar sec. 13 of the Alberta Act makes no reference to an application by "an executor." I must, with respect, say that I entirely disagree with the reasons of O'Halloran, J.A. In my opinion no vested right arises under the Act and no statutory obligation is imposed on a testator. McDonald, J.A. in the *Barker* case, was in complete disagreement with O'Halloran, J.A. In his opinion the Act does not create a legal right but provides for a bounty in the discretion of the court, and there being no legal right there was nothing which could pass to the personal representative. He points out that the question is not whether the proceedings constituted acts *personalis* perishing with the party, but whether the peculiar and anomalous powers given by the Act are such that they can or should be exercised in favour of anyone rather than the petitioner himself. He asks:

> "How can the court be asked to meet the needs of a person who no longer needs anything? How can the court properly provide for the maintenance of a person who can no longer be maintained?"

And he is definite in his conclusion that the Act can be invoked only by living persons for whose proper maintenance and support adequate provision has not been made. Sloan, C.J.B.C., while concurring with O'Halloran, J.A. in the disposition of the appeal expressly refrained from deciding this point. With respect, I may say that I am wholly in accord with the views expressed by McDonald, J.A.

In the Ontario case relied on by counsel for the plaintiff *(Re McCaffery, supra)*, the deceased died in April, 1930. An application for relief was made by his widow on October 28, 1930. Judgment was reserved and reasons for judgment were completed on January 3, 1931, but were not handed to the registrar until January 5. The widow died on January 4. The trial judge directed that his judgment be entered *nunc pro tunc* as of the day of the hearing. The Court of Appeal held that the trial judge had power to make such direction but that he should have considered the intervening change in affairs since the dependant was entitled to take advantage of subsequent events and to have the case disposed of upon the facts as they appeared when judgment came to be given. Accordingly it eliminated the lump sum granted by the trial judge to the widow as such a payment would be not for her future maintenance but only a sum for her to dispose of by will. It allowed a payment of $1,000 to the widow's estate as fairly representing the maintenance she would have been entitled to between the date of the testator's death and her own death, had judgment been delivered at the time of the hearing, and being approximately the amount required to cover her funeral expenses and debts.

It seems to me that this case has little application here. In the *McCaffery* case the application was made during the lifetime of the widow; it was only the court's delay which prevented her from obtaining an effective order and the benefits arising therefrom—and even though this delay deprived her of her effective order she was still not allowed all the benefits she would have received had the order been granted promptly. In this case no application was made during the widow's lifetime—by the time the application was made the widow was dead and it was obvious that no need at all existed for maintenance and support. The circumstances of these two cases are so different that in my view the *McCaffery* case affords no assistance to the plaintiff.

The defendants rely on the judgment of the Saskatchewan Court of Appeal in *Re Smith Estate; Wetzel v. National Trust Co.* (1956) 18 WWR 556. In that case the Court of Appeal gave a judgment allowing the applicant widow twothirds of her husband's estate. It subsequently transpired that the widow had died six days before the delivery of the court's judgment. An application was made to set aside the judgment on the ground that it was a nullity and it was held that the order was invalid as the Act does not permit the court to make an order for the maintenance of a deceased dependant. The court pointed out (as opposed to the views of O'Halloran, J.A. in the *Barker* case) that the Act creates no vested interest in any dependant—merely a right to apply for maintenance when reasonable provisions therefor are not made. Since the purpose of the Act is not to assist a dependant in building up an estate, but has as its sole object the provision of adequate maintenance, it can be invoked only by a living dependant. The court expressed its concurrence with the view of Shaunessy, C.C.J. in *Re Kerby Estate* [1949] OWN 187, a case where no application was made during the dependant's lifetime. Shaunessy, C.C.J. pointed out that nowhere in the Act is any mention made of the personal representative of a deceased dependant, and that no definite interest is given to any dependant but merely a right to apply for maintenance, restricted to the lifetime of the dependant. He analyzes and disagrees with the views of O'Halloran, J.A. in the *Barker* case and concludes: "*The Dependants Relief Act* was intended to authorize a judge to grant relief to living persons only." As I have said the Saskatchewan Court of Appeal expressed its full approval of the views of Shaunessy, C.C.J. and with respect I add my own approval to that of the Saskatchewan court.

In conclusion I would point out that nowhere in the Act does it appear that any right is conferred on anyone but a "dependant" and since the first concern of the court is the need for maintenance and support "dependant" must in my opinion mean a living dependant, since no need for support can exist if the dependant is not living. The controlling section of the Act—sec. 4 (as amended in 1955 by ch. 66) which confers jurisdiction upon the court, clearly indicates that the discretionary jurisdiction is conferred only for the purpose of enabling the court to make adequate provision for the maintenance and support of a dependant. If a dependant dies before such provision is made, the result is that not only the need for maintenance and support disappears, but the dependant also disappears and there is not only no need for maintenance and support (on the existence of which depends the court's jurisdiction) but no person in whose favour any provision could be made. As I intimated in *In re Willan Estate, supra,* [(1951-52) 4 W.W.R. (NS) 114] the Act, derogating as it does from the

> will–making power of a testator, must be construed strictly, and since there is nowhere in the Act any provision or suggestion of a provision that any right devolves upon the personal representative of a deceased dependant, no such provision should be read into the Act, and the right must be confined to those persons on whom it is clearly bestowed by the Act, i.e., "dependants" who in the light of the purpose and intent of the Act must be construed as living dependants. I accordingly find that the widow's right to relief and to apply for relief terminated upon her death, and the application for relief by her executors is dismissed. . . .[81]

As Justice Egbert indicated, *Re Kerby*[82] was also a case of the executors of a deceased dependant being denied permission to apply on behalf of the deceased dependant. The only other case of this ilk is *Currie Estate v. Bowen.*[83] With reference to *Barker v. Westminster Trust Co.* and *McCarvill v. Jones*,[84] and on the basis that dependants' relief legislation exists not only to take care of needy "dependants", but also to enforce a moral obligation to give a fair share of one's estate to one's "dependants", Justice Hutchinson concluded:

> On these authorities I am satisfied that the Wills Variation Act granted Patience Currie the right to claim an equitable share in the estate of her husband. Because the right to advance this claim was granted by statute, it is not founded in tort and as it is broader than a claim for mere support or maintenance, it follows that the cause of action survives the death of Patience Currie, it is not "actio personalis". This right vested in her at the time of Dennis Currie's death (*Walker v. McDermott*, [1931] S.C.R. 94, [1931] 1 D.L.R. 662 [B.C.]). While the statute does not explicitly authorize the claim to be made on her behalf by a personal representative as it did under s. 13 of the Testator's Family Maintenance Act, I find the words in s. 2, "in an action by or on behalf of the wife" authorize the commencement of this action by personal representatives.[85]

Barker v. Westminster Trust Co., *Re McCaffery*, and *Re Smith; Wetzel v. National Trust Co.*, to which Justice Egbert made reference in the *Re McMaster* quote, above, are cases in which the dependant died after commencing the application. There are also *Calladine v. Farrar*,[86] *Wildeman v.*

---

81 *Ibid.* at 605-09.

82 [1949] O.W.N. 187 (Ont. Co. Ct.).

83 (1989), 35 B.C.L.R. (2d) 46 (B.C. S.C.).

84 [1962] S.C.R. 273 (S.C.C.), which did not involve an application on behalf of a deceased dependant.

85 *Supra* note 83 at 49.

86 (1958), 25 W.W.R. 175 (B.C. S.C.).

Co-operative Trust Co.,[87] *Brauer v. Hilton*,[88] *Vien Estate v. Vien Estate*[89] and *Golverk-Berger v. Berger Estate*.[90] In *Barker*, *McCaffery*, *Hawke*, *Calladine*, and *Brauer*, awards were made, varying from as if the applicant were alive[91] to awards taking into account the death of the applicant.[92] In *Smith*, *Wildeman*, *Vien* and *Golverk*, the applications were dismissed, essentially on the reasoning that dependants' relief legislation exists to take care of the need of living dependants; in *Golverk* the judge "regretfully" dismissed the application even though it had been made to provide for the repayment of funds loaned to the applicant when she found herself in desperate straits after the death of her husband when he failed to make adequate provision for her in his will.[93]

(c) Remarriage

There are no Canadian cases in which an issue has been made of the fact,[94] but in *Bailey v. Public Trustee*[95] the Court held that a surviving spouse who had remarried was nonetheless entitled to apply as "[t]he status of a wife is fixed by her position at the moment immediately before the death of the husband and that, being a wife then she is a qualified applicant at any time subsequently."[96] Probably, in assessing need, a court will take into account the income of the spouse of a remarried spouse, although whether this should be a relevant factor is as questionable as it is for an adult child.[97]

---

87 (1973), 39 D.L.R. (3d) 767 (Sask. Q.B.).

88 (1979), 15 B.C.L.R. 116 (B.C. C.A.) at 124.

89 (1985), (*sub nom. Re Vien*) 50 O.R. (2d) 246 (Ont. H.C.), affirmed (1988), 64 O.R. (2d) 230 (Ont. C.A.).

90 (1986), 22 E.T.R. 195 (Ont. Surr. Ct.), amended (May 30, 1986), Doc. York 5345/80 (Ont. Surr. Ct.); note also *Fox v. Grass* (1986), 22 E.T.R. 318 (Ont. Surr. Ct.).

91 *Barker*, *Calladine*, *Brauer*.

92 *McCaffery*, *Hawke* as speculated by *Coffey v. Bennet*, [1961] V.R. 264 (Australia S.C.) at 260.

93 There are also *Swain v Dennison* (1965), 54 W.W.R. 606, (B.C. C.A.), affirmed (1966), 58 W.W.R. 232 (S.C.C.) in which Bull J.A. observed that the interest of a son who died "during the proceedings ceased on his death" and *Fox v. Grass*, *supra* note 90.

94 However, *Simkins v. Blumenthal*, *supra*, note 41 involved a remarried spouse.

95 *Supra*, note 40. Note the commentary of Oosterhoff, A., *Succession Law Reform in Ontario* (Toronto: Carswell, 1979) at 102-03.

96 *Ibid.* at 744.

97 See *infra* Chp. 4, 2. and 2.(c)(ii) at the text accompanying notes 118-19.

(d) Intestacy

Initially, the British Columbia, Alberta, Saskatchewan, Ontario, New Brunswick, and Nova Scotia Acts, were only available if a husband died testate, or at least partially testate in the case of Manitoba. Now only the British Columbia[98] and Nova Scotia[99] Acts are restricted to testacies.[100]

(e) Contracting Out: Releases and Waivers

(i) Generally

It is clear by statutory enablement that ahead of time dower and marital property rights can be waived by clear and unambiguous wording; similarly, by common law such a release of testate and intestate succession expectations is effective.[101] Is the situation the same for dependants' relief applications? The effect of contracting out of the right to make a dependants' relief application is, almost exclusively, an issue with respect to spouses and co-habitees as a result of marriage contracts, co-habitation agreements, and separation agreements. Theoretically, there are strong pro and con arguments respecting the effect which should be given to these releases and waivers. But, by statute and judicial decision, there is no longer any issue, except in Ontario. The Nova Scotia,[102] Prince Edward Island[103] and Yukon[104] Acts expressly make non-binding or invalid any contracting out. The other Acts are silent. Canadian courts have consistently held that, despite a waiver or release of the right to make a dependants' relief application, a dependant is not barred from making such an application.[105]

---

98 *Barker v. Westminster Trust Co.* (1941), 57 B.C.R. 21 (B.C. C.A.) at 45; *Hammond v. Hammond* (1995), 7 B.C.L.R. (3d) 25, (B.C. S.C.) at 29–33.

99 *Specht v. Archibald* (1974), 16 N.S.R. (2d) 354 (N.S. T.D.).

100 Thus, rendering obsolete cases such as *Allaby v. Allaby Estate* (1988), 91 N.B.R. (2d) 102 (N.B. Q.B.).

101 See, *inter alia*, *Re Jutras*, [1932] 2 W.W.R. 533 (Sask. C.A.); *Re Dalton*, [1934] O.W.N. 691 (Ont. H.C.); *Re Knoll*, [1938] O.W.N. 282 (Ont. H.C.); *Re Rist*, [1939] 1 W.W.R. 518 (Alta. C.A.), apparently overriding *Jones v. Kline (Jones) supra*, note 18, on this point; *Cliff v. Schop*, [1948] O.W.N. 338 (Ont. H.C.); *Re Winter*, [1954] O.W.N. 726 (Ont. H.C.); *Re Draper*, [1956] O.W.N. 106 (Ont. H.C.); *Pearson v. Pearson* (1980), 3 Man. R. (2d) 404 (Man. C.A.), leave to appeal refused (1980), 34 N.R. 459n (S.C.C.); *Menrad v. Blowers*, *supra* note 12; *Re Saylor* (1983), 44 O.R. (2d) 188 (Ont. H.C.) at 194; *Cairns v. Cairns* (1990), 72 O.R. (2d) 217 (Ont. H.C.).

102 s. 16(2).

103 s. 16.

104 s. 17.

105 *Re Anderson*, [1934] 1 W.W.R. 430 (Alta. C.A.) at 437; *Re Lewis* (1935), 49 B.C.R. 386 (B.C. C.A.); *Jones v. Kline (Jones)*, *supra* note 18; *Re Rist*, *supra* note

However, a waiver or release is an important factor or circumstance to be considered by the court in dealing with an application.[106] Probably, the refusal of the Supreme Court of Canada to entertain an appeal in *Wagner v. Wagner Estate*[107] puts to rest any question about the effectiveness of waivers or releases everywhere except in some circumstances in Ontario; nonetheless, Justice Lysyk's eloquent trial reasons in *Wagner Estate*[108] should be added to the cases cited in footnote 106 for the proposition that

---

101; *Re Carey*, [1940] O.R. 171 (Ont. C.A.); *McNamara v. Hyde, supra* note 11; *Alberta (Official Guardian) v. LeMasurier*, [1949] 2 W.W.R. 748 (Alta. C.A.); a separation agreement requiring a wife-mother to maintain and support a child does not bar an application by the child; *Re Duranceau*, [1952] O.R. 584 (Ont. C.A.); *Re Edgelow* (1955), 18 W.W.R. 235 (B.C. S.C.); *Pope v. Stevens, supra* note 11; *Re Stannard* (1960), 32 W.W.R. 432 (B.C. S.C.); *Re Edwards Estate* (1961), 36 W.W.R. 605 (Alta. C.A.) in which at 309 Smith C.J.A. added that the judicial approval of a separation agreement "had no legal consequence whatever and added no legal effect to the separation agreement it did not have before approved by" the judge; *Re Hawley, supra* note 11; *Lang v. Chugg* (1965), 51 W.W.R. 666 (Alta. C.A.), in which Justice Kane discusses contracting out and the irrelevance of a consent judgment in respect of a decree of judicial separation, although the Court considered the wording of the alleged contracting out not to include a dependant's relief application; *Re Bérubé*, [1973] 3 W.W.R. 180 (Alta. C.A.); *Collard v. Collard, supra* note 11; *Cooperman v. Cooperman*, [1978] 5 W.W.R. 518 (B.C. S.C.) at 523, but the terms of the separation agreement, creating debts of the estate with priority over a relief order, left no estate from which a relief order could be made; *Re Marquis* (1980), 30 N.B.R. (2d) 93 (N.B. T.D.); *Boulanger v. Singh* (1984), 59 B.C.L.R. 383 (B.C. C.A.); *Stepaniuk v. Koziol Estate* (1985), 60 A.R. 47 (Alta. Q.B.), the mutual agreement was reflected in the spouses' wills; *Wagner v. Wagner Estate* (1991), 62 B.C.L.R. (2d) 1 (B.C. C.A.), leave to appeal to S.C.C. refused (1992), 39 R.F.L. (3d) 399n (S.C.C.); *Webb v. Webb Estate* (1995), 28 Alta. L.R. (3d) 110 (Alta. Surr. Ct.); *Holland v. Holland Estate* (1995), 9 E.T.R. (2d) 119 (B.C. S.C.) at 122; *Siegel v. Siegel Estate* (1995), 177 A.R. 282 (Alta. Q.B.) at paragraph 14. In *Williams v. Moody Bible Institute of Chicago*, [1937] 2 W.W.R. 316 (Sask. C.A.) the courts held an anti-nuptial agreement to be no bar for, *inter alia*, lack of full disclosure. In *Re Bursaw Estate* (1924), 19 Sask. L.R. 137 (Sask. C.A.), set aside (1925), [1931] 3 W.W.R. App. II (S.C.C.) a pre-nuptial waiver was held void for duress.

106 *Re Anderson, supra* note 105 at 438; *Re Lewis, supra* note 105; *Jones v. Kline (Jones), supra* note 18 at 84; *McNamara v. Hyde, supra* note 105 at 75; *Re Stannard, supra* note 105; *Re Edwards Estate, supra* note 105, Johnson J.A.'s dissent; *Collard v. Collard, supra* note 11; *Re Marquis, supra* note 105; *Boulanger v. Singh, supra* note 105; *Wagner v. Wagner Estate, supra* note 105; *Lobe v. Lobe Estate* (1996), 13 E.T.R. (2d) 126 (B.C. S.C.) at paragraphs 24-30, affirmed (1997), 17 E.T.R. (2d) 275 (B.C. C.A.); *Howard v. Howard Estate* (1997), 32 B.C.L.R. (3d) 1 (B.C. C.A.).

107 *Supra* note 105.

108 (1990), 39 E.T.R. 5 (B.C. S.C.) at paragraph 32, reversed (1991), 44 E.T.R. 24 (B.C. C.A.), leave to appeal to S.C.C. refused (1992), 39 R.F.L. (3d) 399n (S.C.C.); similarly, *Farquar v. Farquar* and *Webb v. Webb* quoted in *Dyer v. Dyer* (1984), 18 E.T.R. 44 (Ont. Surr. Ct.) at 49–50.

a waiver or a release is an important factor or circumstance for consideration.

In *Re Stannard*,[109] Justice Norris opined that waivers given after death are no more a bar than those given before death.[110]

In *Richer v. Richer* the court dealt with an application by a 17 year old daughter, at a time when s. 16 of the *Family Law Reform Act* decreed an obligation on parents to provide support to their children until they reached the age of 18. The deceased and the mother of the applicant separated when the applicant was 8; by their separation agreement the deceased agreed to provide support to the child until she became 16. The first question for the court was whether the applicant was qualified to apply as a "child . . . to whom the deceased was . . . under an obligation to provide support immediately before his . . . death". The court decided:

> In order to determine whether or not Anne-Marie Richer was, immediately before her father's death, a dependant as defined in the Succession Law Reform Act, one must consider the effect the 1974 separation agreement on the deceased obligation to provide support to her to age 18. Are the provisions of s. 16 of the Family Law Reform Act, R.S.O. 1980, c. 152, negated by the written agreement made by the deceased to support his daughter to age 16 and his subsequent compliance with it?
>
> I think not. That agreement was entered into by her parents and while it created certain obligations on the respective parties to it, such agreement cannot, in my view, abrogate a dependant's statutory right to support without that dependant's consent. The fact that the applicant made no claim against her father during his lifetime and after the coming into force of the Family Law Reform Act in 1978 . . . is no ban to the present claim.[111]

(ii) Ontario

The situation now is different from what it was under the former *Dependants' Relief Act*.[112] Now the Ontario Act provides:

> **63.** (4) An order under this section may be made despite any agreement or waiver to the contrary.

It would be better if the sub-section were worded "An order under this Part . . ." or if the sub-section were a sub-section of s. 58. Nonetheless, generally, whether contained in a pre-nuptial, co-habitation or separation

109 *Supra* note 105.

110 The court in *Re Close*, [1952] O.W.N. 660 (Ont. C.A.) thought so too.

111 (1984), 17 E.T.R. 102 (Ont. Co. Ct.) at 106–07.

112 See Osterhoff, A., *Succession Law Reform in Ontario* (Toronto: Carswell, 1979) at 109, and "The Effect of Death on Familial Obligations" (1981) 23 R.F.L. (2d) 272 at 298 and Macdonell, Sheard & Hull at 128, note 21.

agreement, or in the minutes of settlement in a divorce proceeding, a waiver should not be a bar to an application.[113] However, by s. 62(1)(m) a waiver is an important factor or circumstance to be considered by the court in dealing with an application.[114]

If there is in existence at the time of the deceased's death a "domestic contract" made pursuant to the *Family Law Act*[115], which provides that the deceased shall pay no support, there is a line of authority that the other party to the contract does not qualify to make a dependants' relief application.[116]

(f) Obtaining a Personal Representation Grant

Not surprisingly, obtaining a grant to administer an estate is not deemed to indicate satisfaction with a testamentary provision or an intestate entitlement so as to bar a dependants' relief application.[117]

(g) Conditional Testamentary Gifts

It is not possible to do an end run around the ineffectiveness of dependants' relief application waivers by inserting a provision in a will that a benefit conferred by the will is revoked if the beneficiary commences

---

113 For ex., *Goldhar v. Goldhar* (1985), (*sub nom. Re Goldhar's Estate*) 21 E.T.R. 189 (Ont. Div. Ct.), reversed (April 8, 1986), Dubin J.A., Houlden J.A., Krever J.A. (Ont. C.A.) and *Swire v. Swire* (1986), 23 E.T.R. (Ont. Surr. Ct.) at 250–51, 265 *et seq*., affirmed (1987), 28 E.T.R. 206 (Ont. Div. Ct.), both pre-nuptial agreements; *Blago v. Aetna Life Insurance Co.* (1988), 30 E.T.R. 283 (Ont. Surr. Ct.) at 297-301, minutes of settlement. Note *Dyer v. Dyer, supra* note 108 at 55; a case involving minutes of settlement in which the court found a waiver to be ineffectually worded, but in an obiter commented that, if the waiver had not been ineffectually worded, "it might well be that there would be no other option but to find the minutes . . . conclusive against" applicant; the obiter is questionable since by the minutes the applicant was receiving support from the deceased at the time of his death and thus was a qualified dependant and the case on its facts does not come within the line of cases continued in note 116, *infra*.

114 *Moores v. Hughes* (1981), 37 O.R. (2d) 785 (Ont. H.C.) at 792; *Dyer v. Dyer, supra* note 108 at 49-54; *Goldhar v. Goldhar, supra* note 113; *Swire v. Swire, supra* note 113; *Blago v. Aetna Life Insurance Co., supra* note 113; *Fune v. Hoy Estate* (1995), 6 E.T.R. (2d) 91 (Ont. Gen. Div.).

115 *Supra* note 66.

116 *Mealey v. Broadbent* (1984), 47 O.R. (2d) 161 (Ont. Div. Ct.); affirmed (1987), 25 E.T.R. 1 (Ont. C.A.), separation agreement; *Smith v. Smith Estate* (1985), (*sub nom. Smith v. Henderson*) 21 E.T.R. 299 (Ont. Surr. Ct.), minutes of settlement; *Taylor v. Taylor Estate, supra* note 16, pre-nuptial agreement and minutes of settlement; *Frye v. Frye, supra* note 10, minutes of settlement. Note also *Gocsei v. Skublak Estate* (1995), 8 E.T.R. (2d) 201 (Ont. Gen. Div.) and Youdan, T., "The Status of a Dependant under Part V of the Ontario Succession Law Reform Act" (1986) 21 E.T.R. 303, esp. at 307-08 and Macdonell, Sheard & Hull at 128.

117 *Williams v. Moody Bible Institute of Chicago, supra* note 105 at 320-21

litigation with respect to the will other than for an interpretation of the will or for advice and directions concerning administration of the estate; such a provision is void for being contrary to the public policy pursuant to which dependants' relief legislation is enacted.[118]

By the way, none of the statutes puts an applicant, who is a beneficiary in a deceased's will or an heir of the estate, upon an election between the testamentary or intestate benefit and applying for relief. In *Re Hull*[119] Justice Laidlaw said:

> Counsel for the appellants argues that the applicant cannot accept benefits under the will of the deceased, and at the same time seek to obtain additional benefits under the Act. I do not agree. The applicant can take under the will whatever rights and benefits are therein given to her. If they are inadequate for her future maintenance, she can apply to the Court for an order to add to them, and the whole, or a portion, of the estate may be charged with payment of an allowance to her. She is not prejudiced in any manner in such an application by the fact that she was given, and accepted, other benefits under the will.

(h) Life Estate with a Power of Encroachment

John Oscar Courtney made a will giving his wife a life interest in the estate and providing:

> In case the revenue from the capital of my estate . . . is not sufficient . . . I invest full power and authority to my Executors to use so much of the capital of my estate as may be necessary for the proper support of my wife . . .

Without asking for the Executors to exercise their encroachment power, the widow applied to be given the whole of the modest estate, *Courtney v. Lister*.[120] It was argued for the remaining beneficiaries that the gift of income coupled with the power of encroachment comprised an adequate provision for the applicant's proper maintenance and support and thus the application should be dismissed, or at least that the application was premature. The court reviewed the various conflicting decisions, *Re Harper*,[121] *Re Rankin*,[122] *Re Lawther*,[123] *Re Stapleton*,[124] and *Re Beyor*,[125] and concluded:

118 *Kent v. McKay* (1982), 38 B.C.L.R. 216 (B.C. S.C.).
119 [1943] O.R. 778 (Ont. C.A.) at 782–83.
120 (1958), 24 W.W.R. 676 (Sask. Q.B.).
121 [1946] 3 W.W.R. 59 (B.C. S.C.).
122 (1950), [1951] O.W.N. 121 (Ont. C.A.).
123 (1947), 55 Man. R. 142 (Man. K.B.) at 157-58.
124 (1953), [1954] O.W.N. 132 (Ont. C.A.).
125 [1949] O.W.N. 289 (Ont. C.A.).

> With great deference I find myself unable to subscribe to the views expressed in the *Stapleton* case, or the solution adopted in the *Harper* case. I can nowhere find that a testator, by any device contained in his will, can supplant or exclude the manifest duty which the legislature, by the terms of the Act of this province, has reposed in the courts. Nor can I read into the Act a condition that a dependant must first resort to other available remedies before seeking the remedies which the Act provides. Were it so, a dependant might well inherit nothing more than the necessity of engaging in repeated, prolonged and costly litigation. The very purpose of our Act is to, at once and finally, secure to a dependant, within the structure of the Act, and in so far as the assets of the estate permit, reasonable provision for the future, where the deceased has failed to do so.[126]

(i) Obtaining a Marital Property Order

Obtaining such an order during the deceased's life is not a bar to a dependants' relief application.[127] And, not infrequently, surviving spouses combine applications pursuant to the marital property and dependants' relief statutes; in such cases the marital propery application should be considered first[128] and it may result in the dismissal of the dependants' relief application.[129]

(j) Accepting Testamentary Benefit

It was argued in *Re Hull*[130] on a late application that an applicant, who has accepted a testamentary benefit cannot apply for an additional benefit. The court disagreed.

---

126 *Supra* note 120 at 683. Note also *Re Hoskins* (1961), 35 W.W.R. 430 (B.C. S.C.) at 431-32; *Cranston v. Cranston* (1962), 40 W.W.R. 321 (Alta. T.D.) at 328; *Re Kirk* (1963), 38 D.L.R. (2d) 746 (B.C. S.C.); *Re Berry* (1966), 58 W.W.R. 187 (Sask. Q.B.); *Re Parks* (1968), 64 W.W.R. 586 (B.C. S.C.); *Re Flahr* (1983), 28 Sask. R. 268 (Sask. Q.B.), at paragraph 5.

127 *Adams v. Irvine, supra* note 11; *Manson v. Shoaf, supra* note 11; note also *The Matrimonial Property Act*, C.S.A. 1999 c.M-9, s. 18 and *The Matrimonial Property Act* S.S. 1998 c.M-6.11, s. 37.

128 See text at note 139, *infra*.

129 For instance, *Re Serdula* (1983), 23 Sask. R. 282 (Sask. Q.B.); *Peslari v. Petruic, supra* note 11; *Penteluk v. Penteluk Estate, supra* note 11. Similarly, *Menrad v. Blowers, supra* note 12 at 316-17; *Krokosh v. Krokosh* (1985), 34 Man. R. (2d) 121 (Man. Q.B.).

130 [1943] O.R. 778 (Ont. C.A.) at 782-83.

(k) Deceased's Domicile at Death

Formerly, it was a requirement of some Acts[131] that an application could be made only if the deceased died domiciled within the province or the territory. This is no longer the situation. A deceased's domicile at death should be relevant only to the dependants' relief law a court is to apply respecting the deceased's movables. However, courts have been willing to entertain applications only if the estate of the deceased owns immovables within the court's territorial jurisdiction and respecting movables only if the deceased died domiciled within the court's territorial jurisdiction.[132]

(l) Residence and Domicile of Dependants

Evidentally, neither residence nor domicile within a court's territorial jurisdiction is required of dependants for *locus standi* to apply.[133]

3. FORUM

By the definition of either "court" or "judge" in all of the Canadian Acts, except the Yukon Act[134], a dependants' relief proceeding is commenced in the superior trial court of the province. The Nova Scotia Act defines "judge" to include "a local judge [of the Trial Division of the Supreme Court] . . . acting within the district for which the local judge is appointed a judge of the county court".

4. WHEN CAN A PROCEEDING BE COMMENCED

Ordinarily, a proceeding is commenced after a grant of representation has been made and this makes sense because then the assets of the estate and the respondents to be served are known.[135] Can a proceeding be

---

131 See for ex., the *Dependants' Relief Act*, R.S.S. 1940, c. 111, s. 3; the *Dependants' Relief Act*, R.S.O. 1970, c. 126, s. 2(1); and the *Dependants' Relief Ordinance*, R.O.Y.T. 1971, c. D-3, s. 3(1).

132 See further Chp. 4, 5(c), *Conflict of Laws*. For Manitoba see also the Manitoba Act, s. 13(3) and (4).

133 *Re McAdam*, *supra* note 44 at 550; *Re Kvasnak*, (1951), 2 W.W.R. (N.S.) 174 (Sask. C.A.); *Hayzel v. Alberta (Public Trustee)*, *supra* note 71; *Zajac v. Zwarycz*, [1965] 1 O.R. 575 (Ont. C.A.), although the application was dismissed on the merits; *Re Parkanski*, *supra* note 61; *Re Quon*, *supra* note 7; *Re Soroka* (1975), 10 O.R. (2d) 638 (Ont. H.C.); *Beasley v. Willet* (1972), 4 N.B.R. (2d) 122 (Man. Q.B.).

134 The Yukon Act also provides for the proceeding to be commenced in the Supreme Court, s.5.

135 See further Schnurr, B., and Woodley, S., "Dependant Support Proceedings" (1995) 14 E.T.J. 159 at 160-61.

commenced before a grant of representation has been made? All of the Acts contain a limitation period section; the sections are worded "no application may be made except within 6 months from the grant of . . ." or variations thereof. Does this wording preclude commencing a proceeding before a representation grant has been made? The judges of the British Columbia Supreme Court and Court of Appeal in *Murgatroyd v. Stewart*[136] split evenly on this issue although, of course, the majority opinion in the Court of Appeal carried the day. For the Court of Appeal majority Chief Justice Martin wrote:

> [the section enabling dependants to apply to court] confers a right in general to make application without reference to any temporal limitation which right is not taken away by [the] subsequent [limitation period section], which is one purely of limitation, as to when the application may be brought, that is to say, within six months from the date of issuance of probate of the will.
>
> Taking that view of the matter, with all respect to the learned Judge below, who did not give any reasons in support of the view that the applicant could not present her application until probate had been granted, it seems to me, with all due respect, legally impossible to dislodge the applicant from the general right which is conferred by [the application enabling section] . . . by resorting to a subsequent section which deals only with limitation of the time within which application may be made . . .

Justice M.A. Macdonald's dissenting view was:

> The short point is this: Has the Court jurisdiction to hear a petition under this Act if it is launched before the will is admitted to probate, in other words, immediately after the death of the testator or at some subsequent period up to six months after probate? Mr. MacInnis submitted that a petition may be launched by one of the beneficiaries mentioned in [the application enabling section] at once after the death of the testator before probate and for six months after the latter date. Mr. Justice D. A. McDonald did not agree with this submission and I think he was right. It was said that if an application should be made six months after probate it would be launched "within six months from the date of the grant;" also if made six months (or any shorter period) before the grant of probate it would again be made "within six months from the date of the grant." Even this novel reading of the section would not make provision for a petition launched immediately after death if probate were not granted until nine months thereafter. Some further support therefore must be found to justify the submission that at any time after death and up to six months beyond the grant of probate this application may be made.
>
> By the plain reading of the section, at all events the construction reasonably necessary to carry out the intendment of the Act, the petition can only be launched during the six-months period immediately following probate and at

136 (1938), [1939] 3 W.W.R. 106 (B.C. C.A.).

> no other period. By preventing applications until probate is granted the right will and testament will be dealt with; by limiting the time to six months thereafter distribution will not be unduly delayed. While support for the construction submitted by the appellant may be found in other statutes, not entirely similar, it is because their intendment is effected by such a construction. It is not appropriate to the Act under review. As stated the intention was that the will should first be authenticated and that distribution should take place within a reasonable time. The Court would then know the nature and extent of the estate, assets and liabilities, with which it had to deal. The will could not be altered fairly without that knowledge.
>
> The submission against this view is that the word "within" in [the limitation period section] should be read as meaning "not later than." That interpretation, as intimated, is supported in some American cases . . ., but a perusal of the Acts considered show why it was adopted. To substitute the words "not later than" for "within" in our [limitation period section] seems to me to be taking a greater liberty with the English language than the facts warrant and strong reasons—found only in the desire to accomplish the purposes of the Act—should be present to justify it. In the case at bar it would not be proper to give it this extended meaning. The Court has no means of knowing what claims may be made on the estate before probate nor for a limited time thereafter. To say, as was suggested, that the Judge might adjourn the hearing until after probate is to concede that such a continuation is not workable without resorting to adventitious aids. This is a tempest in a teapot. There is no good reason for objecting to a proceeding being commenced before a grant of representation has been made, since nothing more can happen with it until the representation grant is made enabling service upon the personal representative. As well, mere commencement of the proceeding does not enable any interim advances to be made to dependants or other successors.

Chief Justice Martin's reasons were adopted in *Re Stafford*[137] with the court adding:

> [A]lthough I think in most cases where probate has not been granted it would be preferable for the plaintiff, before making an application under the Act, to take out a citation . . . calling upon the executor to either prove the will and file an inventory or renounce. . .

In *Stafford* the court had to adjourn the application because there was no reliable inventory of the assets of the estate:

> 16 In the absence of satisfactory evidence as to the nature and value of the assets of the testatrix at the date of her death, I cannot properly exercise the discretion given me by the Act. I do not, however, think the application should be dismissed merely because of the absence of such evidence. A defendant in such proceedings, particularly a defendant who is both the executor and sole

---

137 (1979), 26 N.B.R. (2d) 561 (N.B. Q.B.) at 564, 565.

> beneficiary of the estate, has in my view a duty to candidly disclose to the court the nature and value of the estate. Lack of evidence in such a case "cannot militate against the making of an order" in the plaintiff's favour. See the judgment of Laskin, C.J., in *Harper v. Harper* - Supreme Court of Canada, June 28, 1979. [See 27 N.R. 554].

Without reference to either *Murgatroyd v. Stewart* or *Re Stafford*, in *Gabel v. Gabel Estate*[138] Justice Noble held that a dependants' relief application could not be made before a personal representative of the deceased has been appointed by the court.

5. MARITAL PROPERTY VERSUS DEPENDANTS' RELIEF LEGISLATION

Everywhere in Canada, except British Columbia, Prince Edward Island, and the two territories, a surviving spouse can apply for an accounting and equalization of matrimonial assets.[139] Common sense dictates that if the two applications come together to court the marital property claim should be treated before a dependants' relief application: Justice Mason in *Zubiss v. Moulson Estate* said:[140]

> [18] To which entitlement should the court first address itself when claims are made by a surviving spouse against the estate of the deceased spouse, both for a matrimonial property order under the **Matrimonial Property Act** and an order for maintenance and support under the **Family Relief Act**?
>
> [19] Unless readily apparent that a successful application under the **Family Relief Act** would result in the award of the total estate of the deceased spouse to the surviving spouse for maintenance and support, which is not the case here, it is apparent from a reading of the provisions of both statutes and their inter-relationship that the entitlement to a distribution of matrimonial property under the **Matrimonial Property Act** must be determined first. While s. 18(1) of that Act provides that nothing in the **Matrimonial Property Act** affects the right of a surviving spouse to make an application under the **Family Relief Act** and join it with an application for a matrimonial property order, s. 15 deems that money paid or property transferred to a surviving spouse under a matrimonial property order is not property which is part of the estate of the deceased spouse, and is not subject to a claim against the estate by a benefi-

138 (1995), 127 Sask. R. 275 (Sask. Q.B.) at paragraphs 25-26.

139 R.S.A. 1999, c.M-9, s. 11(1); S.S. 1998, c.M-6.11, s. 30(1); R.S.M. 1987, c. M45, s. 28(1); R.S.O. 1990 c.F-3, s. 5(2); S.N.B. 1997, c.M-1.1, s. 4(1); R.S.N.S. 1989, c. 275, s. 2(g); R.S.N. 1990, c.F-2, s. 2(1)(e).

140 (1987), 80 A.R. 105 (Alta. Q.B.) followed in *Baker v. Baker Estate*, *supra* note 11 at paragraph 37; note also *Edward v. Edward Estate*, *supra* note 8 at paragraphs 42-50, followed in *Olesko v. Olesko Estate* (1990), 87 Sask. R. 61 (Sask. Q.B.) and *Driscoll v. Driscoll Estate*, *supra* note 69 at paragraph 83.

> ciary under the will or under the **Intestate Succession Act**, or by a dependant under the **Family Relief Act**. So any entitlement of the plaintiff to a matrimonial property distribution under the **Matrimonial Property Act** must be determined first because such distribution will reduce the estate of [the deceased spouse] to that effect. Further, under the **Family Relief Act**, before addressing a claim for support by a surviving spouse as a "dependant" against the estate of the deceased spouse, the estate of the surviving spouse must be considered as part of the determination of whether or not the estate of the deceased spouse should be subject to an order granting maintenance. So the size of the plaintiff's estate will have a bearing on any claim by her for maintenance from [the deceased spouse's] estate.

The legislation of some provinces provides that a matrimonial property order has priority over a dependants' relief order.[141] This means fewer assets available to satisfy relief applications. Uniquely, by s. 6(12)(c) of the *Family Law Act*[142] of Ontario, a *Family Law Act* order does not have priority over a dependants' relief order in favour of a child of the deceased.

6. LIMITATION PERIOD; LATE APPLICATIONS

The New Brunswick Act prescribes a four month limitation period "after the death of the deceased".[143] All of the other Acts prescribe a six month limitation period from the "grant" or "issue" of probate or administration for the commencement of the proceeding.[144] All of these Acts, except the British Columbia Act, use the word "grant". In *Re Larsen*[145] the court construed the phrase in the then *Administration Act* of British Columbia, "not later than six months after the date on which administration of the estate was granted", to mean within six months of the day upon which the grant issued, which is the day the grant is entered in the court register, and not the day upon which an order granting administration is signed if that occurs on an earlier date. The court in *Re Hirsch*[146] reached the same conclusion respecting the phrase "issuance of probate". In *Etches v.*

141 The *Matrimonial Property Act*, C.S.A. 1999, c. M-9, s. 15(c); the *Matrimonial Property Act*, C.S.S. 1998, c. M-6.11, s. 35(c); the *Marital Property Act*, R.S.M. 1987, c. M45, s. 41(1)(c); the *Family Law Act*, R.S.O. 1990, c. F-3, s. 6(12)(c); the *Marital Property Act*, S.N.B. 1997, c. M.-1.1, s. 4(6); the *Matrimonial Property Act*, R.S.N.S. 1989, c. 275, s. 12(4); the *Family Law Act*, R.S.N. 1990, c. F-2, s. 21(2).

142 *Supra* note 66.

143 s. 14(1).

144 B.C. s. 3(1) "issue of probate . . . or resealing"; Alta s. 15(1); Sask. s. 4(1); Man. s. 6; Ont. s. 61(1); N.S. s. 14(1); P.E.I. s. 13(1); Nfld. s. 14(1); N.W.T. s. 13(1); Y.T. s. 14(1).

145 [1974] 5 W.W.R. 670 (B.C. S.C.). Note *Re Pedlar Estate*, [1933] 1 W.W.R. 267 (B.C. S.C.) interpreting "grant" in s. 11 of the former *Testators Family Maintenance Act* of B.C. to mean "date the grant . . . is actually completed by the grant being sealed. . .".

146 (1977), 2 B.C.L.R. 216 (B.C. S.C.).

Stephens, the will of Richard Etches named his three children to be the executors of his estate. One child received a grant of probate; subsequently, the other two children received a second grant of probate. One of the latter two children commenced a dependants' relief action within six months of the second grant, but more than six months after the first grant. The court dismissed the action for being late:

> The issue of probate for the purposes of the Act should be interpreted as the issuance of the first Grant of Probate, as that is the date at which the substantive rights of probate arise.[147]

In *Vien Estate v. Vien Estate*[148] the application was made within six months of the resealing of a foreign grant, although more than six months after the original grant. Justice Sirois ruled that in his opinion the limitation ran from the resealing, but if he was wrong he would have exercised his discretion to entertain the late application.

All of the Acts except the British Columbia Act are worded either "No application . . . may be made . . ." or "An application . . . may not be made . . ." or ". . . an application must be made . . .". It was decided in *Re Brown*[149] that an application filed, but not heard, within the limitation period was an application "made" in time. The current British Columbia Act avoids this issue by its use of the word "commenced". *Re Roy*[150] concerned a motion for a spousal allotment pursuant to s. 92 of the then *Administration Act* of British Columbia, not the *Wills Variation Act*, for which there was also a six month limitation period. In connection with the motion, counsel for spouse made a motion for advice and directions as to, *inter alia*, the persons to be served and then, subsequently, out of time filed the actual motion for the allotment order. The court dismissed the motion for being too late, rejecting counsel's argument that the motion for directions should be considered the effectual commencement of the s. 92 proceeding.

Amighetti raises the question, when the limitation runs from the grant of probate, what is meant by "probate". Does it mean probate in common form or probate in solemn form. He thinks that it is arguable that probate means probate in solemn form and "consequently, the limitation period should not apply until an order for solemn form probate has been obtained".[151] I disagree. I think that probate must mean either kind of probate, and when a probate in solemn form occurs after a common form probate,

---

147 (1994), 99 B.C.L.R. (2d) 171 (B.C. S.C.) at 175.
148 *Supra* note 89 at 250.
149 (1956), 19 W.W.R. 616 (B.C. S.C.).
150 (1975), 23 R.F.L. 34 (B.C. S.C.).
151 Amighetti at 143-44.

then obviously the limitation period begins on the effective date of the solemn form probate.

The Ontario Act, s. 74, uniquely requires letters probate or of administration to be served on the Public Trustee if there is a potential applicant who has been institutionalized and the limitation period for the Public Trustee begins to run only from the service.

The British Columbia Act, unlike the other Canadian Acts, expressly requires the writ of summons by which a *Wills Variation Act* proceeding is commenced to be served upon the executor and in some cases on the Public Trustee.[152] The Act does not specify a time frame for service. In *British Columbia (Public Trustee) v. Williams Estate*[153] a writ was issued within the six month limitation prescribed by the Act, but not served until after the six month limitation period had elapsed. The court held that service was required only within the one year prescribed by the Supreme Court Rules for service of writs of summons. The court rejected the argument that not requiring service of a writ also within the six month limitation would delay distribution of estates:

> If an executor of a will is uncertain whether an action has been commenced under the Act within 6 months of the date of the granting of probate a search of all Supreme Court Registries would resolve the uncertainty. If such a wide sweeping search was not practicable, direct communication with, and a request for a "consent" under s. 11 of the Act from, the limited number of persons who would be entitled to apply for relief under the Act would swiftly dispel any uncertainty. The argument that in the absence of an interpretation of s. 10 requiring the writ not only to be issued, but also to be served within the 6-month limitation period would result in an estate not being distributed until the expiration of 18 months from the date of the grant of probate is rejected. As previously indicated, the apprehended delay can be overcome by a search of the court registries or by communication with the limited number of persons who are entitled to apply under the Act.[154]

Most of the Acts contain a section like s. 4(2) of the P.E.I. Act

> **4.** (2) Where an application for an order under section 2 is made by or on behalf of any dependant
>
> (a) it may be dealt with by the court as; and
>
> (b) in so far as the question of limitation is concerned, it shall be deemed to be;
>
> an application on behalf of all persons who might apply.

---

152 s. 3(1)(b) and (c).

153 *Supra* note 78.

154 *Ibid.* at 55-56.

the purport of which is self-evident.[155]

All of the Acts, except those of British Columbia and Manitoba, contain a simple extension section, the import of which is:

> A court, if it considers it just [proper], may allow an application to be made at any time as to any portion [part] of the estate remaining undistributed at the date of the application.[156]

The Manitoba Act is more specific:

> **6.** (3) The court may allow an application to be made at any time as to the portion of the estate remaining undistributed at the date notice of the application is served on the personal representative if the court is satisfied that,
>
> (a) the dependant did not know of the death of the deceased until after the expiry of the limitation period;
>
> (b) the dependant's need for maintenance and support did not arise until after the expiry of the limitation period; or
>
> (c) circumstances beyond the control of the dependant prevented the dependant from making an application within the limitation period.

The British Columbia Act is silent. In *MacDonald v. MacDonald Estate*[157] an applicant persuaded the court to allow his late application to proceed, including the issue that the defendant was estopped from relying on the limitation period.

The legislation involves three possible issues, namely the basis of the exercise of the discretion to entertain a late application, what constitutes a "portion [part] of the estate remaining undistributed", and what is "the date of the application". Regarding the basis upon which a court should exercise its discretion to entertain a late application, in *Re Stewart*[158] Justice Fisher said:

> The Act permits the judge, "if he deems it just", to hear an application, confined to the estate then undistributed, at any time. The judge is thus given a discretion to be exercised on the principle of promoting justice between those interested in the estate. It is clear that he must refuse an application if the delay in applying would work an injustice. Further than that it would seem that he must find that justice, in so far as the principle of the Act defines the kind of justice that the Legislature had in mind, requires that the application should be heard. It is not shown here that any injustice would be caused by

155 B.C. s. 4(1); Alta. s. 16(1)(b); Man. s. 4; Ont. s. 60(2); N.B. s. 15; P.E.I. s. 4(2); Nfld. s. 15; Y.T s. 4.

156 Alta. s. 15(2); Sask. s. 4(2); Ont. s. 61(2); N.B. s. 14(2); N.S. s. 14(2); P.E.I. s. 13(2); Nfld. s. 14(2); N.W.T. s. 13(2); Y.T. s. 14(2).

157 (1996), 11 E.T.R. (2d) 286 (B.C. S.C.).

158 [1944] O.W.N. 380 (Ont. C.A.).

> hearing the application after the delay that has occurred. Further than that, it would appear that the applicant has a prima facie right to have his application heard, and the Court in deciding this preliminary question of discretion is not concerned beyond that.

Justice Kellock added:

> In *Brown v. Dean* et al., [1910] A.C. 373 it was held, under somewhat similar words, that the discretion there in question was not an unfettered one. In my opinion the same may be said of the discretion given by the subsection here under consideration. The learned [trial] judge has construed the subsection as meaning that an applicant for an extension of time must show good cause why the application was not made within three months. In my opinion, this is not the meaning of the statute. The discretion to extend or to refuse to extend the time is to be exercised having regard to what is equitable as between the parties concerned in all the circumstances of the particular case. The existence or non-existence of good reason for delay in applying may, in any given case, be a circumstance to be considered, but the statute does not mean that that is the sole consideration upon which an extension of time is to be granted or refused. Where, as in the case at bar, the applicant is the only person within the statutory class of dependants, and no reason is offered as to why the application should not be permitted to be heard beyond the mere delay, it would appear to be inequitable not to extend the time. It has not been shown that the assets of the estate will be in any way prejudicially affected by remaining undistributed in the hands of the executors pending the disposition of the application on the merits. The beneficiaries under the will will be compensated for any additional delay in distribution by the income earned by the assets of the estate in the meantime.

In *Smith v. Hunter Estate*,[159] Justice Goodfellow said:

> **[3]** In order for an applicant to be successful she must satisfy the court that it is just for her to be permitted to seek under s. 3 an order based upon the testatrix dying without having made adequate provision in her will for the proper maintenance and support of the applicant. The discretion under s. 14(2) [the N.S. extension section] should be exercised judicially in a broad, liberal manner mandated by the statutory use of "may" in both ss. 14(1) [the N.S. limitation section] and 14(2) of the **Act** plus the statutory use of the term "just". The term "just" has been interpreted in many cases in conjunction with other terms where it has been used such as "just and reasonable", "just and proper", "just cause", etc. In **Port Arthur Shipbuilding Co. v. Arthurs et al.**, [1967] 1 O.R. 272 (H.C.), Brooke, J., dealt with the term "just cause for

159 (1993), (*sub nom. Smith v. Hunter*) 126 N.S.R. (2d) 254 (N.S. S.C.) at paragraphs 3-5, 13-14.

discharge" in the context of modern industrial employment and stated at p. 276:

> "The words 'proper' and 'just' have distinctly different meanings, the latter being broader than the former, and probably including it. The word 'proper' according to the **Shorter Oxford English Dictionary** means 'fit, apt, suitable', whereas the word 'just' when used in relation to reward or punishment has the broader meaning which involves a consideration of equitable matters . . ."

[4] It is my view that the word "just" in any context involves the consideration of equitable matters. The interpretation of s. 14(2) should not be made in isolation and bears direct relationship to s. 3 [the N.S. primary jurisdiction section]. Section 3 does not use the term maintenance in quite the same manner as it has been defined or interpreted in statutes such as the **Family Maintenance Act** and the **Divorce Act** dealing with an obligation of support between two parties. Maintenance in s. 3 has to be given a wider context including "fit, apt, suitable" which in themselves incorporate the concept of reasonableness which in many cases includes a determination of whether the testator acted as a morally responsible parent in the circumstances.

[5] Even with this requirement of a broad, liberal interpretation of the word "just" in s. 14(1) "just" cannot be equated with "automatic". What is just will depend upon the circumstances and frequently there are factors such as illiteracy, health considerations, financial or special care needs, some indication of a degree of contribution by the applicant to the testatrix in caring for, providing financial or emotional assistance that the testatrix has failed to recognize, etc. There is no exhaustive list of the factors or combination of factors that may occur in any given factual situation. Usually, however, one or more of the foregoing exists to warrant an extension because there is an indication the situation bears review by the court for consideration whether or not the testatrix, in the circumstances made adequate provision in her will for the proper maintenance and support of the testatrix' dependent, in this case, one of her daughters. . . .

[13] Frequently limitation periods are extended under statutory provisions primarily when it is indicated that there would be no prejudice to the other party arising from the delay. It is not a major factor in this application because most of the prejudice that would otherwise arise is removed by the provision in s. 14(2) whereby any application filed out of time is permitted only as against any portion of the estate remaining undistributed at the date of the application. There may be occasions where delay in itself is prejudicial from an evidentiary point of view or where the distribution could or ought to have taken place earlier to one or more beneficiaries or partial distribution to some beneficiaries has taken place leaving the remainder in possible prejudice, etc.

[14] My determination is solely whether or not it would be just in all the circumstances, and the onus is upon the applicant to convince the court on a balance of probabilities that extending the time frame is "just". This is not a

> particularly heavy onus because of the need to liberally interpret the statute. By the same token it is not an automatic determination. What is required is something akin to the necessity of a pleading setting out facts that should be assumed true and where the pleading would only be struck because it does not set out a reasonable arguable position.

In *Maldaver v. Canada Permanent Trust Co.*[160] Chief Justice Cowan said:

> 16 In my opinion, the limitation of six months provided in that section was intended to avoid delays in administration of estates, and delays in distribution of estates in the hands of personal representatives. These reasons do not apply in the present case, since the estate has been fully administered and distribution of assets is not to be made until the death of the survivor of the two applicants. I am satisfied also that there were good and sufficient reasons for the delay in making the present application, and I consider it just to allow the application to be made at this time. The application is, of course, restricted to the portion of the estate remaining undistributed at the date of the application.

In *Re Kvasnak*[161] Chief Justice Martin, for the majority, said:

> It is argued that the delay in making the application should disentitle the applicant to the extension of time. It is pointed out that letters probate were issued on February 28, 1949, that the six months provided in sec. 14 expired at the end of August, 1949, and that the application was not made until December 14, 1950, about 15 months later. It does appear, even making allowances for the difficulty in getting information from Czechoslovakia, that the application has not been made promptly. However, a mere delay is not a bar to relief so far as the undistributed part of the estate is concerned. Delay is a circumstance to be considered but it is not the sole consideration. To refuse the extension of time on the ground merely of delay would, it seems to me, be unjust. . .

Apparently, courts readily entertain late applications,[162] for there are only five reported Canadian cases of a refusal where there existed undistributed

---

160 (1977), 27 N.S.R. (2d) 248 (N.S. S.C.) at paragraph 16.

161 (1951), 2 W.W.R. (N.S.) 174 (Sask. C.A.) at 179.

162 *Re Hourston*, [1919] 1 W.W.R. 521 (Alta. C.A.); *Re Monkman*, [1920] 1 W.W.R. 376 (Alta. S.C.); *Re Stewart*, *supra* note 158; *Tatko v. Liefke*, *supra* note 7; *Re Pemberton*, *supra* note 11 at 747; *Re La Fleur* (1948), 56 Man. R. 44 (Man. K.B.); *Re Bourne*, *supra* note 65; *Re Kvasnak*, *supra* note 161; *Re Cole*, *supra* note 69; *Re DeRoche Estate*, *supra* note 60; *Re Schurman*, *supra* note 37; *Re Smigelski* (1968), 64 W.W.R. 456 (Alta. C.A.); *Simmonds v. Rehn*, *supra* note 37; *Re Brown*, *supra* note 64; *Re Phillips* (1973), 8 N.B.R. (2d) 188 (N.B. Q.B.); *Re Soroka*, *supra* note 133 at 640; *Garrett v. Zwicker* (1976), 15 N.S.R. (2d) 118 (N.S. C.A.); *Fox v. Fox* (1977), 26 N.S.R. (2d) 463 (N.S. T.D.); *Maldaver v. Canada Permanent Trust Co.*, *supra* note 160; *Adams v. Irvine*, *supra* note 11; *Hiebert v. Ward* (1980), 3 Sask. R. 255 (Sask. Q.B.); *MacDonald v. MacDonald* (1980), 39 N.S.R. (2d) 573 (N.S. T.D.) at paragraph 4; *Coolen v. Coolen* (1980), 43 N.S.R. (2d) 67 (N.S. C.A.) at paragraph 22; *Collins v. Collins Estate* (1981), 34 Nfld. & P.E.I.R. 325 (Nfld. T.D.) at paragraph 10; *Re Deis* (1983), 21 Sask. R. 328 (Sask.

estate.[163] In *Re Kvasnak*[164] Chief Justice Martin, for the majority[165] on an appeal of a decision to entertain a late application, said:

> . . . this court should not assume to substitute its discretion for the discretion . . . exercised by the chamber judge unless it is clear that an injustice would be done by allowing the [extension] order to stand. . .[166]

Of course, some supporting evidence is required,[167] but the courts only occasionally articulate the reason for entertaining a late application;[168] also, "[w]hen the time is extended for one dependant any other dependant [is] . . . granted the same extension".[169]

If there is no undistributed estate a late application must be dismissed.[170] A late application can only relate to assets of the estate which remain within the control of the personal representative of the estate at the

---

C.A.); *Re deBeaudrap* (1983), 44 A.R. 100 (Alta. Q.B.), but the delay in applying figured in the court's dismissal of the application at paragraph 38; *Vien Estate v. Vien Estate*, *supra* note 89; *Ritchot v. Ritchot Estate* (1989), 57 Man. R. (2d) 186 (Man. Q.B.) at paragraphs 25-29, affirmed (1989), 58 Man. R. (2d) 61 (Man. C.A.); *Shapka v. Shapka Estate* (1985), 44 Sask. R. 262 (Alta. Q.B.) at paragraph 8; *Hart (Guardian ad litem of) v. Hart*, *supra* note 51 at paragraph 7; *Hobman v. Hobman* (1993), 117 Sask. R. 255 (Sask. Q.B.).

163 *Daye v. Holmes Estate* (1987), 25 E.T.R. 161 (Ont. H.C.); *Smith v. Hunter*, *supra* note 159 and *Etches v. Stephens*, *supra* note 147, which seem like hardline decisions when compared to other successful late applications: *Gocsei v. Skublak Estate*, *supra* note 116, in which the applicant by a co-habitation agreement had waived his right to apply and in any event the court said that it would have dismissed the application on the merits, and *Roussel v. Hill Estate*, *supra* note 56 at 120, an application on behalf of an 18 year old alleged daughter who was not even eligible to apply.

164 *Supra* note 161.

165 The Court split 3-2, with Justice Gordon writing a very strong dissent.

166 *Supra* note 161 at 176; also *Re Hull*, *supra* note 119 at 782.

167 *Re Jervas* (1953), [1954] O.W.N. 48 (Ont. C.A.).

168 *Re Pemberton*, *supra* note 11, mistakenly took proceedings challenging the validity of the will and then unsuccessfully tried to negotiate a settlement; *Re DeRoche Estate*, *supra* note 60 at 762 "delay will not prejudice an infant, for the presumption of law is he does not understand his rights and is not capable of taking advantage of the rules of law so as to apply them to advantage"; *Collins v. Collins Estate*, *supra* note 162; and *Hobman v. Hobman*, *supra* note 162, change in circumstances; *Ritchot v. Richot Estate*, *supra* note 162, applicant's counsel gave notice within the limitation period that an application might be made; and *Re Bourne*, *supra* note 65 wherein the court accepted as "a good one" the reason simply that the applicant did not seek legal advice until nine years after her husband's death.

169 *Re Deis*, *supra* note 162 at 331.

170 *Re Monkman*, *supra* note 162; *Krogman v. Dickson*, [1928] 2 D.L.R. 948 (Alta. T.D.); *Buzogan v. Banister* (1971), [1972] 1 W.W.R. 1 (Alta. S.C.); *Zaplotinsky v. Zaplotinsky* (1980), 14 Alta. L.R. (2d) 6 (Alta. Q.B.); *Fralick v. Fralick's Estate* (1983), 60 N.S.R. (2d) 90 (N.S. T.D.); *Re Bowie* (1984), 30 Man. R. (2d) 128 (Man. Q.B.); *W. (D.J.) (Litigation Guardian of) v. W. (L.) Estate* (1994), 122 Sask. R. 299 (Sask. Q.B.), affirmed [1966] 2 W.W.R. 593 (Sask. C.A.).

time of service of the application. None of the Acts provide for tracing distributed assets. In *Re Hull*,[171] acknowledging that "[n]o portion which has been distributed to beneficiaries or placed in trust out of the control of the executor is affected in any way", the court disagreed with the submission that this included assets of the estate at the time of the application "in the hands of the trustee named in the will and subject to the trusts thereof".[172] In *Zaplotinsky v. Zaplotinsky*[173] the estate in question comprised land which by the testator's will was to be divided among his widow and children. At the time of the widow's late application the trustee had executed and given to the children transfers of their shares of the land, but the children had not registered the transfers; the court held that the unregistered land transfers constituted a distribution.

The Acts of some provinces deem certain assets to be part of a deceased's estate.[174] In *Re Dolan*[175] the court held that the Ontario Act's deemed asset section "must cease to have any effect" upon the expiration of the limitation period for commencing an application.

For the courts deciding *Fralick v. Fralick's Estate*[176] and *Harvey v. Powell Estate*[177] the legal vesting of the estate in real property constituted a distribution. *Fralick* had to do with a late application by a widower. The estate assets included a house property which, by the deceased's will, was given to the deceased's widower for life and after his death to the deceased's daughter in fee simple. For some years after his wife's death and prior to his application for relief, the widower had been in receipt of the rental income from the house property. The court's reasons do not indicate whether the title to the house property stood in the name of the deceased, the estate, or the widower and daughter. With reference to several dictionary definitions the court said:

> These definitions seem to indicate that in probate matters whether or not the estate assets have been distributed depends on whether the estate still has possession or control of those assets. Cyril Fralick, and not the estate, has received income from the rental property since he has been a resident at the nursing home. In other words the real property has been 'disposed of' or 'distributed' to those entitled under the will. There is nothing further to be done by the executors with regard to this property - it has no further interest

---

171 *Supra* note 119 at 782.

172 Also *Re Hourston, supra* note 162 at 522; *Maldaver v. Canada Permanent Trust Co., supra* note 160.

173 *Supra* note 170.

174 See Chp. 4, 5(a), below.

175 (1983), 43 O.R. (2d) 677 (Ont. Div. Ct.) at 679-80.

176 *Supra* note 170.

177 (1988), 86 N.S.R. (2d) 191 (N.S. T.D.) at 201, additional reasons at (1989), 90 N.S.R. (2d) 265, 230 A.P.R. 265 (N.S. T.D.), affirmed (1989) 95 N.S.R. (2d) 37 (N.S. C.A.).

> in it. The estate has relinquished control over the premises to the tenant for life Cyril Fralick. The daughter has a vested remainder, being entitled to the property on the death of her father and not dependent on any contingency. . . .
>
> In summary the whole of the fee simple has vested. The estate has disposed of all interest in the property to those entitled under the terms of the will. There is nothing further to distribute.[178]

In *Harvey v. Powell Estate* the widow was both the sole executor and beneficiary of her husband's estate if she survived him for thirty days, which she did. In dealing with the issue of what assets of the estate remained undistributed the trial judge said:

> It is therefore necessary to inquire as to which assets of the estate of John Richard Powell were in the possession or under the control of the estate on April 15, 1986. The title of the three items of real property passed to Mildred on June 3, 1985, the date of probate of her husband's estate, since it was more than 30 days after the date of his death. The Dodge truck was still owned by and in the possession of the estate on the date of Mildred's death on July 6, 1986; the actual trade was not concluded until after she died. The R.R.S.P. and interest associated therewith ceased to be under the control of the estate as it was effectively transferred by Mildred via the Royal Bank to Arlene Dunford on April 24, 1985. The Canada Savings Bond and interest coupons are still in the possession of Wayne MacPherson as successor to Mildred as sole executrix of her husband's estate. His camera and furniture are also still in the possession of Wayne MacPherson in the same capacity, but they are included in the Inventory of Mildred's estate. In summary, the assets in the possession or under the control of the estate of John Richard Powell as of the date of the present application are: the Dodge truck, Canada Savings Bond and interest coupons.
>
> Those assets or their money equivalent are available for payment of the shares of the estate directed to be paid to the two claimants.[179]

In *W. (D.J.) (Litigation Guardian of) v. W. (L.) Estate*[180] the deceased gave the residue of his estate to his widow, whom he also named to be his executrix. She liquidated the residue of his estate and invested it in her name. In dismissing a late application the court rejected a submission "that it should not be concluded that Larry's [L.'s] estate has been completely distributed, because the beneficiary to whom the estate was distributed was the same person as the executrix".[181] *Tatko v. Liefke*[182] also had to do with

178 *Supra* note 170 at paragraphs 14 and 15.

179 *Supra* note 177 at paragraphs 49 and 50. See also *Smith v. Hunter*, *supra* note 159 at paragraphs 20-21.

180 *Supra* note 170.

181 *Supra* note 170 at paragraph 22.

182 *Supra* note 7.

the situation where the sole beneficiary is also the executor; the court held that "the household and personal effects and the automobile remained unadministered in the hands of the executor".[183]

Regardless of the precise nature of the application proceeding, probably the "the date of the application" is the date upon which the proceeding is filed in the court office.[184]

While formerly it was the practice in Ontario for leave to be obtained to commence a late application,[185] it is apparent from the reported cases that it is usual for the limitation extension application and the substantive application to be heard together.

7. STAY OF DISTRIBUTION OF THE ESTATE; INTERIM DISTRIBUTION

All of the Acts have a section staying distribution of the estate. The Ontario Act provides:

> **67.** (1) Where an application is made and notice thereof is served on the personal representative of the deceased, he or she shall not, after service of the notice upon him or her, unless all persons entitled to apply consent or the court otherwise orders, proceed with the distribution of the estate until the court has disposed of the application.
>
> (2) Nothing in this Part prevents a personal representative from making reasonable advances for support to dependants who are beneficiaries.
>
> (3) Where a personal representative distributes any portion of the estate in violation of subsection (1), if any provision for support is ordered by the court to be made out of the estate, the personal representative is personally liable to pay the amount of the distribution to the extent that such provision or any part thereof ought, pursuant to the order or this Part, to be made out of the portion of the estate distributed.

---

183 *Ibid.* at 498. Unfortunately, in *Re Gold* (1975), 8 O.R. (2d) 694 (Ont. Surr. Ct.) at 702, although the sole executor beneficiary transferred a bank account to himself before the date of the application, the court overlooked this fact and treated the case as one involving transfers occurring after the date of the application. There is also *Re Brill*, [1967] 2 O.R. 586 (Ont. Surr. Ct.), where the court held that payment by an executrix of the net proceeds of an account to herself as sole beneficiary constitutes distribution of the estate; *Gilles v. Althouse* (1975), [1976] 1 S.C.R. 353 (S.C.C.) and *MacDonald v. MacKenzie Estate*, *supra* note 25; had to do with in-time applications and the courts ordered the widow in *Gilles* and the co-habitee in *MacDonald* to receive the whole estate even though the executrixes and sole beneficiaries had distributed the estate to themselves prior to receiving notice of the relief application.

184 There is some inconclusive discussion of this point in *Re Gold*, *ibid.* at 699-702.

185 For instance, *Re Hull*, *supra* note 119; *Re Ahearn*, [1952] O.W.N. 704 (Ont. H.C.); *Re Jervas*, *supra* note 167.

The Manitoba,[186] Prince Edward Island,[187] Northwest Territories,[188] and Yukon Acts[189] have an identical section. The Newfoundland Act's section[190] is similar, but it does not provide for either interim distribution or advances and it expressly empowers the personal representative to proceed with distribution of the estate until served with notice of an application. The Nova Scotia section[191] is similar to the Ontario section, but in addition to staying distribution once notice of an application has been served it stays distribution until the expiration of six months from the grant of probate or administration; also, it expressly excepts the payment of debts, and funeral and testamentary expenses. The Alberta section[192] is similar to the Ontario section, except that it stays distribution for six months from the grant of probate or administration. The Alberta Act contains an additional section:

> **18.** (1) On notice of any application being given to the executor, administrator or trustee, the estate is subject to the provisions of any order that may be made and the executor, administrator or trustee shall not proceed with the distribution of the estate otherwise than in accordance with that order.
>
> (2) If an executor, administrator or trustee distributes or disposes of any portion of the estate in any manner in contravention of subsection (1) and provision for maintenance and support is ordered by a judge to be made out of the estate, the executor, administrator or trustee is personally liable to pay the amount distributed or disposed of to the extent that the provision or any part of it ought, pursuant to the order or this Act, to be made out of the portion of the estate distributed or disposed of.
>
> **18.** (3) In addition to being personally liable as provided in subsection (2), an executor, administrator or trustee who wilfully contravenes subsection (1) is guilty of an offence and liable
>
> > (a) in the case of a natural person to a fine of not more than $1000 and in default of payment to a term of imprisonment of not more than 60 days, and
> >
> > (b) in the case of a corporation to a fine of not more than $5000.

The Saskatchewan sections[193] are like the Alberta sections. The British Columbia and New Brunswick Acts have simpler sections and the British Columbia Act has an additional unique subsection (2):

---

186 s. 7.

187 s. 9.

188 s. 8, except that it does not enable an interim distribution by consent of all the persons entitled to apply.

189 s. 9.

190 s. 9.

191 s. 9.

192 s. 17.

193 ss. 17-18.

British Columbia:

> **12.** (1) Until 6 months have passed from the issue of probate of the will in British Columbia or the resealing in British Columbia of probate of the will, the executor or trustee must not distribute any portion of the estate to beneficiaries under the will except
>
> (a) with the consent of all persons who would be entitlied to apply, or
>
> (b) if authorized by order of the court.
>
> (2) Until the period referred to in subsection (1) has passed, a title passing by devise to a beneficiary must not be registered in a land title office unless under a similar consent or order, except subject to the liability of being charged by an order made under this Act.

New Brunswick:

> **8.** Where an application is made and notice thereof is served on the executor or trustee of the estate of the deceased, he shall not, after service of the notice upon him, proceed with the distribution of the estate until the judge has disposed of the application.

Although only the Nova Scotia section excepts the payment of debts, and funeral and testamentary expenses, probably the personal representative in the other provinces can pay them with impunity, and indeed probably is obliged to pay them as soon as possible;[194] the estate out of which an award can be made is the net estate, after the payment of the deceased's debts, and funeral and testamentary expenses.[195] Similarly, there is no prohibition in any of the Acts of the personal representative continuing with the administration of the estate.

The Ontario Act, and the other similar Acts, commence: "where an application is made and notice thereof is served on the personal representative . . .". In *Re Gold*[196] the court held that service of the notice upon the estate solicitor sufficed; the court referred to several cases including *Re Consiglio (No. 2)*[197] wherein it was held that if a writ of summons comes to the knowledge or into the possession of the person to be served either directly or indirectly from a third person then that can constitute personal service.

---

194 *In re Simson*, [1950] Ch. 38 (U.K. Ch.) at 42-43.

195 Further, see Chp. 4, 5 *infra*.

196 *Supra* note 183 at 698-99; also *Re Dentinger*, *supra* note 10.

197 [1971] 3 O.R. 798 (Ont. Master), varied [1973] 3 O.R. 329, 36 D.L.R. (3d) 661 (Ont. C.A.).

The British Columbia, Alberta, Saskatchewan, Manitoba, Ontario, Nova Scotia,[198] Prince Edward Island, and Yukon sections enable an interim distribution either with the consent of all parties entitled to apply for a relief order or by court order. The Northwest Territories Act enables an interim distribution only by court order. The New Brunswick and Newfoundland sections are silent on advances and interim distribution. The Alberta, Saskatchewan, Ontario, Nova Scotia, Prince Edward Island, Northwest Territories and Yukon sections enable the personal representative(s) to make "reasonable advances" to "dependants who are beneficiaries"; does "beneficiaries" include heirs on an intestacy? The Manitoba section clearly enables advances in both the testate and intestate situations. An example of an interim distribution order, made for elderly beneficiaries of modest means from a multi-million dollar estate, albeit pursuant to the *Court of Appeal Act*, is *Hecht v. Hecht Estate*;[199] the court said:

> The factors to be considered by the court when deciding whether to exercise its discretion to grant leave to the executors include:
>
> (a) the amount of the benefits sought to be distributed as compared to the value of the estate;
>
> (b) the claim of the beneficiaries on the testator;
>
> (c) the need of beneficiaries for money;
>
> (d) the consent of the residuary beneficiary to the proposes distribution.[200]

The court also took into account the risk of the distribution encroaching on the funds needed to satisfy the possible dependants' relief order. Not to be confused with advances and interim distribution orders are interim relief orders treated in Chp. 5, 2.

The court in *Re Dentinger*[201] indicated that in the circumstances of the case the advances made to the beneficiary should be charged against the beneficiary's share and not against the entire estate as a debt.

The combined effect of the limitation period and stay of distribution sections was described by the Supreme Court of Canada in *Gilles v. Althouse*.[202] The deceased, Michael Gilles, died July 31, 1971, survived by his widow, from whom he had been separated since 1952, and their two

---

198 Query the correctness of *Mollins v. Mollins Estate* (1996), 152 N.S.R. (2d) 386 (N.S. S.C.) at paragraph 4 that "[t]here is no provision for interim payments under the [N.S.] Act". (Additional reasons for *Mollins* at (1996), 152 N.S.R. (2d) 386 at 389 (N.S. S.C.)).

199 (1991), (*sub nom. Hecht v. Reid*) 62 B.C.L.R. (2d) 145 (B.C. C.A.).

200 *Ibid.* at 151.

201 *Supra* note 10 at 24-25.

202 [1976] 1 S.C.R. 353 (S.C.C.).

daughters, whom by his will he named as his executrixes and sole beneficiaries. On August 14, 1971, the widow wrote a letter to one of the daughters, which commenced: "Just a line to let you know I don't want anything to do with that Will. I wouldn't hurt you for love or money so please don't worry about it . . .". The daughters obtained letters probate on August 18, 1971, and distributed the estate to themselves on August 24, 1971. On September 3, 1971, within the limitation period, the widow filed a motion for an order pursuant to the Saskatchewan Act. The trial judge ordered that the widow receive the entire estate. The Court of Appeal reversed that decision on the basis that the estate had been fully distributed by the time the widow filed her motion and served the executrixes with notice thereof. The pertinent sections of the Saskatchewan Act were:

> **15.** No order shall be made unless on an application made within six months from the grant of probate of the will or of administration, but the court may, if it deems it just, allow an application to be made at any time as to any portion of the estate remaining undistributed at the date of the application.
>
> **17.** (1) After service of notice of an application for an allowance under this Act the executor or trustee or the administrator shall not proceed with the distribution of the estate until the application is disposed of.

Reversing the Court of Appeal, Justice Dickson for the Supreme Court of Canada said:

> The argument of the respondents is simply this—if there is no estate there can be no order. It is, of course, apparent that if this submission is valid a testator could readily defeat dependants' relief legislation merely by converting his property to liquid assets and naming as executors and beneficiaries of his estate those whom he favours, to the exclusion of all others. One must look with some misgiving upon a construction which would lead to such result. Dependants' relief legislation properly recognizes that the financial responsibilities of marriage and parenthood do not always terminate at death. The legislation is intended to curb unlimited testamentary disposition to the extent of assuring reasonable provision for the maintenance of those who, in necessitous or other circumstances, have a meritorious claim on the estate of the testator or intestate. Is recovery to depend on the outcome of a race between executors on the one hand, distributing the assets of the estate, and dependants on the other hand, making application to the Court for relief?
>
> It is true, . . . there is nothing in s. 15 which restricts the right of an executor or administrator to distribute an estate during the period of six months following grant of probate of the will or of administration. It is also true there is nothing in the section which expressly or impliedly authorizes him to do so. The construction which the Court of Appeal adopted, in my opinion, renders meaningless, as mere surplusage, the six-month period mentioned in s. 15; on that construction an application for relief, irrespective of the date

> upon which it is lodged, could only affect the portion of the estate remaining undistributed. In my view the true meaning and effect of the section is to afford an applicant a period of six months after probate within which to obtain an order as to the entire estate, but if he or she delays and makes application after expiry of the six-month period the claim can only be against the portion of the estate then remaining undistributed.
>
> . . . . .
>
> Counsel for the respondents placed reliance on s. 16 of *The Dependants' Relief Act, supra.* Counsel submitted that the effect of this section is such that executors are free to proceed with distribution of the estate until such time as they have notice of an application for an allowance under the Act. I find it difficult to accept that submission. Section 16 must be read with s. 15, the combined effect of which in my opinion is to inhibit an executor for a period of six months from distributing the assets of an estate if there is the possibility of an application under the Act; after six months the executor is free to distribute the estate unless and until he receives notice of an application under the Act.
>
> . . . . .
>
> In his factum counsel for the respondents submitted that the respondents had acted precisely within the scope of their duties . . .. I do not agree. At least until expiry of the six-month period Mrs. Gilles was a potential applicant under *The Dependants' Relief Act.* She did not effectively disclaim any rights which she might have under that Act. Executors or administrators have a duty not to distribute before the expiry of the limitation period if the possibility of an application for relief is hanging over the estate; if they do so, they do so at their peril . . .[203]

About the August 14, 1971 letter, Justice Dickson said:

> This letter may have had some bearing on the decision of the executrices to proceed with immediate distribution to themselves of the assets constituting the estate and may tend to negate any allegation of bad faith. It may also be relevant on the question of costs but the letter does not in my opinion amount to an estoppel or disclaimer by the appellant. I understood counsel for the respondents to concede as much during argument.[204]

Apparently, *Gilles v. Althouse* makes inconsequential a unique aspect of the British Columbia stay of distribution section, s.11, above, that it does not require service upon the personal representative of the process by which a relief proceeding is commenced. For all provinces it can be said that,

---

203 *Ibid.* at 356-60. See also *Mazur v. Mazur*, [1980] 3 W.W.R. 289 (Man. C.A.), leave to appeal refused (1980), 5 Man. R. (2d) 180n (S.C.C.); *Re Dentinger, supra* note 10 at 30-32; *Daniel v. Daniel Estate* (1986), 41 Man. R. (2d) 66 (Man. Q.B.) at paragraphs 14-18; *MacDonald v. MacKenzie Estate, supra* note 25 at paragraphs 7-14; *Black v. Keith Estate* (1989), 96 N.B.R. (2d) 322 (N.B. Q.B.).

204 *Ibid.* at 361.

generally speaking, the personal representative cannot make any distribution of the estate until six months after the representation grant; thereafter, the estate can be distributed if the personal representative has not been served with notice of an application.

8. NATURE OF THE PROCEEDING

In all of the Acts, except the British Columbia Act, the proceeding is prescribed to be an "application", made by or on behalf of the dependants or any of them; several of the Acts also provide that the application "may be made" by originating notice,[205] by originating notice of motion[206] by notice of application,[207] or by originating application.[208] The Alberta Court of Appeal in *Tatko v. Liefke*[209] rejected an argument that the proceeding should have been dismissed on the basis that the widow proceeded by way of a statement of claim and not a notice of motion; the Court noted, *inter alia*, the use of the word "may" in the legislation.

An application must be supported by an affidavit, which qualifies the applicant and deals with the circumstances[210] pertinent to the application, including personal information of the applicant, such as age, health, education, employment (prospects), and financial details of income, assets and expenses, the nature of the relationship between the applicant and the deceased, the size, nature and testate or intestate disposition of the estate, and the names of other persons who might qualify as dependants. It should be borne in mind that a relief application can be treated entirely by affidavit evidence,[211] although usually there will be a hearing at which *viva voce* evidence is adduced.

The British Columbia Act prescribes "an action",[212] which by the Supreme Court Rules is commenced by a writ of summons.[213]

Justice Disbery in *Re Hovdebo*[214] said that a dependants' relief action "should stand alone and not be yoked in the same motion with applications for orders respecting matters outside the purview of the Act".

205 Alta. s. 13(1); N.S. s. 4.

206 N.W.T. s. 3.

207 Ont. s. 60; N.B. s. 3.

208 Nfld. s. 4.

209 *Supra* note 7.

210 See Chp. 4.

211 *Re Czajkowski*, [1963] 2 O.R. 513 (Ont. C.A.); *Zeman v. Zeman Estate* (1993), 49 E.T.R. 31 (B.C. S.C.) at paragraphs 51-60; note *Re Jenkins*, [1955] O.W.N. 958 (Ont. Surr. Ct.), reversed [1956] O.W.N. 548, 3 D.L.R. (2d) 561 (Ont. C.A.).

212 s. 2.

213 See Amighetti at 142, 146, 149 *et seq*.

214 (1963), 45 W.W.R. 640 (Sask. Q.B.). See further Chp. 4.

9. PARTIES AND NOTICE

All of the dependants' relief Acts provide for applications to be made by or on behalf of statutorily defined dependants.[215] Most of the Acts either empower or direct the court to treat an application as an application made on behalf of all possible dependants.[216]

The respondent of an application is the personal representative of the estate. When letters probate or of administration have not been issued the citation process can be used to bring about a grant,[217] or perhaps, as in *Re Stafford*[218] if there is a will, the executor appointed in the will can be made the respondent.

Although not all of the Acts require notice to be given, presumably it should be given to all interested persons (other dependants, beneficiaries, and heirs) and perhaps to the Public Trustee if a minor or institutionalized person is involved.[219] The Alberta, Ontario and Nova Scotia sections stipulate that the court cannot make an order until being "satisfied upon oath that all persons who are or may be interested in or affected by the order have been served . . . with notice of the application".[220] While, generally speaking, all persons interested in the application must be given notice and will have status to participate, in *Re Mannion (No. 2)*[221] an application for intervener status made by the Ontario Status of Women Council was dismissed.

In *Ford v. Bell Estate*[222] an application was dismissed because the notice of motion was neither served on the executors nor served six clear days before the notice was returnable, as was required by former s. 6(1) of the Saskatchewan Act; the notice of motion was served on the lawyer retained by the executors, who was the solicitor of record, but who had no instructions to accept the service.

---

215 See further Chp. 3, 1, above.

216 B.C. s. 4(1); Alta. s. 16; Man. s. 4; Ont. s. 60(2); N.B. s. 15; N.S. s. 15; P.E.I. s. 4; N.W.T. s. 2(1); Y.T. s. 4.

217 Schnurr, B. and Woodley, S., "Dependant Support Proceedings" (1995) 14 E.T.J. 159 at 160-61.

218 *Supra* note 137.

219 B.C. s. 3(1)(c), see Amighetti at 146; Alta. s. 13(3); Sask. s. 5; Man. s. 5; Ont. s. 74; N.S. s. 15.

220 *Ibid.* Note *Re Weir* (1962) [1963] 1 O.R. 53 (Ont. C.A.); *Coolen v. Coolen, supra* note 162 at paragraphs 33-35; and *Carey v. Carey* (1981), 36 Nfld. & P.E.I.R. 224 (Nfld. T.D.).

221 (1983), 15 E.T.R. 76 (Ont. C.A.).

222 (1997), 154 Sask. R. 193 (Sask. Q.B.).

None of the Acts deals with pre-hearing matters, such as pleadings, discovery,[223] and whether a hearing will be involved.[224] Of course, these matters may be regulated by rules of court.

10. EVIDENTIARY ISSUES

(a) Onus of Proof

On a dependants' relief application, aside from having to decide whether an applicant qualifies as a dependant,[225] which is seldom an issue, the first determination a court has to make is whether the deceased, by will or by allowing the estate to be distributed as an intestacy, has made adequate or reasonable provision for the proper support or the maintenance and support of applicant. The onus of proof is on the applicant[226] to prove that the will or intestate succession law does not make adequate provision.[227] In connection with this determination, if the deceased has expressed

223 Note *Re Hunt*, [1940] O.W.N. 408 (Ont. H.C.); *Re Hitchin* (1943), 60 B.C.R. 117 (B.C. S.C.).

224 See text at note 211 *supra*.

225 See Chp. 2, text at note 12.

226 There may be more than one applicant and as a result of an application another dependant may ask for his or her situation to be considered; of course, all dependants asking for relief have this onus of proof.

227 *Inter alia*, *Shaw Estate*, [1942] S.C.R. 513 (S.C.C.) at 516; *Re Lawther*, *supra* note 123 at 150; *Pope v. Stevens*, *supra* note 11 at 171; *Simmonds v. Rehn*, *supra* note 37 at 568; *Rill v. Miller*, *supra* note 11 at 213; *Spinney v. Royal Trust Co.*, *supra* note 11 at paragraph 29; *Re Ducherer*, [1977] 6 W.W.R. 495 (Sask. Surr. Ct.) at 497; *Malychuk v. Malychuk* (1978), 6 Alta. L.R. (2d) 240 (Alta. T.D.) at 245; *Re Davies*, *supra* note 10; *Jeffers v. Jeffers*, *supra* note 11 at paragraph 10; *Re Protopappas Estate* (1987), 78 A.R. 60 (Alta. Q.B.) at paragraph 39; *Moroz v. Moroz Estate* (1991), 92 Sask. R. 176 (Sask. Surr. Ct.) at paragraph 1; *Currie v. Currie Estate* (1995), 166 N.B.R. (2d) 144 (N.B. C.A.) at paragraph 12; *Paxman v. Saskatchewan (Public Trustee)*, *supra* note 23 at paragraph 10. By the way, there are numerous cases in which the court has dismissed the application because the applicant failed to fulfill this onus of proof including *Warwick (Guardian ad litem of) v. Warwick Estate* (1996), 11 E.T.R. (2d) 129 (B.C. S.C.); *Modopoulos v. Breen Estate*, *supra* note 10 at paragraph 21; *Hecht v. Hecht Estate* (1993), 81 B.C.L.R. (2d) 239 (B.C. C.A.), additional reasons at (1993), 87 B.C.L.R. (2d) 271 (B.C. C.A.), leave to appeal refused [1994] 2 W.W.R. lxiv (S.C.C.); *Penteluk v. Penteluk Estate*, *supra* note 11; *Pedersen v. Pedersen* (1991), 43 E.T.R. 189 (B.C. S.C.) at paragraphs 17 and 22; *Black v. Kronberger Estate* (1990), 83 Sask. R. 73 (Sask. C.A.); *Driscoll v. Driscoll Estate*, *supra* note 69; *Cross v. Currie Estate* (1987), 81 N.S.R. (2d) 193 (N.S. T.D.); *Swire v. Swire*, *supra* note 113; *Murray v. Murray Estate* (1986), 50 Sask. R. 308 (Sask. Surr. Ct.); *Niebergall v. Niebergall Estate*, *supra* note 11; *Re Champ Estate* (1986), (*sub nom. Re Champ*) 47 Sask. R. 305 (Sask. Q.B.); *Peslari v. Pestruic*, *supra* note 11; *Re deBeaudrap*, *supra* note 162; *Re Serdula*, *supra* note 129; *Carlson v. Carlson* (1983), 49 A.R. 117 (Alta. Q.B.); *Foulon v. Foulon* (1981), 29 A.R.

in one form another reasons for his or her actions, the applicant's onus of proof includes discrediting the deceased's reasons.[228]

In a few cases the court considered that the applicant being left nothing in the deceased's estate discharged the onus for the applicant.[229] The court in *Rill v. Miller* disagreed.[230] Surely, merely being left out of the deceased's will is not sufficient to discharge the onus.

In *Modopoulos v. Breen Estate*,[231] where the applicant was going after proceeds of the sale of a property owned jointly by the deceased and her mother, the court held that the applicant had failed to discharge the onus since the deceased had made the applicant the sole beneficiary of her estate.

If the court decides that adequate provision has not been made, the next determination is what relief order will be reasonable or adequate (just and equitable) for proper support or maintenance; presumably the onus continues to be on the applicant, although the obligation of apprising the court of the composition of the deceased's estate is on the deceased's personal representative.[232] Since the wording of the two matters is the same in all the Acts, that is in each Act, although not among all the Acts, except in the British Columbia Act, it should be needless to say that the same circumstances are to be considered by the court for both matters[233] and the Supreme Court of Canada has said in *Tataryn v. Tataryn Estate* that this is so for the British Columbia Act too.[234]

---

120 (Alta. Q.B.); *Re Flood* (1978), 20 Nfld. & P.E.I.R. 448 (P.E.I. S.C.); *Biblow v. Royal Trust Co.* (1977), 3 A.R. 203 (Alta. T.D.); *Nelson v. Nelson* (1977), 17 N.B.R. (2d) 457 (N.B. C.A.); *Collard v. Collard, supra* note 11; *Nickle v. Jones*, [1974] 3 W.W.R. 385 (Alta. S.C.); *Re Pelletier* (1974), 10 N.B.R. (2d) 365 (N.B. Q.B.); *Keane v. Keane, supra* note 11; *Rill v. Miller, supra* note 11; *Re Wild* (1964), 44 D.L.R. (2d) 91 (Alta. T.D.); *Re Cole, supra* note 69; *Re Lund*, [1946] 3 W.W.R. 732 (Sask. K.B.).

228 See text in Chp. 4, 2(i).

229 *Hiebert v. Ward, supra* note 63 at 260; *Jeffers v. Jeffers, supra* note 11; *Niebergall v. Niebergall Estate, supra* note 11 at 292.

230 *Supra* note 11. Also *Re Dickinson, supra* note 69 at 215-17.

231 *Supra* note 10 at 135.

232 *Re Stafford, supra* note 137 at paragraphs 16-18; also *Re Jones* (1959), 27 W.W.R. 631 (B.C. S.C.) at 638.

233 But some courts have felt compelled to state the obvious; for ex., *Re Lawther, supra* note 123 at 151 and *Spinney v. Royal Trust Co., supra* note 11 at paragraph 21.

234 [1994] 2 S.C.R. 807 (S.C.C.) at 814, reconsideration refused 5 E.T.R. (2d) 210 (note), [1994] 9 W.W.R. lxxiii, 95 B.C.L.R. (2d) xxxiii (S.C.C.).

(b) Other Evidence

In addition to evidence adduced by the parties to an application, most of the Acts[235] provide that the court may direct any other evidence to be given as it considers necessary, proper, or relevant.

(c) Corroboration

There is a rule of evidence embodied in the Evidence Acts of most provinces[236] of which s. 11 of the Prince Edward Island *Evidence Act*[237] is exemplary:

> **11.** In any action or proceeding by or against the heirs, or personal representatives or their assigns of a deceased person, an opposite or interested party to the action shall not obtain a verdict, judgment or decision therein on his own evidence in respect of any matter occurring before the death of the deceased person, unless the evidence is corroborated by some other material evidence.

It has been held that this statutory requirement does not apply to dependants' relief applications, for the reason that the applicant is not seeking "a verdict, judgment or decision . . . in respect of any matter occurring before the death of the deceased person".[238] However, in *Re Murray*[239] Justice Atkins said:

> The petitioner's evidence as to her husband's conduct towards her is wholly uncorroborated. I invited counsel to make submissions on the question of whether or not s. 11 of the *Evidence Act*, R.S.B.C. 1960, c. 134, requiring corroboration in any action or proceeding against the heirs, executors, administrators or assigns of a deceased person had any application. Mr. Bonnell referred me to *Plumb v. Royal Trust Co.* . . . in which Macdonald, J. (Supreme Court of Alberta) held that the corresponding section of the Alberta *Evidence Act* had no application in a proceeding under the *Widows' Relief Act* of that

---

235 Alta. s. 3(2)(b); Man. s. 8(2)(b); Ont. s. 62(2); N.S. s. 5(2); P.E.I. s. 5(1)(b); Nfld. s. 5(2); N.W.T. s. 4(1)(b); Y.T. s. 5(1)(b). The B.C. and N.B. Acts do not contain this provision.

236 Note Sopinka, J., Lederman, S., Bryant, A., *The Law of Evidence in Canada* (Toronto: Butterworths, 1992) at 917-18.

237 R.S. P.E.I. 1974, c. E-10.

238 *Re Blackwell*, *supra* note 11 at 527; also *Plumb v. Royal Trust Co.*, *supra* note 11 at 515; cf. *Re Ruby*, *supra* note 55 at 281–82; and *Baker v. Baker Estate*, *supra* note 11 at paragraphs 23-31, in which the court, without reference to the foregoing cases, seems to proceed on the basis that corroboration is required.

239 (1966), 60 D.L.R. (2d) 76 (B.C. S.C.) at 81.

Province. I am in respectful agreement with this conclusion. However, the fact of the matter is that the petitioner by her evidence makes serious allegations as to the conduct of her late husband. There is no way in which these allegations can be met. They can be made with impunity.

While corroboration is not an absolute statutory requirement prudent common sense requires that evidence such as given by Mrs. Murray, which is wholly uncorroborated, about the conduct of a deceased person should be weighed and considered with the greatest care. The statutory rule requiring corroboration as an absolute condition of acceptance of the evidence of a claimant against the estate of the deceased has no application, nevertheless the nature of the evidence given by Mrs. Murray is such, in my view, as to call into operation the common law rule as to corroboration in cases involving claims against a deceased person's estate. The common law rule, a rule of practice only, does not preclude a claimant succeeding without corroboration, granted that the Court is convinced that the uncorroborated testimony is true. I refer to *Adamson v. Vachon* (1914), 6 W.W.R. 114, and I quote from the judgment of Anglin, J., at p. 120:

> While there is no absolute rule requiring corroboration in the case of a claim against the estate of a deceased person (*In re Griffin* (1898) 1 Ch. 408, 413, 68 L.J. Ch. 220), the uncorroborated evidence of a claimant will be regarded with jealous suspicion (*In re Garnett* (1885) 31 Ch.D. 1), and the court will in general require corroboration (*In re Hodgson*, 31 Ch.D. 177, 183, 55 L.J. Ch. 241). The plaintiff's testimony did not convince the learned Chief Justice who heard it. The court ought to be completely satisfied before allowing such a claim as this: *Rawlinson v. Scholes* (1898) 79 L.T. 350. I am far from being so satisfied.

As to the petitioner's evidence, bearing in mind the petitioner's failure to instruct her counsel fully and her failure to give the evidence she gave before me when testifying before the Magistrate in 1937 and the other factors which I have considered, I am not satisfied that Mrs. Murray's evidence is reliable. I am not completely convinced that it is true.

I should not be taken as having reached the conclusion that the petitioner was deliberately fabricating her evidence. It should, I think, be remembered that the petitioner was giving evidence of her life with her husband 29 years ago. The fact of the matter is that Mrs. Murray did leave her husband in August of 1937 and it seems to me obvious that she could not have been happy in her marriage to him. In this situation it seems to me to be not at all unlikely that recollection has become distorted by time and emotion and perhaps by some need for self-justification.

(d) Solicitor-Client Privilege

Gordon v. Gilroy[240] had to do with whether a lawyer is obliged to produce files pertaining to a will. While there is in this regard an exception to the solicitor-client privilege, in the context of the subject case the Master refused the application for production.

240 (1994), 5 E.T.R. (2d) 289 (B.C. Master). See also *Johal v. Billan* (1995), 10 E.T.R. (2d) 171 (B.C. S.C. [In Chambers]).

4

The Basic Order

1. INTRODUCTION

The seminal New Zealand *Testator's Family Maintenance Act, 1900*, provided:

> **2.** Should any person die, leaving a will, and without making therein adequate provision for the proper maintenance and support of his or her wife, husband, or children, the Court may at its discretion, on application by or on behalf of the said wife, husband, or children, order that such provision as to the said Court shall seem fit shall be made out of the estate of the said deceased person for such wife, husband, or children . . .

In regard to the implementation of this section Justice Edwards made an oft-quoted statement in *Allardice v. Allardice*:[1]

> It is the duty of the court, so far as is possible, to place itself in all respects in the position of the testator, and to consider whether or not, having regard to all existing facts and surrounding circumstances, the testator has been guilty of a manifest breach of that moral duty which a just, but not a loving, husband or father owes towards his wife or towards his children, as the case may be.

His words, "having regard to all existing facts and surrounding circumstances", slightly changed, have been included in the primary jurisdiction section of several of the Canadian dependant's relief Acts.[2] Others among the Acts, such as the Northwest Territories Act,[3] provide:

---

1 (1910), 29 N.Z.L.R. 959 (New Zealand C.A.) at 972, affirmed [1911] A.C. 730 (New Zealand P.C.).

2 Saskatchewan *Dependants Relief Act, 1996*, S.S. 1996, c. D-25.01, s. 9(3) [hereinafter Saskatchewan Act]; New Brunswick *Provision for Dependants Act*, R.S.N.B. 1973, c. P-22.3, s. 2(1) [hereinafter New Brunswick Act]; Nova Scotia *Testators' Family Maintenance Act*, R.S.N.S. 1989, c. 465, s. 3(1); and Newfoundland *Family Relief Act*, R.S.N. 1990, c. F-2, s. 3(1) [hereinafter Newfoundland Act].

3 Northwest Territories *Dependants Relief Act*, R.S.N.W.T. 1988, c. D-4, s. 4(1)(a) [hereinafter Northwest Territories Act]; Alberta *Family Relief Act*, R.S.A. 1980, c. F-2, s. 3(2)(a) [hereinafter Alberta Act]; Prince Edward Island *Dependants of a Deceased Person Relief Act*, R.S.P.E.I. 1988, c. D-7, s. 5(1)(a) [hereinafter Prince Edward Island

4. (1) A judge on hearing an application under this Act may

(a) inquire into and consider all matters that the judge considers should be fairly taken into account in deciding on the application;

The Saskatchewan, Manitoba,[4] Ontario,[5] Nova Scotia, and Newfoundland Acts contain additional specificity.

Saskatchewan

8. (1) In determining whether, and in what way, and from what date, maintenance ought to be provided, the court shall consider the nature of the property representing the deceased's estate and shall not make an order requiring a sale of property that would be improvident having regard to the interests of the dependants and of the person who, apart from the order, would be entitled to that property.

(2) In making an order for maintenance, the court shall consider:

(a) any past, present or future capital or income from any source of the dependant;

(b) the conduct of that dependant in relation to the deceased;

(c) the claims that any other dependant of the deceased may have; and

(d) any other matters that the court considers appropriate.

. . .

(6) The court may refuse to make an order in favour of a dependant whose character or conduct is or has been of a nature that would, in the opinion of the court, disentitle the dependant to the benefit of an order.

Manitoba

Determination of amount
8. (1) In determining the amount and duration, if any, of maintenance and support, the court shall have regard primarily to the financial needs of the dependant and shall consider all of the circumstances of the application, including,

(a) the size and nature of the deceased's estate;

(b) the assets and financial resources that the dependant has or is likely to have in the foreseeable future;

Act]; and Yukon Territory *Dependants Relief Act*, R.S.Y.T. 1990, c. 44, s. 5(1)(a) [hereinafter Yukon Act].

4 *Dependants Relief Act*, S.M. 1989-90, c. 42; C.C.S.M., c. D37 [hereinafter Manitoba Act].

5 *Succession Law Reform Act*, R.S.O. 1990, c. S.26, Part V [hereinafter Ontario Act].

(c) the measures available for a dependent to become financially independent and the length of time and cost involved to enable the dependant to take such measures;

(d) the age and the physical and mental health of the dependant;

(e) the capacity of the dependant to provide for his or her own support;

(f) if the dependant is a spouse, any distribution or division of property that the dependant has received or is entitled to receive under The Homesteads Act or The Marital Property Act;

(g) the assets that the dependant is entitled to receive from the estate of the deceased otherwise than by an order under this Act;

(h) the claims that any other dependant or any other person has upon the estate;

(i) any provision which the deceased while living made for the dependant and for any other dependants;

(j) if the dependant is a child, the child's aptitude for and reasonable prospects of obtaining an education;

(k) if the dependant is a child to whom the deceased stood in loco parentis, the primary obligation of the child's parents to maintain the child and whether the parents have discharged that obligation.

Evidence
8. (2) On the hearing of an application, the court

(a) may inquire into and consider all matters that it considers should fairly be taken into account in deciding the application;

Ontario

Determination of amount
62. (1) In determining the amount and duration, if any, of support, the court shall consider all the circumstances of the application, including,

(a) the dependant's current assets and means;

(b) the assets and means that the dependant is likely to have in the future;

(c) the dependant's capacity to contribute to his or her own support;

(d) the dependant's age and physical and mental health;

(e) the dependant's needs, in determining which the court shall have regard to the dependant's accustomed standard of living;

(f) the measures available for the dependant to become able to provide for his or her own support and the length of time and cost involved to enable the dependant to take those measures;

(g) the proximity and duration of the dependant's relationship with the deceased;

(h) the contributions made by the dependant to the deceased's welfare, including indirect and non-financial contributions;

(i) the contributions made by the dependant to the acquisition, maintenance and improvement of the deceased's property or business;

(j) a contribution by the dependant to the realization of the deceased's career potential;

(k) whether the dependant has a legal obligation to provide support for another person;

(l) the circumstances of the deceased at the time of death;

(m) any agreement between the deceased and the dependant;

(n) any previous distribution or division of property made by the deceased in favour of the dependant by gift or agreement or under court order;

(o) the claims that any other person may have as a dependant;

(p) if the dependant is a child,

> (i) the child's aptitude for and reasonable prospects of obtaining an education, and
>
> (ii) the child's need for a stable environment;

(q) if the dependant is a child of the age of sixteen years or more, whether the child has withdrawn from parental control;

(r) if the dependant is a spouse,

> (i) a course of conduct by the spouse during the deceased's lifetime that is so unconscionable as to constitute an obvious and gross repudiation of the relationship,
>
> (ii) the length of time the spouses cohabited,
>
> (iii) the effect on the spouse's earning capacity of the responsibilities assumed during cohabitation,
>
> (iv) whether the spouse has undertaken the care of a child who is of the age of eighteen years or over and unable by reason of illness, disability or other cause to withdraw from the charge of his or her parents,
>
> (v) whether the spouse has undertaken to assist in the continuation of a program of education for a child eighteen years of age or over who is unable for that reason to withdraw from the charge of his or her parents,

(vi) any housekeeping, child care or other domestic service performed by the spouse for the family, as if the spouse had devoted the time spent in performing that service in remunerative employment and had contributed the earnings to the family's support,

(vii) the effect on the spouse's earnings and career development of the responsibility of caring for a child,

(viii) the desirability of the spouse remaining at home to care for a child; and

(s) any other legal right of the dependant to support, other than out of public money.[6]

Nova Scotia and Newfoundland

Inquiry by judge[7]

5. (1) Upon the hearing of an application made by or on behalf of a dependant under subsection (1) of Section 3, the judge shall inquire into and consider all matters that should be fairly taken into account in deciding upon the application including, without limiting the generality of the foregoing,

(a) whether the character or conduct of the dependant is such as should disentitle the dependant to the benefit of an order under this Act;

(b) whether the dependant is likely to become possessed of or entitled to any other provision for his maintenance and support;

(c) the relations of the dependant and the testator at the time of his death;

(d) the financial circumstances of the dependant;

(e) the claims which any other dependant has upon the estate;

(f) any provision which the testator while living has made for the dependant and for any other dependant;

(g) any services rendered by the dependant to the testator;

(h) any sum of money or any property provided by the dependant for the testator for the purpose of providing a home or assisting in any business or occupation or for maintenance or medical or hospital expenses.

Section 5(1) of the Newfoundland Act is identical to s. 5(1) of the Nova Scotia Act except that the Newfoundland Act contains an additional matter, "(i) rights that a widow or widower has under the *Family Law Act* or a marriage contract made under that Act".[8]

---

6 The initial *Dependants' Relief Act* of Ontario, S.O. 1929, c. 47, in its s. 7 contained a shorter version of the current Act's s. 62.

7 Nova Scotia Act, s. 5(1).

8 Added by S.N. 1979, c. 32, s. 43.

Another circumstance which all of the Acts allow or direct to be considered are any reasons given by a testator.[9]

Prior to the enactment of the detailed Manitoba and Ontario sections, courts had created their own lists of circumstances to be taken into account. Probably, the most quoted list is the one articulated by Chief Justice Williams in *Re Lawther*:[10]

> The judge must consider the character and conduct of the applicant . . .
>
> It would seem proper to enquire whether the applicant is likely to become possessed of, or entitled to, any other provision for her proper maintenance and support . . .
>
> Besides the matters just referred to, the decisions show that the Court will take into consideration the following circumstances:
>
> 1. The size of the testator's estate.
> 2. The size of his family.
> 3. The ages of his dependants.
> 4. The station in life of the testator and his dependants.
> 5. The character and views of the testator.
> 6. The wishes of the testator, if his failure to perform his duty is due to omission or oversight (e.g. an expressed intention, not carried out, to make further provision by will).
> 7. The relative needs and deserts of the claimants (if the estate is small and the claimants are numerous).
> 8. The possibility of changes in existing circumstances.
> 9. The future value of money and rates of interest.
> 10. The opinions and wishes of a just and wise mother about the education and mode of life of the children of herself and the testator.
> 11. The situation arising when the testator has been married more than once.
> 12. The personal income of the dependants.
> 13. The competing moral claims on the bounty of the testator.
> 14. The health and mental capacity of the dependants.
> 15. In the case of a widow, the kind of maintenance to which she had been accustomed during the life of the testator, or to which she would have been accustomed if her husband had then done his duty to her, all this

---

9 British Columbia *Wills Variation Act*, R.S.B.C. 1996, c. 490, s. 5(1) [hereinafter British Columbia Act]; Alta., s. 3(2); Sask., s. 8(3); Man., s. 8(2); Ont., s. 62(3) and (4); N.B., s. 9; N.S., s. 5(3); P.E.I., s. 5(1)(c) and (b); Nfld., s. 5(3); N.W.T., s. 4(1)(c) and (2); Y.T., s. 5(1)(c) and (2). See further Chp. 4, (2) (i).

10 (1947), 55 Man. R. 142 (Man. K.B.) at 152–54. For a list of cases which have referred to the Williams' list see *Canadian Case Citations*, Carswell. Note also *Re Morton Estate* (1934), 49 B.C.L.R. 172 (B.C. S.C.) at 173; *Jones v. Kline (Jones)*, [1938] 3 W.W.R. 65 (Alta. T.D.) at 84; *Re Willan Estate* (1951), 4 W.W.R. (N.S.) 114 (Alta. S.C.) at 135; *Seerey v. Seerey* (1979), 20 A.R. 442 (Alta. Q.B.); *Nickle v. Jones*, [1974] 3 W.W.R. 385 (Alta. S.C.) at 387; and *Pauliuk v. Pauliuk* (1986), 48 Alta. L.R. (2d) 25 (Alta. Q.B.) at 31.

> involving a consideration of (a) the size of the house in which she is to live, (b) the cost of fuel, living expenses, clothing, and replenishing household furnishings, (c) taxes, including income tax, (d) employment of domestic servants and of persons to tend furnace and grounds, if such servants had been employed in the husband's lifetime or become necessary because of his death or the disability of the widow, (e) the necessity for the use of a motor car and the employment of a driver, (f) the need for medical care or treatment, (g) travelling, particularly if it is necessary to winter in a milder climate.
>
> . . . .
>
> The help given by the applicant in amassing the estate . . .

The wording of the Manitoba, Ontario, and Nova Scotia sections indicate that the list of circumstances is not exhaustive. They comprise an "aide memoire or checklist",[11] with which some courts deal *seriatum* in their reasons for judgment. The various detailed lists have been compendiated for the purpose of the following elaboration.

2. VARIOUS CIRCUMSTANCES

(a) Disqualifying[12] Character or Conduct

All of the Acts, except those of Manitoba and Ontario, contain a section virtually identical to s. 3(5) of the Alberta Act:

> The judge may refuse to make an order in favour of any dependant whose character or conduct is such as in the opinion of the judge disentitles the dependant to the benefit of an order under this Act.[13]

The Ontario Act contains s. 62(1)(r):

> In determining the amount and duration, if any, of support, the court shall consider all the circumstances of the application, including . . .
>
> (r) if the dependant is a spouse,
>
> (i) a course of conduct by the spouse during the deceased's lifetime that is so unconscionable as to constitute an obvious and gross repudiation of the relationship.[14]

---

11 *Re Dentinger* (1981), 10 E.T.R. 6 (Ont. Surr. Ct.) at 17.

12 The literature of this area of the law uses the word "disentitling", which is peculiar since no one is entitled to a relief order.

13 B.C. s. 6(b); Sask. s. 8(6); N.B. s. 2(3); N.S. s. 5(1)(a); P.E.I. s. 5(1)(d); Nfld. s. 5(1)(a); N.W.T. s. 4(1)(d); Y.T. s. 5(1)(d).

14 Note *Re Tothivan* (1982), 36 O.R. (2d) 410 (Ont. Surr. Ct.) at 414; *Re Pflanzner* (1983), 15 E.T.R. 144 (Ont. Surr. Ct.) at 148, 155; and Bale, G., "Re Dentinger, Dependants' Relief Legislation and the Changed Emphasis Effected by Part V of the Succession Law Reform Act (Ontario)" (1982) 10 E.T.R. 7 at 9.

There is no similar provision respecting other dependants, but arguably, the court has jurisdiction to disqualify other dependants pursuant to the opening wording of s. 62(1).

The former *Testator's Family Maintenance Act* of Manitoba contained a section like s. 3(5) of the Alberta Act; inexplicably the section was not continued in the current *Dependants Relief Act;* nonetheless, the courts surely have jurisdiction to refuse to make an order for disqualifying conduct pursuant to the opening wording of s. 8(1) of the Manitoba Act which requires the court to "consider all of the circumstances of the application, including . . .".

The phrase used in most of the Acts, as in s. 3(5) of the Alberta Act, above, is "character or conduct". However, almost invariably, the focus is on conduct, not character.[15] The best articulation of disqualifying conduct or, as it is sometimes called, the preclusion doctrine is in Justice Johnson's dissenting reasons in *Re Edwards Estate*:[16]

> I agree with Macfarlane, J., who said (in *Re Edgelow* (1955), 1 D.L.R. (2d) 126 at p. 129) when considering a similar section in the British Columbia Act: "I do not think that that provision is to be limited in its application to bad behaviour in its so-called moral sense." It applies, I suggest, to any conduct which tends to show that the spouse, without reasonable cause, had surrendered the rights and had refused to perform the duties which the marriage confers and imposes. Such considerations as the length of time that the parties lived together, their conduct to each other while living together, why they separated, the terms of the separation agreement, and their relations subsequent to the separation agreement, are all matters which may be considered when this section is in question.

Section 62(1)(r) of the Ontario Act reflects this point of view.

When testators decide to leave a dependant out of a will for reasons of character or conduct, sometimes they make a statement to this effect in the will. These reasons are generally to be considered by the court.[17] However, in *Sobodiuk v. MacLaren*[18] Justice Freedman pointed out:

> It is the opinion of the judge as to the character or conduct of the applicant that governs. It is not the opinion of the testatrix. The latter may well have felt that the applicant was disentitled to share in the estate, and may, for that reason, have left her nothing in the will. But since it is "moral duty" that must

15 In *Re Bailey Estate* (1971), [1972] 1 W.W.R. 99 (B.C. S.C.), affirmed [1972] 3 W.W.R. 640 (B.C. C.A.), the court considered both the applicant's conduct and character, but found them not to be disqualifying; similarly in *Patterson v. Lauritsen* (1984), 58 B.C.L.R. 182 (B.C. S.C.) the court thought that the applicant's homosexuality, long-time un-employment, and drinking problem was of no consequence.

16 (1961), 31 D.L.R. (2d) 308 (Alta. C.A.) at 314-15.

17 See 2(i), below.

18 (1954), (*sub nom. Re Karabin Estate*) 62 Man. R. 334 (Man. Q.B.) at 338–39.

> be appraised, the testatrix cannot be the one to judge thereof according to her own opinion of the character or conduct of the applicant, even if formed in all good faith. This is the function of the court, which must consider the matter objectively and in the light of all the circumstances.
>
> I have reached the conclusion that in this case the applicant's character or conduct falls short, though not by much, of being such as to disentitle her to an order under the Act. I have the right, however, to consider her character and conduct in its relation to and effect upon the moral duty owed to her by the testatrix. Considering these and other factors I believe that the moral duty in this case was minimal in degree.

According to Justices O'Halloran in *Barker v. Westminster Trust Co.*:[19]

> . . . the "character or conduct" must relate to a state of affairs existing at the death of the wife . . . For the statute speaks of character or conduct which "is such." It does not say "which at any time has been such." A statute of this character can hardly contemplate an inquisition into the life of the husband beginning with their marriage in 1911, and because he may have been guilty of an isolated act 10 or 20 years ago and long since forgiven or forgotten, that it can be used now as a bar against his receiving his proper share of an estate; . . .

However, as the quote from Justice Johnson's reasons in *Re Edwards Estate*, above indicates, not infrequently the court reviews the relationship of the deceased and the applicant over a considerable period of time.

One of the most obvious cases illustrating Justice Johnson's articulation of disqualifying conduct, above, is *Re Shirley Estate*.[20] The husband and wife separated by agreement. The wife received a property settlement from the husband. She moved to California and commenced a divorce proceeding. The husband did not co-operate. There was no evidence of any misconduct on the part of the husband. The court said:

> Probably she would have been successful in obtaining the decree but for the intervention of the husband's death which made further prosecution of the action unnecessary. It seems to me that it would be completely incongruous for the wife to obtain the benefit of an order under this Act by reason of the existence of a marriage tie which she had done everything possible to sever. A greater inconsistency I cannot imagine.[21]

---

19 [1941] 3 W.W.R. 473 (B.C. C.A.) at 489; see also *Re Willan Estate*, *supra* note 10 at 118; *Re Cole* (1958), 12 D.L.R. (2d) 406 (N.S. T.D.) at 416–17; and *Re Gosse* (1963), 43 D.L.R. (2d) 664 (Nfld. T.D.) at 668; *Re Pemberton*, [1948] 2 W.W.R. 745 (Sask. K.B.) at 749–50.

20 (1965), 55 W.W.R. 56 (Sask. Q.B.). Note also *Kelly v. Baker* (1996), 15 E.T.R. (2d) 219 (B.C. C.A.), which could have been decided on the basis of disqualifying conduct, rather than as it was on the basis of a justifiable reason for disinheritance.

21 *Ibid.* at 59.

In other cases, commencing divorce proceedings or obtaining a decree *nisi* has been of no consequence.[22] By the Manitoba, Ontario,[23] Prince Edward Island, and the Yukon Acts some divorced spouses are entitled to apply.

Justice Brownridge opined in *Chernoff v. Chernoff*[24] that doubtless a spouse who deserts and is living in adultery at the time of the other spouse's death is disqualified,[25] but desertion alone may or may not be disqualifying; he decided that the desertion by the applicant of the deceased was not disqualifying.[26] As indicated in Chapter 3, while contracting out of the right to make a dependants' relief application does not bar an application it is an important and perhaps disqualifying circumstance.[27]

Absent overwhelming conduct repudiating the relationship on which the applicant is relying, courts have refused to disqualify for: adultery following the deceased spouse's desertion;[28] a "short extra-marital affair";[29] long separation, apparently mutually agreeable;[30] separation at the behest of the deceased spouse;[31] remoteness or estrangement between a parent and

---

22 *Re Keroack* (1957), 65 Man. R. 96 (Man. Q.B.) at 102; *Re Laur* (1975), 7 O.R. (2d) 385 (Ont. Surr. Ct.); *Adams v. Irvine* (1978), 4 R.F.L. (2d) 295 (Sask. Q.B.); *Menrad v. Blowers* (1982), 137 D.L.R. (3d) 309 (Man. Q.B.); *Harry v. Harry Estate* (1988), 67 Sask. R. 279 (Sask. Surr. Ct.); *Sakundiak v. Sakundiak Estate* (1996), 149 Sask. R. 99 (Sask. Q.B.).

23 For ex., *Re Tothivan, supra* note 14, although the application was dismissed for other reasons.

24 (1960), 32 W.W.R. 473 (Sask. Q.B.) at 476, affirmed (1962), 33 D.L.R. (2d) 742 (Sask. C.A.).

25 Also *Re Anderson,* [1934] 1 W.W.R. 430 (Alta. C.A.) at 438. See, for instance, *Re Cassidy* (1965), 54 D.L.R. (2d) 329 (Sask. Q.B.). In *Zubiss v. Moulson Estate* (1987), 80 A.R. 105 (Alta. Q.B.), in dismissing the application the court took into account the fact that, following a mutual separation, the applicant "established a relationship resembling marriage" with another man.

26 Also *Re Gouge* (1938), 52 B.C.R. 544 (B.C. S.C.); *Re MacRobert* (1967), 63 D.L.R. (2d) 650 (N.S. S.C.) in an obiter beginning on 661; *Dmytriw v. Dmytriw* (1975), 22 R.F.L. 382 (Man. Q.B.); *Manson v. Shoaf,* [1980] 5 W.W.R. 106 (Sask. Surr. Ct.); *Niebergall v. Niebergall Estate* (1986), 53 Sask. R. 289 (Sask. Q.B.) at paragraph 18; Cf. *Peill v. Peill,* [1939] 2 W.W.R. 519 (Sask. K.B.); *Re Edgelow* (1955), 18 W.W.R. 235 (B.C. S.C.); *Re Murray* (1966), 60 D.L.R. (2d) 76 (B.C. S.C.); *Re Nixey* (1972), 31 D.L.R. (3d) 597 (Man. Q.B.).

27 See Chp. 3, notes 102-03 and text. Probably, the conduct of signing an agreement containing a waiver or release respecting a dependants' relief application is not as significant as the property consideration received, which is a relevant discrete circumstance. Query *Re Hawley, supra* Chp. 3, note 11 at 359, first sentence.

28 *Belaney v. Perrier,* [1939] 3 W.W.R. 591 (Sask. K.B.); *Re Callegari* (1958), 13 D.L.R. (2d) 585 (B.C. S.C.).

29 *Jensen v. Jensen* (1982), 34 B.C.L.R. 163 (B.C. S.C.); *Re Pflanzner, supra* note 14.

30 *Re Pemberton, supra* note 19; *Re Edwards Estate, supra* note 16, *Re Soroka* (1995), 10 O.R. (2d) 638 (Ont. H.C.). Cf. *Keane v. Keane* (1972), 7 N.B.R. (2d) 187 (N.B. Q.B.).

31 *Re Willan Estate, supra* note 10.

a child;[32] the dysfunctionality of the marriage;[33] the participation of the applicant in a foreign divorce proceeding on advice of counsel to protect her separation settlement;[34] being addicted to gambling and using a power of attorney, just before the deceased died, to take over her modest bank account;[35] a refusal to move the marital home;[36] not enforcing payments pursuant to a separation agreement or otherwise claiming support during the deceased's lifetime;[37] refusing to respond to a dying husband's pleas to visit him;[38] obtaining a personal representation grant to administer the estate;[39] leaving an abusive relationship upon doctor's advice;[40] having been acquitted of her husband's murder;[41] commencing divorce proceedings;[42] and cruelty.[43]

---

32 *Re Tian* (1952), 6 W.W.R. (N.S.) 371 (Sask. Q.B.); *Sobodiuk v. MacLaren*, *supra* note 18. *Re Stewart* (1961), 31 D.L.R. (2d) 601 (B.C. S.C.); *Re Schurman* (1965), 54 D.L.R. (2d) 77 (N.S. S.C.); *Simmonds v. Rehn* (1969), 3 D.L.R. (3d) 565 (Man. Q.B.); *Re Bailey Estate*, *supra* note 15; *Beasley v. Willet* (1972), 4 N.B.R. (2d) 122 (N.B. Q.B.); *Re Harding*, [1973] 6 W.W.R. 229 (B.C. S.C.); *Travagline v. Kendall* (1978), 29 N.S.R. (2d) 442 (N.S. C.A.); *Re Gamble* (1981), 33 N.B.R. (2d) 132 (N.B. Q.B.); *Bartel v. Holmes* (1982), 16 Man. R. (2d) 29 (Man. Q.B.); *Nulty v. Nulty Estate* (1989), 41 B.C.L.R. (2d) 343 (B.C. C.A.) at paragraphs 346, 348; *Kuhn v. Kuhn Estate* (1992), 112 N.S.R. (2d) 38 (N.S. T.D.) at paragraphs 10–14 and 31–36. Cf. *Little v. Little* (1975), 11 N.S.R. (2d) 701 (N.S. T.D.); *Adams v. Perks* (1979), 41 N.S.R. (2d) 14 (N.S. T.D.) at paragraph 6; *Moxon v. Moxon* (1980), 43 N.S.R. (2d) 116 (N.S. T.D.) at paragraph 34; *Re Anderson Estate* (1986), 76 N.S.R. (2d) 251 (N.S. T.D.) at paragraph 39; *Harrison v. Evans Estate* (1987), 28 E.T.R. 53 (B.C. S.C.); *Re Trenton* (1987), 26 E.T.R. 209 (Ont. Surr. Ct.); *Currie v. Currie Estate* (1995), 166 N.B.R. (2d) 144 (N.B. C.A.) at paragraphs 4, 22; *Newstead v. Newstead Estate* (1996), 11 E.T.R. (2d) 236 (B.C. S.C.) at paragraphs 59–72. Cf. *Zajic v. Chomiak Estate* (1990), 63 Man. R. (2d) 178 (Man. Q.B.) at paragraph 25; *Kelly v. Baker*, *supra* note 20.

33 *Re Fisher* (1960), 31 W.W.R. 697 (B.C. S.C.); *Adams v. Broughton* (1982), 20 Alta. L.R. (2d) 390 (Alta. Q.B.).

34 *Downton v. Royal Trust Co.* (1972), [1973] S.C.R. 437 (S.C.C.), in which Justice Laskin for the Court reviews the preclusion doctrine at length.

35 *Greenwood v. Greenwood* (1979), 11 B.C.L.R. 218 (B.C. S.C.).

36 *Chernoff v. Chernoff*, *supra* note 24.

37 *Re Tero*, [1949] 2 W.W.R. 203 (B.C. C.A.); *Plumb v. Royal Trust Co.*, [1943] 3 W.W.R. 513 (Alta. T.D.), affirmed (1944), [1950] 2 W.W.R. 334 (Alta. C.A.).

38 *Re Wilson*, [1937] 1 W.W.R. 161 (Alta. S.C.). Note *Webb v. Webb Estate* (1995), 28 Alta. L.R. (3d) 110 (Alta. Surr. Ct.) at paragraph 59 and *Sakundiak v. Sakundiak Estate*, *supra* note 22 at paragraph 49.

39 *Williams v. Moody Bible Institute of Chicago*, [1937] 2 W.W.R. 316 (Sask. C.A.) at 320-21.

40 *Re Gosse*, *supra* note 19 at 670–71.

41 *Re Emele Estate*, [1941] 2 W.W.R. 566 (Sask. K.B.).

42 See note 22, *supra*.

43 *Re Dupaul* (1941), 56 B.C.R. 532 (B.C. C.A.).

(b) Proximity, Nature, and Duration of the Applicant and Deceased's Relationship

Not infrequently the court is required to consider competing claims. The competition may involve a second wife versus children of the first marriage, the spouse (perhaps separated) versus the children, a spouse parent versus a minor child, children versus children, or an institutionalized dependant versus another dependant. Of course, applicants are always in competition with testamentary beneficiaries or intestate heirs. The proximity, nature, and duration of the relationship that existed between an applicant, a testamentary beneficiary, or an intestate heir and the deceased is a significant circumstance in the prioritization of competing claims and the substance of successful applications.

(i) Proximity

Naturally courts are more sympathetic to widows, minor children, incapacitated adult children and widowers, and perhaps adult capacitated daughters than to capacitated widowers and sons. On occasion courts have acknowledged this.[44]

The Ontario Act in s. 68(1)(g), above, uses the term "proximity". Professor Bale asserts:

> . . . the word "proximity" does not make [the] happiness or unhappiness of the [relationship] relevant. It is the closeness, not the quality, of the relationship which is pertinent.[45]

---

44 *Shaw v. Regina (City)* (1943), [1944] 1 W.W.R. 433 (Sask. C.A.) at 441, affirmed (1944), [1945] S.C.R. 42 (S.C.C.); *Re La Fleur* (1948), 56 Man. R. 44 (Man. K.B.) at 49 *et seq.*; *Re Maitland* (1954), 10 W.W.R. (N.S.) 673 (Alta. C.A.) at 680, 689; *Garrett v. Zwicker* (1976), 15 N.S.R. (2d) 118 (N.S. C.A.) at paragraph 38.

45 Bale, G., "Re Dentinger, Dependants' Relief Legislation and the Changed Emphasis Effected by Part V of The Succession Law Reform Act (Ontario)" (1982) 10 E.T.R. 7 at 9; similarly, *Re McCaffery*, [1931] O.R. 512 (Ont. C.A.) at 517, 525. Nonetheless, Ontario courts do comment on the quality of the relationship pursuant to s. 68(1)(g); for ex., *Re Mannion* (1981), 39 O.R. (2d) 263 (Ont. Surr. Ct.) at 267, varied (1982), 39 O.R. (2d) 609 (Ont. Div. Ct.), affirmed (1984), 45 O.R. (2d) 339 (Ont. C.A.); *Chellew v. Ontario (Public Trustee)* (1983), 45 O.R. (2d) 189 (Ont. Surr. Ct.) at 197; *Dyer v. Dyer* (1984), 18 E.T.R. 44 (Ont. Surr. Ct.) at 59; *McSween v. McSween Estate* (1985), 21 E.T.R. 195 (Ont. Surr. Ct.) at 204.

A. *Spouses*

Generally, widows are "most favoured",[46] "unless there [are] some compelling reasons to the contrary",[47] and second wives, including common law spouses and co-habitees in provinces in which they can apply, should be no less favoured.[48] Widows have been unsuccessful for a variety of reasons: adequate provision made in the will or through *inter vivos* gifts and joint tenancy property, life insurance or pension benefits, or resulting from intestate entitlement, also considering the widow's own assets and ability to earn income;[49] short duration of the marriage, lack of contribution to the creation of the deceased's estate, and *inter vivos* gifts;[50] a marital

---

46 *Re Livingston* (1922), 31 B.C.R. 468 (B.C. S.C.) at 470; *Re Maitland, supra* note 44 at 680; also *Shaw v. Regina (City), supra* note 44; *Pope v. Stevens* (1954), 63 Man. R. 162 (Man. C.A.) at 172–73; *Re La Fleur, supra* note 44; *Re Gosse, supra* note 19 at 671; *Garrett v. Zwicker, supra* note 44 at paragraph 27; *Bennett v. Morrison* (1976), 16 N.S.R. (2d) 476 (N.S. C.A.) at 481; *Simkins v. Blumenthal* (1995), 9 E.T.R. (2d) 53 (B.C. S.C.) at paragraph 19.

47 *Nickle v. Jones, supra* note 10 at 387; also *Biblow v. Royal Trust Co.* (1977), 3 A.R. 203 (Alta. T.D.) at paragraph 6; *Foulon v. Foulon* (1981), 29 A.R. 120 (Alta. Q.B.) at paragraph 30.

48 *Duncan v. Duncan* (1975), 11 O.R. (2d) 539 (Ont. Div. Ct.) at 543; *Re Cooper* (1980), 30 O.R. (2d) 113 (Ont. Div. Ct.) at 122.

49 *Re Cole* (1958), 40 M.P.R. 201 (N.S. T.D.); *Re Wild* (1964), 44 D.L.R. (2d) 91 (Alta. S.C.); *Rill v. Miller* (1969), 9 D.L.R. (3d) 211 (Sask. C.A.); *Re Pelletier* (1974), 10 N.B.R. (2d) 365 (N.B. Q.B.); *Nickle v. Jones, supra* note 10; *Nelson v. Nelson* (1977), 17 N.B.R. (2d) 457 (N.B. C.A.); *Pulham v. Yorkshire Trust Co.* (1979), 16 B.C.L.R. 80 (B.C. S.C.); *Re Tothivan, supra* note 14 at 415; *Re deBeaudrap* (1983), 44 A.R. 100 (Alta. Q.B.); *Niebergall v. Niebergall Estate, supra* note 26; *Murray v. Murray Estate* (1986), 50 Sask. R. 308 (Sask. Surr. Ct.); *Swire v. Swire* (1986), 23 E.T.R. 246 (Ont. Surr. Ct.), affirmed (1987), 28 E.T.R. 206 (Ont. Div. Ct.); *Blago v. Aetna Life Insurance Co.* (1988), 30 E.T.R. 283 (Ont. Surr. Ct.) at 303–04; *Pedersen v. Pedersen* (1991), 43 E.T.R. 189 (B.C. S.C.); *Hecht v. Hecht Estate* (1991), (*sub nom. Hecht v. Reid*) 42 E.T.R. 295 (B.C. S.C.), affirmed (1993), 81 B.C.L.R. (2d) 239 (B.C. C.A.), additional reasons at (1993), 87 B.C.L.R. (2d) 271 (B.C. C.A.), leave to appeal refused [1994] 2 W.W.R. lxiv (S.C.C.); *Warwick (Guardian ad litem of) v. Warwick Estate* (1996), 11 E.T.R. (2d) 129 (B.C. S.C.); *Lobe v. Lobe Estate* (1996), 13 E.T.R. (2d) 126 (B.C. S.C.), affirmed (1997), 17 E.T.R. (2d) 275 (B.C. C.A.); *Modopoulos v. Breen Estate* (1996), 15 E.T.R. (2d) 128 (Ont. Gen. Div.) at 135; *Howard v. Howard Estate* (1997), 32 B.C.L.R. (3d) 1 (B.C. C.A.). Cf. *Dyer v. Dyer, supra* note 45.

50 *Carlson v. Carlson* (1983), 49 A.R. 117 (Alta. Q.B.); *Foulon v. Foulon, supra* note 47; *Re Marquis* (1980), 30 N.B.R. (2d) 93 (N.B. T.D.); *Biblow v. Royal Trust Co., supra* note 47; *Montgomery v. Flood* (1979), 5 E.T.R. 16 (B.C. S.C.); *Howard v. Howard Estate, supra* note 49.

property order;[51] adequate provision made in a separation agreement even though the separated widow had spent most of what she received,[52] also considering the short duration of the marriage, the minimal contribution made to the creation of deceased's estate, and the modest size of the estate;[53] long time separation;[54] desertion.[55]

There are several widow cases which stand out.[56]

Applications by widowers are rare; there have been only nineteen reported cases.[57] Probably, conventional wisdom at one time was reflected in a statement made by Justice Farwell in *Re Silvester*[58] which has been quoted in several of the Canadian cases:

---

51 *Re Serdula* (1983), 23 Sask. R. 282 (Sask. Q.B.); *Peslari v. Petruic* (1984), 33 Sask. R. 315 (Sask. Q.B.); *Driscoll v. Driscoll Estate* (1988), 88 N.S.R. (2d) 1 (N.S. T.D.); *Penteluk v. Penteluk Estate* (1991), 95 Sask. R. 128 (Sask. Surr. Ct.), varied (1992), 100 Sask. R. 178 (Sask. C.A.), leave to appeal refused (1992), 105 Sask. R. 79 (note) (S.C.C.). Note also *Menrad v. Blowers, supra* note 22 at 317; *Krokosh v. Krokosh* (1985), 34 Man. R. (2d) 121 (Man. Q.B.).

52 *Black v. Kronberger Estate* (1990), 83 Sask. R. 73 (Sask. C.A.).

53 *Re Anderson, supra* note 25; *Collard v. Collard* (1976), 28 R.F.L. 252 (Sask Surr. Ct.); *Howard v. Howard Estate, supra* note 49.

54 *Keane v. Keane, supra* note 30; cf. *Re Edwards Estate* (1961), 36 W.W.R. 605 (Alta. C.A.); *Re Soroka* (1975), 10 O.R. (2d) 638 (Ont. H.C.).

55 See the cf. cases cited, *supra*, in note 26; note that the first group of cases contained in note 26 indicate that desertion is not necessarily fatal to an application.

56 Pre-*Tataryn*: *Re Gosse, supra* note 19; *Moore v. Moore* (1976), 27 R.F.L. 314 (Sask. Surr. Ct.); *Re Protopappas Estate* (1987), 25 E.T.R. 241 (Alta. Q.B.); *Baker v. Baker Estate* (1992), 136 A.R. 94 (Alta. Q.B.), additional reasons at (1993), 138 A.R. 1 (Alta. Q.B.), despite a couple of case name mis-spellings. Post-*Tataryn*: *Siegel v. Siegel Estate* (1995), 177 A.R. 282 (Alta. Q.B.), a widow; *Ostrander v. Kimble Estate* (1996), 146 Sask. R. 64 (Sask. Q.B.), a co-habitee.

57 Successful: *Re Stigings* (1924), 34 B.C.R. 347 (B.C. S.C.); *Re Dupaul* (1941), 56 B.C.R. 532 (B.C. C.A.); *Barker v. Westminster Trust Co.* (1941), 57 B.C.R. 21 (B.C. C.A.); *McNamara v. Hyde* (1943), 59 B.C.R. 70 (B.C. C.A.); *Re Blackwell*, [1948] O.R. 522 (Ont. C.A.); *Re Fisher, supra* note 33; *Cranston v. Cranston* (1962), 40 W.W.R. 321 (Alta. T.D.); *Re Becker* (1964), 46 D.L.R. (2d) 574 (Alta. S.C.); *Re Day* (1977), 26 N.S.R. (2d) 361 (N.S. T.D.); *Re Davies* (1979), 27 O.R. (2d) 98 (Ont. Surr. Ct.); *Kiss v. Palachik* (1981), 34 O.R. (2d) 484 (Ont. C.A.), affirmed [1983] 1 S.C.R. 623 (S.C.C.); *Jensen v. Jensen, supra* note 29; *Walker v. Dubord* (1992), 67 B.C.L.R. (2d) (B.C. C.A.); *Webb v. Webb Estate, supra* note 38; *Tweedale v. Tweedale Estate* (1995), 1 B.C.L.R. (3d) 167 (B.C. C.A.). Unsuccessful: *Re Lund*, [1946] 3 W.W.R. 732 (Sask. K.B.); *Stadnyk v. Bulycz* (1961), 36 W.W.R. 680 (Sask. C.A.); *Collier v. Yonkers* (1967), 61 W.W.R. 761 (Alta. C.A.); *Re Flood* (1978), 20 Nfld. & P.E.I.R. 448 (P.E.I. S.C.). Note also *Re Tian, supra* note 32, and *Re Cameron* (1979), (*sub nom. Simpson v. Montreal Trust Co.*) 4 E.T.R. 257 (Sask. Surr. Ct.) in which the courts took into account the situation of the widower, and *Amatniaks v. Benkis Estate* (1992), 46 E.T.R. 204 (Ont. Gen. Div.) and *Paxman v. Saskatchewan (Public Trustee)* (1996), 146 Sask. R. 312 (Sask. Q.B.), successful applications by common law husbands.

58 [1941] Ch. 87 (Eng. Ch. Div.) at 89.

> I do not consider that in the ordinary way applications by husbands for this sort of assistance should readily be entertained. Prima facie a husband should be able to maintain himself and ought not to ask the Court to give him, out of his wife's estate, more than she has thought fit to provide for him. There are of course exceptional cases in which such an application may be justified, but personally I should not be very willing to assist husbands in cases of this sort, unless the circumstances were indeed exceptional.

One would expect that widowers would have been mostly unsuccessful applicants. However, in the *Silvester* case and in fifteen of the nineteen Canadian cases, the widowers have been successful. In four of the fifteen cases the widower's circumstances were not exceptional; they were earning employment income and were not in actual need or of adequate assets.[59] Surely current conventional wisdom is expressed by Justice Ungoed-Thomas in *Re Clayton*:[60]

> I come now to the position of a husband in making a claim. The Act . . . expressly provides that a surviving husband may be a dependant entitled to claim for maintenance from his wife's estate. The difference in capacity for self-maintenance of a woman on the one hand, and of a man on the other hand, is becoming increasingly less; and the historical prima facie inclination in favour of a maintenance order for a widow as contrasted with a widower will doubtless become, as it appears to have become even in very recent years, correspondingly less, too. I certainly do not see in the Act . . . a greater onus of proof on the surviving husband than on the surviving wife. It is simply a question in each case, be the claimant husband or wife, whether in all the circumstances as established in evidence, the deceased's failure to make any, or enough, provision for the surviving spouse is unreasonable; and I, for my part, find no material assistance nowadays from contemplating the sex of the claimant, or considering it as a circumstance on its own when all the material circumstances have to be considered.

B. *Children*

All of the reported cases involving minor children have resulted in a relief order for the child or children directly, or indirectly in the order made for the surviving spouse-parent. As for whether the court should make a discrete order for a dependant minor child, as compared to taking into account responsibility for the child in an order made for the surviving spouse-parent, this was an issue in *Bosch v. Perpetual Trust Co. Ltd.*[61] Both

59 *McNamara v. Hyde*, *supra* note 57; *Re Blackwell*, *supra* note 57; *Re Fisher*, *supra* note 33; *Walker v. Dubord*, *supra* note 57.

60 [1966] 2 All E.R. 370 (U.K. Ch.) at 372.

61 [1938] A.C. 463 (New South Wales P.C.).

the widow and two minor sons applied for a relief order. The trial court made an order for the widow, but dismissed the sons' applications. Lord Romer for the Privy Council said that if the widow "appears to be a just and wise mother, her opinions and her wishes are not to be excluded from the circumstances . . . to which . . . the Court has to pay attention, and this is especially the case where the children are of tender age".[62] Lord Romer continued

> . . . the provision for her made by [the Supreme Court of New South Wales] was not made subject to any condition as to her contributing thereout anything to the maintenance, education or advancement of the appellant children. That she would in fact do so if the present state of affairs were to continue may be readily conceded. But there can be no certainty that the present state of affairs will not in the future be materially altered. The widow, for instance, might remarry and have further children. Her second husband might be a man of slender means, and the provision made for her by the [trial] order . . . might be no more than sufficient to enable her to make provision for the proper maintenance of her second husband and the children of her second marriage. It cannot, therefore, be predicted that the appellants will benefit in any way by the order in question. In these circumstances it is not, in their Lordships' opinion, a valid reason for refusing to increase the appellants' legacies that an increase has been made in the provisions made by the testator for his widow. In considering all the circumstances of the case, the learned judge should have borne in mind that the circumstances as they exist at present will not necessarily remain unchanged, and in omitting to do so he has, in their Lordships' opinion, inadvertently misdirected himself.[63]

The Privy Council made discrete orders in favour of the sons, but not at the expense of the widow's order. This issue has arisen in several Canadian cases with varying results.[64] In many cases apparently the issue never arises with an application being made by only the surviving spouse parent and an order made, perhaps reflecting that it is for the benefit of infant children too.[65]

---

62 *Ibid.* at 482.

63 *Ibid.*

64 *Re Denton,* [1950] 2 W.W.R. 848 (Alta. S.C.); *Re Finlan,* (1951), 1 W.W.R. (N.S.) 656 (Alta. S.C.), reversed (1951), 3 W.W.R. (N.S.) 671 (Alta. C.A.); *Re Brown* (1969), 70 W.W.R. 543 (Sask. Q.B.); *Re Ducherer,* [1977] 6 W.W.R. 495 (Sask. Surr. Ct.); *Alberta (Public Trustee) v. Buchholz* (1980), 24 A.R. 287 (Alta. C.A.); *Cameron (Public Trustee of) v. Cameron Estate* (1991), (*sub nom. British Columbia (Public Trustee) v. Cameron Estate*) 58 B.C.L.R. (2d) 71 (B.C. S.C.), varied (1991), (*sub nom. British Columbia (Public Trustee) v. Cameron Estate*) 58 B.C.L.R. (2d) 82 (B.C. C.A.).

65 For ex., *Dilworth v. Dilworth* (1984), 54 A.R. 261 (Alta. Q.B.) at paragraph 29.

Another minor children issue respecting Acts which define children as dependants with an age limitation (the Alberta, Saskatchewan, Manitoba, Prince Edward Island, the Northwest Territories, and the Yukon Acts) is whether a relief order should take into account possible post-majority needs. The cases are divided on this issue. In *Re Denton* the deceased left "everything I own to my wife". He was survived by his wife and five minor children. The Public Trustee applied for a relief order on behalf of the children. Justice Ford said:

> There are five children of the deceased. At the time of his death their ages ranged from 11 years to two months. They are, therefore, dependants of the testator within the terms of sec. 2(c) of *The Testators Family Maintenance Act*, 1947, ch. 12 (Alta.) and the application is properly made on their behalf.
>
> The section reads :
>
> > "'Dependant' means the wife or husband of the testator, a child of the testator who at the time of the testator's death is under the age of nineteen years, and a child over that age who by reason of mental or physical disability is unable to earn a livelihood."
>
> It was urged that these words limit the period of the proper maintenance and support of a dependant child to the age of 19 years, but that the limitation does not apply after that age where disability from earning a livelihood exists. I cannot accept the view that the scope of the Act is limited to such an extent. Its purpose, as gathered from the language of the whole Act, is so much more far-reaching than such an interpretation would allow as to point to an intention to make a child under the age of 19 years at the time of the testator's death a dependant, in as broad a sense as one over that age who is unable to earn a livelihood by reason of mental or physical disability. Quite clearly the latter would continue to be a dependant by reason of such disability and, in my opinion, the former does not cease to be one merely by reaching the age of 19 years. I think that such an interpretation would defeat much of the purpose of the Act in respect of dependant children, as it cannot be discovered on such an application whether or not a child under the age of 19 years and capable at that time will be able to maintain itself after passing the age of 19 since it may become mentally or physically incapable at any time. This fact being a contingency is an aid to interpretation.
>
> It may be noted that in at least two statutes, Ontario and Saskatchewan, the definition of a dependant child contains age limits of 16 and 21 years respectively, but that the phrase "at the time of the testator's death," which appears in the Alberta statute, is not included. I think that the phrase, if it has any effect, accentuates the importance of the description as defining who shall be a dependant child on whose behalf an application may be made for relief, and not as also limiting maintenance and support to the age of 19 years. No express

> limitation as to age is contained in sec. 4, and I cannot think that it is to be implied in the word "dependant" by reason of the definition.[66]

Justice Ford ordered a portion of the estate to be set aside for the children from which they were to receive the income until they reached the age of 25 years.

Justice Marshall expressed this opposing point of view in *Pauliuk v. Pauliuk*:[67]

> While I am well aware of the desire of prodigal parents to provide post-secondary education for their children, I believe that a very substantial portion of people obtaining such education at the present time receive little or no assistance from their parents. Most educational institutions and various levels of government provide some financial assistance for higher education. In addition, numerous students do not pursue their studies immediately after high school but often pursue such education after marriage and even while raising a family. I believe it is of some relevance that the deceased did not appear to have a higher education nor was there any other indication that the other adult children have pursued such. I believe it is inequitable that a child less than 18 at the death of the testator should be entitled to a substantially greater benefit than a child who has passed the magic milestone. Under the circumstances, I am going to make an award for each of the children which will enable them to live in the nature and style to which they have been accustomed from the date of the death of the deceased until the children reach the age of 18.[68]

The Manitoba Act in s. 8(1)(j) and the Ontario Act in s. 62(1)(p)(i) expressly list as a relevant consideration "if the dependant is a child, the child's apttitude for and reasonable prospects of obtaining an education". So, it is not surprising that there are several Ontario cases in which the

---

66 *Supra* note 64 at 849-50; See also *Re Finlan, supra* note 64; *Re Cameron, supra* note 57; *Hiebert v. Ward* (1980), 3 Sask. R. 255 (Sask. Q.B.); and probably *Alberta (Public Trustee) v. Raniseth Estate* (1990), 80 Alta. L.R. (2d) 274 (Alta. Q.B.)

67 *Supra* note 10 at 33.

68 See also Litman, M., "Re Cameron, Limitations on the Use of Future Contingencies in Calculating Awards made Under Dependants Relief Legislation" (1979) 4 E.T.R. 257; *Re Bourne*, [1950] O.W.N. 807 (Ont. Surr. Ct.); probably *Re Gilbert* (1965), 51 W.W.R. 701 (Sask. Q.B.); *Rill v. Miller, supra* note 49; *Biblow v. Royal Trust Co., supra* note 47; probably *Prefontaine v. Co-operative Trust Co.*, [1977] 5 W.W.R. 478 (Sask. C.A.); *Alberta (Public Trustee) v. Buchholz, supra* note 64 at paragraphs 23–33; *Cook v. Hrychuk Estate* (1987), 71 Sask. R. 303 (Sask. C.A.); *Re Alainga Estate*, [1995] N.W.T.R. 392 (N.W.T. S.C.) at paragraph 20; *Hoeppner (Litigation Guardian of) v. Misiewicz Estate* (1995), (*sub nom. Hoeppner v. Misiewicz Estate*) 106 Man. R. (2d) 24 (Man. Q.B.).

courts have taken into account post-secondary education.[69] In *Richer v. Richer*[70] the court decided that the cost of pursuing competitive ice dance training, while attending high school, came within the wording:

> If the legislators intended to restrict that term [i.e., education] to pure scholastic endeavours, they would have done so. Her training coupled with her academic efforts come squarely within the educational objective listed in the applicable section of the Act.

The Alberta, Saskatchewan, Manitoba, Prince Edward Island, Northwest Territories and Yukon Acts distinguish between minor and adult children. Generally, under these Acts adult children must be unable to provide for themselves for some reason to receive a relief order.[71] Regarding the British Columbia, Ontario, New Brunswick, Nova Scotia, and Newfoundland Acts, which do not distinguish between minor and adult children, a starting point may be Chief Justice Williams' statement in *Re La Fleur*:[72]

> Infant children usually receive some measure of relief, directly or indirectly, by increased allowances to a parent. Adult daughters, married or single, receive relief more often than it is refused to them. . . . But the position of adult sons, who are not physically or mentally disabled, is different.
>
> . . . .
>
> The applicable principles to be extracted from the *Allardice* case would appear to be that the applicant [son], who has for some years maintained himself, might well be expected to be able to fight the battle of life without extraneous aid, and that only if the means of the testator were great and the fight was a great struggle, might the court properly give aid.[73]

Surely the different treatment of adult capacitated daughters and sons reflected in Chief Justice Williams' statement is dated. Indeed, in *Barr v. Barr*[74] Justice Dickson, as he then was, disagreed with Chief Justice Williams:

---

69 *Re Tothivan*, *supra* note 14 at 415–16; *Chellew v. Ontario (Public Trustee)*, *supra* note 45; *Re Pflanzner*, *supra* note 14 at 155–56; *McSween v. McSween Estate*, *supra* note 45 at 204; *Neumann (Next Friend of) v. Neumann Estate* (1996), 15 E.T.R. (2d) 159 (Ont. Gen. Div.) at 163, additional reasons at (June 13, 1996), Doc. Barrie G11103 (Ont. Gen. Div.).

70 (1984), 17 E.T.R. 102 (Ont. Co. Ct.) at 107-08.

71 More specifically see the text in Chp. 3 at notes 59-61. The Saskatchewan Act includes "need or other circumstances" (s. 2(1)).

72 [1948] 1 W.W.R. 801 (Man. K.B.) at 810–11.

73 Williams reviewed the cases involving incapacitated sons and capacitated sons where the estate was great and dismissed the applicant son's application. Also *Rutledge v. Jackson* (1981), 26 B.C.L.R. 239 (B.C. S.C.).

74 (1971), 25 D.L.R. (3d) 401 (Man. C.A.) at 413; also *Simmonds v. Rehn*, *supra* note 32 at 570.

> If the learned Chief Justice meant to suggest that an order in favour of adult sons could only be made in the two situations mentioned then, with respect, I cannot agree as there are a number of cases, additional to those mentioned by him, in which orders were made in small estates in favour of adult sons who were without disability.

Chief Justice MacKeigan in *Garrett v. Zwicker*[75] questioned "whether today's moral and social standards permit a court to discriminate in favour of adult daughters against adult sons to the extent the courts did in *Allardice v. Allardice*". Also noteworthy is Justice Grant's comment in *Re Joudrey Estate*:[76]

> [36] I consider today it is unrealistic in assessing the assets of a married [daughter] to give great weight to the assets and earning potential of her husband. The state of matrimony today does not import the security which it was once thought to bring.

Aside from institutionalized adult children,[77] the adult children cases can be divided into three categories, namely incapacitated children,[78] (needy) capacitated children (who have a moral claim),[79] and unsuccessful

75 *Supra* note 44 at paragraph 37.

76 (1989), (*sub nom. Badiuk v. Joudrey Estate*) 90 N.S.R. (2d) 181 (N.S. T.D.).

77 For some of whom relief orders have been made and for some not; see, *infra*, notes 155-156.

78 *Re Dickinson* (1944), 60 B.C.R. 214 (B.C. S.C.); *Corkum v. Corkum* (1976), 18 N.S.R. (2d) 501 (N.S. C.A.); *Maldaver v. Canada Permanent Trust Co.* (1977), 27 N.S.R. (2d) 248 (N.S. T.D.); *Re McKinnon* (1977), 20 N.B.R. (2d) 268 (N.B. Q.B.); *Malychuk v. Malychuk* (1978), 6 Alta. L.R. (2d) 240 (Alta. T.D.); *MacDonald v. MacDonald* (1980), 39 N.S.R. (2d) 573 (N.S. T.D.); *Leard v. Maki* (1982), 36 B.C.L.R. 92 (B.C. S.C.); *McCaw v. McCaw* (1983), 29 Sask. R. 39 (Sask. Surr. Ct.); *Linden v. Linden* (1985), 35 Man. R. (2d) 73 (Man. Q.B.); *Zeman v. Zeman Estate* (1993), 49 E.T.R. 31 (B.C. S.C.); *Newstead v. Newstead Estate*, *supra* note 32. Note also *Re Bowers* (1955), 19 W.W.R. 241 (Alta. S.C.) and *Re DeRoche Estate* (1964), 51 W.W.R. 120 (Sask. Q.B.) at 123, an application of a daughter who was a minor at the time of her father's death, but whose application was treated, perhaps wrongly, as an application of an adult child, since she had reached her majority after making the application.

79 The Alberta, Manitoba, Prince Edward Island, Northwest Territories and Yukon Acts restrict success in this category; British Columbia courts have been the most accommodating. *Re Tiefenbach* (1950), 58 Man. R. 398 (Man. K.B.); *Trainor v. Toronto General Trusts Corp.* (1953), 61 Man. R. 154 (Man. C.A.); *Walker v. Rivalin* (1963), 43 W.W.R. 321 (Man. Q.B.); *Re Schurman*, *supra* note 32; *Re Parkanski* (1966), 56 D.L.R. (2d) 475 (Sask. Q.B.); *Re Parks* (1968), 64 W.W.R. 586 (B.C. S.C.); *Simmonds v. Rehn*, *supra* note 32; *Barr v. Barr*, *supra* note 74; *Beasley v. Willet*, *supra* note 32; *Mitchell v. Mitchell* (1970), 3 N.S.R. (2d) 455 (N.S. T.D.); *Re Parker* (1972), 9 N.S.R. (2d) 28 (N.S. T.D.); *Re Michalson* (1972), [1973] 1 W.W.R. 560 (B.C. S.C.); *Re Phillips* (1973), 8 N.B.R. (2d) 188 (N.B. Q.B.); *Garrett v. Zwicker*, *supra* note 44; *Maldaver v. Canada Permanent Trust Co.*, *supra* note 78; *Re Radcliffe* (1977), 2 B.C.L.R. 220 (B.C. S.C.); *Travagline v. Kendall*, *supra* note 32; *Re Holt* (1978), 85 D.L.R. (3d) 543 (B.C. S.C.), in which astonishingly the court thought it pertinent to refer to the applicant as "a

applications.[80] A moral claim will usually be based upon contribution to the creation of the deceased's estate or to the deceased's welfare. Some

---

strikingly beautiful woman...While at the university she was elected Miss U.B.C."; *Adams v. Perks*, *supra* note 32; *Re Stafford* (1979), 26 N.B.R. (2d) 561 (N.B. Q.B.); *Dutka v. Dutka* (1980), 7 Man. R. (2d) 211 (Man. Q.B.); *Moxon v. Moxon*, *supra* note 32; *Re Gamble*, *supra* note 32; *Hall v. Hall* (1981), 10 Man. R. (2d) 168 (Man. Q.B.); *Morris v. Morris* (1982), 41 B.C.L.R. 239 (B.C. C.A.), leave to appeal refused (1983), 48 N.R. 79n (S.C.C.) (also, Bale, G., "Morris v. Morris, Duty Owed to Able-Bodied Adult Children under Testator's Family Maintenance Legislation and Need to Adopt an Objective Approach" (1983-84) 14 E.T.R. 35 to be read bearing in mind *Tataryn*); *Bartel v. Holmes*, *supra* note 32, an outrageous decision, which can only be explained by the fair share gloss which had been put on the former *Testators' Family Maintenance Act*; *Cox v. Nova Scotia (Public Trustee)* (1983), 56 N.S.R. (2d) 657 (N.S. T.D.); *McCaw v. McCaw*, *supra* note 78; *Dalziel v. Bradford* (1985), 62 B.C.L.R. 215 (B.C. S.C.); *Crilley v. Beckingham* (1986), 74 N.B.R. (2d) 91 (N.B. Q.B.); *Miller v. Rankin Estate* (1986), 72 N.S.R. (2d) 441 (N.S. T.D.); *Braidwood v. Maxwell* (1987), 28 E.T.R. 15 (B.C. S.C.); *Schofield Estate v. Schofield* (1988), 84 N.S.R. (2d) 404 (N.S. C.A.); *Re Joudrey Estate*, *supra* note 76 at paragraph 40; *Black v. Keith Estate* (1989), 96 N.B.R. (2d) (N.B. Q.B.); *Nulty v. Nulty Estate*, *supra* note 32; *Brammall v. Brammall Estate* (1991), 40 E.T.R. 169 (B.C. S.C.); *Plut v. Plut Estate* (1991), 41 E.T.R. 49 (B.C. C.A.); *Baim v. Shaner* (1991), 41 E.T.R. 241 (B.C. S.C.); *Lindsay v. Jones* (1991), 5 B.C.A.C. 112 (B.C. C.A.); *Kuhn v. Kuhn Estate*, *supra* note 32; *Hart (Guardian ad litem of) v. Hart Estate* (1993), (*sub nom. Hart v. Hart Estate*) 124 N.S.R. (2d) 333 (N.S. S.C.); *Jones v. Jones Estate* (1993), 125 N.S.R. (2d) 263 (N.S. S.C.); *McGhie v. Muzylowski Estate* (1993), 49 E.T.R. 178 (B.C. S.C.), affirmed (1994), 45 B.C.A.C. 65, 72 W.A.C. 65 (B.C. C.A.); *Redmond v. Redmond Estate* (1996), 155 N.S.R. (2d) 61 (N.S. S.C. [In Chambers]); *Huang v. Chan* (1996), 11 E.T.R. (2d) 156 (B.C. S.C.); *Mann v. Mann Estate* (1996), 13 E.T.R. (2d) 203 (B.C. S.C.), additional reasons at (February 14, 1997), Doc. Vancouver A942728 (B.C. S.C.); *McRae v. Royal Trust Corp. of Canada* (1997), 16 E.T.R. (2d) 223 (B.C. S.C. [In Chambers]).

80 *Re La Fleur*, *supra* note 44; *Re Becker*, *supra* note 57; *Re Dawson* (1945), 61 B.C.R. 481 (B.C. S.C.); *Re Bowers*, *supra* note 78; *Re Taylor* (1960), 33 W.W.R. 699 (Sask. C.A.); *Re Hornett* (1962), 33 D.L.R. (2d) 289 (B.C. S.C.); *Little v. Little*, *supra* note 32; *Adams v. Perks* (1979), 41 N.S.R. (2d) 14 (N.S. T.D.); *Coolen v. Coolen* (1980), 43 N.S.R. (2d) 67 (N.S. C.A.); *Moxon v. Moxon*, *supra* note 32; *Sloane v. Bartley* (1980), 7 Man. R. (2d) 222 (Man. C.A.); *Rutledge v. Jackson*, *supra* note 73; *Minkler v. Pinder* (1984), (*sub nom. Re Plummer*) 18 E.T.R. 297 (B.C. S.C.); *Krokosh v. Krokosh*, *supra* note 51; *Walsh v. Clifford* (1985), 68 N.B.R. (2d) 231 (N.B. Q.B.); *Cross v. Currie Estate* (1987), 81 N.S.R. (2d) 193 (N.S. T.D.); *Rollins v. Beyea Estate* (1987), 81 N.B.R. (2d) 58 (N.B. Q.B.); *Rafuse v. Rafuse Estate* (1990), (*sub nom. Re Rafuse Estate*) 97 N.S.R. (2d) 46 (N.S. T.D.); *Zajic v. Chomiak Estate*, *supra* note 32; *Fedon Estate v. Fedon* (1991), 74 Man. R. (2d) 84 (Man. Q.B.), affirmed (1992), 78 Man. R. (2d) 103 (Man. C.A.); *Jones v. Jones Estate*, *supra* note 79; *Bell v. Roy Estate*, [1993] 4 W.W.R. 40 (B.C. C.A.); *Knysh v. Knysh Estate* (1994), 94 Man. R. (2d) 266 (Man. Q.B.), additional reasons at (1994), 94 Man. R. (2d) 274 (Man. Q.B.); *Moore v. Moore Estate* (1994), 93 B.C.L.R. (2d) 64 (B.C. C.A.); *Spinney v. Spinney Estate* (1995), 165 N.B.R. (2d) 69 (N.B. Q.B.); *Robicheau v. McGibbon* (1995), 165 N.B.R. (2d) 255 (N.B. Q.B.); *Currie v. Currie Estate*, *supra* note 32; *Vielbig v. Waterland Estate* (1995), 1 B.C.L.R. (3d) 76 (B.C. C.A.); *Wilson v. Kosok* (1996), 146 Sask. R. 105 (Sask. Q.B.) at paragraphs 16–18; *Kelly v. Baker*, *supra* note 20; *Chernecki v. Vangolen* (1996), 28 B.C.L.R. (3d)

courts have found a moral claim as a result of estrangement following a divorce or separation and a failure to provide support during the minority of a child.[81] Where *Tataryn v. Tataryn Estate*[82] is the law a moral claim exists "if the estate permits" whether or not[83] there has been a normal familial relationship.

Perhaps worthy of note are cases dealing with the competing claims of a second spouse and the children of a first marriage[84] and of a cohabitee and the children of a wife.[85] In one of these cases, *Re Cole*,[86] Chief Justice Isley said:

> The following features of this application should be noted:
>
> (1) The applicant was the second wife of the testator. She married him when he was about seventy-seven years of age and she was about forty-five. The residuary legatees are the children and grandchildren of the testator's first wife

---

33 (B.C. C.A.).

81 See text at note 95, *infra*.

82 [1994] 2 S.C.R. 807 (S.C.C.), reconsideration refused (1994), 95 B.C.L.R. (2d) xxxiii (S.C.C.).

83 For ex., *Newstead v. Newstead Estate, supra* note 32, *Mann v. Mann Estate, supra* note 79.

84 *Re Schmalz* (1927), 38 B.C.R. 264 (B.C. S.C. [In chambers]); *Walker v. McDermott* (1930), [1931] S.C.R. 94 (S.C.C.); *Williams v. Moody Bible Institute of Chicago, supra* note 39; *Alberta (Official Guardian) v. LeMasurier*, [1949] 2 W.W.R. 748 (Alta. C.A.); *Pope v. Stevens, supra* note 46 at 172–73; *Re Rusk Estate* (1957), 6 D.L.R. (2d) 700 (Sask. C.A.); *Re Cole, supra* note 49 at 213–18; *Re Carnduff* (1957), 22 W.W.R. 160 (Sask. C.A.); *Re Green* (1959), 17 D.L.R. (2d) 74 (N.S. S.C.); *McCarvill v. Jones*, [1962] S.C.R. 273 (S.C.C.); *Re Wild* (1964), 44 D.L.R. (2d) 91 (Alta. S.C.); *Re Becker, supra* note 57; *Mitchell v. Mitchell, supra* note 79; *Garrett v. Zwicker, supra* note 44; *Bennett v. Morrison, supra* note 46; *Re Sleno* (1977), 78 D.L.R. (3d) 155 (B.C. S.C.); *Biblow v. Royal Trust Co., supra* note 47; *Fox v. Fox* (1977), 26 N.S.R. (2d) 463 (N.S. T.D.); *Nelson v. Nelson, supra* note 49; *Re Cameron, supra* note 57; *Montrose v. Montrose* (1980), 39 N.S.R. (2d) 339 (N.S. T.D.); *Moxon v. Moxon, supra* note 32; *Albert v. Albert* (1982), 24 Alta. L.R. (2d) 258 (Alta. Q.B.); *Morris v. Morris, supra* note 79; *Re Dentinger, supra* note 11; *McCaw v. McCaw, supra* note 78; *Daniel v. Daniel Estate* (1986), 41 Man. R. (2d) 66 (Man. Q.B.); *Michalyshen v. Michalyshen Estate* (1986), 45 Man. R. (2d) 178 (Man. Q.B.); *Edward v. Edward Estate* (1987), 57 Sask. R. 67 (Sask. C.A.) at paragraph 14; *Rollins v. Beyea Estate, supra* note 80; *Driscoll v. Driscoll Estate, supra* note 51; *Alberta (Public Trustee) v. Raniseth Estate, supra* note 66; *Siegel v. Siegel Estate, supra* note 56; *Sakundiak v. Sakundiak Estate, supra* 22; *Glanville v. Glanville* (1997), 17 E.T.R. (2d) 181 (B.C. S.C.), esp. at paragraph 38, additional reasons (July 3, 1997), Doc. New Westminster S0-32693 (B.C. S.C.), reversed in part (December 22, 1998), Doc. Vancouver CA023360 (B.C. C.A.).

85 *Re Schurman, supra* note 32; *Hiebert v. Ward, supra* note 66; *Re Gamble, supra* note 32; *Farrar v. Scammell* (1982), 11 E.T.R. 316 (Sask. Q.B.); *Pauliuk v. Pauliuk, supra* note 10; *Vernon v. Dieleman Estate* (1992), 46 E.T.R. 242 (Ont. Gen. Div.), varied (1997), 16 E.T.R. (2d) 68 (Ont. C.A.).

86 *Supra* note 49 at 213–14

who lived with him about fifty years and doubtless helped him accumulate the property that he had at the time of his second marriage and at the time of his death. In a New Zealand case referred to in the Canadian Bar Review, Volume 18, 1940, pages 473 and 474, the learned judge, Fair J., refused the application of a second wife, saying:

"One factor of importance in all these cases where there has been a second marriage of the testator is the period during which his second wife lived with him. The applicant in this case was the second wife of the testator. She has been married to him for some five years at the time of his death. Her moral claim on his bounty and on his consideration is not nearly so great as that of the widow who has lived with the testator for the whole of his married life, assisted to build up his estate, managed his household during the whole of that time, cared for and brought up his children and generally acted as his partner in the business of life."

"Where there has been a remarriage the children are, I think, entitled to say, 'we are successors not only to our father's rights, but in a measure, to our mother's rights.' The position of the second wife must correspondingly be less strong in her claim for consideration either as against the testator himself or under the Act, than the position of a first wife."

By comparison, in *Re Marsh*[87] the deceased made his adult children of his first marriage the residuary beneficiaries of his modest estate; they unsuccessfully argued for an award of a periodic payment to the deceased's widow, on the basis that if the widow were given the whole of the estate probably she would leave any residue to her own children.

Respecting minor children of a deceased from successive marriages or relationships, in *McSween v. McSween Estate*[88] Judge Carnwath said:

I adopt the principle that the children of both marriages have an equal claim to support from their father, and a father is entitled, and should be required, to treat all his children fairly and equally. . . .

At first blush the two children of the applicant [former wife] would appear to be better off than the two children of the respondent [widow]. The four children were treated equally under the will. . . . However, in examining the relative positions of the children of the first marriage and the children of the second marriage one cannot ignore the financial circumstances of the respective mothers. The applicant's annual income is $21,000 approximately and she has net assets of $14,000 approximately. The respondent's annual income can be conservatively estimated at three times this amount or $60,000 approximately and she would appear to have net assets of $800,000.

---

87 [1950] 2 W.W.R. 238 (Sask. K.B.) at 240.

88 *Supra* note 45 at 207; also *Barton v. Barton Estate* (1991), 42 E.T.R. 213 (Ont. Gen. Div.).

> I find that the very legitimate claims of the respondent and her two children to support from the deceased's estate have been more than adequately met. I find further that, appearances to the contrary, the four children were not equally treated by the deceased in the sense that his first two children will be living in a household with a total annual income for 1985 of $31,800 approximately while the children of the second marriage will be living in a household with annual income of $60,000 approximately. There is a corresponding gulf between the net assets of the two households. The standard of living that will be enjoyed by the children of the respondent will far outstrip the standard of living to be enjoyed by the children of the applicant.

(ii) Nature

Frequently in reciting the facts courts describe at some length or at least briefly, the relationship between the parties and the deceased; but frequently such courts do not refer subsequently to these relationships in their analysis of the facts or their reasons for the decision.[89] Only in the Nova Scotia Act, s. 5(1)(c), above, is there a specific reference to "the relations of the dependant and the testator" and this may explain why this circumstance is described and discussed most frequently in Nova Scotia cases. The Ontario Act in s. 68(1)(g), above, lists "proximity and duration of the dependant's relationship with the deceased". Pursuant to this section Ontario courts refer to the nature of the relationship.[90]

Although the absence of a normal relationship has been fatal to the success of an application, more often it has not.[91] In *Corkum v. Corkum*[92] Chief Justice MacKeigan wrote:

> 17 . . . [the moral] duty, to help the helpless dependant, is not dissolved by the lack of a warm or close relationship between the child and the father, as in the present case, or even by a positively hostile relationship between them, as in *Re Beasley and Willett* . . .
>
> 18 I do not suggest that the degree of love displayed is irrelevant. Where a warm and loving relationship exists, 'proper maintenance' for a child may be much greater than the minimal amount which cold paternal duty might dictate, always having in mind the size of the estate and the moral strength of other claims. Such a relationship may indeed be vitally important in considering the

---

89 For instance, *Re Osland* (1977), 1 E.T.R. 128 (B.C. S.C.); *MacDonald v. MacDonald*, *supra* note 78; *Crilley v. Buckingham*, *supra* note 79.

90 *Supra* note 45.

91 See text at, and the cases cited in, note 32 earlier in this chapter; also note the text at, and the cases cited in, notes 28-31 and 33-43.

92 *Supra* note 78 at paragraphs 7–18.

> father's duty to an adult child who is not disabled and is in no dire or desperate need, but who could certainly use some help. In such a case, and *Zwicker v. Garrett* was such a case, moral duty may well require that, if the size of the estate and the claims of others permit, something 'adequate' be given to that child so that 'proper maintenance' is thus supplied.

In *Sobodiuk v. MacLaren*[93] Justice Freedman wrote:

> There was considerable evidence—much of it controversial—dealing with the relations between the applicant and her mother. I have no difficulty in concluding that the ties binding Minerva and Michael to their mother were much more solid and substantial than those between the applicant and her mother . . . . Minerva and Michael were born of this happy union. They took their place as units in the Karabin household. The closest of bonds linked them to both their parents until their respective deaths. The applicant, on the other hand, maintained a relationship with her mother which was decidedly checkered in character. At times mother and daughter were not on speaking terms. Such periods of strain came with disturbing frequency. They marred and blighted the relationship. This is not to say that there were not happier intervals. Indeed there were such from time to time but, considering the relationship as it emerges from the evidence in its entirety, I must conclude that too often it was one of remoteness and estrangement.
>
> These facts are of importance in determining whether there was a breach of the moral duty on the part of the testatrix . . . . In appraising the extent of the moral duty that was owed by the testatrix to the applicant, therefore, I am justified in taking into account the strained and disturbed pattern of their relationship. I do not say that circumstance obliterated such moral duty. I do feel, however, that it whittled it down very considerably.

Dutka v. Dutka[94] had to do with a father who became separated from his wife before his son was born. The father and son had no contact until the son "sought out and found" the father, when the son was 27. A "warm and genuine" relationship quickly materialized; The father gave his son $5,000.00 and there was evidence of his intention to make a new will leaving his whole estate to his son. However within a couple of months the father died, with a will made before the reunion leaving his estate to his mother and siblings. The son was not "needy in the sense of being impoverished" and he had not contributed to the creation of his father's estate as had his father's siblings with whom his father had a close and supportive relationship and whose economic circumstances were modest. On the basis of the short but "warm and genuine" relationship the son had with his father

93 *Supra* note 18 at 337. Note also *Re Dickinson, supra* note 78 at 218–19; *Re Schurman, supra* note 32 at 83; *Re Lukie* (1976), 1 B.C.L.R. 1 (B.C. C.A.); and *Linden v. Linden, supra* note 78 at paragraphs 8–12, 18–20.

94 *Supra* note 79.

and the father's thwarted intentions, the court awarded the son $45,000.00 of a $160,000.00 estate.

There is a pod of cases in which the deceased and an applicant child were more or less estranged and the deceased provided little or no financial support following a divorce or separation. Two points of view have been expressed regarding the significance of the estrangement and failure to provide financial support. In *Re Joudrey Estate*[95] the deceased and his applicant adult child had a sporadic relationship; at the time of his death "little or no relationship existed".[96] The deceased did not leave the applicant any of his $87,000.00 estate. The applicant and her husband were employed, although their "means" were "very modest".[97] In awarding her $18,500.00 Justice Grant said:

> [33] I consider the testator had a moral and legal obligation to support the applicant at least until age 16.
>
> . . . . .
>
> [40] I consider the testator was under a high moral obligation to right an old wrong to the applicant. Whatever the relations between the testator and his estranged wife may have been was between them but the maintenance of the daughter of the marriage was clearly an obligation of the testator which he failed to meet.[98]

By comparison in *Little v. Little*[99] in regard to an applicant, who "for a period of more than fifty years . . . had virtually no contact with his father who lived only a short distance away" and who as a result of a perceived insult had no contact with his father for the last seven years of the deceased's life, the court said:

---

95 *Supra* note 76, distinguished in *Rafuse v. Rafuse Estate*, *supra* note 80 at paragraph 26 *et seq*. and *Jones v. Jones Estate*, *supra* note 79 at paragraphs 35–36. In *Rafuse* the lack of a relationship seemed to be of no consequence to the court, but the modest size of the estate and the contribution to the deceased's welfare in the final days of his life by his mother, his sole beneficiary, resulted in the dismissal of the applications. In *Jones* the lack of a relationship was fatal for a non-needy son, but the need of a daughter overcame it.

96 *Ibid.* at paragraph 38.

97 *Ibid.* at paragraph 41.

98 Similarly, *Re Stubbe* (1972), [1973] 1 W.W.R. 354 (B.C. S.C.) at 355–56; *Corkum v. Corkum*, *supra* note 78; *Re Gamble*, *supra* note 32; *Cox v. Nova Scotia (Public Trustee)*, *supra* note 79; *Redmond v. Redmond Estate*, *supra* note 79. Note also *Harrison v. Evans Estate*, *supra* note 32; *Martin v. McIlwain Estate* (1992), 66 B.C.L.R. (2d) 195 (B.C. S.C.); *Newstead v. Newstead Estate*, *supra* note 32 at paragraphs 49–58; *Pattie v. Standal Estate* (1997), 42 B.C.L.R. (3d) 211 (B.C. S.C.) at paragraph 26.

99 *Supra* note 32 at paragraph 8. *Similarly, Moxon v. Moxon*, *supra* note 32; *Hamling v. Brooks* (1985), (*sub nom. Re Wheeler*) 19 E.T.R. 102 (B.C. S.C.); *Price v. Lypchuk Estate* (1987), 26 E.T.R. 259 (B.C. C.A.); and *Cummine v. Cummine Estate* (1991), 91 Sask. R. 304 (Sask. Q.B.) at paragraph 13.

11 After reviewing all of the circumstances I am satisfied that there is no moral obligation which would be recognized by a wise and just parent in these circumstances as requiring any provision to be made by the testator for the maintenance and support of the applicant. The normal relationship between father and son ceased to exist and was never revived over the years. At the time the testator made his Will he had no obligation to the applicant or his other children.

Regarding the Ontario Act, and perhaps all of the other Acts except the Nova Scotia Act, Professor Bale suggests[100] that the quality of a relationship is only relevant respecting spouses by virtue of the Ontario Act, s. 62(1)(r)(i) which reads:

(r) if the dependant is a spouse,

(i) a course of conduct by the spouse during the deceased's lifetime that is so unconscionable as to constitute an obvious and gross repudiation of the relationship.

(iii) Duration

Courts have commented on the length, short[101] or long[102] of the marriage, usually connecting it to the lack of contribution the applicant made to the creation of the deceased's estate.

(c) Circumstances of the Applicant

(i) Age and Health

Aside from its being a component of the definition of child in some of the Acts,[103] age *per se* as a circumstance to be considered respecting need and moral obligation is only relevant in regard to minor children. In a few cases courts

---

100 Bale, G., "Re Dentinger, Dependants' Relief Legislation and the Changed Emphasis Effected by Part V of The Succession Law Reform Act (Ontario)" (1982) 10 E.T.R. 7 at 9.

101 *Re Anderson, supra* note 25 at 434 and 438; *Re Urquhart* (1956), 20 W.W.R. 177 (B.C. S.C.) at 180; *Nickle v. Jones, supra* note 10 at 388; *Collard v. Collard, supra* note 53; *Biblow v. Royal Trust Co., supra* note 47 at 206; *Montgomery v. Flood, supra* note 50; *Foulon v. Foulon, supra* note 47; *Carlson v. Carlson, supra* note 50 at 119; *Driscoll v. Driscoll Estate, supra* note 51 at paragraph 14.

102 *Dowsett v. Dowsett*, [1948] O.W.N. 685 (Ont. H.C.) at 692–93; *Moore v. Moore, supra* note 56 at 320 and 321; *Moores v. Hughes* (1981), 37 O.R. (2d) 785 (Ont. H.C.) at 792; *McMacken v. McMacken* (1984), 47 O.R. (2d) 701 (Ont. Div. Ct.); *Re Protopappas Estate, supra* note 56 at paragraph 55; *Vernon v. Dieleman Estate, supra* note 85 at paragraph 45 [46 E.T.R. 242].

103 See Chp. 3, 1.(b), above.

have made equal orders for minor children,[104] but usually unequal orders are made reflecting the ages of the children involved.[105] Age is often mentioned together with the need of the applicant and inability of the applicant to be employed. Two of the stereotypical dependants for whom dependants' relief legislation exists are the aged spouse of modest means, perhaps in poor health,[106] and the middle-aged, unemployable spouse or child.[107] In

---

104 *Re Denton, supra* note 64; *Farrar v. Scammell, supra* note 85; *Butt v. Chittock Estate* (1995), [1996] N.W.T.R. 104 (N.W.T. S.C.); *Surminsky (Litigation Guardian of) v. Ulmer Estate* (1997), (*sub nom. Surminsky v. Ulmer Estate*) 159 Sask. R. 217 (Sask. Q.B.).

105 *Re Finlan* (1951), 3 W.W.R. (N.S.) 671 (Alta. C.A.); *Re Gilbert, supra* note 68; *Rill v. Miller, supra* note 49; *Prefontaine v. Co-operative Trust Co., supra* note 68; *Hiebert v. Ward, supra* note 66; *Alberta (Public Trustee) v. Buchholz, supra* note 64; *McSween v. McSween Estate, supra* note 45; *Pauliuk v. Pauliuk, supra* note 10; *Cook v. Hrychuk Estate, supra* note 68; *Alberta (Public Trustee) v. Raniseth Estate, supra* note 66; *Hart (Guardian ad litem of) v. Hart Estate, supra* note 79.

106 *Re Schmalz, supra* note 84; *Re Morton Estate, supra* note 10, although the court was not generous; *Re Ponzir,* [1950] 2 W.W.R. 1009 (Alta. S.C.), affirmed [1950] 2 W.W.R. 1201 (Alta. C.A.); *Re Maitland, supra* note 44 at 675, 680; *Pope v. Stevens, supra*, note 46 at 171; *Cranston v. Cranston, supra* note 57; *Re Kirk* (1963), 38 D.L.R. (2d) 746 (B.C. S.C.); *Re Becker, supra* note 57; *Re Berry* (1966), 58 W.W.R. 187 (Sask. Q.B.); *Re Quon* (1969), 4 D.L.R. (3d) 702 (Alta. Q.B.); *Spinney v. Royal Trust Co.* (1973), 9 N.S.R. (2d) 699 (N.S. T.D.); *Re Leggatt* (1974), 10 N.B.R. (2d) 86 (N.B. Q.B.); *Re Soroka, supra* note 30; *Bennett v. Morrison, supra* note 46; *Davidson v. Allen* (1976), 14 N.B.R. (2d) 60 (N.B. S.C.); *Moore v. Moore, supra* note 56 at 323; *Re Day, supra* note 57; *Re Kiel* (1979), 24 A.R. 469 (Alta. Q.B.); *Coolen v. Coolen, supra* note 80 at paragraph 15; *Albert v. Albert, supra* note 84; *Watt v. Watt* (1982), 16 Sask. R. 127 (Sask. Q.B.) at paragraph 19; *Re Flahr* (1983), 28 Sask. R. 268 (Sask. Q.B.); *Re Nalywayko* (1984), 17 E.T.R. 151 (Ont. Surr. Ct.); *Vernon v. Dieleman Estate, supra* note 85; *Webb v. Webb Estate, supra* note 38.

107 *Re McDonald,* [1937] 2 W.W.R. 22 (Alta. S.C.); *Re Dickinson, supra* note 78; *Re Barclay* (1952), 5 W.W.R. (N.S.) 308 (Alta. S.C.); *Re Maitland, supra* note 44 at 680; *Re Rusk Estate, supra* note 84; *Re Green, supra* note 84 at 77–78; *Rybe v. Alberta (Public Trustee)* (1959), 36 W.W.R. 133 (Alta. C.A.); *Chernoff v. Chernoff, supra* note 24; *Re Hawley* (1962), 38 W.W.R. 354 (Sask. Q.B.) at 359; *Re Gosse, supra* note 19; *Re Bateman* (1965), 55 D.L.R. (2d) 763 (Sask. Q.B.); *Re Osland, supra* note 89; *Corkum v. Corkum, supra* note 78; *Re Ducherer, supra* note 64 at 496; *Malychuk v. Malychuk, supra* note 78; *Re Berger* (1978), 6 B.C.L.R. 241 (B.C. S.C.); *MacDonald v. MacDonald, supra* note 78; *Re Deis* (1981), 9 Sask. R. 257 (Sask. Q.B.) at paragraph 18, reversed (1983), 21 Sask. R. 328 (Sask. C.A.); *Moores v. Hughes, supra* note 102 at 788, 792; *Adams v. Broughton, supra* note 33; *Cox v. Nova Scotia (Public Trustee), supra* note 79; *McCaw v. McCaw, supra* note 78; *Chityala v. Chityala Estate* (1986), 71 A.R. 200 (Alta. Q.B.); *Rollins v. Beyea Estate, supra* note 80; *Burnett v. Noble Estate* (1990), 72 O.R. (2d) 583 (Ont. Surr. Ct.); *Holland v. Clements Estate* (1991), 43 E.T.R. 299 (Ont. Gen. Div.) at paragraphs 25–32; *Lindsay v. Jones, supra* note 79; *Smallman v. Smallman Estate* (1991), 41 E.T.R. 86 (Ont. Gen. Div.); *Wilson v. Kosok, supra* note 80 at paragraph 23.

Mitchell v. Mitchell,[108] regarding an application by an adult son, the court expressed concern for the widow, who was the residuary beneficiary:

> The widow is now 74 years of age and apparently not in the best of health. It is obvious that she has no way to augment her income if it were decreased by a reduction in her capital or interest rates.

On the other hand, the youthfulness of a widow and her ability to provide for herself is also relevant.[109]

Poor health, when coupled with need or inability to be fully employed has been the basis for relief orders.[110]

(ii) Financial

As the Manitoba Act states,

> **8.** (1) . . . the court . . . shall consider . . .
>
> (b) the assets and financial resources that the dependant has or is likely to have in the foreseeable future;
>
> (c) the measures available for a dependant to become financially independent and the length of time and cost involved to enable the dependant to take such measures;

The Saskatchewan, Ontario, Nova Scotia and Newfoundland Acts, above, contain similar provisions and so do the common law lists of relevant circumstances.[111] Thus, it is incumbent upon an applicant and the vigilant respondent to provide the court with complete, detailed evidence of the applicant's current and future financial means, including *inter vivos* settlements or gifts received from the deceased and non-estate benefits derived from the deceased's death, such as joint tenancy property and insurance and pension proceeds;[112] also the onus is on the applicant to

---

108 *Supra* note 79 at 461.

109 *Re Cole, supra* note 49 at 218–19; *Rill v. Miller, supra* note 49; *Foulon v. Foulon, supra* note 47; *Driscoll v. Driscoll Estate, supra* note 51.

110 *Re Morton Estate, supra* note 10; *Re Dickinson, supra* note 78; *Re Salthammer* (1946), [1947] 2 D.L.R. 135 (Sask. K.B.); *Downton v. Royal Trust Co.* (1970), 1 Nfld. & P.E.I.R. 203 (Nfld. T.D.), reversed (1971), 1 Nfld. & P.E.I.R. 528 (Nfld. C.A.), reversed (1972), 3 Nfld. & P.E.I.R. 576 (S.C.C.); *Re McKinnon, supra* note 78; *Re Protopappas Estate, supra* note 56 at paragraphs 33–35; and the cases dealing with institutionalized dependants, Chp. 4, 2(d)(ii). Similarly, *Plumb v. Royal Trust Co., supra* note 37.

111 *Supra* note 10.

112 Illustrative cases include: *Re Jenkins Estate* [1956] O.W.N. 548 (C.A.); *Re Smith*, [1958] O.W.N. 415 (Ont. H.C.); *Re Green, supra* note 84 at 77–78; *Re Michalson, supra* note 79; *Re Leggatt, supra* note 106 at paragraph 5; *Re Pelletier, supra* note 49 at paragraph 10; *Moore v. Moore, supra* note 56 at 317–18; *Foulon v. Foulon, supra* note 47 at paragraphs 10–12, 17–25; *Albert v. Albert, supra* note 84, pages 260, 264;

inform the court of the financial means of competitors.[113] Ample financial means can[114] result in the dismissal of an application,[115] although not necessarily.[116]

On occasion courts have been unsympathetic to applicants who put themselves behind the financial eight ball.[117]

Although, regarding adult children applicants courts do take note of the financial means of the applicant's spouse,[118] surely the comment of Justice Grant in *Re Joudrey Estate*,[119] is pertinent. In *Barnsley v. Barnsley*[120] the court ruled that the foster parents of a child with Downs Syndrome were not required to answer interrogatories about their financial situation, although they were required to answer questions regarding "information about the child's situation, including the childs relationship [to them] . . .

Dyer v. Dyer, *supra* note 45 at 55–56; *Dilworth v. Dilworth*, *supra* note 65; *Griffin v. McCarthy Estate* (1989), 36 E.T.R. 129 (B.C. S.C.); *Niebergall v. Niebergall Estate*, *supra* note 26; *Chityala v. Chityala Estate*, *supra* note 107 at paragraph 4; *Pauliuk v. Pauliuk*, *supra* note 10 at 31–32; *Edward v. Edward Estate*, *supra* note 84 at paragraphs 12–13; *Rutherford v. Rutherford Estate* (1988), 26 B.C.L.R. (2d) 140 (B.C. S.C.); *Baker v. Baker Estate*, *supra* note 56; *Kuhn v. Kuhn Estate*, *supra* note 32 at paragraph 40. In *Morris v. Morris*, *supra* note 79, *Harrison v. Evans Estate*, *supra* note 32, and *Purser v. Purser Estate* (1988), 31 E.T.R. 299 (B.C. S.C.), substantial gifts given by the deceased to one child or a couple of children was a factor in the court making an order in favour of another child or other children.

113 *Garrett v. Zwicker*, *supra* note 44 at paragraph 45.

114 Pursuant to the Manitoba Act financial means should result in dismissal.

115 See the cases listed *supra* in notes 49-51 and the *Lund*, *Stadnyk*, and *Flood* cases in note 57.

116 *Re McCann* (1962), 40 W.W.R. 254 (Sask. C.A.); *Mitchell v. Mitchell*, *supra* note 79; *Re Michalson*, *supra* note 79; *Granfield v. Williams* (1981), 29 B.C.L.R. 150 (B.C. C.A.); *Dyer v. Dyer*, *supra* note 45.

117 For ex., *Niebergall v. Niebergall Estate*, *supra* note 26 at paragraphs 19–22; *Black v. Kronberger Estate* (1989), 81 Sask. R. 106 (Sask. Q.B.) at paragraph 12, affirmed (1990), 83 Sask. R. 73 (Sask. C.A.); *Pedersen v. Pedersen*, *supra* note 49; note also *Stadnyk v. Bulycz* (1961), 36 W.W.R. 241 (Sask. Q.B.) at 252, varied (1961), 36 W.W.R. 680 (Sask. C.A.). Cf. *Wagner v. Wagner Estate* (1991), 62 B.C.L.R. (2d) 1 (B.C. C.A.), leave to appeal to S.C.C. refused (1992), 39 R.F.L. (3d) 399n (S.C.C.).

118 For ex., *Walker v. McDermott*, *supra* note 84 at 96; *Laventure v. Killey* (1953), 61 Man. R. 198 (Man. Q.B.) at 200; *Re Michalson*, *supra* note 79; *Re Osland*, *supra* note 89; *Re Holt*, *supra* note 79; *Coolen v. Coolen*, *supra* note 80 at paragraphs 19 and 21; *Moxon v. Moxon*, *supra* note 32; *MacDonald v. MacDonald*, *supra* note 78 at paragraphs 9, 43, 46; *Bartel v. Holmes*, *supra* note 32 at paragraph 2; *Griffin v. McCarthy Estate*, *supra* note 112; *Miller v. Rankin Estate*, *supra* note 79 at paragraphs 20, 23; *Crilley v. Beckingham*, *supra* note 79 at paragraph 9; *Rollins v. Beyea Estate*, *supra* note 80 at paragraph 4; *Spinney v. Spinney Estate*, *supra* note 80 at paragraphs 12–13.

119 See text at note 76.

120 (1996), 13 E.T.R. (2d) 310 (B.C. S.C. [In Chambers]) at paragraph 16.

and any expectation the child might have to benefit from the relationship which was known to the testator immediately prior to his death". The second part of this decision is troubling. While evidence of a testator's reasons is admissible, I hope that the court would treat it only as explanatory and not excusatory. Surely, an explanation of benefit from a foster relationship is too tenuous to be given much, if any, weight.

(iii) Dependants

In *Leard v. Maki*[121] Chief Justice MacEachern said:

> I consider that the question of the whether adequate provision for the plaintiff existed at the time of the testator's death requires a consideration not just of the plaintiff's needs, but also his family's needs, for their needs are his responsibility.

(d) Applicant's Need, Including Standard of Living

(i) Need and Standard of Living

Regardless of whether the court's jurisdiction is based solely, primarily, or perhaps only partly on the need of the applicant, the court will want to know about the need of the applicant. Indeed, the Ontario Act in s. 62(1)(e), quoted at the beginning of the chapter, lists the "dependant's needs". In his list of relevant circumstances, quoted near the beginning of this chapter,[122] Chief Justice Williams in *Re Lawther Estate* included:

> 15. In the case of a widow, the kind of maintenance to which she had been accustomed during the life of the testator, or to which she would have been accustomed if her husband had then done his duty to her, all this involving a consideration of (a) the size of the house in which she is to live, (b) the cost of fuel, living expenses, clothing, and replenishing household furnishings, (c) taxes, including income tax, (d) employment of domestic servants and of persons to tend furnace and grounds, if such servants had been employed in the husband's lifetime or become necessary because of his death or the disability of the widow, (e) the necessity for the use of a motor car and the employment of a driver, (f) the need for medical care or treatment, (g) travelling, particularly if it is necessary to winter in a milder climate.

---

121 *Supra* note 78 at 98. See also Chp. 3 the text at and cases cited in note 69. In *Albert v. Albert, supra* note 84 at 265, in calculating the amount of the relief the court included a monthly payment the widow had been making to her own disabled daughter.

122 See text at note 10.

Useful detailed lists of expenses can be found in a few cases.[123]

Of course, it is not only immediate need with which the court should be concerned, but also future need. This is evident in the cases involving middle aged, unemployable spouses and adult children[124] and minor children for whom the courts took into account post-majority needs,[125] statutory provisions respecting the financial means of the applicant, such as s. 8(1)(b) and (c) of the Manitoba Act, quoted at the beginning of the chapter, the illustrative cases cited respecting the applicant's financial means,[126] and in the common law lists of relevant circumstances, such as number 8 in Chief Justice Williams' list in *Re Lawther*, quoted at the beginning of the chapter. In *Re Rusk Estate*[127] Justice Culliton said:

> In disposing of this application, consideration must be given not only to the applicant's immediate requirements for maintenance but also to her requirements for future maintenance difficult as it is to determine with all the probabilities and uncertainties.

In *Laventure v. Killey*[128] the applicant was the adopted daughter of the testatrix. She was married; her husband was employed and his income looked after their current needs. At age 51 the court was of the view that she "would not be able to earn her own living should she be required to do so by some stroke of ill fortune". She was given a $500.00 legacy by the testatrix's will. About her need Justice Maybank said:

> . . . the "need" to be shown by an applicant is not necessarily a present, or an immediate, or an imminent condition. The expression "taking into consideration all the circumstances of the case," which is used in the statute, warrants a consideration of future possibilities. I am persuaded that the scheme of this statute is the prevention of preventable penury, present or apprehended. . . .
>
> My conclusion is that a case cannot be made out for varying the will in favour of the applicant to allow her something for present maintenance. But her future has to be considered and it is possible that, in days ahead, she will experience need. Her husband's death and his retirement upon a meagre pension are two

---

123 *Re Lawther, supra* note 10 at 159; *Re Cole, supra* note 49 at 206; *Re Green, supra* note 84 at 77; *Spinney v. Royal Trust Co., supra* note 106 at paragraphs 12–15; *Moore v. Moore, supra* note 56 at 317; *Fox v. Fox, supra* note 84 at 465; *Albert v. Albert, supra* note 84 at 260; *Niebergall v. Niebergall Estate, supra* note 26 at paragraph 8; *Swire v. Swire, supra* note 49 at 256; *Blago v. Aetna Life Insurance Co., supra* note 49 at 292.

124 *Supra* note 107. Also the cases cited in note 110 and cases of elderly spouses such as *Re Rist*, [1938] 3 W.W.R. 101 (Alta. S.C.) at 108.

125 *Supra* text at note 66.

126 *Supra* note 112.

127 (1957), 6 D.L.R. (2d) 700 (Sask. C.A.) at 705.

128 *Supra* note 118.

possibilities that would put her in need of support. Prolonged illness of her husband is another.[129]

The court issued an order suspending the distribution of the estate, but allowing the residuary beneficiary to receive the income generated by the residue of the estate for the time being. In arriving at his disposition of the case, Justice Maybank said, probably out of step with his Manitoba colleagues at that time and certainly in later years, "that it is a sine qua non for an applicant to show actual need before the court will vary a testator's will"; *Laventure* on its facts and the court's disposition of the case can be compared to *Walker v. McDermott*.

Olesko v. Olesko Estate[130] is a case in which the relief order was made solely to take care of a future need of the widow, who had been given by her husband's will a life estate in the matrimonial home. She testified that likely she would not be able to continue to live in the home in future and requested the court to order that she be given a fee simple estate. The court complied.

To what extent should the court contemplate future needs? In *Laventure* Justice Maybank considered the possibility of the applicant's husband's death, retirement, or prolonged illness. In *Re Denton*[131] and *Re Cameron*[132] with minor children applicants the courts took into account the possibility that the applicants might become physically or mentally unable to earn a livelihood. In *Coolen v. Coolen*[133] the trial judge thought that "the testator should have devised his homestead property outright to his widow, so that if she were forced to go into a nursing home the property could be sold and the proceeds used to pay her way". The Court of Appeal disagreed. In *Re Marsh*[134] the court considered the widow's "future needs, in case of illness or disability [and that] at her age she may wish to move to a more temperate climate". In *Re Dentinger* the applicant was 64, employed, and in good health; the court considered that she might be "forced to retire due to advancing age or indifferent health . . . lose her employment earnings, but gain an additional pension under the Canada Pension Plan, to which she contributes".[135] The *Cameron* decision prompted Professor Litman to advocate the adoption of a reasonable foreseeability test:

---

129 *Ibid.* at 203-04.

130 (1990), 87 Sask. R. 61 (Sask. Q.B.).

131 *Supra* note 64.

132 *Supra* note 57.

133 *Supra* note 80 at paragraphs 15, 16, and 18; similarly *Olesko v. Olesko Estate*, *supra* note 130 at paragraph 18.

134 *Supra* note 87 at 240.

135 *Supra* note 11 at 18; also *McSween v. McSween Estate*, *supra* note 45 at 213–14.

> It is this writer's view that if a contingent event is the type of event which a reasonable person would take stock of and which would influence his planning if his resources permitted, then it ought to be taken into account . . .[136]

The reasonable foreseeability concept has been expressly adopted in several of the decisions determining that the date of assessment of the relevant circumstances is the date of death.[137] In an annotation[138] to the *Dentinger* decision Professor Bale wrote:

> Determining which future contingencies should be taken into account in deciding upon an award has always been a difficult issue. . . . The assessment of future contingencies which influence only the quantum of the award has become a little less difficult because the order is no longer final in Ontario but may be varied, discharged or suspended at any subsequent date (now s. 65). In Ontario and other provinces which permit the order to be varied, it is submitted that only clearly foreseeable future events which diminish the need of the applicant should be taken into account in quantifying the award. If unlikely contingencies do occur, which decrease the need of dependant, these may be considered in an application to diminish the order. Contingencies which determine whether to make any award at all remain as difficult as ever. Also, contingencies which may increase the need of the applicant will not necessarily be solved through a future upward variation of the order, since the assets remaining undistributed may not be sufficient to support the upward variation.

Finally on need, in *Bates v. Bates*[139] the court heard actuarial evidence in support of the widow's claim. Despite Professor Bale's assertion to the contrary, this was not the first case in Canada in which such evidence was addressed; Professor Bale provided a worthwhile annotation to the case on actuarial evidence.[140]

Standard of living may be a consideration for all dependant applicants, but it is most often mentioned with regard to spouse applicants. The court should concern itself with what was the standard of living during joint lives of the deceased and an applicant spouse, whether the deceased spouse while alive could have provided a better standard of living, what standard of living can the applicant enjoy with what is to be received from the deceased's

---

136 Litman, M., "Re Cameron, Limitations on the Use of Future Contingencies in Calculating Awards made Under Dependants Relief Legislation" (1979) 4 E.T.R. 257 at 259. Also Amighetti at 118.

137 *Re Novikoff Estate* (1968), 66 W.W.R. 164 (B.C. S.C.); *Re Bowe*, [1971] 4 W.W.R. 234 (B.C. S.C.) at 237; *Lynds v. Lynds* (1986), 73 N.B.R. (2d) 296 (N.B. C.A.) at paragraph 19; *Landy v. Landy Estate* (1991), 60 B.C.L.R. (2d) 282 (B.C. C.A.) at 287–92.

138 Bale, G., "Re Dentinger, Dependants' Relief Legislation and the Changed Emphasis Effected by Part V of The Succession Law Reform Act (Ontario)" (1982) 10 E.T.R. 7 at 8–9.

139 (1981), 9 E.T.R. 235 (B.C. S.C.), affirmed (1982), 11 E.T.R. 310 (B.C. C.A.); also *Burnett v. Noble Estate*, *supra* note 107.

140 *Ibid.* at 236.

estate, together with the applicant's income and assets and, if necessary, what improvement can the court make, given the assets of the deceased's estate and the competing claims for the deceased's assets?[141] These concerns are derived from several judicial statements:

Allardice v. Allardice,[142] Chief Justice Stout:

> The question what principles the Court should follow is raised in this appeal . . . In my opinion these rules may be summarized as follows: 1, That the Act is something more than a statute to extend the provisions of the Destitute Persons Act . . . "Support," it has been held, at all events, in the case of a widow, does not mean merely having a supply of food and clothing. It means, it has been held, such kind of maintenance as the widow during the life of her husband has been accustomed to. The matter that should be considered, both as to widow and children, is how she or they have been maintained in the past.

Allen v. Manchester,[143] Justice Salmond:

> It may probably be said with truth that the proper maintenance which a testator owes to his widow in cases where there are no competing moral claims of other dependants is such maintenance as will enable her, taken in conjunction with her own means, to live with comfort and without pecuniary anxiety in such state of life as she was accustomed to in her husband's lifetime, or would have been so accustomed to if her husband had then done his duty to her.

Walker v. McDermott,[144] Justice Duff:

> What constitutes " proper maintenance and support " is a question to be determined with reference to a variety of circumstances. It cannot be limited to the bare necessities of existence. For the purpose of arriving at a conclusion, the court on whom devolves the responsibility of giving effect to the statute, would naturally proceed from the point of view of the judicious father of a family seeking to discharge both his marital and his parental duty; and would of course (looking at the matter from the point of view), consider the situation of the child, wife or husband, and the standard of living to which, having regard to this and the other circumstances, reference ought to be had. If the court comes to the decision that adequate provision has not been made, then the court must consider what provision would be not only adequate, but just and equitable also; and in exercising its judgment upon this, the pecuniary magnitude of the estate, and the situation of others having claims upon the testator, must be taken into account.

---

141 *Spinney v. Royal Trust Co.* (1973), 19 R.F.L. 191 (N.S. T.D.); *Nelson v. Nelson, supra* note 49; *Pulham v. Yorkshire Trust Co., supra* note 49.

142 *Supra* note 1 at 969.

143 [1922] N.Z.L.R. 218 (New Zealand S.C. In Banco) at 222. Similarly, *Re Protopappas Estate* (1987), 78 A.R. 60 (Alta. Q.B.) at 64, 65.

144 *Supra* note 84 at 96. Also *Re Marsh, supra* note 87 at 240; *McCarvill v. Jones, supra* note 84 at 280.

Re Cole,[145] Chief Justice Ilsley:

> It may be noted that [in *Walker v. McDermott*] Duff J. did not say that there is a failure to make adequate provision for the proper maintenance and support of a dependant if the provision made does not enable the dependant to enjoy the same standard of living provided by the testator in his lifetime. I do not think that this is necessarily so even in a case where the estate is sufficient. That standard of living should, of course, be considered but it should be considered having regard to the claims of the other dependants and other circumstances.
>
> The question is of importance in this case because one of the applicant's main grounds was that unless further provision is made for her out of the estate she will not be able to enjoy the kind of maintenance which she was accustomed to during her husband's lifetime. As noted below, I am not sure that she is right about this. It is, I think, quite possible that she may be able with the provision that was made for her to enjoy a standard of living which is as high as that to which she has been accustomed, although the nature of her daily activities and even perhaps her place of residence might necessarily be different.

Similarly, in *Nelson v. Nelson*[146] the deceased purchased homes in Saint John and Florida in the names of himself and his wife in joint tenancy. Also, he built a home in Hampstead, near Saint John, on a lot which he conveyed to his wife. In his will, aside from a small bequest to his wife, he created a $150,000.00 trust fund from which she was to receive the income for life with a power of encroachment. The residue of his estate, approximately $350,000.00, he gave to his two adult daughters by his first marriage. His widow had assets of her own, which together with pension benefits produced for her an annual income before income tax of $8,381.00. Chief Justice Hughes, dismissing her application for a relief order:

> 2 . . . Mrs. Nelson testified that they had a good marriage and enjoyed a relatively high standard of living, entertaining a great deal and spending about five and one-half months each year in Florida . . .
>
> . . . . .
>
> 13 . . . the principal contention made on behalf of Mrs. Nelson is that her husband's will fails to provide her with sufficient income to maintain her in the manner in which she would normally be maintained by a husband in Mr. Nelson's financial circumstances. Her counsel submitted that, although Mr. Nelson in his lifetime gave his wife two residences, he failed to make any adequate provision which would enable her to live in them. I agree with counsel's observation but I do not think that this fact establishes that the testator thereby failed in his moral duty to provide his wife with proper

145 *Supra* note 49 at 209.
146 *Supra* note 49.

maintenance and support. This view was expressed by Ilsley, C.J., in *In Re Cole Estate* (1958), 40 M.P.R. 201, at 209. Mr. Nelson built the house at Hampstead to satisfy his own wants and I think it is doubtful whether he ever intended that Mrs. Nelson should live there after his death. . . .

14 I agree with the submission made on behalf of Mrs. Nelson that her proper maintenance and support should include provision for her living part of the year in Florida and part in New Brunswick. It is obvious she cannot maintain the Hampstead property in the way her husband did on the income which she receives from her own investments and what is provided for in her husband's will. She testified that in the last year of her husband's lifetime the Hampstead property cost about $11,800 to maintain. This included the wages of a caretaker totalling about $5,400 and the maintenance and operation of a large truck and two tractors. She expressed the opinion that a caretaker was necessary for anyone who was occupying the property and that she could not live there unless she had somebody to do the work of the caretaker. I do not think Mrs. Nelson's request for an income to maintain the Hampstead property is reasonable. Evidence was adduced that she could lease an adequate apartment in Saint John with all the usual services except telephone service for less than $3,800 per year. Without the financial burden of maintaining the Hampstead property Mrs. Nelson's requirements would be reduced by at least $8,000 a year. She has an annual income from her own investments of $8,381. There was evidence that the trust fund directed to be set up by her husband's will should yield between 9 1/2% and 10% per annum. Taking the lower yield of 9 1/2% the trust fund should produce annually about $14,250. The Hampstead property, while not readily saleable has a substantial value. . . . For purposes of estimating the probable income available to Mrs. Nelson in the event she should decide to sell the Hampstead property I would assume she should realize a net price of $85,000, which if invested at 9½% per annum, would yield $8,075. Assuming the sale of the property and the investment of the proceeds I would infer that Mrs. Nelson's gross annual income would be somewhat in excess of $30,000 which after payment of Federal and Provincial income taxes would give her an income in excess of $18,000 a year. Counsel for Mrs. Nelson submitted that to award a greater share of the estate to Mrs. Nelson would cause no hardship to the testator's daughters who are the residuary beneficiaries of the estate. Evidence was adduced that during Mr. Nelson's lifetime he assisted them financially in purchasing homes and that he also gave them the common shares in the private holding company of Cramp Investments Ltd. as well as some of the preferred shares in the company. Of the latter Mrs. Himmelman held 1,100 shares of a par value of $10 and Mrs. Magnusson 2,100. In 1974 the company declared a dividend of $100,000 which was paid out of the tax paid distributed surplus of the company to Mrs. Magnusson and Mrs. Himmelman. As of June 30, 1976 the common shares held by them had an estimated total of $162,000. It would be a fair inference therefore that each of the testator's two daughters will ultimately receive approximately $250,000 while his wife received two prop-

> erties having a saleable value of probably $125,000 and the income from the $150,000 trust fund.
>
> 15 In my opinion Mrs. Nelson can maintain a reasonably high standard of living with her own resources and the provision which her husband has made for her, although that standard may in the future be somewhat reduced by continued inflation . . . . For my part I am unable to say [that Mr. Nelson] failed in a moral and legal duty to her.[147]

Bosch v. Perpetual Trust Co. Ltd.,[148] Lord Romer:

> The amount to be provided is not to be measured solely by the need of maintenance. It would be so if the Court were concerned merely with adequacy. But the Court has to consider what is proper maintenance, and therefore the property left by the testator has to be taken into consideration.

Courtney v. Lister,[149] Justice Davis:

> Mr. Bence submits that the applicant is not entitled to a higher standard of life than she enjoyed during her married life. That, of course, is not always true, as she may have been entitled to enjoy a higher standard of life than she did enjoy.[150]

Nickle v. Jones,[151] Chief Justice Milvain:

> In approaching my task I bear in mind the principles laid down in many cases. I am sure a widow is in a preferred position [to the] . . . other dependants and beneficiaries, unless there be some compelling reasons to the contrary. I am sure also that our statute does not mean bare subsistence, or just enough to get along on, but that the provision must be such as will on a just and equitable basis furnish adequate provision for the dependant. The court must give thought to the way of life followed by the deceased and his family during life, to the relationship and its duration between the deceased and the dependant, in this case a wife. The court must consider the independent means, if any, of the dependant, as a sensible testator must or should have done. Consideration must be given to the estate of the testator, its nature and extent and the obvious desires and wishes expressed in the will. The court shall not be motivated to increasing the estate of the dependant unless that be consistent with the needs and equity of all the surrounding circumstances.

---

147 Similarly, *Pulham v. Yorkshire Trust Co.*, *supra* note 49.

148 *Supra* note 61 at 478.

149 (1958), 24 W.W.R. 676 (Sask. Q.B.) at 683.

150 Also *Re Duranceau*, [1952] O.R. 584 (Ont. C.A.) at 592; *Re Kirk*, *supra* note 106 at 748, 750–51; *Moore v. Moore*, *supra* note 56 at 321–22; *Re Berger*, *supra* note 107 at 250; *Adams v. Broughton*, *supra* note 33 at 394; *Pauliuk v. Pauliuk*, *supra* note 10 at 32; *Re Protopappas Estate*, *supra* note 143 at paragraphs 47, 55.

151 *Supra* note 10 at 387.

Bennett v. Morrison,[152] Chief Justice Mackeigan:

13 As I had occasion to emphasize in *Zwicker v. Garrett*, supra:

> The dependant claimant need not, however, show need in the sense of actual want in order to qualify for consideration under the Act, and need not show actual dependency upon the testator. The need is relative, relative to the extent of the estate and the strength of other claims. I agree, as did Dickson, J.A., in *Barr v. Barr*, supra (25 D.L.R. (3d) at p. 411), with Gresson, P., of the New Zealand Court of Appeal in *Re Harrison (Deceased), Thomson v. Harrison*, [1962] N.Z.L.R. at p. 13:
>
> > 'It is rather unfortunate that there has crept into the cases over the years a disposition sometimes to consider first the "need" of the applicant and then to turn to a consideration of the extent of the estate and other claims there might be upon the testator. These considerations do not admit of separate consideration; they are interrelated. The "need" of an applicant, or rather his or her needs—the plural form is I think preferable—cannot be considered *in vacuo*. What has to be assessed are the merits of the claim having regard to the applicant's circumstances as at the date of the death of the testator; relations between the testator and the applicant in the past; and the extent of his estate and the strength of other claims.'

14 The question of "need" is not a mere subsistence test, but is rather the correlative of the moral or ethical claim. The "first obligation", to provide adequately for the wife, must be translated as a duty, so far as the size and nature of the estate permit, to provide "such kind of maintenance as the widow during the life of her husband has been accustomed to." (*Allardice v. Allardice*, [1911] A.C. 730 at 732, quoting Stout, C.J., in the New Zealand court).

15 Bissett, J., in *Mitchell v. Mitchell Estate* (1972), 3 N.S.R. (2d) 455, at p. 462, said:

> . . . the widow must have enough to live in a way at least comparable with that which she maintained as the wife of the testator.

. . . . .

17 Locke, J., in *McCarvill v. Jones et al.*, [1962] S.C.R. 273, at p. 280, stated:

> The respondent should, in my opinion, receive sufficient to maintain her in the manner in which a wife would normally be maintained by a husband financially situated as was the present testator . . . .

Re Davies,[153] Judge Dymond:

---

152 *Supra* note 46.

153 (1979), 27 O.R. (2d) 98 (Ont. Surr. Ct.) at 102-03.

> Some examination of dictionary definitions of the word "support" may be helpful . . .
>
> . . . . .
>
> These definitions lead me to the conclusion that "support" . . . includes not only furnishing food and sustenance and supplying the necessaries of life, but also the secondary meaning of giving physical or moral support. . . . I am inclined to the view that the word "support" . . . include[s] what might by some be considered as non-essentials or luxuries.

The statements quoted above from *Allardice*, *Allen*, *Walker*, and *Bosch* have been quoted in countless Canadian cases.

In the "on the other hand" category, *Re Anderson* was the application of a longtime separated, needy wife, who had co-habited with her husband for only three months. *Inter alia*, Justice McGillivray said:

> I may add that it does not appear that this woman's status in society was in any way changed by her marriage and she certainly did not live with her husband long enough to have formed more expensive habits or tastes as a result of the marriage.[154]

(ii) Persons Receiving Sustenance from Government and Other Sources

Is it relevant that a dependant, who has no assets other than perhaps an abatable pension, is being sustained by the government, perhaps in a mental hospital or chronic care facility, or by a pension? This issue has troubled the courts since 1919. It has created a terrible bramble patch of judicial opinion and conflicting decisions in a dozen Canadian cases and more than a dozen other Commonwealth cases. There would be an understandable difference between decisions made pursuant to Acts, the purposes of which are to take care of financial need and to enforce a moral duty to give a fair share of one's estate to defined dependants, and Acts, the sole purpose of which is to take care of financial need. However, all of the decisions have been made regarding dual purpose Acts. The cases can be divided very roughly into two camps. One camp reflects the point of view that no relief order should be made, especially regarding modest estates, unless the dependant personally can and will benefit from the award; in other words, no relief award should be made if it will be used simply to reimburse or defray the costs of sustenance or it will result simply in the reduction of a pension or welfare payment.[155] The other camp reflects the

---

154 *Supra* note 25 at 438.

155 *Re Cousins* (1951), 59 Man. R. 372 (Man. K.B.) at 379–81 and 386; *Re Taylor*, [1950] 1 W.W.R. 1055 (B.C. S.C.); *Re Pfrimmer Estate* (1968), 64 W.W.R. 762 (Man. Q.B.), reversed (1968), 66 W.W.R. 574 (Man. C.A.), leave to appeal refused (1968), 2 D.L.R. (3d) 720 (Man. C.A.); *Re Page Estate* (1969), 67 W.W.R. 407 (B.C. S.C.); *Re Kinloch*,

point of view that courts should make a relief award for a dependant who is being sustained by the government or a pension taking into account all the circumstances except the circumstance that the dependant may realize no personal benefit because the award may be utilized entirely to defray the costs of care provided by the government or to reduce a pension or welfare payment.[156] A maddening aspect of the reasons for judgment is that they do not expressly reflect upon all of the relevant factors. For instance, it is not always evident that the court considered the current physical and mental condition of the dependant in question and the dependant's prospects for recovery in terms of whether if an award is made the dependant can actually benefit from it. Consideration of whether an award will be used wholly or partly to defray costs of care or to abate a pension or welfare payment is seldom indicated. The practical approach in taking instructions for a will is to advise an appropriate bequest conditional upon its use to provide for additional comforts.

(e) Applicant's Contributions to Deceased's Welfare and Creation of Deceased's Estate

Unless the court's jurisidiction is strictly need based, as it is under the Manitoba Act, then certainly the contribution of the applicant (and anyone else who may be in line to succeed to the deceased's estate) to the creation

---

[1972] 2 W.W.R. 445 (Alta. S.C.); *Re Millar* (1976), 12 Nfld. & P.E.I.R. 440 (P.E.I. S.C.); *Re Deis* (1981), 11 E.T.R. 68 (Sask. Q.B.), reversed (1983), 13 E.T.R. 88 (Sask. C.A.). Note also *Alberta (Public Trustee) v. Jacobson Estate* (1987), 58 Alta. L.R. (2d) 355 (Alta. Q.B.).

156 *Re Cousins, supra* note 155; *Re Brousseau* (1952), 7 W.W.R. (N.S.) 262 (B.C. S.C.); *Re Barclay, supra* note 107; *Re Pfrimmer Estate* (1968), 66 W.W.R. 574 (Man. C.A.), leave to appeal refused (1968), 2 D.L.R. (3d) 720 (Man. C.A.); *Hawker v. Hawker* (1980), 8 Sask. R. 433 (Sask. Q.B.); *Re Deis* (1983), 21 Sask. R. 328 (Sask. C.A.); *Penty v. Mott* (1984), 16 E.T.R. 175 (B.C. S.C.); *Lynds v. Lynds, supra* note 137. The *Brousseau* and *Pfrimmer* decisions, because they were for the personal benefit of the applicant and despite their reference with approval to *Cousins*, might well be cases which should be included in the other camp, *supra* note 155. Note also *Canderton v. Barclays Bank* (1970), 114 Sol. Jo. 208 (Eng. Ch. D.); *Millward v. Shenton*, [1972] 2 All E.R. 1025 (U.K. C.A.); *Hiebert v. Ward, supra* note 66 at paragraph 9; *Watt v. Watt, supra* note 106; *Newstead v. Newstead Estate, supra* note 32 at paragraphs 73–85; *Barnsley v. Barnsley* (1996), 28 B.C.L.R. (3d) 165 (B.C. S.C. [In Chambers]); *Willott v. Willott Estate* (1997), 42 B.C.L.R. (3d) 223 (B.C. S.C.) at paragraphs 61–76; *Stone (Public Trustee of) v. Stone Estate* (1997), (*sub nom. Stone v. Stone Estate*) 209 A.R. 138 (Alta. C.A.); *Re Penner* (1997), (*sub nom. Re Penner Estate*) 161 Sask. R. 317 (Sask. Q.B.).

of the deceased's estate[157] or to the welfare of the deceased[158] is a relevant circumstance as is the lack of any contribution.[159] Insofar as dependants are

157 Widows, qualified cohabitees, labour and financial direct and indirect: *Re Wilson, supra* note 38 at 163; *Re Rusk Estate, supra* note 84 at 701; *Re Gosse, supra* note 19 at 672; *Moore v. Moore, supra* note 56 at 315, 320–21; *Koziol v. Zoltenko* (1978), 20 A.R. 89 (Alta. T.D.) at paragraph 4; *Sing v. Sing* (1977), 23 N.S.R. (2d) 251 (N.S. T.D.) at paragraphs 8–10, 16; *Re Cooper, supra* note 48 at 116–19; *Re Dentinger, supra*, note 11 at 29; *Morris v. Morris, supra* note 79 at 244, 257; *Re Pflanzner, supra* note 14 at 149, 155; *Re Nalywayko, supra* note 106 at 156–57; *Michalyshen v. Michalyshen Estate, supra* note 84 at paragraphs 9–12, 25, 48; *Re Protopappas Estate, supra* note 143 at paragraph 55; *Burnett v. Noble Estate, supra* note 107; *Vernon v. Dieleman Estate* (1992), 46 E.T.R. 242 (Ont. Gen. Div.) at paragraph 26, curiously, stated with respect to a constructive trust issue and not the dependants' relief issue, varied (1997), 16 E.T.R. (2d) 68 (Ont. C.A.); *Butt v. Chittock Estate, supra* note 104 at paragraphs 14–16; *Nelson v. Stroshein Estate* (1997), 161 Sask. R. 311 (Sask. Q.B.). Widows labour: *Jones v. Kline (Jones), supra* note 10 at 66, 84; *Re Lawther, supra* note 10 at 154; *Dmytriw v. Dmytriw, supra* note 26 at 383; *Montrose v. Montrose, supra* note 84 at paragraph 38; *Re Mannion, supra* note 45 at 267–68; *Crerar v. Crerar Estate* (1997), 40 B.C.L.R. (3d) 274 (B.C. S.C.), varied (1998), 111 B.C.A.C. 194 (B.C. C.A.). Widowers, labour and financial, direct and indirect: *Re Dupaul, supra* note 57 at 534; *Barker v. Westminster Trust Co., supra* note 57 at 39–40; *Kiss v. Palachik*, [1983] 1 S.C.R. 623 (S.C.C.) at 637–39; *Paxman v. Saskatchewan (Public Trustee), supra* note 57 at paragraph 14. Child(ren), labour and financial, direct and indirect: *Re Parker, supra* note 79; *Miller v. Rankin Estate, supra* note 79 at paragraphs 42, 44, 47, 52; *Guzzo v. Catlin Estate* (1989), 38 B.C.L.R. (2d) 41 (B.C. C.A.). Child(ren), labour: *Re Dawson, supra* note 80 at 482–83; *Pope v. Stevens, supra* note 46 at 166–67, 172; *Re Rusk Estate, supra* note 127 at 703; *Walker v. Rivalin, supra* note 79 at 323–26, 332–33; *Simmonds v. Rehn, supra* note 32 at 571; *Re Pfrimmer Estate, supra* note 156 at 575; *Mitchell v. Mitchell, supra* note 79 at 460–63; *Barr v. Barr, supra* note 74 at 412–18; *Re McKinnon, supra* note 78 at 269–70; *Re Sleno* (1977), 78 D.L.R. (3d) 155 at 157, 163; *Travagline v. Kendall, supra* note 32 at paragraphs 7 and 10; *Valouch v. Valouch*, [1982] B.C.W.L.D. 924 (B.C. S.C.); *Schofield Estate v. Schofield, supra* note 79; *Kaetler v. Kaetler Estate* (1990), 51 B.C.L.R. (2d) 238 (B.C. C.A.) at 246; *Huang v. Chan, supra* note 79; *McRae v. Royal Trust Corp. of Canada, supra* note 79. Non-dependants: *Laventure v. Killey, supra* note 118; *Simmonds v. Rehn, supra* note 32; *Rafuse v. Rafuse Estate, supra* note 80.

158 *Re Marsh, supra* note 87 at 240; *Laventure v. Killey, supra* note 118 at 202; *Walker v. Rivalin, supra* note 79; *Re Kirk, supra* note 106 at 748; *Re Osland, supra* note 89 at 142; *Moore v. Moore, supra* note 56 at 315; *Adams v. Perks, supra* note 32 at paragraph 7; *MacDonald v. MacDonald, supra* note 78 at paragraphs 15 and 52. *Montrose v. Montrose, supra* note 84; *Bates v. Bates, supra* note 138 at 239–40; *Re Mannion, supra* note 45; *Griffin v. McCarthy Estate, supra* note 112 at 137; *Nulty v. Nulty Estate, supra* note 32 at 349; *Paxman v. Saskatchewan (Public Trustee), supra* note 57; *Nelson v. Stroshein Estate* (1997), 161 Sask. R. 311; *Sakundiak v. Sakundiak Estate, supra* 22 at paragraph 52. Note also *Cross v. Currie Estate, supra* note 80 at paragraph 29.

159 *Re Anderson, supra* note 25 at 438; *Re Rist*, [1938] 3 W.W.R. 101 (Alta. T.D.) at 108–09, affirmed [1939] 1 W.W.R. 518 (Alta. C.A.); *Re Dawson, supra* note 80 at 484; *Dowsett v. Dowsett, supra* note 102 at 692–93; *Re Urquhart, supra* note 101 at 180; *Re Cole, supra* note 49; *Re Bérubé*, [1973] 3 W.W.R. (Alta. C.A.) at 182; *Nickle v. Jones, supra* note 10 at 388; *Biblow v. Royal Trust Co., supra* note 47 at 206; *Montgomery v. Flood,*

concerned, this principle is codified in the Ontario Act in s. 62(1)(h)-(j), and in the Nova Scotia and Newfoundland Acts in s. 5(1)(g) and (h), both quoted at the beginning of this chapter. One statement worth remembering is that of Justice Barry in *Davidson v. Allen,*[160] which had to do with the application of a 78 year old widow of a 60 year marriage:

> 11 . . . It's one thing to say that the Plaintiff didn't contribute financially to the house or the accumulation of assets, but that's just grossly inaccurate, too. The mere fact of her being at home bringing up six children with limited resources, is probably a contribution that far exceeded the value of the estate and had the whole estate been left to Mrs. Davidson she probably wouldn't have received as much as she should have for the services that she performed.

Some courts have discounted the contributions of minor children to family enterprises,[161] while others have taken it into account.[162] Generally, courts do not engage in a tit-for-tat accounting respecting a contribution made to the deceased's welfare or to the accumulation of the deceased's estate, as Justice Diskery indicated in *Stadnyk v. Bulycz.*[163]

> The applicant's affidavit sets forth with considerable detail certain expenditures made and work done by the applicant upon his wife's property during the 12 years of their married life. He states that he built a chicken barn, a cement cistern, a new kitchen with kitchen cupboards, made certain repairs to the house and had the farm buildings wired for electrical power. He further deposes that he spent approximately $1,710.88 for materials for these projects and performed much of the labour required himself. His affidavit further sets out that the testatrix and himself jointly purchased two beds and a washing machine, and that he himself purchased a water heater for $113 and a davenport and chair for $174.10.
>
> Learned counsel for the applicant strongly urged that these matters were relevant in determining whether or not the applicant should be granted an order under the Act, stressing that if no order was made the applicant would not be reimbursed for his work and expenditure.

---

supra note 50 at 25; *Moxon v. Moxon, supra* note 32 at paragraph 35; *Foulon v. Foulon, supra* note 47 at 127; *Carlson v. Carlson, supra* note 50 at 119; *Driscoll v. Driscoll Estate, supra* note 51.

160 *Supra* note 106. Also *Pattie v. Standal Estate, supra* note 98 at paragraph 23.

161 *Re Rusk Estate, supra* note 84 at 700, 704; *Barr v. Barr, supra* note 74 at 401, 415; *Moxon v. Moxon, supra* note 32 at paragraph 36; *Huang v. Chan, supra* note 79 at paragraph 18; *McRae v. Royal Trust Corp. of Canada, supra* note 79 at paragraph 58; *Crerar v. Crerar Estate, supra* note 157 at paragraph 21.

162 *Walker v. Rivalin, supra* note 79; *Schofield Estate v. Schofield, supra* note 79 at paragraph 4; *Kaetler v. Kaetler Estate, supra* note 157 at 240, 246.

163 *Supra* note 117 at 247.

> If this contention were accepted then it would be only equitable for the court to inquire into the benefits the applicant received from the testatrix during their marriage, such as the use and occupation of her home for 12 years, the income from her farm which was used for their joint benefit, and the value of her work and services in the home and on the farm. Counsel might remember that while it is stated in the *Book of Proverbs*, ch. 31, v. 10, that the price of a virtuous woman is "far above rubies" no such valuation is placed upon a husband.
>
> However the law does not, in my opinion, require the court to explore, evaluate and balance off such matters upon applications of this nature; and the provisions of *The Dependants' Relief Act* are not intended to afford a surviving spouse an opportunity to recover from the estate of the predeceasing spouse for moneys spent and work done for their joint benefit during their married life. In *In re Lund Estate* [1946] 3 WWR 732, McNiven, J., as he then was, is reported on p. 735 as follows:
>
>> "The application seemingly is made on the basis that the husband is entitled to an allowance from the estate as of right or, alternatively, that he has a right to be compensated for moneys expended during their married life for living expenses and maintenance of her home. In my opinion neither basis is tenable."

The Ontario *Dependants Relief Act* of 1929[164] in s. 9 empowered the court to fix the value of "personal assistance or the gift or loan of money or real or personal property towards the advancement of the testator in any business or occupation . . . [given by a dependant] and may direct that the applicant shall rank as a creditor upon the estate therefor. . .". The current Ontario Act contains no such provision.

(f) Claims by Any Other Dependant or Person

Courts note whether the applicant is the only person who qualifies as a dependant.[165]

---

164 S.O. 1929, c. 47.

165 *Barker v. Westminster Trust Co., supra* note 57 at 38 and 47; *Shaw v. Regina (City), supra* note 44 at 442, 445; *Re Willan Estate, supra* note 10 at 135; *Re Carnduff, supra* note 84 at 164; *Re Rusk Estate, supra* note 84 at 702; *Re McCann, supra* note 116; *Re Kirk, supra* note 106 at 749–50; *Walker v. Rivalin, supra* note 79 at 334; *Re Gosse, supra* note 19 at 671; *Re Norton* (1964), 44 D.L.R. (2d) 617 (Alta. S.C.) at 621; *Re Becker, supra* note 57 at 579; *Re Wild, supra* note 49 at 94; *Re Bateman, supra* note 107; *Re Parks, supra* note 79 at 594; *Beasley v. Willet, supra* note 32; *Re Michalson, supra* note 79 at 567; *Re Stubbe, supra* note 98 at 356, "[the petitioner] is the only blood relative. . . . That fact may not, of itself, be of great significance. . .; *Spinney v. Royal Trust Co., supra* note 106; *Moore v. Moore, supra* note 56 at 320, 323; *Corkum v. Corkum, supra* note 78 at paragraph 10; *Re Radcliffe, supra* note 79 at 224; *Re Berger, supra* note 107 at 250; *Jeffers v. Jeffers* (1982), 20 Sask. R. 52 (Sask. Q.B.) at paragraphs

Each of the Saskatchewan, Manitoba, Ontario, Nova Scotia, and Newfoundland Acts state that the court is to consider, *inter alia*, the claims of any other *dependant*. In *Re McCann*[166] the testator left his estate to his wife and *adult child*. The trial judge dismissed an application by the widow "having regard to all the claims on his bounty, and the just requirements of his widow . . . and considering her independent means, capacity to earn and present salary, health and other relevant factors".[167] On appeal the court held that the trial judge was wrong to consider "the moral claim of the son" because he was not a statutory dependant. Curiously, notwithstanding the trial judge's other reasons for dismissing the widow's application, the court gave her the whole of the testator's undisclosed estate. The Manitoba Act, uniquely directs the court to consider:

> **8.** (1)(h) the claims that any other dependant *or any other person* has upon the estate; (emphasis added)

This codifies earlier Manitoba decisions and mirrors decisions in other provinces, including Saskatchewan, below. In light of these decisions, the Court of Appeal's strict application in *Re McCann* of then s. 9(6), now s. 8(2), quoted at the beginning of this chapter, seems harsh.

The moral claim of testamentary beneficiaries and intestate heirs who are not statutorily defined dependants is a pertinent consideration,[168] which is also reflected in the relevance of the deceased's intentions[169] and the

---

9 and 11; *Re Flahr, supra* note 106 at paragraph 5; *Swire v. Swire, supra* note 49 at 249; *Re Protopappas Estate* (1987), 78 A.R. 60 (Alta. Q.B.) at paragraphs 14, 55; *Cook v. Hrychuk Estate, supra* note 68 at paragraph 5; *Re Joudrey Estate, supra* note 76 at paragraph 38; *Nulty v. Nulty Estate, supra* note 32 at 347; *Baker v. Baker Estate, supra* note 56 at paragraph 80; *Sakundiak v. Sakundiak Estate, supra* note 22 at paragraph 50.

166 *Supra* note 116.

167 *Ibid.* at 255.

168 *Re Elworthy*, [1928] 1 W.W.R. 737 (B.C. S.C. [In Chambers]); *Re Pedlar Estate*, [1933] 1 W.W.R. 267 (B.C. S.C.); *Re Hoffman*, [1931] 1 W.W.R. 293 (B.C. S.C.); *Re Dawson, supra* note 80; *Re La Fleur, supra* note 44 at 54; *Re Johnson*, (1955), 17 W.W.R. 88 (Sask. Q.B.); *Re Cole, supra* note 49 at 217; *Re Wild, supra* note 49 at 94; *Re Schurman, supra* note 32; *Simmonds v. Rehn, supra* note 32 at 571; *Re Quon, supra* note 106 at 707; *Re Pelletier, supra* note 49; *Collard v. Collard, supra* note 53 at 256; *Re Osland, supra* note 89 at 142; *Menrad v. Blowers, supra* note 22 at 318; *Dilworth v. Dilworth, supra* note 65; *Pauliuk v. Pauliuk, supra* note 10 at 32; *Cook v. Hrychuk Estate, supra* note 68 at paragraphs 5–6; *Rafuse v. Rafuse Estate, supra* note 80; *Simkins v. Blumenthal, supra* note 46; *Pattie v. Standal Estate, supra* note 98 at paragraph 23; *Ostrander v. Kimble Estate, supra* note 56 at paragraphs 44–45.

169 *Infra* at page 153 of this text.

oft-expressed judicial reluctance to make a (new) will for the deceased.[170] However, in *Re Garajczki*[171] a majority of the Saskatchewan Court of Appeal decided that the claim of the needy, deserted widow out-weighed the moral claim of the testamentary beneficiary, the deceased's illegitimate infant daughter, who was living with her paternal grandparents. About the competing claims Justice Culliton for the majority said:

> It was admitted on argument that the right which the infant Marilyn Laliberte has in the estate arises from her claim as a beneficiary under the will. Being an illegitimate child, she has no claim as a dependant. . . . It was argued, however, that the deceased had a moral obligation to his illegitimate daughter and having accepted that obligation by providing for her in his will, the court was bound to give some effect to that provision. In support of this argument counsel relied upon the following statement of Williams, C.J.Q.B. in *In re Testator's Family Maintenance Act; In re La Fleur Estate* [1948] 1 WWR 801, at 815. . .:
>
> > "It is also clear from the authorities that a mistress and illegitimate children have a moral claim on the testator which the courts are bound to recognize if benefits are given to them under the will."
>
> In my opinion the foregoing statement cannot be so literally interpreted, nor do I think the learned chief justice intended that it should be so understood. It is inevitable, in the very nature of the legislation, when relief is granted to a dependant, the rights of other beneficiaries must be affected. In this same judgment the learned chief justice said, "A widow occupies the most favoured position."
>
> It may well be, in the proper application of the Act, the relief granted to a widow would eliminate entirely the benefits given to all other beneficiaries including other dependants. This the court has the power to do. I am sure the learned chief justice did not intend that the court's right to do so would be restricted if a beneficiary happened to be a mistress or an illegitimate child of the deceased.
>
> I think the learned chief justice meant no more than that the court must have regard for the testator's provision for his mistress or illegitimate children and that the moral aspect of the relationship between them is not to be considered as a reason for defeating such provision. My view that such is the correct interpretation is strenghtened by a review of the judgment of Coady, J. in *In re Testator's Family Maintenance Act*; *In re Shadforth Estate* [1943] 1 WWR 793, 58 BCR 317, one of the authorities quoted and relied upon by the learned chief justice. Subsec. (6) of sec. 8 of the Act provides in part,
>
> > "the Court shall also have regard to the testator's reasons so far as ascertainable for making the disposition made by his will."

---

170 *Infra* at page 166 of this text.

171 (1960), 32 W.W.R. 145 (Sask. C.A.).

> The statement of Williams, C.J.Q.B. makes it clear that the court, in the application of this statutory discretion, should draw no inferences detrimental to the beneficiary where the testator has provided for a mistress or illegitimate child, because in so doing he met a moral obligation resting upon him. On the other hand, I must say that a testator by providing for his mistress or illegitimate child cannot diminish or defeat the rights of those in whose favour the Act is intended to operate.
>
> As already stated, the net value of the estate is $6,605. This amount will be substantially reduced by administration and litigation costs. It also appears very doubtful whether the assets will realize the value placed upon them for succession duty purposes. It is thus obvious if the applicant received the entire estate, this amount, together with what she has, will fall far short of making reasonable provision for her maintenance. Under these circumstances I think the learned chamber judge should have ordered that the entire estate be given to the applicant and that the assets be transferred to her in the due course of administration and I now so order.[172]

In *Paxman v. Saskatchewan (Public Trustee)*[173] the 76 year old deceased died intestate survived by her 85 year old common law husband applicant and several niece and nephew heirs. For two reasons, the court awarded one-half of her $75,000.00 estate to the common law husband, whose assets totalled $433,000.00 and whose income exceeded his expenses:

> [13] . . . [Besides the common law husband] there are no other "dependants". . . . The claims of the nieces and nephews do not compete with applicant's claim under the **Act**. The nieces and nephews . . . are relatives with whom the deceased had no contact, and apparently no relationship. They did not know the deceased, nor she them. They were only located through the efforts of an heir locator . . . .
>
> [14] [Her common law husband] cared for [her] and was reliable and kind to her in the last years of her life. . . He paid for their groceries, their household expenses, the couple's recreational and vacation activities, and purchased some of the deceased's clothing and footwear.

Courts have expressed annoyance with opposition to applications by non-dependant testamentary beneficiaries, particularly institutions.[174]

---

172 *Ibid.* at 150-52. The trial judge awarded the widow one-half of the estate. The two dissenting Court of Appeal justices would have awarded $1,000.00 to the daughter and the balance to the widow. For a similar case see *Renwick v. Currie*, [1948] 2 W.W.R. 683 (Sask. C.A.).

173 *Supra* note 57.

174 For ex., Re *Norton, supra* note 165 at 622–23.

(g) Size and Nature of the Estate

(i) Size

Although only the Manitoba Act mentions it, certainly the "pecuniary magnitude of the estate" (one of two circumstances specified by Justice Duff in *Walker v. McDermott*[175]) is a very pertinent circumstance.

In *Garrett v. Zwicker*[176] Chief Justice McKeigan said:

> 21 A large estate thus permits a wider definition of the needs which the testator has a moral obligation to meet if he can, and at the same time supplies the means to satisfy that duty without preventing him from adequately providing by his will for other dependents who have equal or greater claims upon his bounty. As Lord Romer said in *Bosch*, [1938] A.C. at p. 478 "Where, therefore, the testator's estate is a large one the Court will be justified in such a case in making provision to meet contingencies that might have to be disregarded where the estate is small."

Similarly, Justice O'Halloran in *Barker v. Westminster Trust Co.*[177] said, with reference to *Walker v. McDermott*:

> The larger the estate the larger the share to which the daughter would be entitled . . .[178]

Also in *Re Willan Estate*[179] Justice Egbert stated:

> . . . in the case of an application by a widow when the estate is large and there are no other dependants with conflicting moral claims, the court should not be "too meticulous in fixing the amounts which should be considered reasonable for a widow to spend in providing for her needs.

And finally Chief Justice Martin in *Shaw v. Regina (City)*,[180] observed:

> Where the testator has a family and only a small estate he may not be able to provide any one of his dependants with adequate maintenance and at the same time the provision made for them may be reasonable and proper when all the circumstances including the size of his estate are considered. In the case of small estates where there are numerous persons having a claim upon the bounty of the testator and some dependant complains of unjust distribution, the duty of the Court is to endeavour to see that the estate is justly divided among such persons after giving due consideration to the relative needs and

---

175 *Supra* note 84 at 96. Also *Re Lawther, supra* note 10 and the other cases cited in note 10.
176 *Supra* note 44 at paragraph 21.
177 *Supra* note 57 at 36.
178 For ex., *Re Holt, supra* note 79.
179 *Supra* note 10 at 136. Similarly, *Re Protopappas Estate, supra* note 165 at paragraph 55.
180 *Supra* note 44 at 439. Also *Martin v. McIlwain Estate, supra* note 98 at paragraph 52.

> deserts of the claimants. In the case, however, of a large estate where the applicant for relief complains that the testator out of his wealth has not made a provision reasonably sufficient for the maintenance of the dependant, the Court has placed upon it the duty of deciding to what extent a wealthy man should go in making provision for the maintenance of his dependants.

Obviously, the larger the estate the greater is the ability of the court to order more than adequate relief[181] and, in the case of more than one applicant, to do so without having to choose between or among the applicants or to significantly affect the claims of non-dependant beneficiaries.[182] However, in a few cases widows have not been successful notwithstanding the large size of their husband's estate. This was so because either the testamentary provision was considered reasonable or the widows were considered to have adequate financial means of their own.[183] Not surprisingly courts have awarded quite modest estates entirely to the surviving spouse.[184]

(ii) Nature

The Manitoba Act in s. 8(1)(a), quoted at the beginning of the chapter, makes a bare reference to the nature of the estate.[185] In *Cook v. Cook*,[186] the court used the then *Testator's Family Maintenance Act* to enable the family farm, owned by the deceased spouse, to be kept intact by the widow

---

181 *Bosch v. Perpetual Trust Co., supra* note 61 at 476.

182 *Granfield v. Williams, supra* note 116 at 154.

183 *Nelson v. Nelson, supra* note 49; *Foulon v. Foulon, supra* note 47; *Re deBeaudrap, supra* note 49; *Hecht v. Hecht Estate, supra* note 49; *Lobe v. Lobe Estate, supra* note 49.

184 *Re Mays*, [1943] 3 W.W.R. 479 (Alta. S.C.); *Re Salthammer, supra* note 110; *Renwick v. Currie, supra* note 172; *Re Marsh, supra* note 87; *Re Ponzir, supra* note 106; *Courtney v. Lister, supra* note 149; *Rybe v. Alberta (Public Trustee), supra* note 107; *Re Garajczki, supra* note 171; *Re Hawley, supra* note 107; *Cranston v. Cranston, supra* note 57; *Re Becker, supra* note 57; *Re Flahr, supra* note 106; *Rollins v. Beyea Estate, supra* note 80 at paragraph 9; *Edward v. Edward Estate, supra* note 84 at paragraph 11. Note also Jayne, A., "Re Ducherer, The 'Comparatively Small' Problem of the Dependants' Relief Act and the 'Small Estate' " (1978) 2 E.T.R. 146 and *Re Trott*, [1949] 2 W.W.R. 738 (Man. K.B.) in which the court denied the widow an $11,000.00 estate, merely increasing her testamentary income payment; *Re Blackmore*, [1948] 56 Man. R. 88 (Man. K.B.) in which the court ordered a constructively deserted, disinherited widow to receive only $1,800.00 of a $2,000.00 estate, leaving $200.00 for a will-directed requiem mass; *Re Wild, supra* note 49, in which the court dismissed an application by a widow respecting a $5,600.00 estate; *Re Elworthy, supra* note 168, in which "the smallness of the estate" was a factor in the court dismissing an application by a non-needy daughter; *Koski v. Koski Estate* (1994), 3 E.T.R. (2d) 314 (B.C. S.C.) in which the court ordered a needy widow only $20,000.00 of a $65,000.00 estate.

185 As does *Nickle v. Jones, supra* note 10 at 387.

186 (1981), 121 D.L.R. (3d) 190 (Man. Q.B.).

pursuant to s. 47 of Manitoba's *Trustee Act*,[187] free of any personal liability for losses incurred. Section 8(1) of the Saskatchewan Act is unique:

> **8.** (1) In determining whether, and in what way, and from what date, maintenance ought to be provided, the court shall consider the nature of the property representing the deceased's estate and shall not make an order requiring a sale of the property that would be improvident having regard to the interests of the dependants and of the person who, apart from the order, would be entitled to that property.

Regardless of the silence of the other Acts, surely the nature of the estate is a relevant circumstance and the wording of the primary jurisdiction section in all of the Acts respecting the circumstances to be considered is inclusive. The nature of the estate is relevant when the estate is composed entirely or largely of an asset or assets which the court is not awarding (solely) to the applicant(s) and of which the court does not want to force the liquidation.[188] As Justice Burchell aptly put it in *Cross v. Currie Estate*:[189]

> [28] It appears to me that most of the court decisions, and their disposition to interfere with the will of a testator, is influenced by the size of the estate and its liquidity. Here, for all practical purposes, the estate is comprised of real estate alone. If there was to be any change in the disposal of property under the will, the real estate would have to be sold. This would be such an inordinate interference with this will that it should only occur in the gravest and most cogent of circumstances.

(h) External Economic Indicators and Variables

In *Re Ducherer*[190] Judge Walker said:

> It is important to keep in mind not only the widow's present requirements . . . but also her requirements for future maintenance in uncertain economic times.

---

187 R.S.M. 1987, c. T 160.

188 *Re McDonald, supra* note 107; *Re Finnimore* (1956), 17 W.W.R. 668 (Sask. C.A.); *Re Carnduff, supra* note 84; *Garrett v. Zwicker, supra* note 44 at paragraphs 4, 46–48; *Re Ducherer, supra* note 64; *Re Kiel, supra* note 106 at paragraph 7; *Collins v. Collins Estate* (1981), 34 Nfld. & P.E.I.R. 325 (Nfld. T.D.) at paragraph 23; *Re deBeaudrap, supra* note 49 at paragraph 38; *Moroz v. Moroz Estate* (1991), 92 Sask. R. 176 (Sask. Surr. Ct.).

189 *Supra* note 80 at paragraph 28.

190 *Supra* note 64 at 499.

Courts have taken into account the cost of living (index),[191] interest rates,[192] business conditions,[193] inflation,[194] and increasing income taxes.[195] However, in *Morris v. Morris*[196] the British Columbia Court of Appeal refused an application by the respondent to adduce further evidence of a change in circumstances because of fluctuating real estate prices and interest rates.

(i) Deceased's Intentions (Reasons)

All of the Acts,[197] except the Nova Scotia Act, contain provisions like those contained in s. 5(1) and (2) of the British Columbia Act:

> **5.** (1) In an action under section 2 the court may accept the evidence it considers proper of the testator's reasons, so far as ascertainable,
> (a) for making the dispositions made in the will, or
> (b) for not making adequate provision for the wife, husband or children,
> including any statement in writing signed by the testator.
> (2) In estimating the weight to be given to a statement referred to in subsection (1), the court must have regard to all the circumstances from which an inference may reasonably be drawn about the accuracy or otherwise of the statement.

The section in the Nova Scotia Act, s. 5(3), is like British Columbia's s. 5(1), but it does not contain the wording of British Columbia's. 5(2).

---

191 *Re Willan Estate, supra* note 10 at 136; *Moore v. Moore, supra* note 56 at 321; *Albert v. Albert, supra* note 84 at 265; *Re Trenton, supra* note 32 at 224; *Ostrander v. Kimble Estate, supra* note 56 at paragraph 54.

192 *Re Protopappas Estate, supra* note 165 at paragraph 29.

193 *Re Morton Estate* (1934), 49 B.C.R. 172 (B.C. S.C.) at 177.

194 *Re Fraser* (1964), 50 W.W.R. 268 (B.C. C.A.) at 277; *Malychuk v. Malychuk, supra* note 78 at 250; *Re Berger, supra* note 107 at 250; *Moores v. Hughes, supra* note 102 at 792; *Bates v. Bates, supra* note 139; *Pauliuk v. Pauliuk, supra* note 10 at 32; *Burnett v. Noble Estate, supra* note 107 at 590; *Ostrander v. Kimble Estate, supra* note 56. Note *Dyer v. Dyer, supra* note 45 at 57, 59.

195 *Shaw v. Regina (City), supra* note 44 at 445; note also *Re Lawther, supra* note 10 at 162 and *Vernon v. Dieleman Estate, supra* note 85 at paragraph 46.

196 *Supra* note 79 at 254–56 [41 B.C.L.R. 239].

197 Alta. s. 3(2)(c) and (3); Sask. s. 8(3)-(5); Man. s. 8(2)(c) and (3); Ont. s. 62(3) and (4); N.B. s. 9; PEI s. 5(1)(c) and (2); Nfld. s. 5(3); NWT s. 4(1)(c) and (2); YT s. 5(1)(c) and (2).

The evidence will usually come from an express statement in the testator's will;[198] also, it may be derived from written or oral statements made by the testator to the testator's lawyer, family, friends, or other persons,[199] from facts, including the provisions of the deceased's will, from which the deceased's reasons may be inferred,[200] and, as in *Kelly v. Baker*, from correspondence between family members.[201]

---

198 For example, *Re Pemberton, supra* note 19; *Re Willan Estate, supra* note 10; *Chernoff v. Chernoff, supra* note 24; *Re Cassidy, supra* note 25 at 337; *Re Nixey, supra* note 26 at 598–99; *Re Michalson, supra* note 79 at 565; *Montgomery v. Flood, supra* note 50 at 23; *Rutledge v. Jackson, supra* note 73; *Braidwood v. Maxwell, supra* note 79; *Harrison v. Evans Estate, supra* note 32; *Kallasmaa v. Pesonen* (1987), 29 E.T.R. 38 (B.C. S.C.); *Nulty v. Nulty Estate, supra* note 32; *Webb v. Webb Estate, supra* note 38 at paragraphs 26–28; *Warwick (Guardian ad litem of) v. Warwick Estate, supra* note 49; *Huang v. Chan, supra* note 79; *Kelly v. Baker, supra* note 20; *Willott v. Willott Estate, supra* note 156 at paragraphs 35 and 55.

199 *Re Lawther, supra* note 10 at 155–56; *Re Bérubé, supra* note 159, statement made to someone; *Patterson v. Lauritsen, supra* note 15 and *Re Joudrey Estate, supra* note 76; *Redmond v. Redmond Estate, supra* note 79 at paragraph 12, lawyer's notes or recollection of instructions; *Granfield v. Williams, supra* note 116, an unusual case of a deceased's statement to his lawyer of concern for his wife being the basis for the court making an order for the disinherited widow; *Fox v. Fox, supra* note 84 at paragraph 10; *Re Osland, supra* note 89 at 137; *Re Holt, supra* note 79, *Montrose v. Montrose, supra* note 84; *Morris v. Morris, supra* note 79; *Re Grant* (1970), [1971] 1 W.W.R. 555 (B.C. S.C.); *Re Bailey Estate, supra* note 15 at 102; *Montgomery v. Flood, supra* note 50; *Re Davies, supra* note 57 at 105; *Re Cooper, supra* note 48 at 122; *Re Mannion, supra* note 45 at 265; *Valouch v. Valouch, supra* note 157; *Dyer v. Dyer, supra* note 45 at 58; *Re Protopappas Estate, supra* note 165 at paragraphs 23–25; *Zajic v. Chomiak Estate, supra* note 32; *Kuhn v. Kuhn Estate, supra* note 32 at paragraphs 42, 43, 46; *Fedon Estate v. Fedon, supra* note 80; *Zeman v. Zeman Estate, supra* note 78; *Webb v. Webb Estate, supra* note 38; *Currie v. Currie Estate* (1995), 9 E.T.R. (2d) 1 (N.B. C.A.) at paragraph 6, and *Butt v. Chittock Estate, supra* note 104, testimony of family and friends; *Bell v. Roy Estate* (1993), 75 B.C.L.R. (2d) 213 (B.C. C.A.), letter addressed by testatrix to the court; *Gaudet (Litigation Guardian of) v. Young Estate* (1995), 7 E.T.R. (2d) 146 (Ont. Gen. Div.) at paragraph 9, an unsigned note.

200 *Smallwood v. Martins Bank Ltd.*, [1951] Ch. 369 (Eng. Ch. Div.); *Re Barclay, supra* note 107 at 312; *Stadnyk v. Bulycz, supra* note 117 at 250–51 [36 W.W.R. 241]; *Walker v. Rivalin, supra* note 79 at 325, 328–29; *Re Bateman, supra* note 107 at 767; *Re Pelletier, supra* note 49 at paragraph 15; *Moore v. Moore, supra* note 56 at 320–21; *Travagline v. Kendall, supra* note 32 at paragraph 7; *Re Cooper, supra* note 48 at 121–22; *Re Mannion, supra* note 45; *Re Pflanzner, supra* note 14 at 152–53; *Bartel v. Holmes, supra* note 32; *Re Johnson,* (1982), 52 N.S.R. (2d) 508 (N.S. T.D.) at paragraphs 20–23; *Carlson v. Carlson, supra* note 50 at paragraphs 13–14; *Michalyshen v. Michalyshen Estate, supra* note 84 at paragraphs 45–46; *Cook v. Hrychuk Estate, supra* note 68 at paragraph 6; *Black v. Kronberger Estate, supra* note 117; *Cummine v. Cummine Estate, supra* note 99 at paragraph 13; *Moroz v. Moroz Estate, supra* note 188 at paragraph 19. Note also *Niebergall v. Niebergall Estate, supra* note 26 at paragraphs 16–17.

201 *Supra* note 20, at paragraphs 24-35.

Certainly, the court must consider the testator's reasons or motions carefully[202] and objectively;[203] on the latter point in *Bell v. Roy Estate*[204] Justice Goldie, for the Court, said:

> 38 Moreover, it is apparent from subs. [(2) of the B.C. Act, above] that the weight to be given evidence of the testator's reasons is affected by its accuracy and not by morally acceptable or unacceptable content. I do not say the legislature swept away any objectively determined moral duty. I do say, however, that the actual intentions of the testator are to be given an effect which is largely denied by reliance upon the notionally objective reasonable testator.

Similarly, in *Kelly v. Baker*[205] Justice Finch said:

> The law does not require that the reason expressed by the testator in her will or elsewhere, for disinheriting the appellant be justifiable. It is sufficient if there were valid and rational reasons at the time of her death—valid in the sense of being based on fact; rational in the sense that there is a logical connection between the reasons and the act of disinheritance.

If the reasons "are unfounded it is open to [indeed incumbent upon] the [applicant] to discredit them by credible evidence".[206] Of course courts will disregard rebutted, unreasonable, or incredible reasons.[207]

When a lawyer takes instructions for a will, one of the matters to be considered is whether the instructions are vulnerable to a dependants' relief application. If they are, the lawyer should advise the client of the opportu-

---

202 *Swain v. Dennison* (1965), 54 W.W.R. 606 (B.C. C.A.) at 612, affirmed (1966), 58 W.W.R. (S.C.C.); *Brauer v. Hilton* (1979), 15 B.C.L.R. 116 (B.C. C.A.) at 122; *Morris v. Morris, supra* note 79 at 254; *Patterson v. Lauritsen, supra* note 15 at 331; *Griffin v. McCarthy Estate, supra* note 112 at 137.

203 *Nulty v. Nulty Estate, supra* note 32, quoting the trial judge on page 346.

204 *Supra* note 199.

205 *Supra* note 20 at paragraph 58. Also *Pattie v. Standal Estate, supra* note 98 at paragraph 19. Cf. *Valouch v. Valouch, supra* note 157, wherein the court said that the "first function was to ascertain whether the statement is true, that is whether there is any basis in fact for making such a statement and secondly whether the testator's position is a *reasonable* one in all the circumstances" (italics added).

206 *Re Searle*, [1948] 2 All E.R. 426 (Eng. Ch. D.); *Re Grant, supra* note 199 at 557; *Bell v. Roy Estate, supra* note 199 at paragraph 36; *Huang v. Chan, supra* note 79 at paragraph 11.

207 *Re Dickinson, supra* note 78 at 218; *Re Willan Estate, supra* note 10 at 121–22; *Chernoff v. Chernoff, supra* note 24; *Walker v. Rivalin, supra* note 79; *Re Bailey Estate, supra* note 15; *Re Michalson, supra* note 79; *Re Osland, supra* note 89; *Re Holt, supra* note 79; *Koziol v. Zoltenko* (1978), 20 A.R. 89 (Alta. T.D.) at paragraph 4; *Travagline v. Kendall, supra* note 32; *Patterson v. Lauritsen, supra* note 15; *Dalziel v. Bradford, supra* note 79 at 230–31; *Re Joudrey Estate, supra* note 76 at paragraphs 29–32; *Nulty v. Nulty Estate, supra* note 32; *Brammall v. Brammall Estate, supra* note 79 at paragraphs 34–39 and 42; *Redmond v. Redmond Estate, supra* note 79.

nity to state reasons in the will, and if the client persists,[208] of the opportunity to state reasons in the will; this advice should be documented to head off a possible negligence action by a specific gift beneficiary whose gift is subsequently reduced by a successful dependants' relief application.

(j) Intestate and Marital Property Entitlements

Initially, dependants' relief in Saskatchewan and Alberta was limited to widows' relief and the relief was related to intestate entitlement. For Saskatchewan this was provided by the addition in 1910 of ss. 11a and 11g to the *Devolution of Estates Act*:[209]

> **11a.** The widow of a man who dies leaving a will by the terms of which his said widow would in the opinion of the judge before whom the application is made receive less than if he had died intestate leaving a widow and children may apply to the supreme court for relief.
>
> **11g**. On any such application the court may make such allowance to the applicant out of the estate of her husband disposed of by will as shall in the opinion of the judge be equal to what would have gone to such widow under this Act had her deceased husband died intestate leaving a widow and children.

Subsequently, s. 11a was enlarged to include husbands and children and the reference to intestacy was deleted. The enactment of the *Dependants Relief Act* (repealing the *Widows Relief Act*, which had continued the sections inserted into the *Devolution of Estates Act*) made it clear in s. 8(2) that a widow could be awarded no less than her intestate entitlement;[210] this section was repealed in 1990-91.[211]

The *Married Women's Relief Act* of Alberta contained a section[212] which was identical to s. 11a of the Saskatchewan *Devolution of Estates Act*; also by s. 8 the court was empowered to make "such allowance . . . as may be just and equitable in the circumstances". The Supreme Court of Canada in *McBratney v. McBratney*[213] interpreted s. 8 to limit the court's jurisdiction to awarding no more than the widow's intestate entitlement. In 1947 when the *Married Women's Relief Act* was replaced by the *Testators Family Maintenance Act*[214] the category of dependants was enlarged to include husbands and children and the relationship to intestacy was dropped.

208 *Kuhn v. Kuhn Estate*, *supra* note 32 at paragraph 42.
209 By *Devolution of Estates Amendment Act*, S.S. 1910-11, c. 13.
210 R.S.S. 1940, c. 111. There was no such minimum provision for a widower.
211 S.S. 1990-91, c. 15, s. 4.
212 S.A. 1910 (2nd Sess.), c. 18, s. 2.
213 (1919), 59 S.C.R. 550 (S.C.C.).
214 S.A. 1947, c. 12.

Similarly, by s. 11 of the *Dependants' Relief Act* of Ontario, 1929,[215] the value of any order could not exceed that person's intestate entitlement.

Other than dated decisions made pursuant to now repealed original Saskatchewan and Alberta legislation,[216] only in four reported cases has the order been based in part upon the applicant's intestate entitlement: *Mitchell v. Mitchell,*[217] *Michalyshen v. Michalyshen Estate,*[218] *Re Sentner Estate*[219] and *Holland v. Clements Estate.*[220] In *Re Hoskins Estate*[221] Justice Wilson considered the widow's intestate entitlement:

> While I do not regard the law which governs the distribution of an estate in intestacy as a governing factor it is not irrelevant, I think, to say that on an intestacy the wife would have taken the entire estate.[222]

However, that was not what he awarded her.

Although I agree that an applicant's intestate entitlement is relevant, but not governing, the prevailing view is probably that expressed by Justice Egbert in *Re Willan Estate*:[223]

> In *Barker v. Westminster Trust Co.* [1941] 3 WWR 473, 614, 57 BCR 21 (reversing [1940] 3 WWR 239) the British Columbia Court of Appeal allowed the petitioning husband the whole of the deceased wife's estate. The judgment is interesting because of the remarks of O'Halloran, J.A. as to the measure of relief to be granted when the testator has failed to make adequate provision.

---

215 S.O. 1929, c. 47.

216 *Re Baker* (1919), 13 Sask. L.R. 109 (Sask. C.A.); *Re Clark,* [1922] 2 W.W.R. 691 (Alta. C.A.); *Re Bursaw Estate* (1924), 19 Sask. L.R. 137 (Sask. C.A.), set aside (1925), [1931] 3 W.W.R. App. II (S.C.C.); *Williams v. Moody Bible Institute of Chicago, supra* note 39; *Re Wilson, supra* note 38; *Re Emele Estate, supra* note 41; *Plumb v. Royal Trust Co., supra* note 37; *Re Pemberton, supra* note 19; *Re Daneliuk* (1951), 2 W.W.R. (N.S.) 45 (Sask. C.A.); *Re Carnduff, supra* note 84; *Re Maxwell* (1961), 38 W.W.R. 23 (Sask. Q.B.); *Re Bateman, supra* note 107; *Re Gilbert, supra* note 68; *Manson v. Shoaf, supra* note 26; *Jeffers v. Jeffers, supra* 165.

217 *Supra* note 79 at 460 and 463.

218 *Supra* note 84.

219 (1985), 54 Nfld. & P.E.I.R. 181 (P.E.I. S.C.) at paragraph 45, reversed (but not on this point) (1986), 63 Nfld. & P.E.I.R. 151 (P.E.I. C.A.).

220 *Supra* note 107 at paragraphs 40-41. Also, at least O'Halloran J.A. in *Barker v. Westminster Trust Co., supra* note 57.

221 (1961), 35 W.W.R. 430 (B.C.S.C.) at 431.

222 Similarly, *Re Hull,* [1943] O.R. 778 (Ont. C.A.) at 785; *Raymond v. Public Trustee,* [1985] N.W.T.R. 304 (N.W.T. S.C.) at 306; and *MacDonald v. MacKenzie Estate* (1989), 78 Nfld. & P.E.I.R. 76 (P.E.I. T.D.) at paragraph 37.

223 *Supra* note 10 at 131–32; also *Cranston v. Cranston, supra* note 57 at 324–26; *Re Anderson, supra* note 25 at 438; *Re Mannion, supra* note 45 at 271; *Re Dentinger, supra* note 11 at 30; *Bates v. Bates* (1982), 11 E.T.R. 310 (B.C. C.A.); *Re deBeaudrap, supra* note 49 at paragraph 39; *Daniel v. Daniel Estate, supra* note 84 at paragraphs 25–26; *Hecht v. Hecht Estate, supra* note 49 at paragraphs 92–97 [42 E.T.R. 295]; *Pedersen v. Pedersen, supra* note 49 at paragraph 27.

He holds that the allowance to be made should be measured by the portion of the estate the applicant would have received had the testator died intestate:

> "However, there is a standard for the guidance of the Judge. It is the standard set up by law for the distribution of intestate estates. . . . the policy of the law of this province as to what constitutes 'proper maintenance' is reflected in the statutory provision applicable to intestate estates. . . . the intestacy provisions of the *Administration Act* provide a convenient and recognized standard for determining whether adequate provision has been made for the husband. . . . It is the norm by which the actions of the testatrix may be judged."

With all respect, I think there is nothing in the statute of British Columbia which justifies such an interpretation being placed upon it but, if there is, I must still express my emphatic dissent from these views if it is sought to apply them to the Alberta Act. There is nothing, in my opinion, in the language of the Alberta Act which would justify a rule that when the applicant is entitled to relief she shall be entitled to such share of the estate as she would have received in the case of intestacy, nor indeed to any fixed share of the estate. The discretion of the court is unfettered and the court may, "in its discretion," order that "such provisions as it deems adequate," be made for the "proper maintenance and support of the dependants." However, so far as I can ascertain, these views of O'Halloran, J.A. have not been followed by the courts of British Columbia and, indeed, in *In re McPhee Estate* [1947] 1 WWR 741, Macfarlane, J. expressly stated that the Act does not say that the estate should be divided as if there were an intestacy. "I think what the Act intended to provide was just what it says—"adequate provision for her proper maintenance and support." In Saskatchewan the Act contains statutory provisions for the granting of not less than the widow would have received had her husband died intestate, so that the Saskatchewan decisions on this point are of no value when considering the Alberta Act.

In *Bates v. Bates*[224] the British Columbia Court of Appeal, without reference to the view expressed by Justice Egbert in *Re Willan*, expressed a similar view. Justice Seaton for the court also dealt with the relevance of marital property legislation:

> There is another case cited to us in the same argument upon which I would like to comment: *Richards v. Person*, . . . [1982] 2 W.W.R. 668, (S.C.). In that case, which was under the Wills Variation Act, the learned trial Judge referred to the Family Relations Act, . . . and said at p. 671:
>
> > "Counsel for the daughter and her sons says it would be improper for a court to have regard to the statutory policy governing distribution of matrimonial assets inter vivos, as laid down by the Family Relations Act, in considering what would be a just and equitable distribution on death.

---

224 *Supra* note 223 at 314.

> Counsel argues that the court ought not to look for help to other statutes which do not directly deal with the question in issue in determining the contemporary attitude or 'commonsense of the community'.
>
> It seems to me that where, as here, the court is vested with broad discretion, and required to do that which appears just, it ought always to seek guidance by reference to contemporary custom, and particularly to those rules which the community has adopted as part of the statute law. Where the community has declared that spouses should, prima facie, share certain assets equally on a divorce or voluntary separation, that is something which a court can hardly ignore in deciding what allocation of such assets would be 'adequate, just and equitable' upon death."

To that I say that what a spouse's duty is during that spouse's lifetime may be quite different than the duty upon death. The Family Relations Act is there to divide assets between two living persons both of whom will need to be supported in the future and will need capital in the future. That is not the situation under the Wills Variation Act and I see no guidance that can be obtained from the Family Relations Act when considering the position of the parties under the Wills Variation Act.[225]

Justice Seaton's comment is relevant to not only British Columbia, but also Prince Edward Island and the two territories which, like British Columbia, do not have matrimonial property legislation applicable to dissolution of marriage by death. On the other hand, it is noteworthy that, contrary to Justice Seaton's view, all of the other provinces have made their matrimonial property legislation applicable to dissolution of a marriage by death, essentially on the same basis as it is to an *inter vivos* breakdown or dissolution of a marriage. The Alberta Act, s. 4, also makes relevant "[t]he benefits to which a spouse is entitled under The Dower Act. . .".

Only in Ontario is the limitation period for an accounting and equalization application shorter than the dependants' relief application limitation period.[226] However, there is a generous extension provision,[227] making it likely that an accounting and equalization application could be made at the same time as a dependants' relief application. The legislation of Alberta and Saskatchewan does not provide for the extension of the accounting and equalization application limitation period. Thus, it is possible in these two provinces for there to be the situation of a dependants' relief application coming before a court with the spouse being unable to apply for an accounting and equalization of matrimonial property. Nonetheless, in con-

---

225 *Ibid.*; also *Moore v. Moore*, *supra* note 56 at 321 and *Re Mannion* (1984), 45 O.R. (2d) 339 (Ont. C.A.) at 342–43, decided at a time when the *Family Law Act* of Ontario did not provide for an equal division of family property upon death.

226 *Family Law Act*, R.S.O. 1990, c. F-3, s. 7(3)(c), six months from death compared to six months from the grant of probate or administration for a dependants' relief application.

227 *Ibid.*, s. 2(8).

sidering the spouse's actual or deemed application, surely a court would consider relevant what was the spouse's matrimonial property entitlement.

(k) Maintenance Payments

In *Hoeppner (Litigation Guardian of) v. Misiewicz Estate*[228] the deceased left his estate to his wife and their two children. An application was made on behalf of another infant child of the deceased, for whom the deceased had been paying court ordered maintenance which ceased on his death. The court approved a settlement which continued the maintenance until the child reached the age of 19. The Public Trustee opposed the settlement; he argued that by treating the application like a claim for loss of financial support under the *Fatal Accidents Act* the settlement should have been for a larger amount. The court agreed with counsel proposing the settlement that a dependants' relief application differs from a *Fatal Accidents Act* claim because with the former the court must consider the interests of other dependants of the deceased within the context of the deceased's estate.

In *Moores v. Hughes*,[229] with reference to current Ontario Act, s. 62(1)(m), the court considered, *inter alia*, a maintenance settlement, adjusted for inflation, in determining the quantum of the relief order.

(l) Will the Applicant Benefit from an Order?

In at least three cases,[230] the courts have dismissed an application because it was not proved that the applicant would benefit from an order. In two of the cases the applicants lived behind the Iron Curtain. In *Zajac v. Zwarycz*[231] Justice Alyesworth for the Court said:

> . . . all that was disclosed was that the appellant lived in Soviet Russia, was the widow of the deceased, occupied a house upon a collective farm and worked upon that farm. Among the things that the learned trial Judge was required to consider in the case were under s. 7 (*b*) of the Act, the circumstances of the person on whose behalf the application is made and under s. 7 (*g*) generally any matter that the Judge deems should be fairly taken into account in deciding upon the application. We think there were in proof insufficient circumstances of the person on whose behalf the application was

228 *Supra* note 68.

229 *Supra* note 102 at 792; note also *McMacken v. McMacken, supra* note 102 at 704; *Dyer v. Dyer, supra* note 45 at 59.

230 Note also Chp. 4, 2(d)(ii) at note 155, *supra*.

231 [1965] 1 O.R. 575 (Ont. C.A.) at 576–77; similarly *Hayzel v. Alberta (Public Trustee)* (1963), 44 W.W.R. 582 (Alta. T.D.) at 587. Cf. *Re Parkanski, supra* note 79; *Re Soroka, supra* note 30.

made, to enable the Judge properly to decide that an order under the Act was warranted. Furthermore, we think it is inherent in the Act itself when one considers the objects of the Act as disclosed by the provisions thereof, that the Judge hearing the application should be satisfied upon the material before him that if an order is made in favour of the defendant, substantial benefits will accrue to that dependant. We are reinforced in that view of the Act by the provisions of cl. (*g*) of s. 7 already referred to. In applications under the Act emanating from sources such as the source from which this application originates, we think it is incumbent upon the trial Judge to see that the circumstances of the person on whose behalf the application is made, are proven with sufficient particularity and fullness to enable him to determine whether or not an order under the Act will serve the purpose which the Act envisions, namely as I have said, that substantial benefit will accrue under the order to the recipient. This we think is particularly so where the only material before the Court on behalf of the applicant is documentary evidence and where little or no opportunity is available for cross-examination.

In *Re Smigelski*[232] the major assets of the estate were two quarter sections of farmland valued at $28,500.00, one of which was the home quarter in which the widow applicant had a dower interest. The deceased died intestate; the heirs were the widow and children. The widow who was living on her old age pension and welfare applied. Justice Johnson commented:

The application . . . asks that the balance of the estate, which is the lands, be made available to provide maintenance and support for the widow. If the matter had stopped there the courts would have had little difficulty in granting the application and making the order. In an estate of this size, it is obvious that the whole estate will likely be needed to provide adequate maintenance and support. However, in the affidavit filed in support of her application, as well as in her evidence given at the hearing, it was made quite clear that the respondent wanted these lands transferred to herself so she could transfer them over to her son. The application would appear to be in furtherance of a plan that had been put in motion earlier. A draft of an agreement between the widow and the four children prepared in June, 1966, provides for a transfer of all the land to [the son] . . . .

The learned judge who heard the application granted the order asked for and directed that the lands be conveyed to the respondent. . . .

In his judgment the learned judge said: "Whatever she does with her property which she is entitled to I think is her own affair."

It is, of course, clear that *The Family Relief Act* cannot be used to rearrange the succession to an estate, or to prefer one beneficiary over another. If an applicant under this Act asks for more than he is to receive out of the estate,

---

232 (1968), 64 W.W.R. 456 (Alta. C.A.) at 458–460.

and it is brought to the attention of the judge that the property sought, if received, will be immediately transferred away to someone else, the judge hearing the application should see to it that the applicant gets at least equivalent value and is not worse off after the order is made than he was before. . . .

What was the position before the order was made? The widow owned a one-third interest in all the lands and had a life estate in one quarter. . . . If she carries out her intention, the widow will have disposed of all these interests in the property and will have only such rights as may be given to her by her son.

What is it she will get in return? If the documents that I have mentioned had been signed by all the beneficiaries of the estate and had been carried into effect, she would have received only the rights given to her by the following clause in the agreement:

> "2. It is agreed that the said Mary Smigelski shall be entitled to live upon the said land, except the twenty (20) acre portion hereinafter referred to, for her lifetime and shall be entitled to file a Caveat or other encumbrance against the title to the said lands to protect her interest thereunder."

The son . . . was called as a witness by the learned judge and he stated that he proposed to place a mortgage on the property sufficient to raise enough money to build two houses on the land—one for his mother and one for himself—and with the balance of the money go into the stock-raising business. There is no evidence as to whether a mortgage of this size could be obtained. [The son] certainly, has no experience in stock raising. In all the years that he and his mother worked the farm, the profits from this operation were never sufficient to provide more than a bare living. It is difficult to see how these lands will suddenly produce enough to pay off the proposed mortgage and at the same time provide a living for anyone.

Even the right to continue to live on the lands given by the proposed agreement is one which cannot be adequately protected. Those who have had experience in trying to enforce such a right, even when it is protected by "a caveat or other encumbrance," will readily agree that such a security is of little value. In any case, no mortgage company would lend on a title having such an encumbrance upon it. If it is to appear on the title it will have to be postponed to any mortgage that might be obtained.

At the close of argument, we intimated that we would, if the respondent would agree, make an order for the sale of the lands and direct that the proceeds be used to provide an income for the widow which would be adequate for her needs. Her consent to such an order would have to be made because of her dower interest in one of the quarters. We invited counsel for the respondent to consult with his client and suggest a method of securing this income and we adjourned the hearing to a later court. When the case was again spoken to, her counsel advised us that the respondent did not want the land sold and that she wished to live on the land. Another agreement similar to the one mentioned earlier was submitted to the court. This was somewhat more favourable to the respondent than the earlier one but the court considered that it did not provide for "the proper maintenanceand support" of the respondent.

In allowing the appeal and annulling the order appealed from, we intimated that we would allow the application to stand, to be again considered when a new proposal was brought forward.

3. DATE(S) OF ASSESSMENT

As discussed earlier,[233] there are potentially two basic determinations for a court to make on a dependants' relief application: (i) did the deceased make adequate or reasonable provision for the proper support or maintenance (and support) of the eligible dependant(s) and (ii) if not, what provision will be reasonable or adequate (, just, and equitable) for the proper support or maintenance of the dependant(s)? What is the date or what are the dates as of when the court is to assess the circumstances in making these determinations? In *Re Hull* [234] the court indicated that the date for the first determination in the case of a deceased who dies testate is the date of the making of the will and the date for the second determination is the date of death. Justice Egbert in *Re Willan Estate*[235] rejected *Re Hull,* choosing the date of "the application", meaning the date of the hearing, presumably for both determinations; for support, he referred to several decisions including *Re Jones*.[236]

Justice Rae in *Re Novikoff Estate*[237] chose the date of death for both determinations, allowing that the circumstances to be taken in account include those which the deceased could reasonably have foreseen at the date of death.[238] In choosing the date of the deceased's death, Justice Rae

---

233 At pages 6, 97 of this text.

234 *Supra* note 222 at 785; however, note s. 58(4) of the current Ontario Act and *Re Davies, supra* note 57 at 106.

235 *Supra* note 10 at 130.

236 [1934] 3 W.W.R. 726 (B.C. S.C.).

237 *Supra* note 137.

238 Two earlier decisions were decided using the date of death: *Re Hornett, supra* note 80 at 291, citing *Dun v. Dun*, [1959] A.C. 272 (Australia P.C.) and thus presumably including circumstances reasonably foreseeable, and *Re Brown, supra* note 64. Note also *Re Cole, supra* note 19 at 416. In *Novikoff*, using the date of death plus reasonable foreseeability the court refused to take into account a post-death increase in real estate values; also *Morris v. Morris, supra* note 79 at 254–56. Cf. *Koziol v. Zoltenko, supra* note 157.

considered *Calladine v. Farrar*,[239] in which the court chose the date of the commencement of the relief proceeding, *Re Jones*, above, and *Re Urquhart*,[240] in which the courts used the date of the hearing, in all three cases for both determinations. Chief Justice Wilson who decided *Calladine v. Farrar* and *Re Urquhart* changed his mind for a third time in *Re Bowe*[241] when he chose to base his decision upon the "circumstances . . . existing and reasonably foreseeable at the date of . . . death". Most of the subsequent cases have used the date of death.[242] Other cases which have used the date of the hearing include: *Shaw v. Regina (City)*,[243] *Re Martin*,[244] *Malychuk v.*

239 (1958), 25 W.W.R. 175 (B.C. S.C.).

240 *Supra* note 101, although the judge preferred the date of death.

241 *Supra* note 44 at 445.

242 *Re Bailey Estate, supra* note 15 at 101; *Mitchell v. Mitchell, supra* note 79 at 460; *Spinney v. Royal Trust Co., supra* note 106 at paragraph 30; *Re Lukie,* [1976] 6 W.W.R. 395 (B.C. C.A.); *Maldaver v. Canada Permanent Trust Co.* (1982), 53 N.S.R. (2d) 500 (N.S. T.D.) (cf. *Maldaver v. Canada Permanent Trust Co.* (1977), 27 N.S.R. (2d) 248 (N.S. T.D.)); *Morris v. Morris, supra* note 79; *Re deBeaudrap, supra* note 49 at paragraphs 36, 45; *Lynds v. Lynds, supra* note 137 at paragraph 19; *Re Protopappas Estate, supra* note 165 at paragraphs 49–52; *Purser v. Purser Estate, supra* note 112 at 305; *Bell v. Roy Estate,* [1989] B.C.W.L.D. 1938 (B.C. S.C.), affirmed [1993] B.C.W.L.D. 619 (B.C. C.A.); *Walker v. Dubord* (1991), 41 E.T.R. 307 (B.C. S.C.) at 319, affirmed (1992), 45 E.T.R. 209 (B.C. C.A.); *Hecht v. Hecht Estate, supra* note 49 at paragraphs 23–26; *Pedersen v. Pedersen, supra* note 49 at paragraphs 24–26; *Wagner v. Wagner Estate, supra* note 117 at 11; *Lindsay v. Jones, supra* note 79 at paragraph 9; *Landy v. Landy Estate, supra* note 137 at 287–92; *Moore v. Moore Estate, supra* note 80 at paragraph 15; *Huang v. Chan, supra* note 79 at paragraph 15; *Willott v. Willott Estate, supra* note 156 at paragraph 54, "or perhaps more precisely at the time she last had testamentary capacity"; *McRae v. Royal Trust Corp. of Canada, supra* note 79 at paragraphs 28–33. Note the following commentaries: Bale, G. "Limitation on Testamentary Dispositions in Canada (1964) 42 C.B.R. 367 at 367-379; Litman, M., "Maladaver v. Canada Permanent Trust Co., Relevant Date for Determining Adequacy of Provision Made by Testator for Purposes of Dependants Relief Legislation" (1977-78) 1 E.T.R. 41; and Bale, G., "Maladaver v. Canada Permanent Trust Co., Power to Vary Orders Under Testator's Family Maintenance Legislation and the Relevant Date to Determine Adequacy on an Initial Application" (1982-83) 12 E.T.R. 231 at 234. In stating the date of assessment to be the date of death a few of these cases expressly include reasonably foreseeable circumstances; by reference to cases such as *Dun, Novikoff*, and *Bowe*, it may be surmised that some of the other cases, although expressing the point simply in terms of the date of death, mean to include reasonably foreseeable circumstances.

243 *Supra* note 44 at 445.

244 (1962), 40 W.W.R. 513 (Man. C.A.).

Malychuk,[245] *Maldaver v. Canada Permanent Trust Co.*,[246] *Re Stafford*,[247] and *Griffin v. McCarthy Estate*.[248]

The Manitoba Act stipulates the date of the hearing for the determination of what will be a reasonable provision for maintenance and support,[249] the second question; the first question under the Manitoba Act is "financial need", presumably also to be determined as of the date of the hearing. The Ontario Act in s. 58(4) stipulates the date of the hearing for the determination of the "adequacy of provision for support under subsection (1)", which presumably means both questions posed in subsection (1); the Act codifies *Re Brill*.[250]

Insofar as it is a purpose of dependants' relief legislation to enforce a moral obligation of spouses and parents to give a fair share of their estates to the surviving spouse and child or children, the most logical date for determining the deceased's performance is the date of the deceased's death, the last date upon which the deceased could have assessed his or her moral obligation. But, it is also a purpose of dependants' relief legislation to take care of financial need; in this regard the most logical date for assessing the circumstances is the date of the hearing of the application.[251] Furthermore, in all of the Acts there is a section giving the court the power to vary an order on the basis of subsequent circumstances.[252] Since courts can look at subsesquent circumstances to vary an order, it seems only logical that they should look at the circumstances extant at the time of the hearing in making an initial order.

Justice Bouck in *Griffin v. McCarthy Estate* said:

> However, it does not seem to matter what date a court selects, since I may examine all matters in the past and the future to determine entitlement under the statute.[253]

This view is too optimistic. The date selected does matter. Even if the assessment as of the date of death is to include matters reasonably foreseeable, such foresight could not have foreseen the subsequent paralyzing

---

245 *Supra* note 78 at 245.

246 (1977), 27 N.S.R. (2d) 248 (N.S. T.D.) c.f. *Maladaver v. Canada Permanent Trust Co.* (1982), 53 N.S.R. (2d) 500 (N.S. T.D.).

247 *Supra* note 79.

248 *Supra* note 112.

249 Man, s. 2(3) codifying *Re Martin*, *supra* note 244.

250 [1967] 2 O.R. 586 (Ont. Surr. Ct.) at 591 and supercedes *Re Hull*, *supra* note 222. Note Oosterhoff, A., *Succession Law Reform in Ontario* (Toronto: Carswell, 1979) at 97-98.

251 Note Bale, G., "Limitation on Testamentary Dispositions in Canada" (1964) 42 C.B.R. 367 at 376-78.

252 B.C., s. 13; Alta., s. 6(b); Sask., s. 20(1); Man., ss. 14 and 15; Ont., s. 65; N.B., s. 6; N.S., s. 7; PEI, s. 7; Nfld., s. 7; NWT, s. 6; YT, s. 7.

253 *Supra* note 112 at 137.

polio of one of the applicants in *Re Urquhart*[254] and it did not include the subsequent health problems of the petitioners in *Re Bowe*[255] and *Re Bailey Estate*.[256]

4. DRAWING A NEW WILL: TESTAMENTARY AUTONOMY

Courts frequently remind themselves and the litigants that the function of the court is not to make a (new) will for the deceased and that if the court must make a relief order it must make the order which will least disrupt what otherwise will be the succession to the deceased's estate,[257] even if inexplicably the estate has been left largely to strangers.[258] Recently in dealing with the British Columbia Act, the Supreme Court of Canada said that after adequate, just and equitable provision for the deceased's dependants, testamentary autonomy is the other interest protected by the Act:

> The other interest protected by the Act is testamentary autonomy. The Act did not remove the right of the legal owner of property to dispose of it upon death. Rather, it limited that right. The absolute testamentary autonomy of the 19th century was required to yield to the interests of spouses and children to the extent, and only to the extent, that this was necessary to provide the latter with what was "adequate, just and equitable in the circumstances." And if that testamentary autonomy must yield to what is "adequate, just and equitable", then the ultimate question is, what is "adequate, just and equitable" in the circumstances judged by contemporary standards. Once that is established, it

---

254 *Supra* note 101.

255 *Supra* note 137.

256 *Supra* note 15.

257 For instance, *Re Morton Estate, supra* note 10 at 176; *Re Fergie* (1939), 54 B.C.R. 431 (B.C. S.C.) at 433; *Shaw v. Regina (City)* (1944), [1945] S.C.R. 42 (S.C.C.) at 51; *Re McPhee*, [1947] 1 W.W.R. 741 (B.C. S.C.) at 744; *Stadnyk v. Bulycz, supra* note 117 at 248; *McCarvill v. Jones, supra* note 84 at 280; *Swain v. Dennison, supra* note 202 at 612; *Re Smigelski, supra* note 232 at 458; *Re Brown, supra* note 64 at 547; *Simmonds v. Rehn, supra* note 32 at 568; *Re Parker, supra* note 79 at paragraph 11; *Mitchell v. Mitchell, supra* note 79 at 460; *Barr v. Barr, supra* note 74 at 410 ; *Re Pelletier* (1973), 8 N.B.R. (2d) 188 at paragraph 14; *Moore v. Moore, supra* note 56 at 322; *Sing v. Sing, supra* note 157 at paragraph 19; *Adams v. Perks, supra* note 32 at paragraph 3; *Montgomery v. Flood, supra* note 50 at 26; *Montrose v. Montrose, supra* note 84 at paragraph 45; *Bates v. Bates, supra* note 139 at 244; *Morris v. Morris, supra* note 79 at 254; *Cox v. Nova Scotia (Public Trustee), supra* note 79 at paragraph 14; *Re Pflanzner, supra* note 14 at 152; *Cross v. Currie Estate, supra* note 80 at paragraph 21; *Braidwood v. Maxwell, supra* note 79 at 27; *Griffin v. McCarthy Estate, supra* note 112 at 137; *Zajic v. Chomiak Estate, supra* note 32 at paragraphs 18, 75; *Hutton v. Lapka Estate* (1991), 62 B.C.L.R. (2d) 371 (B.C. C.A.) at paragraph 35, leave to appeal refused (1992), 68 B.C.L.R. (2d) xxxi (S.C.C.).

258 *Re Kirk, supra* note 106 at 752.

> cannot be cut down on the ground that the testator did not want to provide what is "adequate, just and equitable".
>
> I add this. In many cases, there will be a number of ways of dividing the assets which are adequate. . . . In other words, there will be a wide range of options, any of which might be considered appropriate in the circumstances. Provided that the testator has chosen an option within this range, the will should not be disturbed. Only where the testator has chosen an option which falls below his or her obligations as defined by reference to legal and moral norms, should the court make an order which achieves the justice the testator failed to achieve. In the absence of other evidence a will should be seen as reflecting the means chosen by the testator to meet his legitimate concerns and provide for an ordered administration and distribution of his estate in the best interests of the persons and institutions closest to him. It is the exercise by the testator of his freedom to dispose of his property and is to be interfered with not lightly but only in so far as the statute requires.[259]

The origin of this judicial sentiment is a statement by Chief Justice Stout in *Allardice v. Allardice*:[260]

> The question what principles the Court should follow is raised in this appeal . . . In my opinion these rules may be summarized as follows: . . . 2 that the Act is not a statute to empower the Court to make a new will for the testator; 3 that the Act allows the court to alter a testator's disposition of his property only in so far as it is necessary to provide for proper maintenance and support . . .

However, as Justice Egbert commented in *Re Willan Estate*:[261]

> May I . . . say that, with the greatest respect, I think it unfortunate that Stout, C.J. made the statement that "the Act is not a statute to empower the Court to make a new will for the testator." As appears by the words in his judgment which immediately follow this statement, it is clear that he intended to modify this statement by saying "except in so far as this may be necessary for the purpose of providing for the proper maintenance and support of a dependant," and that it was with this modification that his statement was approved by the Privy Council. Unfortunately, in some later cases the statement is made baldly without any modification, as if it were one of those immutable legal maxims with which Dr. Broom so lovingly deals, and, put in this bald and unqualified manner, the statement, in my opinion, amounts not only to a closing of the

259 *Tataryn v. Tataryn Estate*, *supra* note 82 at 815–16. Since *Tataryn* this statement has been considered in *Vielbig v. Waterland Estate*, *supra* note 80 at paragraphs 28–39, *Mann v. Mann Estate*, *supra* note 79 at paragraph 14 *et seq.*, in which the court distinguished *Vielbig* in a proceeding to vary a will to give effect to the dispository scheme; *Chernecki v. Vangolen*, *supra* note 80 at paragraphs 18–19; *Crerar v. Crerar Estate*, *supra* note 157 at paragraph 42 *et seq.*

260 *Supra* note 1 at 969 also Cooper J. at 975.

261 *Supra* note 10 at 126.

> court's eyes to the realities of the situation, but also to the enunciation of a principle which is palpably untrue. The Act *does* confer power upon a court to make a new will for the testator and every time a court grants an application made under this Act it does in fact make a new will for the testator. It is true that the power should be exercised sparingly, and for the purpose, and the purpose only, designated by the Act. As Rand, J. in his dissenting judgment in *Shaw v. Sasktoon* [1945] SCR 42 (affirming *Shaw v. Regina and Saskatoon and Toronto Gen. Trusts Corpn.* [No. 3] [1944] 1 WWR 433) says:
>
> > "It should be remarked that relief legislation of the nature of that in question, which in recent years has appeared in various parts of the world, is not intended to convert courts into will-making or will-destroying bodies. The principle that the distribution of property at death shall lie not only in the right but also in the discretion and judgment of the owner is trenched upon only within well-defined limits."
>
> However, with the greatest respect, it seems to me futile to deny that the Act does confer upon the court the very power which it, in fact, actually confers. Accordingly, in my opinion, the rule enunciated by Stout, C.J., and affirmed by the Privy Council, should never be stated without the inclusion of the qualification, which I am sure that both Stout, C.J., and the Privy Council intended should be included.

Similarly, Justice Barry said in *Davidson v. Allen*:[262]

> . . . While I have no right to remake a will, nevertheless sometimes I get the impression that that is what the Court does.[263]

Believe Justices Egbert and Barry. The simple statement that the court does not have the jurisdiction to make a new will is not helpful. As Justice Bull pointed out in *Swain v. Dennison*,[264] a testator's intentions are entitled to careful consideration; but courts must and do draw new wills for testators to do justice pursuant to dependants' relief legislation. But, doing justice does not mean necessarily equal treatment of capacitated adult children, among whom a testator has shown preferences.[265]

In *McSween v. McSween Estate*[266] Judge Carnwath observed:

> On the question of manner of payment, I should make reference to a concept found in many of the reported cases. The concept, simply put, is that when the Court has decided to exercise its discretion and make an order for support, the Court should endeavour to observe the original scheme of the will, that is to

---

262 *Supra* note 106 at paragraph 8

263 Also Carrothers J.A. in *Re Lukie, supra* note 242 at 428.

264 *Supra* note 202 at 612.

265 *Re Dawson, supra* note 80 at 485; *Brammall v. Brammall Estate, supra* note 79 at paragraphs 40–41; *Plut v. Plut Estate, supra* note 79 at paragraph 13; *Chernecki v. Vangolen, supra* note 80 at paragraph 21.

266 *Supra* note 45 at 204.

say, the testator's intention as to the manner in which his estate should be distributed. I am in complete agreement with this principle so long as it works no economic disadvantage either to the residuary beneficiaries of the estate or the dependants in whose favour an order is made. Once again, I refer to the fact that the adequacy of provision for support shall be determined as of the date of the hearing of the application. There are too many examples in our legislative history of the drastic changes possible in tax planning to blindly follow the scheme of the testator in a will that may have been written several years prior to the application. What may have seemed the best plan of attack at that time may at the time of the application invite the imposition of an unforeseen tax liability. Should that situation arise, I would not feel constrained to compound the difficulty by framing an order in such a way as to follow the intentions of the testator, and in the same breath, increase the tax burden of the estate. I would endeavour with the assistance of counsel to frame the order in such a way as to attract the minimum imposition of tax.

5. ASSETS AVAILABLE FOR A RELIEF ORDER

(a) Generally

All of the Acts provide in the primary jurisdiction section for a relief order to be made "out of the estate". So, what comprises the estate? Only the Saskatchewan Act defines estate:

> **2.** (1) "estate" means all the property of which a deceased had power to dispose by will, otherwise than by virtue of a special power of appointment, less the amount of the deceased's funeral, testamentary and administration expenses and debts and liabilities that are payable out of his estate on his or her death;

Similarly, in connection with a section contained in several of the Acts, which provides that the "incidence of any [order] . . . shall . . . fall rateably upon the whole estate . . .", Justice Gushere said in *Downton v. Royal Trust Co.*:[267]

> 3 Noel, J. [the trial judge], found that:
>
> > The defendants' submission that "the whole estate" means the value of all assets at the time of death, is not acceptable. Clearly, "the whole estate", which is subject to an award under the *Family Relief Act*, does

---

267 (1980), 34 Nfld. & P.E.I.R. 308 (Nfld. C.A.) at 309; also *Flannigan v. Ontario (Registrar of Motor Vehicles)*, [1950] O.W.N. 789 (Ont. Master) at 790; *Kuhn v. Kuhn Estate*, *supra* note 32 at paragraph 21. Note the curious case of *Re Carnduff*, *supra* note 84 at 164, in which the assets of the deceased's estate included the assets of his first wife's estate, which at his death were in his name as the administrator of her estate; their children had relinquished and assigned to him their interests in the assets.

> not include the value of liabilities or the award. It can only mean the whole estate which is distributable to beneficiaries.
>
> We are in complete agreement with the learned judge on this point. The "whole estate" must mean the net estate available for distribution to beneficiaries, and, in our view, to interpret the phrase in any other way would lead to a totally illogical, and often inequitable, result. "The whole estate of the deceased", from which an award under s. 10 of the *Family Relief Act* is to be deducted, can only mean the value of a deceased's estate after deduction of the liabilities of the estate, including expenses properly incurred in its winding-up.

Liabilities of the estate will include a matrimonial property equalization order[268] and a continuing maintenance order.[269] In *Royal Trust Co. v. Downton* the deceased had two insurance policies on his life designating his second wife as beneficiary. With the consent of his second wife the deceased assigned the policies to a bank to secure indebtedness. The insurer paid some of the proceeds to the bank. The second wife claimed reimbursement from the estate as a creditor ahead of the relief order made in favour of the deceased's first wife. The court disagreed.[270]

Generally, life insurance[271] and pension proceeds[272] payable to a designated beneficiary, joint tenancy assets,[273] and whatever assets it takes to satisfy a marital property equalization payment[274] are not comprised within the estate. Similarly, aside from statutory stipulation to the contrary, assets

268 *Matrimonial Property Act*, C.S.A. 1999, c. M-9, s. 15(c); *Matrimonial Property Act*, C.S.S. 1998, c. M-6.11, s. 35(c); *Marital Property Act*, R.S.M. 1987, c. M45, s. 41(c); *Family Law Act*, R.S.O. 1990, c. F-3, s. 6(12)(c); *Marital Property Act*, C.S.N.B. 1997, c. M-1.1, s. 4(6); *Matrimonial Property Act*, R.S.N.S. 1989, c. 275, s. 12(4); *Family Law Act*, R.S.N. 1990, c. F-2, s. 21(2).

269 *Family Maintenance Act*, C.S.S. 1998; c. F-6.2, s. 9(1)(a); *Family Maintenance Act*, R.S.M. 1987, c. F20, s. 10(1)(h); *Family Law Act*, R.S.O. 1990, c. F-3, s. 34(4); *Family Services Act*, C.S.N.B. 1998, c. F-2.2, s. 116(1)(a) and (6); *Family Law Act*, S.P.E.I. 1995, c. 12, s. 34(3); *Family Law Act*, R.S.N. 1990, c. F-2, s. 40(5); *Family Property and Support Act*, R.S.Y.T. 1986, c. 63, s. 36(4).

270 (1977), 19 Nfld. & P.E.I.R. 455 (Nfld. T.D.), affirmed (1980), 34 Nfld. & P.E.I.R. 308 (Nfld. C.A.).

271 *Re Matheson* (1916), 9 W.W.R. 996 (Alta. S.C. [In Chambers]); *Dalton v. Macdonald* (1938), 52 B.C.R. 473 (B.C. C.A.); *Flannigan v. Ontario (Registrar of Motor Vehicles), supra* note 267; *Kerslake v. Gray*, [1957] S.C.R. 516 (S.C.C.); *Re Gilbert, supra* note 68; *Farrar v. Scammell, supra* note 85; *Harry v. Harry Estate, supra* note 22; *King v. King* (1990), 68 Man. R. (2d) 253 (Man. Q.B.).

272 *Flannigan v. Ontario (Registrar of Motor Vehicles), supra* note 267; *Berezowsky v. Berezowsky* (1975), 23 R.F.L. 26 (Sask. Q.B.); *Re Luther Estate* (1990), 89 Sask. R. 262 (Sask. C.A.).

273 *Re Maxwell, supra* note 216; *Albert v. Albert, supra* note 84.

274 *Baker v. Baker Estate, supra* note 56 at paragraph 80. Also note Chp. 3, 2(i), above.

given *inter vivos* are beyond the reach of a relief order.[275] And, if the estate is insolvent, there is no estate.[276]

Ontario, Prince Edward Island, Northwest Territories and Yukon Acts have included sections which serve two purposes, namely obviating avoidance of the Act and increasing the assets available for the fulfilment of a relief order.

Ontario[277]

> **72.** (1) Subject to section 71, for the purpose of this Part, the capital value of the following transactions effected by a deceased before his or her death, whether benefitting his or her dependant or any other person, shall be included as testamentary dispositions as of the date of the death of the deceased and shall be deemed to be part of his or her net estate for purposes of ascertaining the value of his or her estate, and being available to be charged for payment by an order under clause 63(2)(f),
>
> (a) gifts *mortis causa*;
>
> (b) money deposited, together with interest thereon, in an account in the name of the deceased in trust for another or others with any bank, savings office, credit union or trust corporation, and remaining on deposit at the date of the death of the deceased;
>
> (c) money deposited, together with interest thereon, in an account in the name of the deceased and another person or persons and payable on death under the terms of the deposit or by operation of law to the survivor or survivors of those persons with any bank, savings office, credit union or trust corporation, and remaining on deposit at the date of the death of the deceased;

---

275 *Re Emele Estate, supra* note 41; *Dower v. Alberta (Public Trustee)* (1962), 38 W.W.R. 129 (Alta. T.D.) at 141; *Collier v. Yonkers, supra* note 57; *Re Dentinger, supra*, note 11 at 24; *Chickeness v. Shields* (1984), 32 Sask. R. 61 (Sask. Q.B.); *Zajic v. Chomiak Estate, supra* note 32; *Hecht v. Hecht Estate, supra* note 49 at paragraphs 27–64. Note also *Du Moulin v. Du Moulin* described in (1939), 17 C.B.R. 233 (Ont. C.A.) at 237 and *Re Becker, supra* note 57 which involved a potentially interesting issue about whether a trust property was an asset of the estate, which the court could not answer; perhaps the court should have disposed of the matter as did the court in *Re Stafford, supra* note 79.

276 *Re Thomson Estate*, [1942] 2 W.W.R. 46 (Sask. C.A.). Cf. *Re McIntyre*, [1925] 3 W.W.R. 172 (Alta. T.D.).

277 Superceding *Flannigan v. Ontario (Registrar of Motor Vehicles), supra* note 267. For additional commentary, see Goodman, W., "Dependants' Relief—Property Passing Outside of Administered Estate Considered 'Estate' for Purposes of Legislation" (1983) 6 E.T.Q. 226, Oosterhoff, A., *Succession Law Reform in Ontario* (Toronto: Carswell, 1979) at 118 and Macdonell Sheard & Hull, 4th ed. at 145.

(d) any disposition of property made by a deceased whereby property is held at the date of his or her death by the deceased and another as joint tenants;

(e) any disposition of property made by the deceased in trust or otherwise, to the extent that the deceased at the date of his or her death retained, either alone or in conjunction with another person or persons by the express provisions of the disposing instrument, a power to revoke such disposition, or a power to consume, invoke or dispose of the principal thereof, but the provisions of this clause do not affect the right of any income beneficiary to the income accrued and undistributed at the date of the death of the deceased;

(f) any amount payable under a policy of insurance effected on the life of the deceased and owned by him or her; and

(g) any amount payable under a designation of beneficiary under Part III.

(2) The capital value of the transactions referred to in clauses (1) (b), (c) and (d) shall be deemed to be included in the net estate of the deceased to the extent that the funds on deposit were the property of the deceased immediately before the deposit or the consideration for the property held as joint tenants was furnished by the deceased.

(3) Dependants claiming under this Part shall have the burden of establishing that the funds or property, or any portion thereof, belonged to the deceased.

(4) Where the other party to a transaction described in clause (1) (c) or (d) is a dependant, he or she shall have the burden of establishing the amount of his or her contribution, if any.

(5) This section does not prohibit any corporation or person from paying or transferring any funds or property, or any portion thereof, to any person otherwise entitled thereto unless there has been personally served on the corporation or person a certified copy of a suspensory order made under section 59 enjoining such payment or transfer.[278]

(6) Personal service upon the corporation or person holding any such fund or property of a certified copy of a suspensory order shall be a defence to any action or proceeding brought against the corporation or person with respect to the fund or property during the period the order is in force.

(7) This section does not affect the rights of creditors of the deceased in any transaction with respect to which a creditor has rights.

Part III of the Ontario Act has to do with a host of benefit, pension, profit sharing and savings plans. An illustrative case applying s. 72 to pension and life insurance proceeds and a joint bank account is *Moores v.*

---

278 See text of Chp. 5.1, preceding note 6, below, and Macdonell, Sheard & Hull at 145.

Hughes.[279] It was argued in vain in *Moores* that s. 72(1)(f) and (g) do not apply to proceeds that have been paid because the sections are worded "payable". The court said:

> The argument centres on the word "payable" in cls. (*f*) and (*g*) of s. 72(1). With deference, I can see no merit in that argument. It is evident that as a practical matter payments will be made (as they were here) shortly after, if not immediately as in the case of joint bank accounts, the death of the deceased. The insurance company, the trustees of a pension fund, a bank, or anyone paying or transferring funds or property covered by s. 72 is not prohibited from doing so and is freed of any liability unless there has been service made of a suspensory order enjoining such payment or transfer as provided for in s. 59 of the Act. The fact that no suspensory order was obtained, hardly an unlikely situation, does not render the proceeds unavailable. In short, the word "payable" includes "paid" for the purposes of this legislation.
>
> Furthermore, the combined effect of s. 72 and s. 63(2)(f) together with s. 78(2) and s. 66 manifest the Legislature's intention to ensure the availability of such funds or property. I interpret these sections and the general scheme of the statute to enable the court to trace funds or property included in s. 72 if necessary to persons to whom they may have been paid or transferred. If such authority is not present the aim of the Act can be frustrated simply because payment was made, as here, before the proceedings could conceivably have been instituted. No prejudice results from the payment because whether the funds are held by the insurance company or trustee or beneficiary, the result is the same. In each case it is available for inclusion in the net estate under s. 72.[280]

Also, the court decided not to charge its relief order against the pension proceeds:

> In this case I propose to make a charging order only against the proceeds of the insurance or so much thereof as I consider necessary for the protection of the dependant. The pension plan has been converted to the income annuity in favour of Anne and to interfere with that at this time would involve serious tax ramifications. I would not want to jeopardize the tax deferral that has been effected by converting the pension plan proceeds into the registered annuity. If, however, I considered it necessary to do so, to give effect to s. 62, I would.[281]

---

279 *Supra* note 102, overruled in respect of the group life policy proceeds by *Re Urquhart Estate* (1991), 3 O.R. (3d) 699 (Ont. Div. Ct.); note also *Dunn v. Dunn Estate* (1993), 12 O.R. (3d) 601 (Ont. Div. Ct.) regarding life, not group life, insurance proceeds. Concerning s. 72(1)(g), *Moore* was distinguished in *Smallman v. Smallman Estate*, *supra* note 107 at paragraphs 12–23.

280 *Ibid.* at 791.

281 *Ibid.*

In *Holland v. Clements Estate*[282] the deceased owned the "matrimonial home" with his son, who had not contributed anything to the purchase or maintenance of the home. The deceased lived in the home with the applicant, his co-habitee, who wanted to continue to live in the home, although she had been evicted by the son. The court pointed out that while the capital value of the home is by s. 72 deemed to be part of the deceased's estate "for the purpose of ascertaining the value of his estate and being available to be charged for payment [of an order] .... Section 72(2) appears to exclude the adding of joint property to the estate for the purpose of permitting the possession or use of the such property ...". In *Modopoulos v. Breen Estate*[283] the court pointed out that the "mere fact of joint tenancy is not sufficient to engage the operation of s. 72" (1)(d). It must be that the deceased made a disposition resulting in a joint tenancy. The deceased had been a joint tenant owner of a property purchased by her mother, with title taken in the names of the mother and the deceased as joint tenants.

In *Re Dolan*[284] the court had to decide whether joint tenancy property was available to a late applicant. The court held that it is not:

> In *Moores v. Hughes* ... it was held that certain assets, being proceeds of insurance policies and joint bank accounts, were to be included as testamentary dispositions as at the date of the death and deemed to be part of the net estate for purposes of ascertaining the value of the estate and being available to be charged for payment by an order under s. 63(2)(*f*) of the Act. I agree with Robins J.'s statement, at p. 791 O.R., ... as follows:
>
> > Furthermore, the combined effect of s. 72 and s. 63(2)(*f*) together with s. 78(2) and s. 66 manifest the Legislature's intention to ensure the availability of such funds or property. I interpret these sections and the general scheme of the statute to enable the court to trace funds or property included in s. 72 if necessary to persons to whom they may have been paid or transferred. If such authority is not present the aim of the Act can be frustrated simply because payment was made, as here, before the proceedings could conceivably have been instituted. No prejudice results from the payment because whether the funds are held by the insurance company or trustee or beneficiary, the result is the same. In each case it is available for inclusion in the net estate under s. 72.
>
> In my opinion, joint tenancy properties referred to in s. 72(1)(d) are in a similar position. Therefore, the joint property is deemed to form part of the net estate for the purposes of ascertaining the value of the estate.

---

282 (1988), 30 E.T.R. 93 (Ont. Surr. Ct.) at 97.

283 *Supra* note 49 at 135; given this decision, the court in *Holland v. Clements Estate*, *supra* note 282, may have erroneously charged the joint tenancy property involved in that case.

284 (1983), 43 O.R. (2d) 677 (Ont. Div. Ct.) at 679. See also *Cimetta v. Cimetta Estate* (1989), 68 O.R. (2d) 251 (Ont. H.C.) and Simmonds, D., "Succession Law Reform in Ontario: An Old Cat needs a New Kick" (1991) 10 E.T.J. 297 at 308–310.

The present case does not deal with the situation of an asset that was part of the estate that has been distributed without reference to s. 72, and I make no pronouncement whatsoever upon it.

Section 61 requires that an application for an order under s. 58 must be made within six months from the grant of letters probate of the will. In the present case, no such application was brought. However, s. 61(2) provides that the court may allow an application to be made at any time as to any portion of the estate remaining undistributed at the date of the application. In my opinion, the joint property was distributed by law of survivorship on death, but, by virtue of s. 72, is brought back into the estate for the purpose of an application that was brought within time. The present application was not brought within time and therefore no valid claim can be made against the joint property because it has been distributed.

Once the six-month time-limit expires, unless an application under s. 58 has been previously brought, s. 72 must cease to have any effect; and the automatic distribution by operation of the law of joint tenancy must be given its usual full effect. If it were otherwise, then s. 72 would mean that those classes of assets referred to in the section would remain subject to an application under s. 58 forever. This unusual and impractical result cannot be what the Legislature intended.

Prince Edward Island and the Yukon

The comparable section to the Ontario Act, s.72, above, in the Prince Edward Island Act is s. 19 and in the Yukon Act is s. 20. The Prince Edward Island and Yukon sections are very similar to the Ontario Act, differing in these ways: The preambles of ss. 19(1) and 20(1) do not contain at their end the clause contained at the end of the preamble of the Ontario Act's s. 72(1), above, "and being available to be charged for payment. . ." of a relief order. There is no s. 19(1)(g) in the Prince Edward Island Act or s. 20(1)(g) in the Yukon Act comparable to Ontario's s. 72(1)(g), above. The Prince Edward Island Act has an additional section, not contained in the Ontario Act:

20. (1) Where, upon an application for an order under section 2, it appears to the court that

(a) the deceased has within one year prior to his death made an unreasonably large disposition of real or personal property

(i) as an immediate gift while the donor and donee are alive, whether by transfer, delivery, declaration of revocable or irrevocable trust or otherwise, or

(ii) the value of which at the date of the disposition exceeded the consideration received by the deceased therefor; and

(b) there are insufficient assets in the estate of the deceased to provide adequate maintenance and support for the dependants or any of them,

the court may, subject to subsection (2), order that any person who benefited, or who will benefit by the disposition pay to the executor, administrator or trustee of the estate of the deceased or to the dependants or any of them, as the court may direct, such amount as the court deems adequate for the proper maintenance and support of the dependants or any of them.

(2) The amount that a person may be ordered to pay under subsection (1) shall be determined in accordance with the following rules:

(a) no person to whom property was disposed of is liable to contribute more than an amount equal to the extent to which the disposition was unreasonably large;

(b) if the deceased made several dispositions of property that were unreasonably large, no person to whom property was disposed of shall be ordered to pay more than his proportional share based on the extent to which the disposition was unreasonably large;

(c) the court shall consider the injurious effect on a person to whom property was disposed of from an order to pay in view of any circumstances occurring between the date of the disposition of the property and the date on which the transferee received notice of the application under section 2;

(d) if the person to whom the property was disposed of has retained the property he shall not be liable to contribute more than the value of his beneficial interest in the property;

(e) if the person to whom property was disposed of has disposed of or exchanged the property, in whole or in part, he shall not be liable to contribute more than the combined value of any remaining original property and any remaining proceeds or substituted property;

(f) for the purposes of clauses (d) and (e) "value" is the fair market value as at the date of the application under section 2.

(3) In determining whether a disposition of property is a disposition of an unreasonably large amount of property within the meaning of subsection (1), the court shall consider

(a) the ratio of value of the property disposed of to the value of the property determined under this Act to comprise the estate of the deceased at the time of his death;

(b) the aggregate value of any property disposed of under prior and simultaneous dispositions and for this purpose the court shall consider all dispositions drawn to its attention whether made prior or subsequent to one year prior to the death of the deceased;

(c) any moral or legal obligation of the deceased to make the disposition;

(d) the amount, in money or moneys worth, of any consideration paid by the person to whom the property was disposed;

(e) any other circumstance that the court considers relevant.

The Yukon Act has an identical section, s. 21.

The Northwest Territories

The Northwest Territories Act has s. 19, differing from Ontario's s. 72, above, in two respects: s. 19(f) does not apply to an insurance policy containing an irrevocable beneficiary designation and there is no s. 19(g) comparable to Ontario's s. 72(1)(g), above. Similar to the Prince Edward Island and Yukon Acts, the Northwest Territories Act contains a simpler additional section respecting large *inter vivos* gift transfers of property:

> **21.** Where
>
> (a) the estate of a deceased is insufficient to provide appropriate maintenance to the dependants of the deceased, and
>
> (b) the deceased, within three years before the date of his or her death, made a transfer of property that in the opinion of the Supreme Court was unreasonably large,
>
> if the Supreme Court considers it just in the circumstances, the Supreme Court may, on the application of the dependants or any of them, order the transferee to contribute to the maintenance of the dependant or dependants of the deceased.

There is controversy as to whether group life insurance policies come within Ontario's s. 72(1)(f) and the comparable sections in the other Acts. Holding that they do is *Re Alaingna Estate*;[285] to the contrary are *Re Sentner Estate*,[286] *Re Urquhart Estate*,[287] and *Juarez (Litigation Guardian of) v. Juarez*.[288]

Recently in Manitoba there was a spate of cases, two of which were applications pursuant to the former *Testator's Family Maintenance Act*, which were in conflict on whether proceeds of a retirement savings plan, payable to a designated beneficiary upon the death of the plan owner, were payable to the beneficiary directly[289] or through the estate like a specific bequest;[290] if the latter, the proceeds were available to creditors and *Testator's Family Maintenance Act* applicants. In 1992, the *Retirement Plan*

---

285 [1995] N.W.T.R. 392 (N.W.T. S.C.); also *Moores v. Hughes*, *supra* note 102, *Blago v. Aetna Life Insurance Co.*, *supra* note 49, and *Barton v. Barton Estate*, *supra* note 88, all of which have been overruled by *Re Urqhart Estate*, *supra* note 279, and the trial decision in *Re Sentner Estate*, which was overruled by the P.E.I.C.A., *infra* note 286.

286 (1986), 63 Nfld. & P.E.I.R. 151 (P.E.I. C.A.).

287 *Supra* note 279, which presumably overrules not only *Moores v. Hughes*, *supra* note 102, but also *Blago v. Aetna Life Insurance Co.*, *supra* note 49 and *Barton v. Barton Estate* (1991), 37 R.F.L. (3d) 330 (Ont. Gen. Div.) which did not consider the *Urquhart* Div. Ct. decision. For a comment on *Urquhart* see Norwood, D., "Re Urquhart Succession Law Reform Act—Group Life Insurance Proceeds—Designated Beneficiary—Conflict of Laws—Domicile" (1993) 12 E.T.J. 3.

288 (1996), 27 O.R. (3d) 706 (Ont. Gen. Div.); for a comment see McMurtry, H., "Group Life Insurance and the SLRA" (1997) 16 E.T.J. 193.

289 *Daniel v. Daniel Estate*, *supra* note 84 and *King v. King*, *supra* note 271, both *Testators' Family Maintenance Act* cases.

290 *Waugh Estate v. Waugh* (1990), 63 Man. R. (2d) 155 (Man. Q.B.) and *Pozniak Estate v. Pozniak* (1993), 88 Man. R. (2d) 36 (Man. C.A.), both cases concerning the payment of debts of the estate.

Beneficiaries Act of Manitoba was re-enacted.[291] According to *Clark Estate v. Clark*,[292] the new Act provides for such proceeds to be paid directly to the designated beneficiary. However, the court added that "it does not necessarily follow that those moneys are immune from the claims of creditors of the estate", because there is no provision in the *Retirement Plan Beneficiaries Act* like that in the *Insurance Act* exempting the proceeds from claims by creditors. *Clark* was not a *Dependants Relief Act* case and thus the court did not indicate whether "creditors" includes successful *Dependants Relief Act* applicants.

(b) Contracts to Make a Testamentary Gift

All of the Acts,[293] except those of British Columbia and Manitoba, contain a section like s. 71 of the Ontario Act:

> **71.** Where a deceased
>
> (a) has, in his or her lifetime, in good faith and for valuable consideration, entered into a contract to devise or bequeath any property; and
>
> (b) has by his or her will devised or bequeathed that property in accordance with the provisions of the contract,
>
> the property is not liable to the provisions of an order made under this Part except to the extent that the value of the property in the opinion of the court exceeds the consideration therefor.

This legislation supersedes a Privy Council decision, *Dillon v. Public Trustee of New Zealand*,[294] which decided that such a contract was not enforceable against the deceased's estate ahead of the court's jurisdiction to make a relief order. The Alberta section was argued unsuccessfully in *Re Edwards Estate*.[295] Chief Justice Smith for the majority stated:

> . . . the son contends that *bona fide* and for valuable consideration, the testator entered into a contract to devise "the place" to him.
>
> The burden, in my view, lies upon the son to establish such a contract as alleged and that it was *bona fide* and for valuable consideration. I am unable to come to the conclusion that the son established that his father entered into a contract to devise and bequeath to him the father's farm as a going concern

291 S.M. 1992, c. 31.

292 (1997), 115 Man. R. (2d) 48 (Man. C.A.).

293 Alta. s. 12; Sask. s. 10; N.B. s. 16(1); N.S. s. 16; P.E.I. s. 14; Nfld. s. 16; N.W.T. s. 14; Y.T. s. 15. The former *Testators' Family Maintenance Act* of Man. contained such a section; it was not continued in the current Manitoba *Dependants Relief Act*.

294 [1941] A.C. 294 (New Zealand P.C.).

295 (1961), 36 W.W.R. (NS) 605 (Alta. C.A.) at 610.

> or devise to him the land or any part of it. It seems much more probable to me that the deceased satisfied any obligation to his son by transferring to the son during his lifetime the assets already referred to and by allowing the son the use for some years of some of his land and to retain part of the proceeds of the crops therefrom.

The section is deficient in that it does not apply if the deceased has not performed his side of the contract. There is another Privy Council decision, *Schaefer v. Schuhmann*,[296] in which the Council, not following its decision in *Dillon*, decided that such a contract was enforceable against the deceased's estate ahead of the court's jurisdiction to make a relief order. Is this the law of British Columbia and Manitoba, and the other provinces if the testator has not devised or bequeathed the property in question? Presumably, the other contracting party will have an unlimited option for specific performance or damages ahead of the court's jurisdiction to make a relief order.[297]

About the issue of consideration it has been said:

> The Act does not say as of what date the property is to be valued. Presumably, the consideration must bear a close relation to the value of the property when the agreement was entered into, but having regard to the expected date of performance, that is, to the age of the testator. In other words, the consideration may be less than the actual value because of the expected delay in performance but, on the other hand, the agreement must take into account the probable increase in value during that time. Because of inflationary increases in property values, courts may be tempted to have undue regard to the value of the property at the time of the testator's death.[298]

(c) Conflict of Laws

On an intestacy the law governing succession to immovables is the law of the place where the immovables are situate and the law governing succession to movables is the law of the deceased's domicile at death.[299] Respecting wills, dependants' relief legislation has to do with intrinsic validity;[300] the intrinsic validity of a will respecting immovables is gov-

---

296 [1972] A.C. 572 (New Zealand P.C.).

297 *Re Johnson*, *supra* note 168; *Phillips v. Spooner*, [1979] 2 W.W.R. 473 (Sask. Q.B.), varied (1980), [1981] 1 W.W.R. 79 (Sask. C.A.). Also McRae, D., "Contracts to Leave Property by Will and Dependants' Relief" (1972) 20 Chitty's L.J. 298; Hull, R., "Contracts to Make Wills and Dependants' Relief Legislation" (1974) 1 E.T.Q. 240; and Oosterhoff, A., "The Effect of Death on Familial Obligations" (1981) 23 R.F.L. (2d) 272 at 288.

298 Oosterhoff, *ibid.* at 287-88.

299 Castel, J., *Canadian Conflict of Laws*, 3rd ed. (Toronto and Vancouver: Butterworths, 1997) at 490.

300 *Pouliot v. Cloutier*, [1944] S.C.R. 284 (S.C.C.) at 288.

erned by the law where the immovables are situate and respecting movables by the law of the testator's domicile at death.[301] Also, regarding immovables, an issue respecting succession can be decided only in the court where the immovables are situate.[302]

So, on a dependants' relief application it should follow that the court would consider an application in terms of the law of the forum regarding immovables situate within the court's territorial jurisdiction and the law of the deceased's domicile at death regarding movables situate within the court's territorial jurisdiction. This is not what has happened. Courts have consistently made orders only in regard to immovables situate within their territorial jurisdiction and movables if the deceased died domiciled within their territorial jurisdiction, thus requiring in cases when the deceased died domiciled elsewhere than within the court's territorial jurisdiction insofar as movables are concerned a second application in that other jurisdiction.[303] This has been enshrined in s. 13 of the Manitoba Act. No court has ever applied the law of a deceased foreign domicile at death in making an order to encompass movables within the court's territorial jurisdiction.

6. TAX IMPLICATIONS

Earlier in the chapter, it was pointed out that the tax burden of an applicant is a factor to be considered in the determination of an applicant's need[304] and that at least one court has taken into account increasing taxes.[305] Here the point is, as apparently occurred in *Dilworth v. Dilworth*,[306] that the court ought to be made aware of the tax implications of differing ways in which the court might provide relief.

7. LUMP SUM, PERIODIC(AL) PAYMENT, SPECIFIED PROPERTY TRANSFER

All of the Acts empower the court to order a lump sum or periodic(al)

---

301 Castel, *supra* note 299 at 496-97.

302 *Ibid.* at 433.

303 *Ostrander v. Houston* (1915), 8 Sask. L.R. 132 (Sask. C.A.); *Re Rattenbury* (1935), 51 B.C.R. 316 (B.C. S.C.); *Williams v. Moody Bible Institute of Chicago*, *supra* note 39 at 322; *Re Elliott* (1941), 56 B.C.R. 465 (B.C. C.A.); *Re Puliver* (1982), 39 O.R. (2d) 460 (Ont. H.C.), although in this case the court allowed an application for an interim order to proceed even though the deceased's domicile at death was in doubt.

304 See Chief Justice Williams' list of needs stated in *Re Lawther*, Chp. 4, 2(d)(i), above.

305 *Shaw v. Regina (City)*, *supra* note 44 at 445.

306 *Supra* note 65.

payment, or the transfer of specified property.[307] The empowering sections vary from the British Columbia Act's very simple s. 7:

> **7.** In making an order the court may, if it thinks fit, order that the provision for the testator's wife, husband or children is to consist of a lump sum or a periodic or other payment.[308]

to the Alberta Act's s. 5(3) and (4):

> **5.** (3) Provision for maintenance and support may be made out of income or capital or both and may be made in one or more of the following ways, as the judge sees fit:
>
> (a) an amount payable annually or otherwise;
>
> (b) a lump sum to be paid or held in trust;
>
> (c) a specified property to be transferred or assigned, absolutely or in trust for life, or for a term of years to or for the benefit of the dependant.
>
> (4) When a transfer or assignment of property is ordered, the judge
>
> (a) may give all necessary directions for the execution of the transfer or assignment by the executor or administrator or such other person as the judge may direct, or
>
> (b) may grant a vesting order.

and the Ontario Act's s. 63(2) and (3):

> **63.** (2) Provision may be made out of income or capital or both and an order may provide for one or more of the following, as the court considers appropriate,
>
> (a) an amount payable annually or otherwise whether for an indefinite or limited period or until the happening of a specified event;
>
> (b) a lump sum to be paid or held in trust;
>
> (c) any specified property to be transferred or assigned to or in trust for the benefit of the dependant, whether absolutely, for life or for a term of years;
>
> (d) the possession or use of any specified property by the dependant for life or such period as the court considers appropriate;
>
> (e) a lump sum payment to supplement or replace periodic payments;
>
> (f) the securing of payment under an order by a charge on property or otherwise;

---

307 B.C. s. 7; Alta. s. 5(3) and (4); Sask. ss. 7 and 14; Man. s. 9(2) and (3); Ont. s. 63(2) and (3); N.B. s. 5(3) and (4); N.S. s. 6(2) and (3); P.E.I. s. 6(2) and (3); Nfld. s. 6 (3) and (4); N.W.T. s. 5(3) and (4); Y.T. s. 6(2) and (3).

308 Does "other payment" include ordering a specified property transfer?

(g) the payment of a lump sum or of increased periodic payments to enable a dependant spouse or child to meet debts reasonably incurred for his or her own support prior to an application under this Part;

(h) that all or any of the money payable under the order be paid to an appropriate person or agency for the benefit of the dependant;

(i) the payment to an agency referred to in subsection 58(3) of any amount in reimbursement for an allowance or benefit granted in respect of the support of the dependant, including an amount in reimbursement for an allowance paid or benefit provided before the date of the order.

(3) Where a transfer or assignment of property is ordered, the court may,

(a) give all necessary directions for the execution of the transfer or assignment by the executor or administrator or such other person as the court may direct; or

(b) grant a vesting order.

The Saskatchewan, New Brunswick, Nova Scotia, Prince Edward Island, Newfoundland, Northwest Territories, and Yukon Acts contain sections identical or virtually identical to s. 5(3) and (4) of the Alberta Act. Manitoba's s. 9(2) and (3) are the same as Alberta's s. 5(2) and (3), except that Manitoba's s. 9(2) includes in addition:

9. (2) . . . .

(d) the possession or use of specified property by the dependant for life or such period as the court considers appropriate;

(e) the securing of payment under an order by a charge on property or otherwise;

(f) in any other way that the court considers appropriate.

There are three virtues to an order comprising periodic payments. First, it is an oft-quoted principle that dependants' relief legislation does not exist for the purpose of creating an estate for an applicant.[309] Second, another oft-quoted principle is that the court should not re-write the testator's will

---

309 *Re Morton Estate, supra* note 10 at 178; *Shaw v. Regina (City), supra* note 44 at 444; *Re Lawther,* [1947] 1 W.W.R. 577 (Man. K.B.) at 593; *Trainor v. Toronto General Trusts Corp., supra* note 79 at 163; *Wetzel v. National Trust Co.* (1956), 18 W.W.R. 556 (Sask. C.A.) at 560; *Re McMaster* (1957), 21 W.W.R. 603 (Alta. S.C.) at 608; *McCarwill v. Jones* (1959), 30 W.W.R. 498 (B.C. S.C.) at 508, reversed (1961), 36 W.W.R. 337 (B.C. C.A.), affirmed (1962), 37 W.W.R. 597 (S.C.C.); *Re Hoskins, supra* note 221 at 431; *Stadnyk v. Bulycz, supra* note 117 at 248; *Nickle v. Jones, supra* note 10 at 387; *Moore v. Moore, supra* note 56 at 322; *Albert v. Albert* (1982), 24 Alta. L.R. (2d) 258 (Alta. Q.B.) at paragraph 85; *Niebergall v. Niebergall Estate, supra* note 26 at paragraph 21.

or interfere with intestate succession any more than is absolutely necessary;[310] a periodic payment will result in the least interference with the otherwise intended testate or intestate distribution of the capital of the deceased's estate, except that it may hold up completion of the administration of the estate.[311] Third, a periodic payment, which can be varied, protects a dependant against significant changes in conditions, avoiding the misfortune which befell Mrs. Bowie, for whom the court ordered the purchase of an inadequate annuity and allowed the rest of the estate to be distributed.[312] In this regard the Supreme Court of Canada in *McCarvill v. Jones*[313] indicated a preference for periodic payments in the case of a large estate capable of generating the necessary income.

A lump sum order may be reasonable to enable the applicant to pay off debts[314] or acquire practical accommodation;[315] or as Justice Fisher stated in *Re McCaffery*:[316]

> To grant a lump sum may be advantageous in some cases, as it would enable the executors to go on and administer and wind up the estate, instead of holding it up for years for final distribution;[317]

However, Justice Fisher immediately added:

> . . . on the other hand, the recipients of a lump sum may die within a short time, or their circumstances may change by their marriage or by coming into possession of sufficient property out of which they can be properly maintained[318]

and he proceeded to order modest lump sum payments to cover immediate debts and needs, plus an appropriation from the estate capital to yield stipulated periodic payments to the applicants; presumably, the balance of

---

310 See Chp. 4, 4, above. Note that in *Re Marsh, supra* note 87, an argument by adult children of the deceased for a periodic payment award, based in effect upon this principle and that relief orders should not create an estate for the applicant, was unsuccessful probably due to the modest size of the estate.

311 *Re Duranceau, supra* note 150 at 593; *Trainor v. Toronto General Trusts Corp., supra* note 79 at 163; *Pope v. Stevens, supra* note 46 at 177.

312 See Chp. 5, 1 at note 6, below.

313 *Supra* note 84 at 280–81.

314 Note the Ontario Act, s. 63(2)(g), *above*, and *Re Pflanzner, supra* note 14 at 155.

315 *Spinney v. Royal Trust Co., supra* note 106 at paragraph 40; *Re Beyor* (1949), [1950] O.W.N. 117 (Ont. C.A.) at 120, regarding the purchase of furniture.

316 *Supra* note 45 at 523–24.

317 *Re Schmalz, supra* note 84; *Re Leggatt, supra* note 106 at paragraph 6; *McMacken v. McMacken, supra* note 102 at 704; *Chityala v. Chityala Estate, supra* note 107 at paragraphs 2, 3; *Re Protopappas Estate, supra* note 56 at 256.

318 *Supra* note 316 at 524. Also *Pope v. Stevens, supra* note 46 at 85 and *Re Norton, supra* note 165 at 623-24.

the estate could be distributed.[319] As mentioned earlier, when a lump sum is ordered, including the purchase of annuity, or when the estate is ordered to invest a specified amount to provide stipulated periodic payments and the balance of the estate is allowed to be distributed, there is no protection for the applicant against the ordered relief being insufficient for whatever reason.

On occasion courts refuse to make a lump sum order because the court thinks that the applicant is not competent to deal with it.[320] On the other hand, in *Re Parks,*[321] the court upset a discretionary trust, created probably with good intentions, and awarded in part a lump sum. The applicant was the deceased's widow who was "barely capable of caring for herself".[322] Chief Justice Wilson decided:

> In the case of the mother real need is shown. This lady of 77, after a lifetime of meagrely rewarded service, is, in effect, given nothing from this estate save the upkeep of her house and such part of the income from the estate as her daughter, the executrix, shall, in her discretion, see fit to award her. I have no doubt that the testator was justified in deciding not to give her outright the whole corpus of the estate. His own treatment of her in respect of money had left her financially inexpert. But I do not think that he should have placed this faithful wife in a position where she has virtually to account to her daughter for all her needs beyond those covered by her old age pension. I think she should have a sum of cash at her command and that the income from the rest of the estate should be hers by right and not at the discretion of her daughter. I think, also, that there should be an entitlement to encroach on capital if this is necessary to keep this old lady in her declining years. The widow is the only person in this litigation who qualifies as a dependant and a person in need, and her requirements are paramount.
>
> She should be given the sum of $5,000 in cash. The income from the rest of the estate should be hers absolutely for her life. If need is shown, the corpus of the estate may be encroached upon to support the widow, to pay any large and unusual medical expenses or to provide for her care in a nursing home.[323]

Similarly, in *Holland v. Clements Estate*[324] while the court was concerned about the applicant's ability to deal with a lump sum award because of her "problem with alcohol", the court awarded a lump sum instead of a

319 Similarly *Re Soroka, supra* note 30.

320 *Re Rist, supra* note 159 at 109; *Belaney v. Perrier, supra* note 28 at 601; *Ostrander v. Kimble Estate, supra* note 56 at paragraphs 51–52; similarly, *Re Quon, supra* note 106 at 708.

321 *Supra* note 79.

322 *Ibid.* at 588.

323 *Ibid.* at 593-94. See also the somewhat similar *Linden v. Linden, supra* note 78.

324 (1991), 43 E.T.R. 299 (Ont. Gen. Div.) at paragraph 44.

periodic payment because of demonstrated hostility towards the applicant on the part of the executor.

In the odd case, where "the value of the . . . assets is problematical and the ultimate amount of . . . liabilities is incapable of absolute determination", of course it will be unwise for the court to award a fixed sum either in terms of a lump sum or an annuity; in such a case a periodic payment will be the appropriate order, which in all provinces can be varied subsequently.[325]

In *Coolen v. Coolen*[326] the deceased had devised the family home to his wife for life, with the remainder going to his daughter subject to a right of purchase in another child. The daughter applied, seeking an order giving her an unconditional remainder interest. The court dismissed her application because "[i]t is hardly necessary to say that the Act cannot be invoked for such a purpose". Surely what the daughter was seeking, if deserving, came within the court's jurisdiction as worded in s. 5(3)(c) of the Alberta Act, above?

Incidentally, there have been approximately 200 reported dependants' relief orders made in Canada.[327] Approximately 160 or 80% of the orders have been lump sum orders, including a couple that were for the purchase of an annuity.[328] Included in the periodic orders were a couple for the purchase of an annuity with the balance, if any, upon the death of the dependant to be repaid to the estate.[329] In addition there have been approximately 15 orders that comprised or involved specific property transfers.

The Saskatchewan Act contains a unique section:

Trust fund for certain dependants

9. (1) In this section:

"allowance" means an allowance paid by way of a trust fund;

"dependant" means a child of a deceased who is 18 years or older at the time of the deceased's death and who alleges or on whose behalf it is alleged that:

(i) by reason of mental or physical disability, he or she is unable to earn a livelihood; or

---

325 Note *Re Clark, supra* note 216 at 694–95.

326 (1980), 43 N.S.R. (2d) 67 (N.S. C.A.) at paragraph 23.

327 That is including for British Columbia only orders from 1991 and for Ontario only orders pursuant to the *Succession Law Reform Act*. By the way, Feeney, T., *The Canadian Law of Wills Probate*, 3rd ed. (Toronto: Butterworths, 1987) at 271, is certainly misleading in stating that periodic orders are "the more usual manner in which an award is made".

328 B.C. 21; Alta. 29; Sask. 43; Man. 21; Ont. 14; N.B. 8; N.S. 20; Nfld. 3. These numbers are approximate.

329 B.C. 1; Alta. 13; Sask. 9; Man. 3; Ont. 9; N.B. 1; N.S. 3. These numbers are approximate.

(ii) by reason of need or other circumstances, he or she ought to receive a greater share of the deceased's estate than he or she is entitled to without an order;

"trust fund" means a trust fund established pursuant to subsection (2),

(2) Subject to subsections (3) to (7), the court may order the establishment of a trust fund for a dependant for the purpose of paying an allowance:

(a) to help the dependant achieve independence;

(b) to meet the special needs of the dependant;

(c) to provide occasional gifts to the dependant; or

(d) to do all or any combination of the things mentioned in clauses (a) to (c).

(3) In determining the amount of an allowance that may be paid to a dependant, the court shall consider that any assistance provided to or on behalf of the dependant pursuant to *The Saskatchewan Assistance Act* and any other similar assistance programs funded by the Government of Saskatchewan will continue to be provided to the dependant.

(4) The capital of and income from a trust fund is not to be considered as an asset or income of the dependant for the purpose of determining the dependant's eligibility for assistance pursuant to *The Saskatchewan Assistance Act* or any other similar assistance program funded by the Government of Saskatchewan.

(5) If there is no other suitable person to be appointed as trustee and the public trustee consents to be appointed, the court may appoint the public trustee as trustee for a trust fund.

(6) If the public trustee is appointed as trustee of a trust fund pursuant to subsection (5), the public trustee may charge the same fee for administering the trust fund that the public trustee could charge pursuant to *The Public Trustee Act* for performing similar services respecting the property of a dependent adult.

(7) The Lieutenant Governor in Council may make regulations limiting the amount of a trust fund.

In *Re Penner*[330] Justice McIntyre said:

The purpose of a s. 9 trust fund is to enhance the dependant's quality of life without affecting their entitlement to public assistance.

330 (1997), (*sub nom. Re Penner Estate*) 161 Sask. R. 317 (Sask. Q.B.) at paragraph 9.

8. CONDITIONS AND RESTRICTIONS; INCIDENCE OF ORDERS

All of the Acts[331] contain sections similar to ss. 5(1) and (2), 8-9 of the Alberta Act:

> **5.** (1) The judge in any order making provision for maintenance and support of a dependant may impose any conditions and restrictions he sees fit.
>
> (2) The judge may in his discretion order that the provision for maintenance and support be made out of and charged against the whole or any portion of the estate in the proportion and in the manner that to him seem proper.
>
> **8.** A judge at any time
>
> (a) may fix a periodic payment or lump sum to be paid by a legatee, devisee or beneficiary under an intestacy to represent, or in commutation of, the proportion of the sum ordered to be paid that falls on the portion of the estate in which he is interested,
>
> (b) may relieve that portion of the estate from further liability, and
>
> (c) may direct
>
> (i) in what manner the periodic payment is to be secured, or
>
> (ii) to whom the lump sum is to be paid and in what manner it is to be dealt with for the benefit of the person to whom the commuted payment is payable.
>
> **9.** Unless the judge otherwise determines, the incidence of any provision for maintenance and support that is ordered pursuant to this Act falls ratably
>
> (a) on the whole estate of the deceased, or
>
> (b) if the jurisdiction of the judge does not extend to the whole estate, on that part of the estate to which the jurisdiction of the judge extends,
>
> and the judge may relieve any part of the deceased's estate from the incidence of the order for maintenance and support.

(a) Conditions and Restrictions

Not to be confused with the occasionally quite complex provisions for the fulfilment of an award, the infrequent exercise of the power to impose conditions and restrictions is more easily treated with a few illustrations than summarized:

---

331 B.C. ss. 6, 8-10; Sask. ss. 6(2), (3), 11-13; Man. ss. 9(1), 10, 12; Ont. ss. 63(1), 66, 68, 69; N.B. ss. 4, 5(1), (2), 7, 10, 12; N.S. ss. 6(1), (2), 8, 10; P.E.I. ss. 6(1), 8, 10, 11; Nfld. ss. 6(1), (2), 8, 10; N.W.T. ss. 5(1), (2), 7, 9, 10; Y.T. ss. 6(1), 8, 10, 12.

In *Re Bateman*[332] the testator left $15,000.00 of his $34,000.00 estate to his widow and the balance to five non-dependant brothers. At the time by the Saskatchewan Act the widow was entitled at least to her intestate entitlement. In connection with its order the court said:

> On an intestacy the widow would have received $10,000 plus one-third of the residue . . . Her share will be about $18,000. I shall refer to it as "the primary amount". It shall be paid out to her at the rate of $250 per month from January 1, 1966. She is also entitled to relief against the terms of the will to the full balance of the estate and this allowance will continue to be paid after her share has expired as long as the estate lasts.
>
> In the event that she shall die before the primary amount has, with interest, been paid to her then the balance thereof shall be paid to her estate.
>
> In the event that she shall remarry before the primary amount has, with interest, been paid to her, the payments shall continue only until the primary amount is finished.
>
> In the event that she shall remarry after the primary amount has, with interest, been paid to her, the payments shall forthwith terminate.
>
> In the event of her death or remarriage, the residue of the estate remaining, after allowing for the balance of her primary amount, if any, may be distributed.
>
> I direct that the value of the household goods bequeathed to the wife shall be over and above the primary amount provision I have ordered.

In *Re Ducherer*[333] the deceased died intestate survived by a widow and eight children, three of whom were minors. In making its order the court said:

> In my view, the maintenance which the widow requires to enable her to live with comfort and without pecuniary anxiety in the state of life to which she was accustomed in the deceased's lifetime, taking into consideration her own limited means, can be met by granting her the entire estate of the deceased, except for the share of the infants. I direct payment and transfer to the widow, in the due course of administration, of all that portion of the estate other than the shares of the three infants, subject to all outstanding indebtedness, costs of administration and the cost of this application. . . .
>
> I may give such "consequential directions as [I think] fit for the purpose of giving effect to an order". A "consequential direction" means a direction traceable directly or indirectly to the main order made, namely, the order above. Section 9(5) provides that I "shall have regard to the nature of the property representing . . . estate and shall not order any provisions necessitating a realization that would be improvident having regard to the interests of the dependants and of the person who, apart from the order, would be entitled to that property." In result, in terms of specific assets, to give effect to the

332 *Supra* note 107 at 768.
333 *Supra* note 64 at 499.

order made above, I direct, under s. 9(4), payment and transfer to the widow, in the due course of administration, of all assets of the estate except the following land: SE 33-44-24-W3; NE 15-43-24-W3. I direct, under s. 9(4), "assignment" of that land to the widow for a term ending on the day on which the youngest infant attains majority, when it shall be dealt with, free of the assignment, by the adminstratrix as the share of the estate of the deceased of the infants. They may wish, at this point, to transfer it to their mother—who knows. The widow will pay taxes and upkeep on the land during the term.

In *Re Kiel*[334] the deceased's estate was composed of a house in Barrhead, Alberta, and a section of farmland. By his will he gave the house to his widow and a quarter of the section of farmland to each of his four children. To provide better for the widow the court said:

7. Being mindful of the size of the estate, the widow's probable needs, and the income the estate is capable of generating it is still unnecessary to interfere with the testator's disposition of the four quarter-sections in order to amply protect the widow during her remaining years, but I do order the sum of $10,000.00 per annum to be paid by the estate for her better maintenance and support. These monies shall be secured by a charge against the farmlands described in the application for probate and the income generated by them. This sum shall be paid in semi-annual instalments of $5,000.00 each, commencing October 15, 1979. In addition, the estate will pay to Mrs. Kiel a sum equal to the municipal tax levy upon her Edmonton home so long as she chooses to reside within it. A similar direction is made with respect to the cost of insuring the home. These sums will be payable when the levies and invoices are received by her.

In *Spinney v. Royal Trust Co.*[335] the testator in his will made several specific bequests; he left the income from the residue to his wife with the remainder going to King's College. The court agreed that it was reasonable to have the matrimonial home sold and the widow given in its place a lump sum, plus a stipulated income for life, charged against all of the remaining assets of the estate, thus postponing until her death the payment of the specific bequests.

In *Re Gilbert*[336] the nature of the estate assets, which included farmland, farm machinery, and trucks, was not a factor in the awards made by the court for the widow and children, but in regard to payment of the awards the court ordered the assets converted "into cash . . . as expeditiously as possible, having regard, however, to the principle that there be no improvi-

---

334 *Supra* note 106. Similarly, in *Moores v. Hughes*, *supra* note 102, the court charged non-estate assets for the payment of the relief order.

335 *Supra* note 106.

336 *Supra* note 68 at 704.

dent disposal of assets. The sale of the farm lands [to] be subject to the approval of the court".

In *Re Trott*[337] the diseased by his will gave his widow all his "furniture, books, provisions and other household effects", plus one third of the residue of his estate to be paid out as $300.00 immediately and the balance at $40.00 per month. The court decided:

> There will be an order that the trustee pay forthwith to the applicant the sum of $300 referred to in the will, and that the trustee further pay to the applicant, out of the estate, on January 1, 1950, and on the first day of each and every month thereafter, the sum of $75, until the death or remarriage of the applicant or until the estate shall have been exhausted, whichever be the earlier, provided that such payments shall first be paid out of the share of the applicant, as provided by the will, until her share shall have become exhausted and thereafter out of the remainder of the estate and the interests of all parties therein shall abate accordingly.
>
> I do further order that the trustee shall hold the assets of the estate, after payment of proper debts, funeral and testamentary expenses, and other proper charges, to secure the above-mentioned payments to the applicant and upon the death or remarriage of the applicant the balance of the estate, if any, as abated, shall be distributed as in the will directed.

In *Re Tian*[338] the only asset of the deceased's estate was a $4,000.00 house. By her will she made her husband the sole beneficiary. On an application by her minor child, of whom her widower was the step-father, the court ordered:

> . . . that the estate . . . shall pay to the official guardian of this province, on behalf of the . . . applicant, . . . the sum of $50 monthly until the sum of $2,000 shall have been paid over . . . .
>
> The house property belonging to the estate . . . shall stand charged with the payment of the sums so provided.
>
> I assume from the information given me at the hearing that [the widower] is desirous of retaining the said property as his home. In order to permit of this and in order to assist in making it unnecessary for the said property to be sold in order to provide the funds for the payments as aforesaid, I direct that [he] may advance to the estate the monthly sum so payable and be entitled to reimbursement from the estate for the moneys so advanced. Should he die before the full amount of $2,000 is paid over the balance then payable under the terms of this order shall be realized out of the assets of the estate and paid over to the official guardian forthwith. Should the applicant predecease [his stepfather] and die before the full amount of the $2,000 has been paid over then the balance not then due and payable under the terms of this order shall revert to the estate and be distributed as by the will provided.

---

337 *Supra* note 184 at 742–743.

338 *Supra* note 32 at 373.

In *Crilley v. Beckingham*[339] the widower testator left the bulk of his estate to a granddaughter, the respondent on an application by the testator's daughter. In making an order in favour of the daughter the court added:

> [37] The provisions of the **Act** also allow me to set certain conditions and there is one which I would impose on the distribution of funds to the respondent. In August 1984, the respondent borrowed $730 from her brother, Edward Crane, prior to leaving for college in Welland, Ontario. That money has not been repaid to the brother and no doubt he needs it to further his studies at the university. I direct the trustee to pay this sum to the brother, out of the respondent's share of the estate, before distributing the funds to the respondent.

In *Albert v. Albert*[340] the testator divided his estate equally among his widow and two daughters. In addition to her one-third of the estate the court awarded the widow a periodic payment to be increased or decreased annually according to the cost of living index.

In *Re Davies*[341] the widower was awarded the right to live in the family home subject to several conditions, including that he pay the taxes, the utilities, the insurance, the costs of maintenance, and for all repairs.

In *Chellew v. Ontario (Public Trustee)*[342] the court made an award with conditions to a daughter for her post secondary education:

> . . . I am deciding to award the applicant the sum of $700 per month for as long as she is in full-time attendance at a college or university, in Canada or outside Canada and within three months thereafter or for a period of three years following December 1, 1983, whichever date shall come first . . . .
>
> . . . . .
>
> The applicant shall be required to continue to apply for student grants in each year. Any student grants received by her shall be paid to the respondent and added to the estate of the deceased.

(b) Incidence

(i) Generally

As is provided in s. 9 of the Alberta Act, above, which is typical of the legislation in all of the provinces, unless the court otherwise orders, the incidence of an order falls rateably upon the whole estate to which the jurisdiction of the court extends. The whole estate is the net estate available for distribution to the beneficiaries after the payment of the deceased's

339 *Supra* note 79.
340 *Supra* note 84 at 265.
341 *Supra* note 57 at 107.
342 *Supra* note 45 at 199.

debts and the costs of administering the estate.[343] In an annotation to *Re Osland*[344] Professor Bale wondered whether the judge's award of "$10,000.00 from this estate" meant that the award was payable out of the residue or also out of two specific bequests. Without any doubt, with such simple orders, which comprise the overwhelming majority of orders, their incidence falls rateably upon the whole estate and when there is a will this means upon all of the testamentary gifts.

Regarding s. 9(b), courts have consistently considered that their jurisdiction extends only to immovables situate within their territorial jurisdiction and to movables if the deceased died domiciled within their territorial jurisdiction.[345]

The deceased's will in *Re Randle*[346] after providing for the payment of debts, liabilities, and funeral and testamentary expenses, created a trust in connection with which there was a bequest to his widow, a bequest and a devise to one of his sons, named George, and a residuary gift to his other children. The widow applied successfully pursuant to the *Family Relief Act*; she was awarded a lump sum in lieu of her bequest. The trial judge ordered her award to be paid out of the residue, thus exonerating the bequest and devise to George. On an appeal Justice Haddad said:

> Where it is asserted that any particular part of an estate should be relieved from bearing its proportionate share of such maintenance and support, in my opinion the onus is on the person making that assertion to show that it is equitable and fair that such relief be granted.
>
> Counsel for the respondent also submitted that the terms of the will manifest a scheme intended by the testator to give his son George all of the assets identified with the testator's farming business. In consequence thereof he argued that in considering which parts of the estate should bear the burden of the maintenance and support for a dependant the presumed wishes of the testator should be the governing factor. And to give effect to those wishes the scheme of distribution according to the tenor of the will should be preserved. That was the ratio in the decision in *Re Schmidt*, [1952] O.R. 532, . . . where an application was brought by a widow under the Ontario statute, The Depen-

---

343 The text earlier in this Chp. at 5(a) and, as indicated there by the Acts of Ontario, Prince Edward Island, the Northwest Territories, and the Yukon there is a statutory enlargement of what comprises the estate.

344 Bale, G., "Re Osland, Testator's Family Maintenance in British Columbia—Fair Share of Estate or Equitable Maintenance and the Dilemma Still Confronting the Courts by the Supreme Court of Canada Decision in Walker v. McDermott," (1977-78) 1 E.T.R. 129 at 134.

345 Further see Chp. 4, 5(c), above.

346 (1976), 1 Alta. L.R. (2d) 52 (Alta. C.A.).

dants' Relief Act, R.S.O. 1950, c. 101. . . , conceived to accomplish a purpose similar to that of The Family Relief Act of this province. There the testator, after making certain specific bequests in his will, directed that the net income from the residue of his estate be paid to his widow until her death or remarriage and thereafter that the residue be divided equally between two charitable institutions. The trial Judge made an order charging the whole estate to produce an allowance to the widow of $2,400 annually. On appeal from that order it was the submission of the appellant that in providing for an allowance to the widow, resort should be primarily to the residue of the estate until it is exhausted. The Court held that in the circumstances of that case the order of the learned trial Judge was not appropriate, and in substitution therefor an order was made directing the executors to pay to the widow the net income from the residue with power to mortgage or sell the assets of the residue should that become necessary to ensure payment to her of $2,400 per annum.

There are distinguishing aspects of the *Schmidt* case which do not necessarily make the ratio thereof applicable to this one. The first and most important feature is that the Ontario Act had no provision similar to s. [9] of our Act. Secondly, the testator in the *Schmidt* case clearly intended by his will that the residue of his estate be earmarked and set apart to provide for the widow's maintenance and support.

I do not go so far as to say the scheme of the will should not be given some weight, but in my opinion, the test to be applied in deciding whether a part of the estate should be relieved from bearing its fair share of the incidence of the support and maintenance is to determine whether a reasonable testator would have provided for that relief. The test is an objective one, and unless the judge is satisfied that a reasonable testator, in the circumstances of the testator whose will is being considered, would have relieved any part of an estate from contributing its fair share, he should not interfere with the prima facie rule enunciated by the Legislature in s. [9].

The Court has found that the testator has not acted reasonably in making adequate provision for a dependant, and accordingly it is in its function to exercise its discretion and interfere with the will to ensure that adequate provision for maintenance and support is provided, and in doing so it should endeavour to determine what a fair and reasonable testator would do. No reason has been shown why the directions set out in s. [9] should not apply.

Accordingly, I am of the view that the obligation for payment of the [relief order] ought to be spread equitably across the whole estate. It should not be absorbed by residue alone.[347]

Courts seldom exonerate testamentary gifts or assets from the fulfilment of orders. It is not clear from the reports of those cases whether the exoneration was requested or considered by the court on its own and

347 *Ibid.* at 59-60.

whether the court considered the matter along the lines of the principles stated by Justice Haddad in *Randle*. For instance, in *Podolski v. Podolski*,[348] where the testator expressly directed that any award was to be paid out of the residue, and in *Pauliuk v. Pauliuk*,[349] where the court was of the "opinion that . . . the testator's intention was that the residue . . . should go to [the residuary beneficiary] after the specific devises and bequests as well as the debts were paid",[350] the courts simply gave effect to the testator's direction or perceived intention without comment upon its reasonableness. Similarly in *Davison v. Parks*,[351] treating a relief order as if it were a specific bequest, the court refused to order exoneration for an infant's residuary gift, because the will directed the testamentary gifts to be paid "in the order set out in the will"; the court gave no indication that it considered the reasonableness of the direction.

Courts have given exoneration relief to protect the share of a widow,[352] an infant,[353] a non-statutory beneficiary, who had made a significant contribution to the creation of the deceased's estate and to the deceased's welfare,[354] and to avoid "serious tax ramifications".[355] In *Dutka v. Dutka,*[356] presumably because the applicant "consented" to a specific bequest made to his mother in his father's will, the court ordered the lump sum it awarded to the applicant to be paid "as if by special [sic] bequest", with the result that only the residue bore the incidence of the award.

In *Walker v. Rivalin*[357] the recipients of several specific legacies essentially had a no more deserving relationship with the deceased than did the residuary beneficiary. The court refused to exonerate these specific legacies, simply because the court did "not deem it just".

---

348 (1979), 4 E.T.R. 161 (Man. Q.B.).

349 *Supra* note 10.

350 *Ibid.* at 34.

351 [1919] 2 W.W.R. 100 (Sask. C.A.).

352 *Re Cousins, supra* note 155 at 392.

353 *Reinsch v. Crown Trust Co.* (1956), 19 W.W.R. 63 (Man. Q.B.); *Re Ducherer, supra* note 64 at 499–500; cf. *Davison v. Parks, supra* note 351; *Moores v. Hughes, supra* note 102 at 793. In *Royal Trust Co. v. Downton, supra* note 267 at paragraphs 9–10, the court gave time to infant appellants to consider making an application for exoneration.

354 *Re Barclay, supra* note 107 at 312; *Re Schurman, supra* note 32 at 84; *Simmonds v. Rehn, supra* note 32 at 571; *Re Quon, supra* note 106 at 708; *Redmond v. Redmond Estate, supra* note 79 at paragraph 34.

355 *Moores v. Hughes, supra* note 102 at 791.

356 *Supra* note 79 at paragraphs 1 and 47; similarly *Re Ducherer*, supra note 64.

357 *Supra* note 79.

In *Re Nalywayko*[358] an Ontario Surrogate Court ordered its award to fall rateably upon the specific and residuary legatees. The Court said that "[w]hile this . . . may represent a significant change from past practice it is my opinion that the Court is merely giving effect to the plain meaning of the words in s. 68(1) which in my view represent a significant legislative change".[359] Regarding the past practice the court referred to *Re McCaffery*,[360] wherein the trial judge had exempted from the incidence of the award a specific bequest and Justice Riddell in the Court of Appeal said:

> [The exemption of the bequest] is exceptionable; the power of the Judge being to charge "the whole or any portion of the estate in such proportion and in such manner as to him seems proper" . . . he should have first exhausted the residuary estate before reducing the special devise and legacies.[361]

The *Nalywako* court also referred to *Re Schmidt*, above, and *Re Randle*, above, and "adopt[ed] the reasoning of *Re Randle* as being applicable to the instant case".

Finally, in *Re Lawther*[362] Chief Justice Williams dealt with the incidence of an award against two parcels of land in this way:

> By section 11, the incidence of any provision for maintenance and support ordered shall, unless the Judge otherwise determines, fall rateably on the whole estate of the testator. I think this general rule should be applied here, but it is somewhat difficult to apply it in the case of the two pieces of land specifically devised. It is impossible to work out the exact figures but a reasonable approximation can be arrived at. If the net estate is approximately $36,000.00, the aggregate value of the two farms is $4,260.00 ($2,300.00 and $1,960.00) or something over 11 per cent. The amounts that will be paid out of capital under the terms of this order will be a minimum of $1,425.00 a year and will yearly increase. I think a proper disposition would be to direct that the property devised to Leslie L. Langford be charged with payment of the sum of $90.00 a year during the lifetime of the applicant, and the property devised to Alice Goodbun be charged with payment of the sum of $75.00 a year during the same period. These amounts will be paid to the executors to be received by them as capital and used to reimburse the estate pro tanto for the amounts paid to the applicant under the terms of this order. I direct each of the devisees to execute a proper charge on her property to secure the payment of these sums. The contingent shares of the residue to which these devisees may become entitled will also stand charged respectively with the payment of these sums.

358 *Supra* note 106.
359 *Ibid.* at 157–58.
360 *Supra* note 45.
361 *Ibid.* at 519.
362 *Supra* note 10 at 162.

(ii) Matrimonial Property Equalization Orders

As indicated earlier,[363] generally a matrimonial property equalization order and a continuing maintenance order enjoy priority over a dependants' relief order. However, *Gaudet (Litigation Guardian of) v. Young Estate*[364] was an application by a child of the deceased's comon law wife, who, it was agreed, qualified as a dependant of the deceased. The deceased's second wife submitted that any order the court made in favour of the applicant should be subject to her outstanding claim for equalization of net family assets pursuant to the *Family Law Act* of Ontario.[365] In connection with her equalization claim, the second wife had obtained a preservation order. Relevant to her submission is s. 6(12)(c) of the *Family Law Act*:

> (12) The spouse's entitlement under section 5 has priority over . . .
>
> > (c) an order made against the estate under Part V (Support of Dependants) of the *Succession Law Reform Act*, except an order in favour of a child of the deceased spouse.

The court did not agree with her submission. The court reviewed conflicting recent cases concerning priority between an equalization claimant and third party creditors of the estate and decided:

> 17 In any event, as regards dependant claimants, it is abundantly clear that while the *Family Law Act* provides that a spouse's entitlement to equalization of net family properties has priority over any order against the estate made in favour of a dependant of the deceased spouse, it is quite different where that dependant is a child of the deceased spouse. Where the dependant is a child, the *Family Law Act* provides that the child's claim, under the *Succession Law Reform Act*, is not subordinate to the spouse's entitlement to an equalization of net family properties. Section 1(1) of the *Family Law Act* defines a "child" as:
>
> > includ[ing] a person whom a parent has demonstrated a settled intention to treat as a child of his or her family . . .
>
> 18 I do not interpret s. 6(12)(*c*) of the *Family Law Act* as meaning that the claims of the entitled spouse and those of the dependent child rank equally. Rather, I am of the view that the legislature intended that the dependent child's claim has priority over that of the entitled spouse.

---

363 *Supra*, notes 268-69.

364 (1995), 7 E.T.R. (2d) 146 (Ont. Gen. Div.).

365 R.S.O. 1990, c. F.3.

(c) Ademption

When ordering relief for a dependant who is a testamentary beneficiary of the deceased's estate the court can make the relief order to be in addition to or instead of the dependant's testamentary share. The court should be advised to make this clear to avoid further litigation.[366]

366 For ex., *Re Barker* (1983), 41 O.R. (2d) 377 (Ont. C.A.).

5

Other Orders

Besides the basic order and supplementary directions, which courts are empowered to give pursuant to their primary jurisdiction, Chapter 2, above, courts are empowered to make suspensory, interim, and variation orders.

1. SUSPENSORY

With the exception of the British Columbia[1] and Saskatchewan[2] Acts, all of the Acts[3] have a section like s. 3 of the Manitoba Act[4]:

> **3.** On an application by or on behalf of a dependant, the court may make an order suspending in whole or in part the administration of the deceased's estate, for such time and to such extent as the court may decide.

Notice of a relief application must be served on the personal representative(s) of the deceased's estate, if only to bring into operation the stay of distribution provision contained in all of the Acts.[5] Such service obviates the necessity of obtaining a suspensory order at the initiation of a relief

---

1 *Wills Variation Act*, R.S.B.C. 1996, c. 490 [hereinafter British Columbia Act].

2 *Dependants' Relief Act*, 1996, S.S. 1996, c. D-25.01 [hereinafter Saskatchewan Act]. See *Re Finnimore* (1956), 17 W.W.R. 668 (Sask. C.A.) at 674.

3 Alberta *Family Relief Act*, R.S.A. 1980, c. F-2, s. 3(4) [hereinafter Alberta Act]; Ontario *Succession Law Reform Act*, Part V, R.S.O. 1990, c. S.26, s. 59 [hereinafter Ontario Act], which supercedes *Re McCaffery*, [1931] O.R. 512 (Ont. C.A.) and *Re Rice*, [1952] O.W.N. 465 (Ont. H.C.) at 468; New Brunswick *Provision for Dependants Act*, R.S.N.B. 1973, c. P-22.3, s. 2(2) [hereinafter New Brunswick Act]; Nova Scotia *Testators' Family Maintenance Act*, R.S.N.S. 1989, c. 465, s. 3(2) [hereinafter Nova Scotia Act]; Prince Edward Island *Dependants of a Deceased Person Relief Act*, R.S.P.E.I. 1988, c. D-7, s. 3 [hereinafter Prince Edward Island Act]; Newfoundland *Family Relief Act*, R.S.N. 1990, c. F-2, s. 3(2) [hereinafter Newfoundland Act]; Northwest Territories *Dependants Relief Act*, R.S.N.W.T. 1988, c. D-4, s. 2(2) [hereinafter Northwest Territories Act]; Yukon Territory *Dependants Relief Act*, R.S.Y.T. 1990, c. 44, s. 3 [hereinafter Yukon Act].

4 *Dependants Relief Act*, S.M. 1989-90, c. 42; C.C.S.M., c. D37 [hereinafter Manitoba Act].

5 Above, Chp. 3, 7.

application, except to deal with an apprehended distribution before the relief application can be served. In Ontario, Prince Edward Island, the Northwest Territories, and the Yukon, the Acts of which contain a section deeming certain assets to be available for the fulfilment of a relief order, the section, for example s. 72(5) of the Ontario Act, requires a suspensory order to be served on the holder of the deemed assets:

> (5) This section does not prohibit any corporation or person from paying or transferring any funds or property, or any portion thereof, to any person otherwise entitled thereto unless there has been personally served on the corporation or person a certified copy of a suspensory order made under section 59 enjoining such payment or transfer.

However, in *Re Urquhart Estate*[6] a widow applied for a suspensory order respecting the payment of insurance proceeds payable pursuant to a group life policy on the death of her husband. The policy was between the company for which the husband had worked and Canada Life Assurance Company. The husband had named his son as his beneficiary. The widow sought the suspensory order pursuant to ss. 59 and 72(1)(f) of the Ontario Act:

> **59.** On an application by or on behalf of the dependants or any of them, the court may make an order suspending in whole or in part the administration of the deceased's estate, for such time and to such extent as the court may decide.
>
> . . . . .
>
> **72.** (1) Subject to section 71, for the purpose of this Part, the capital value of the following transactions effected by a deceased before his or her death, whether benefitting his or her dependant or any other person, shall be included as testamentary dispositions as of the date of the death of the deceased and shall be deemed to be part of his or her net estate for purposes of ascertaining the value of his or her estate and being available to be charged for payment by an order under clause 63(2)(f). . . .
>
> > (f) any amount payable under a policy of insurance effected on the life of the deceased and owned by him or her; and . . .

The court dismissed the application, because (i) the policy did not come within s. 72(1)(f) since the husband was not the owner of the policy and (ii) even if he were the owner of the policy, s. 72 does not make the proceeds an asset of the estate; the section merely deems the proceeds to be part of the estate for the purpose of ascertaining the value of the estate. By the wording of suspensory order sections, including s. 59 of the Ontario Act, an order can only be made to suspend "the administration of the deceased's estate". Regarding the court's second conclusion, the conflict-

---

6 (1991), 3 O.R. (3d) 699 (Ont. Div. Ct.).

ing wording of ss. 59 and 72(5) of the Ontario Act begs an application of the golden rule of interpretation to give effect to s. 72(5).

A suspensory order can also be useful in place of or to supplement a relief order. *Laventure v. Killey*[7] is a good example. The testatrix by her will gave a small legacy to her adopted daughter, the applicant, a licence to occupy her house and a small allowance to her sister, and the residue of her modest estate to a church. The daughter was not in financial need. However, the court was mindful of her possible future need:

> My conclusion is that a case cannot be made out for varying the will in favour of the applicant to allow her something for present maintenance. But her future has to be considered and it is possible that, in days ahead, she will experience need. Her husband's death and his retirement upon a meagre pension are two possibilities that would put her in need of support. Prolonged illness of her husband is another. Had the testatrix viewed these possibilities in a cool, judicial manner (even setting aside love) she would have seen, I think, that there was something she could do to avoid them and that a moral duty rested upon her to do so. In such a case she would have attempted to set up a guard against these eventualities for the woman she had, so long ago, adopted as her own child. I consider that this attempt should be made now.
>
> In the event of the applicant being widowed she will have her own home. Such a home will not be of much use to her without an allowance for fuel, light, taxes, repairs, etc. Besides these requirements of mere shelter she will need income for the other necessities of life. The desired income I would place at $100 per month. Now I do not know whether upon the death of Mr. Laventure, in case he predeceases his wife, there will be insurance moneys and, while the couple at present have no considerable savings, I do not know whether that will still be the case if and when the applicant's husband predeceases her. The income of $100 per month which I envisage should be obtained from interest of a fund so far as possible with resort to the body of the fund if necessary. This fund should be considered as being made up of whatever assets the applicant (then a widow) may have from any source (excepting the home and its contents) plus the whole estate of the deceased testatrix. The interest from this corpus, so far as possible, should be used to provide the income mentioned and any deficiency should be made up out of the fund itself; and should such a cutting into the body of the fund be necessary, that part which is not the estate of the testatrix should be used first.
>
> The eventuality of the husband of the applicant necessarily retiring from employment should be dealt with in a similar manner. In this case the combined income of husband and wife should be $150. Income from all sources must be considered. It is possible that even after retirement no augmentation from testatrix' estate will be necessary. For instance, the hus-

7 (1953), 61 Man. R. 198 (Man. Q.B.). Also, *Re Hannah* (1931), 39 O.W.N. 499 (Ont. C.A.).

> band may retire and receive a pension of $75 per month but may immediately take up some other remunerative activities which will give him another $75 per month. Upon retirement of Mr. Laventure the income of him and his wife should be computed and their assets totalled. The home and contents should not be taken into consideration but should be excepted as in the death eventuality already dealt with. Income from their assets and income from the estate funds combined should go to the applicant up to the amount of $150 per month, and if such income should be less than that amount the deficiency should be made up out of, first, the assets of the couple themselves and, second, out of the principal of the estate.
>
> I would make no change in the will so far as the bequest to [the sister] is concerned, and likewise would leave undisturbed the $500 legacy to the applicant. There is no reason why St. John's Cathedral should not have and use the interest of or from the estate of the testatrix until necessity arises for its use under one of the eventualities mentioned.
>
> I have spoken of the possibility of serious loss of income through prolonged illness, but I do not think the present is the right time to deal with that possibility. Under the Act the opportunity exists to bring such a matter before the court if and when it should develop. I think it would be better to leave it that way and, if necessary, I reserve to the applicant her right to ask for consideration in such an eventuality.[8]

Re Bowie[9] is a case in which unfortunately the court did not make use of a suspensory order. Mr. Bowie's will provided for his wife several bequests plus the creation of a trust fund to yield a specific annual payment. The will provided several other bequests and gave the residue of the fairly large estate to a Foundation. Mrs. Bowie applied for relief pursuant to the then *Testator's Family Maintenance Act*. The court ordered the trust fund to be increased to provide for a larger annual payment. This was done and the executor and trustee transferred the residue to the Foundation where, incidentally, it remained intact. Subsequently, Mrs. Bowie had the annual payment increased at the expense of capital. When the trust fund was nearly exhausted she made another application to have the annual payment made out of Foundation funds. The court dismissed her application because there was no estate left undistributed out of which to fund an order. There could have been the residue of the estate if the court dealing with Mrs. Bowie's initial application had not only ordered the trust fund to be increased, but also had suspended the distribution of the residue as did the court in *Laventure*, above.

---

8 *Ibid.* at 204–05.

9 (1984), 30 Man. R. (2d) 128 (Man. Q.B.).

In *Alberta (Official Guardian) v. LeMasurier*[10] the trial judge issued a suspensory order setting aside $5,000.00 of the estate for an adopted child for which he could apply "for his use arising from sickness or other necessity" until he reached 18 years. The Court of Appeal awarded the child a higher lump sum unconditionally.

Even though a suspensory order has been made, the court can release part of the estate from the suspensory order, as did the court in *Laventure*, above. *Hecht v. Hecht Estate*[11] had to do with an application to permit one gift in a will to be implemented notwithstanding the existence of a suspensory order. The court granted the application on the basis that the beneficiaries had established need and hardship because of delay in the administration of the estate, and the risk that the money in question would be needed to satisfy a relief order was remote.

Although, the British Columbia Act does not provide for suspensory orders, British Columbia courts in effect make them.[12]

2. INTERIM RELIEF ORDERS[13]

The Ontario Act empowers the court to make an interim relief order:

> **64.** Where an application is made under this Part and the applicant is in need of and entitled to support but any or all of the matters referred to in section 62 or 63 have not been ascertained by the court, the court may make such interim order under section 63 as it considers appropriate.[14]

The Manitoba Act[15] contains a similar section.

Does the phrase "entitled to support" mean that an interim relief order cannot be made when an application for relief is opposed? *Re Puliver*[16] had to do with a motion by the executors of the deceased's estate for an order staying the application of the widow for an interim order. Respecting the phrase "entitled to support", the executors raised three questions concern-

---

10 [1949] 2 W.W.R. 748 (Alta. C.A.) at 748.

11 (1990), 39 E.T.R. 165 (B.C. S.C.); see also (1991), (*sub nom. Hecht v. Reid*) 62 B.C.L.R. (2d) 145 (B.C. C.A.).

12 See *Re Savannah* (1963), 43 W.W.R. 569 (B.C. S.C.).

13 Not to be confused with interim advances or interim distribution orders which are treated earlier in Chp. 3, 7.

14 In *Bailey v. Bailey Estate* (1986), (*sub nom. Bailey v. Hunt*) 57 O.R. (2d) 241 (Ont. H.C.) at 245, it was decided that "it is most appropriate that a master of the Supreme Court of Ontario should hear a motion for interim support. . .". Section 10 supercedes *Re Boucher*, [1971] 1 O.R. 49 (Ont. C.A.); *Holland v. Clements Estate* (1988), 30 E.T.R. 93 (Ont. Surr. Ct.) was an application for an interim relief order more remarkable for other aspects of the case.

15 S.M. 1989-90, c. 42, s. 11.

16 (1982), 39 O.R. (2d) 460 (Ont. H.C.).

ing the widow's entitlement to support, including the deceased's domicile at death. Justice Van Camp construed the phrase liberally:

> The only jurisdiction to award interim relief must be found in the statute. It did not leave it to the Court to make such order as it thought fit and just. I must pay heed to the requirement that the applicant be in need of and entitled to support. I may interpret that section strictly and require that there may be no doubt as to entitlement. Such an interpretation would effectively deprive dependants of any interim relief if any question were raised as to entitlement except as to quantum.
>
> Section 10 of the *Interpretation Act*, R.S.O. 1980, c. 219, provides that every Act is deemed to be remedial and is to receive such liberal construction as will best ensure the attainment of its object. Those words were used again by Mr. Justice Zuber when he was considering the meaning of the word "entitled" in the *Insurance Act* and said in *Brown v. Bowwkamp*, 8 O.R. (2d) 363 at 366, 58 D.L.R. (2d) 59, [1976] I.L.R. 1-722:
>
>> The word entitled as used in s. 226h(2) must be interpreted in the light of the purpose sought to be accomplished.
>
> The Act before me provides for support of dependants and it provides for interim support. Consequently, it is my opinion that where the applicant has put forward substantial evidence to support her claim as a dependant, and that the testator was domiciled in Ontario, application for interim relief should be heard even if those questions are in issue on the final hearing of the substantive application.
>
> I have recognized that when domicile is determined and when the other matters are determined it may be that the applicant will have received funds under an interim order to which she would not be entitled. In light of the assets that she has, in light of the relationship to the testator, I do consider that no order for security for repayment of amounts made under the order should be made.[17]

Presumably, the courts in those provinces, the legislation of which does not expressly empower interim relief orders, do not have the jurisdiction to make them.[18]

---

17 *Ibid* at 462–63.

18 *Mollins v. Mollins Estate* (1996), 152 N.S.R. (2d) 386 (N.S. S.C.) at paragraph 4, additional reasons at (1996), 152 N.S.R. (2d) 386 at 389 (N.S. S.C.) confirms this for Nova Scotia. However, note *Chityala v. Chityala Estate* (1986), 71 A.R. 200 (Alta. Q.B.) at paragraph 2.

3. VARIATION

All of the Acts[19] contain a section identical or similar to s. 65 of the Ontario Act:

> Where an order has been made under this Part, the court at any subsequent date may,
>
> (a) inquire whether the dependant benefitted by the order has become entitled to the benefit of any other provision for his or her support;
>
> (b) inquire into the adequacy of the provision ordered; and
>
> (c) discharge, vary or suspend the order, or make such other order as the court considers appropriate in the circumstances.

The Saskatchewan and Manitoba sections are the similar ones. The Saskatchewan section provides:

> **20.** (1) The court may at any time discharge, vary or suspend an order or make any other order that it considers just in the circumstances, on the ground that a material fact was not disclosed to the court when the order was made.
>
> (2) An application for an order under subsection (1) may be made by or on behalf of a
>
> (a) dependant;
>
> (b) beneficiary under the will; or
>
> (c) a person entitled pursuant to *The Intestate Succession Act*, 1996 to share in the estate of the deceased.

About s. 20(1) and the unique wording "on the ground that a material fact was not disclosed to the court when the order was made", Justice Grotsky in *Shapka v. Shapka Estate*[20] said:

> [1] . . .
> THE ISSUES
>
> 4. Is the applicant entitled to apply, under s. 19 of the Act, for an order varying the order of Noble, J., on the ground that a material fact was not disclosed to Mr. Justice Noble when he heard the application and made the order, now sought to be varied?
>
> 5. If the answer to issue #1 is "YES", then, in the circumstances, is the previously undisclosed fact so material in nature that the court ought to vary the order, in the manner requested by the applicant: to direct that

19 B.C. s. 14; Alta. s. 6(6); Sask. s. 20; Man. ss. 14-15; N.B. s. 6; N.S. s. 7; P.E.I. s. 7; Nfld. s. 7; N.W.T. s. 6; Y.T. s. 7.

20 (1985), 44 Sask. R. 262 (Sask. Q.B.).

> the whole of the estate of the deceased situated in Saskatchewan be paid to the applicant? . . .

THE APPLICANT SUBMITS

[13] That a material fact was not disclosed to the court on the original application when the order, now sought to be varied, was made . . .

THE PUBLIC TRUSTEE SUBMITS

[14] That the material fact sought now to be brought forward by the applicant was available when the original application was heard. Further, and in any event, if the alleged "new" material fact(s) had been brought forward at the original hearing, the order then made, would still have been made.

THE LAW

[15] What is the meaning to be ascribed to s. 19 of the Dependants' Relief Act?

[16] The mischief rule for statutory interpretation is discussed in Maxwell on Interpretation of Statutes at pp. 40-42 and Craies on Statutes (7th Ed.), at pp. 96-98.

[17] Briefly stated, the rule calls on the court to consider the problem or mischief which the statutes seek to remedy, and then to suppress the mischief, and advance the remedy.

[18] By s. 19 of the Act, the legislature intended to suppress the non-disclosure of material facts contrary to a party's interest. A s. 19(2) party, contrary in interest to the party not making disclosure of a material fact is, by s. 19(1) permitted to seek an order such as is by it permitted: discharge, vary or suspend, when the material fact is discovered by that party. For example, if the executors here had failed to make full disclosure of the assets of the estate, the widow, the applicant, if unaware of their existence, and not a party to their non-disclosure, would have been entitled under s. 19 of the Act to seek variation based on such non-disclosure.

[19] I have considered and read the able oral and written submission of counsel. As well, the authorities to which each has referred me. I am satisfied that the facts which the applicant submits are "new" and "material" and which she asserts were not disclosed to the court on the original application were facts of which she had knowledge, or which were available to her, prior to the original application. This is evident from a reading of her own affidavit submitted in support of that application. If material facts were not disclosed to the court on the original application such non-disclosure was the act of the applicant. Not by any person with a contrary interest. Such a non-disclosure is not the mischief intended to be remedied by an application under s. 19 of the Act.

[20] In the circumstances, the applicant is not entitled to apply under s. 19 of the Act for an order varying the order made by Noble, J.

Section 14 of the Manitoba Act reads:

Application to discharge, suspend or reduce order

14. (1) At any time subsequent to the making of an order of provision for maintenance and support, an application to have the order discharged, suspended or reduced may be made to the court by or on behalf of any of the following persons:

(a) the deceased's personal representative;

(b) a person entitled under the deceased's will or under The Intestate Succession Act;

(c) a dependant.

Power of court to discharge, suspend or reduce

14. (2) In an application under subsection (1), the court shall consider

(a) whether the dependant who benefitted by the order has become entitled to any other provision for his or her maintenance and support; and

(b) the reasonableness of the maintenance and support ordered;

and may discharge, suspend or reduce the provision made under the order.

Exception

14. (3) Specified property that was ordered transferred absolutely to a dependant or a lump sum ordered to be paid directly to a dependant is not subject to an order under subsection (2).

There are three points to note. First, although only the Manitoba and Saskatchewan sections, ss. 14(1) and 20(2) respectively, specify who can apply for a discharge, variation or suspension order, surely what they specify goes without stipulation in the other provinces. Second, s. 14(2) of the Manitoba Act uses the word "reduced" not the word "varied"; in all the other Acts the phrase used, as in s. 65 of he Ontario Act, is "discharge, vary or suspend". The word "vary" seems to empower the court to reduce or increase an order. For Manitoba increasing orders is empowered quite elaborately in s. 15:

Order for increased provision

15. (1) Subject to subsections (2) and (3), at any time subsequent to the making of an order of provision for maintenance and support, a dependant in respect of whom the order was made may apply to the court for an order increasing the amount of provision.

When increased provision may be made

15. (2) The court may make an order increasing the amount of provision if it is satisfied that

(a) since the date of the order circumstances have so changed that undue hardship will be caused to the applicant if the increase is not ordered; and

(b) it would not be inequitable to order increased provision having regard to the implications in respect of other persons interested in the estate.

Exception

15. (3) An order may be made under this section only as to that portion of the estate remaining undistributed at the date notice of the application for increased provision is served on the personal representative.

Third, similar to s. 14 of the British Columbia Act and s. 6(b) of the Alberta Act, s. 14(3) of the Manitoba Act restricts the kinds of orders with which the court can deal. Section 14 of the British Columbia Act begins "If the court has ordered periodic payments, or that a lump sum be invested for the benefit of a person" and s. 6 of the Alberta Act reads ". . . a judge . . . (b) may, when periodic payments have been ordered. . .". Probably in all of the other provinces the court will only vary to increase an order if there is undistributed estate,[21] and the court will not discharge, reduce, or suspend either an absolute lump sum payment or a property transfer.

Section 7(1) of the Nova Scotia and Newfoundland Acts are worded identically to s. 65 of the Ontario Act, above. Section 7(2) of the Nova Scotia Act reads:

(2) The judge may, when proceeding under subsection (1), include as relevant the fact that the dependant was

(a) the surviving spouse of the testator and has remarried;

---

21 Note *Re Bowie, supra* note 9, which was decided when s. 7 of the former *Testators Family Maintenance Act* of Manitoba empowered the court to "discharge, vary, or suspend" orders.

(b) an unmarried child of the testator who has married;

(c) an infant child of the testator who has attained the age of majority;

or

(d) a disabled child of the testator who has ceased to be disabled.

Section 7(2) of the Newfoundland Act is quite similar. In *Maldaver v. Canada Permanent Trust Co.*[22] Justice Hollett commented upon s. 7(2) of the Nova Scotia Act; at the time, current s. 7 was s. 6:

> 5. There are two points that emerge in this case. First, I am persuaded from looking at the case law and looking at the actual provisions of Section 6 of the Nova Scotia Act that section 6 does not contemplate increasing an Order that has already been made. It is to be noted that Section 6(2) deals with situations which would warrant a decrease. Secondly, the case law persuades me that the date of death is the proper time to make the determination as to the adequacy of the provisions made by the testator for the dependent. That date least interferes with the intention of the testator as expressed in the words of his Will. If the Legislature intended to authorize a court to vary a testator's will on a regular basis by a succession of applications so as to increase the payments to be made to a dependent based on the circumstances that exist at the time of the various applications, I think the provisions of the legislation would have been made much clearer than those in the Nova Scotia Act. As indicated, the provisions in Section 6(2) seem to contemplate a downward revision only of an Order that was made in the first instance. . . .

22 (1982), 53 N.S.R. (2d) 500 (N.S. T.D.).

6

Other Claims

Although courts readily combine marital property and dependants' relief applications, for the most part courts have refused to deal with matters beyond their jurisdiction under their dependants' relief Act. It is understandable in the circumstances why the court in *Re Hovdebo*[1] refused to deal with a requested change of executors. However, Justice Disberey added:

> This request in the notice of motion is an entirely separate and distinct matter from the application by the widow for relief under *The Dependants' Relief Act* . . . and should not have been included in the same application. When an application is made by a dependant under *The Dependants' Relief Act* such should stand alone and not be yoked in the same motion with applications for orders respecting matters outside the purview of the Act.

In his will Helmer Salthammer, *inter alia*, directed "that all indebtedness owing to me by my brother Jack . . . be cancelled".[2] Helmer's widow made a relief application. In ordering that she receive the whole estate Justice Disberey wrote:

> Counsel both for the applicant and the Trust Company thought the indebtedness of Jack Salthammer to the estate might well be cancelled because he is and has been for years in very poor health and in consequence the probability of getting payment was very remote. I do not think I have the power to cancel that indebtedness. My duty is confined to making an allowance to the widow that is reasonable, just and equitable in the circumstances. Under the disposition of the matter that I am making, the widow or the executor with her consent can absolve Jack Salthammer of his indebtedness and I think it advisable to be done in that way, if it is done.
>
> I give to the widow all of the estate of the said Helmer Salthammer, deceased, and the will is changed accordingly.[3]

---

1 (1963), 45 W.W.R. 640 (Sask. Q.B.).

2 *Re Salthammer* (1946), [1947] 2 D.L.R. 135 (Sask. K.B.) at 136.

3 *Ibid.* at 138. Similarly, *Re Becker* (1964), 46 D.L.R. (2d) 574 (Alta. S.C.).

Similarly, in *Rollins v. Beyea Estate*,[4] not only did the court dismiss the applications of two adult daughters, but also the court said that it did not come within its jurisdiction under the then *Testators Family Maintenance Act* to relieve the daughters of their indebtedness to the estate.

In *Re Ponzir*[5] the deceased in his will devised his homestead to a friend, who "had furnished materials and labour to a value of several hundred dollars for the construction of the house on the lot". In awarding the homestead to the widow, the court acknowledged that the friend could obtain a judgment for the materials and labour he supplied which would give him rights against the homestead upon the death of the widow, but left it up to the friend to commence a separate action to that end.

In *Pauliuk v. Pauliuk*[6] the court refused to consider a *quantum meruit* claim by a woman who cared for the deceased during his terminal illness.

In *Stadnyk v. Bulycz*[7] the court refused to deal with an allegation that the applicant had removed certain chattels in violation of an agreement made between the applicant and the executrix:

> I do not feel that this is a matter which should be dealt with on an application of this nature, and this judgment in no way affects the rights of the parties with respect thereto.

In *Maldaver v. Canada Permanent Trust Co.*[8] the court awarded two daughters an increase in the per weekly legacy provided in their father's will. Their counsel expressed their wish that the court not make an award for them which would require use of the capital estate. The will apparently restricted the trustee of the estate to depositing the proceeds of sale of the assets in a certain institution. The court opined that the deposit provision was "unduly restrictive" and stated that the power of investment given by the will "can be varied to increase the income substantially, without affecting the security of capital", enabling the court's order to be paid without encroaching on the capital; but, a separate application would have to be made.

---

4 (1987), 81 N.B.R. (2d) 58 (N.B. Q.B.) at paragraph 10.

5 [1950] 2 W.W.R. 1009 (Alta. S.C.), affirmed [1950] 2 W.W.R. 1201 (Alta. C.A.); also *Rybe v. Alberta (Public Trustee)* (1959), 36 W.W.R. 133 (Alta. C.A.) and *Moroz v. Moroz Estate* (1991), 92 Sask. R. 176 (Sask. Surr. Ct.). Note *Crilley v. Beckingham* (1986), 74 N.B.R. (2d) 91 (N.B. Q.B.) at paragraph 37.

6 (1986), 48 Alta. L.R. (2d) 25 (Alta. Q.B.) at 28. Cf. *Re Johnson* (1955), 17 W.W.R. 88 (Sask. Q.B.) at 91.

7 (1961), 36 W.W.R. 241 (Sask. Q.B.) at 253, varied (1961), 36 W.W.R. 680 (Sask. C.A.). Cf. *Spinney v. Royal Trust Co.* (1973), 9 N.S.R. (2d) 699 (N.S. T.D.) at paragraphs 8–9 and 45–47, and *Coolen v. Coolen* (1980), 43 N.S.R. (2d) 67 (N.S. C.A.) at paragraphs 24–42; *Menrad v. Blowers* (1982), 137 D.L.R. (3d) 309 (Man. Q.B.) at 319–20.

8 (1977), 27 N.S.R. (2d) 248 (N.S. T.D.) at paragraphs 17–18.

In *Re Rusk Estate*[9] the court acknowledged that it could not deal with entitlement to a disputed asset.

However, there are cases in which courts have dealt with extraneous claims, as the "cf." cases in footnotes 6 and 7 exemplify. Also, in *Royal Trust Co. v. Downton*[10] the court dealt with the claim of a life insurance beneficiary to be a creditor of the estate entitled to reimbursement ahead of the relief order. The deceased, with the consent of the beneficiary, had assigned the insurance policy to a bank. Pursuant to the assignment the insurer paid some of the proceeds to the bank to satisfy the deceased's indebtedness to the bank.

9 (1957), 6 D.L.R. (2d) 700 (Sask. C.A.) at 703.
10 (1977), 19 Nfld. & P.E.I.R. 455 (Nfld. T.D.), affirmed (1980), 34 Nfld. & P.E.I.R. 308 (Nfld. C.A.).

7

Costs

1. GENERALLY

There may be a widespread impression that commonly costs are awarded to the applicant(s) and the respondent(s) out of the estate on a solicitor and client basis or at least on a party and party basis. Actually, there is a range of costs law or policy prevalent across Canada, which ranges from treating dependants' relief proceedings the same as other litigation, to treating dependants' relief proceedings the same as other estate litigation, to usually ordering costs of all parties to be paid out of the estate on either a party and party or solicitor and client basis. A careful recording and analysis of the costs dispositions in the reported cases resulted in few general insights. It is impossible to determine the real situation in any province, except British Columbia, because of the significant number of cases in which the report is silent as to costs,[1] because of the variety of costs orders,[2] and because of the lack of consistency.

In all of the provinces and territories, except Saskatchewan and Ontario, the jurisdiction to order costs in dependants' relief proceedings derives from the legislation and common law respecting costs generally. Probably, the existence of costs sections in the Saskatchewan and Ontario dependants' relief Acts is of no particular significance and does not make the costs jurisdiction of the courts of those provinces any different

---

1 This is true for Alta., Sask., Man., Ont., N.B., and N.S.; there is not the critical mass of reported cases for P.E.I., Nfld., the N.W.T., and the Y.T. to allow for generalization.

2 The variety of costs orders include; all parties to receive their costs out of the estate on either a party and party or a solicitor and client basis; the executor to receive costs on a solicitor and client basis, other parties to receive costs on a party and party basis, all out of the estate; only the executor to receive costs on either a solicitor and client or party and party basis out of the estate; without costs in various wordings; the applicant(s) to pay the costs of the respondent(s) or vice versa on a solicitor and client or party and party basis; or one respondent to pay the costs of the other parties; and fixed costs orders.

from that of the courts elsewhere in Canada. Nonetheless, dealing first with Saskatchewan, its Act[3] provides:

> **21.** The court may:
>
> (a) direct that the costs of any application be paid out of the estate or in any other manner that it considers just; and
>
> (b) fix the amount of the costs, exclusive of necessary disbursements, at a lump sum having regard to the value of the estate and the amount of any maintenance applied for or directed by the order.

In *Peill v. Peill*,[4] decided at a time when the predecessor to the current Saskatchewan Act did not contain a section comparable to the current s. 21, the court said that, regarding costs, the widow applicant "is in just the same position as any female plaintiff in any ordinary litigation;"[5] accordingly, the court dismissed the widow's application with costs to the respondents against the widow. In *Re Day*,[6] when the Saskatchewan Act contained a section comparable to the current s. 21, Justice Graham expressly disagreed with *Peill* and said:

> . . . I think the matter of costs is in the discretion of the judge hearing the application and each case must be dealt with on its merits.

While acknowledging that the widow applicant "had some, if not sufficient, grounds to justify her application", he dismissed her application without costs and ordered that the respondent's costs be paid out of the estate on a solicitor and client basis. However, in *Wildeman v. Co-operative Trust Co.*[7] the court said:

> It seems that the courts have generally allowed costs . . . to an unsuccessful widow . . . where the Court felt that she had been entitled to a full review by the Court of the circumstances.

In *Re Champ Estate*[8] Justice Geatros, with reference to cases, but not *Peill* or *Day*, said regarding costs that dependants' relief applications ought to be treated according to the principles which govern estate litigation generally. The applicant was the guardian *ad litem* of the deceased's mentally handicapped son. Although Justice Geatros dismissed the application, pointing out that the applicant had acknowledged that the deceased had made reasonable provision for his son, nonetheless he did order a lump

3 *Dependants' Relief Act, 1996*, S.S. 1996, c. D-25.01, s. 21 [hereinafter Saskatchewan Act].

4 [1939] 2 W.W.R. 519 (Sask. K.B.).

5 *Ibid.* at 526; one can only wonder what the position of a male plaintiff was.

6 (1952), 4 W.W.R. (N.S.) 644 (Sask. K.B.) at 647.

7 (1973), 39 D.L.R. (3d) 767 (Sask. Q.B.) at 768; also *Collard v. Collard* (1976), 28 R.F.L. 252 (Sask. Surr. Ct.) at 256.

8 (1986), (*sub nom. Re Champ*) 47 Sask. R. 305 (Sask. Q.B.)

sum approximating 17% of the solicitor and client costs claimed by the applicant to be paid out of the estate; the costs order was based upon cases in which courts have said that litigation by a next friend must be encouraged.

So far as the case reports are indicative, Saskatchewan judges are inclined to order party and party costs to all parties. An exemplary case is *Edward v. Edward Estate*.[9] An unsuccessful respondent, who was awarded party and party costs out of the estate, unsuccessfully appealed, *inter alia*, trying to have the costs order changed to solicitor and client costs; the court dismissed the appeal with "no order as to costs" for the appeal.

The *Succession Law Reform Act* of Ontario[10] provides:

> **75.** The court may direct that the costs of the application be paid out of the estate or otherwise as it thinks proper, and may fix the amount of the costs payable by any party, exclusive of necessary disbursements, at a lump sum having regard to the value of the estate and the amount of any support applied for or directed by its order.

There is no Ontario case which deals at length with costs generally in dependants' relief proceedings. However, in *Re Dentinger*[11] the court said:

> Had this estate not been distributed, and having regard to the issues and amounts involved, I would have ordered the costs of both the applicant and the respondents to be paid from the estate on a solicitor-and-client basis and on the Supreme Court scale.

The Court made an award to the widow applicant and ordered the respondents to pay her costs on a solicitor and client basis on the Supreme Court scale. The respondents were the two executrices, who had prematurely distributed the estate to themselves and their two siblings, who were the other respondents, all of whom advanced a common position to the widow's application. The "issues and amounts involved" were not extraordinary. In *Assaf v. Koury*,[12] after quoting the section in the *Judicature Act*, which empowers judges to order costs generally, and the predecessor to s. 75, the court said:

> In my opinion the jurisdiction with respect to costs under either Act should be governed by the same principles even though there is some difference in the wording of the two sections.

This statement was made in connection with a dismissal of an application and a "vigorous" submission that the court should order the executors' costs to be paid on a solicitor and own client basis by the son of the

9 (1987), 57 Sask. R. 67 (Sask. C.A.).
10 R.S.O. 1990, c. S.26, Part V, s. 75 [hereinafter Ontario Act].
11 (1981), 10 E.T.R. 6 (Ont. Surr. Ct.) at 32–33.
12 (1980), 16 C.P.C. 202 (Ont. H.C.).

applicant, who had promoted and financed the application, as well as other improper litigation against the estate; the court complied. The *Dentinger* and *Assaf* cases are at odds with each other. Macdonell, Sheard and Hull[13] say:

> In practice when the Court has concluded that the dependant was entitled to have the circumstances reviewed, the costs of all parties are most commonly ordered to be paid out of the estate on a solicitor and client basis.

So far as the case reports are indicative they bear out this statement, although there are cases in which only party and party costs were awarded and in 40% of the cases the report does not indicate the costs disposition.

This is not so for Alberta, if *Baker v. Baker Estate*[14] is representative. The case involved a widow left destitute by her husband who by his will gave his estate to three of his four children. The Court discussed the issue of costs at length and took the position that the widow's dependants' relief application should be treated on the same basis as any other estate litigation, *inter alia* allowing the widow costs from the estate on a party and party basis and refusing costs to the executrix insofar as her opposition to the application related to her status as one of the beneficiaries. So far as the case reports are indicative, Alberta judges are much more inclined to order costs on a party and party basis; still, in a significant number of cases solicitor and client costs have been ordered.

The Alberta Act contains a unique section[15]:

> (4) No costs of or incidental to an application, other than the executor's or administrator's costs, shall be ordered to be paid out of the estate in any case where the value of the net estate, as finally determined by the clerk of the court in fixing probate or administration fees, is less than $5000.

There is no Manitoba judicial discourse on costs in dependants' relief applications, but there is *Manitoba (Public Trustee) v. Ballen*,[16] concerning the removal of an executor, in which the Court of Appeal said:

> [12] A general principle this court has long embraced is that solicitor and client costs will be awarded only in the "rare and exceptional case." . . .
>
> [13] That principle has been applied in estate proceedings . . . .

---

13 Hull, R. and Hull I., eds. *Macdonell, Sheard and Hull on Probate Practice*, 4th ed. (Toronto: Carswell, 1996) at 149. Schnurr, B. and Woodley, S. suggest that the usual order is party and party costs: "Dependant Support Proceedings" (1995) 14 E.T.J. 159 at 166; note also Schnurr, B., "Estate Litigation—Who Pays The Costs?" (1991) 11 E.T.J. 52 at 62.

14 (1992), 136 A.R. 94 (Alta. Q.B.), further reasons regarding costs and expenses at (1993), at 138 A.R. 1 (Alta. Q.B.).

15 *Family Relief Act*, R.S.A. 1980, c. F-2, s. 13(4) [hereinafter Alberta Act].

16 (1992), (*sub nom. Re Balan's Estate*) 76 Man. R. (2d) 241 (Man. C.A.).

> [14] Another general principle that emerges from the cases is that an executor is to be indemnified against all reasonable costs and expenses incurred by him/her in the course of the administration of the estate. . . .
>
> . . . . .
>
> [16] The costs of all parties to estate proceedings have been ordered to be paid out of an estate when it was necessary to apply to the court to construe a testamentary document; to determine who were the heirs of an intestate deceased; or to determine the capacity of a testator or the circumstances of the execution of his/her will. . . .
>
> . . . . .
>
> [18] At the same time, parties cannot count on their costs being paid out of the estate . . . .
>
> . . . . .
>
> [20] In other cases, courts have ordered parties to pay costs to the estate, and even on a solicitor and client basis.

Similarly, in *Harvey v. Powell Estate*[17] Justice Nathanson, perhaps reflecting the state of costs in Nova Scotia, said:

> [3] The various awards of costs that follow are based upon the application of three guidelines.
>
> [4] First is the equitable principle that costs are in the discretion of the court. That general principle is now enshrined in Civil Procedure Rule 63.02(1). . . .
>
> [5] The second guideline is the rule that the costs of a personal representative, such as the executor of an estate, are usually payable out of the fund that he or she holds. That rule is stated in Civil Procedure Rule 63.12(1). . . ..
>
> [6] The third guideline is derived from a review of decided cases of claims against estates, including claims pursuant to dependents relief legislation. Although it cannot be described as a rule, the trend in such cases appears to be that successful claimants against estates are normally awarded costs on a party and party basis rather than on a solicitor and client basis.

There is a significant number of cases in which applications and appeals have been dismissed "without costs" or similar words. However, analysis of them proved to be of no instructive value. For instance, some of them are unsuccessful applications by widows, not only by the facts resulting in a summary dismissal, but also in some of them only after substantial consideration; there are other unsuccessful applications by widows in which costs were awarded to the widow, including some in which consideration of the application was given short shrift.

---

17 (1989), 90 N.S.R. (2d) 265 (N.S. T.D.), affirmed (1989), 95 N.S.R. (2d) 37 (N.S. C.A.).

A few applications and appeals have been dismissed with costs against the applicant or appellant.[18] But with each situation there are other cases in which costs have been ordered out of the estate or in which "without costs" orders have been made. In at least five cases respondents have been ordered personally to pay the applicant's costs. *Re Blackmore*[19] involved an application by an abused, constructively deserted, disinherited widow, who suffered from polio and supported herself by doing needlework. Her husband left his $2,000.00 estate to a couple of friends, who were appointed by his will to be his executors, to various relatives, none of whom should have had any reason to expect the testamentary gift, and to a church for a requiem mass. The court in awarding the widow $1,800.00, left intact the provision for the requiem mass and said about costs:

> The executors will have their costs of and incidental to this application, which I fix at $40.00, to be paid out of the balance of the estate remaining after the sum of $1,800.00 has been paid to the applicants.
>
> The beneficiaries, other than the pastor of St. Mary's Cathedral, will pay the applicant's costs of and incidental to this application, which I fix at $100.00. I feel that under the circumstances of this most distressing case, with which they must all have been familiar, the beneficiaries should have been willing that this small estate should go to one who had been so badly treated and who

---

18 *Re Lund*, [1946] 3 W.W.R. 732 (Sask. K.B.) non-needy widower, modest estate; *Re Wild* (1964), 44 D.L.R. (2d) 91 (Alta. T.D.) non-needy widow, modest estate; *Re DeRoche Estate* (1964), 51 W.W.R. 120 (Sask. Q.B.), adult daughter; *Alberta (Public Trustee) v. Buchholz* (1980), 24 A.R. 287 (Alta. C.A.), unsuccessful appeal by Public Trustee on behalf of minor children; *Mealey v. Broadbent* (1984), 47 O.R. (2d) 161 (Ont. Div. Ct.), affirmed (1987), 25 E.T.R. 1 (Ont. C.A.), not qualified widow; *Daye v. Holmes Estate* (1987), 25 E.T.R. 161 (Ont. H.C.), late application; *Frye v. Frye* (1992) , 41 R.F.L. (3d) 145 (Ont. Gen. Div.), affirmed (1996), 23 R.F.L. (4th) 283 (Ont. C.A.), not qualified widow; *W. (D.J.) (Litigation Guardian of) v. W. (L.) Estate* (1994), 122 Sask. R. 299 (Sask. Q.B.), affirmed (1996), 137 Sask. R. 286 (Sask. C.A.), late application; *Roussel v. Hill Estate* (1996), 14 E.T.R. (2d) 111 (Ont. Gen. Div.), late application. Also *Assaf v. Koury*, *supra* note 12. In *Cameron (Public Trustee of) v. Cameron Estate* (1991), (*sub nom. British Columbia (Public Trustee) v. Cameron Estate*) 58 B.C.L.R. (2d) 82 (B.C. C.A.) at 82, leave to appeal a costs order was granted to the Public Trustee conditional on the Public Trustee undertaking to pay "the special costs of the estate, no matter what the outcome of the appeal.

19 (1948), 56 Man. R. 88 (Man. K.B.). Also *Tatko v. Liefke*, [1946] 1 W.W.R. 497 (Alta. C.A.), a $2,450.00 estate awarded all to the applicant widow; *Moore v. Hughes* (1981), 37 O.R. (2d) 785 (Ont. H.C.) probably because of the modest size of the estate and the fact that the respondent had received substantial wealth outside of the estate from the deceased; *Cowan v. Cowan Estate* (1988), 30 E.T.R. 216 (B.C. S.C.), affirmed (1990), 37 E.T.R. 308 (B.C. C.A.) because of a fabricated counter-claim; and *Olesko v. Olesko Estate* (1990), 87 Sask. R. 61 (Sask. Q.B.) against the Public Trustee who unsuccessfully opposed a widow's application.

was in such dire need. They should, at least, not have opposed this application.[20]

As to British Columbia, Amighetti, after quoting statements from *Re Lukie*[21] and *Re Bowe*[22] to the effect that the general rule concerning costs applies to dependants' relief proceedings, wrote:

> Since the *Re Bowe* decision the courts' approach to the legislation has changed dramatically [and] The rules [concerning costs] now give the courts a complete discretion as to costs . . . *Re Bowe* is probably no longer good law. The trend now seems to be one of awarding costs to the plaintiff regardless of the outcome at trial. . . .[23]

Apparently, the law of costs has not so evolved, as indicated by the following quote from *Lee v. Lee Estate*.[24] The testator left his estate to the grandchildren of his deceased daughter. Three adults, claiming to be sons of the testator, applied for a variation of the will. Genetic testing proved that the claimants were not sons of the testator, although he had treated them as his sons; the testator's daughter, their sister, thought that they were her full brothers, and their mother told them that the testator was their father. Their action was summarily dismissed and the matter of costs was referred to Master Horn, who wrote:

> I find that it was reasonable for the claimants to suppose that they were the sons of Edward Lee and that it was reasonable in light of the investigations made by their respective solicitors to commence litigation based upon this assumption. Whether if they were the sons of Edward Lee, it was reasonable to seek an order making provision for them out of his estate, I cannot say. There was little material before me which would assist in determining that question.
>
> Upon the basis that the outcome of this litigation, namely dismissal of the action because none of the claimants were the sons of Edward Lee, was entirely unexpected, it is suggested that costs of the claimants should be allowed out of the estate, either on a solicitor and client basis or upon a party and party basis. In short, the claimants, as unsuccessful parties to this litigation, wish to have their costs against a successful party, the estate.
>
> An order for costs in favour of a completely unsuccessful party against a completely successful party is a most exceptional order. The general rule is that costs follow the event and, while a court may depart from this rule, any departure is usually in the way of depriving a successful party of costs and

---

20 *Ibid.* at 98.

21 (1976), 1 B.C.L.R. 1 (B.C. C.A.).

22 [1971] 4 W.W.R. 234 (B.C. S.C.).

23 Amighetti, L., *The Law of Dependants' Relief in British Columbia* (Toronto: Carswell, 1991) at 162.

24 (1993), 84 B.C.L.R. (2d) 341 (B.C. Master).

not of awarding costs to an unsuccessful party. In either case, the usual rule should not be departed from simply because an unsuccessful party did not expect to lose. . . .

In probate or administration actions or in proceedings for the construction of wills, the rule may be more frequently departed from. In such cases where the validity of a will or the capacity of the testator to make a will or the meaning of a will is in issue, it is sometimes the case that the costs of all parties are ordered to be paid out of the estate. This is upon the principle that where such an issue must be litigated to remove all doubts, then all interested parties must be joined and are entitled to be heard and should not be out of pocket if in the result the litigation does not conclude in their favour. The estate must bear the cost of settling disputes as a cost of administration . . . . The question to be asked in such case is whether the parties were forced into litigation by the conduct of the testator or the conduct of the main beneficiaries.

But the case is different where the litigation does not relate to the validity of the will or the capacity of the testator or the construction of the will. Actions brought under dependants' relief legislation presume the validity of the will and the capacity of the testator and that his intentions are clear. There are not doubts to be settled. The remedies provided by such legislation are directed to the maintenance and support of the dependants of the testator and are based on public policy. The legislation does not invalidate the will, it merely permits the court to vary the provisions made by the testator. So an unsuccessful action under such legislation cannot be said to have been caused by a testator, or to have been necessary to enable the estate to be distributed. The action does not benefit the estate.

This difference between probate actions or administration actions or proceedings for the construction of a will and an action under the *Wills Variation Act* has been indirectly adverted to by the Court of Appeal of British Columbia in *Lukie v. Helgason* . . . . There the testator made no provision in his will for two of five children of his first marriage. These two children sought an order under the *Testator's Family Maintenance Act* to vary the terms of the will. The order was granted at first instance and the beneficiaries of the will appealed. On appeal the appeal was allowed. The order of the trial judge was set aside. As to the question of costs in the court below, two members of the court ordered that the plaintiffs, being unsuccessful parties, pay the costs of the defendants in the court below. Robertson J.A. said this at p. 15:

> I look without favour on any idea that persons without meritorious claims under the Act to share in the estate of a testator may have a try at getting part of his estate without risk to themselves and at the expense of the persons whom the testator wished to benefit.

Carrothers J.A., who concurred in making the order for costs, said this at p. 35:

> Costs should follow the event and the respondents should pay the costs of the appellants throughout on a party-and-party basis.

Taggart J.A., while concurring in the order dismissing the appeal, dissented as to costs and said at p. 26:

> As to costs I would not interfere with the disposition made by the trial judge of the costs of the trial.

The disposition of the trial judge was that all costs should be paid by the estate on a party and party basis.

The difference between these two types of action have been directly adverted to by Wilson C.J.S.C. in *Re Bowe Estate* . . . . He said, at pp. 239-40:

> Under The Testator's Family Maintenance Act there is no question of ambiguity or of the creation of a difficulty by the testator or of the petitioner being "led into the contest by the state in which the deceased left his papers". There is a simple assertion and denial of a claim under a statute. If the unsuccessful petitioner recovers costs from the estate it is frequently the effect that the successful litigants pay them through the diminution of the estate caused by the payment of the petitioner's costs.
>
> Therefore good cause must be shown for departing from O. 65 which says that costs will follow the event. This means not just that an unsuccessful petition [sic] will not ordinarily recover costs, it means that he will ordinarily pay costs.
>
> In *Re Edgelow* (1955), 18 W.W.R. 235, 1 D.L.R. (2d) 126 (B.C.), the late MacFarlane J. appeared to have no doubt that the ordinary Rule that costs followed the event was applicable to proceedings under the statute. He did, on the ground of her poverty, excuse the unsuccessful petitioner from the payment of costs to the estate, but he did not award her costs from the estate . . .
>
> But I am not prepared to accept the idea that because there are conflicting decisions referred to on a trial the usual Rule as to costs must necessarily be abrogated. This is not the result in ordinary litigation and I see no reason for a special Rule in cases under The Testator's Family Maintenance Act.

In two cases costs have been awarded in an action under the *Wills Variation Act*, or its predecessor, to an unsuccessful party on the grounds that the testator was at fault.

In *Re Tero Estate*, [1949] 2 W.W.R. 127 (B.C.S.C.), an applicant widow was denied relief on the grounds that there was no obligation to support her even if she were a wife, which was disputed. Nevertheless, the court gave her costs from the estate because [p. 128]:

> . . . the difficulties that have arisen were caused by the fault of the testator and that, if he is to have the luxury of three wives living at the same time, he or his estate should pay the costs of litigation which arises as a result.

What the court was referring to was the fact that the testator had married his third wife without having gone to the trouble of divorcing his second wife or of ascertaining whether she had divorced him.

In *Aussem v. Longmore* . . ., Cashman L.J.S.C. dismissed the action by the widow and by one daughter and allowed the claim by a second daughter. One counsel appeared for the widow and another for the two daughters. He gave costs on a solicitor and client basis against the estate in favour of both daughters, though one was unsuccessful, and gave party and party costs against the estate in favour of the widow, although she was unsuccessful. The grounds were principally that the main beneficiary had not been forthcoming in disclosing the extent of the deceased estate. Judgment was not reserved. The only authority on costs mentioned was *Lukie v. Helgason*, which was distinguished, but the judgment referred to a memorandum of counsel in which, it appears from an examination of the file, the only cases referred to were *Trites v. Johnson* . . . and *Re Dingwall* . . ., neither of which case was a proceeding under dependants' relief legislation but were estate actions. The principles applied by Cashman L.J.S.C. were derived from these two cases. His Honour Judge Cashman was apparently not referred to the decision of Chief Justice Wilson in *Re Bowe Estate*.

Faced with strong statements by two members of the British Columbia Court of Appeal and of the Chief Justice of the Supreme Court I feel compelled to hold that considerations which may be appropriate for awarding costs to an unsuccessful party in ordinary estate litigation are not appropriate in litigation under the *Wills Variation Act*.

Accordingly, the general rule must apply, which is that only in extraordinary circumstances will a successful party be made to pay the costs of an unsuccessful party. I find no such extraordinary circumstances here.

The next question is whether the claimants should pay costs.

It does not require extraordinary circumstances before a court may deprive a successful party of costs. Though R. 57(9) no longer requires "good cause" to be shown to depart from the normal rule as to costs, it does not follow that the rule may be departed from for no cause at all. There is a discretion to be exercised, which must be exercised judicially, meaning that there must be reason for the departure. . . .

In this case I conclude that the claimants ought not to pay costs, not because the successful parties have done any wrong, but because the deceased knew that the claimants went by the name of Lee and knew that they believed that they were his sons and did nothing to dispel that illusion in his lifetime, and may have fostered it. . . .

In these circumstances I conclude that all parties should bear their own costs.[25]

In *Vielbig v. Waterland Estate*[26] the Court of Appeal quoted extensively from Master Horn's articulation of the law in dismissing "with costs against the appellant in the court below and in this Court" an appeal of a trial judgment dismissal of the plaintiff's claim. The plaintiff was an adult daughter who, while not very well off financially, had not been dependent on the testator and to whom the testator owed no special moral obligation. In his will the testator treated her equally with her wealthy brother. Earlier in *Hecht v. Hecht Estate*,[27] on an unsuccessful appeal the Court of Appeal said:

> Although Mrs. Hecht was unsuccessful in the Supreme Court in her petition under the *Wills Variation Act*, the trial judge made no order for costs. The reason the trial judge gave was that the testator had misled Mrs. Hecht at the time she executed a marriage agreement as to the size of his estate.
>
> Mr. Nathanson, counsel for Mrs. Hecht, submitted that same reason should be the basis for an order of no costs in this court. The petitioner, however, failed in the Supreme Court because the trial judge found that the testator had made adequate provision for her in his will. Once the finding on that threshold test was made by the trial judge, the appellant was in the same position of any other appellant, that is to say, liable to pay costs if unsuccessful on the appeal.[28]

An examination of post *Lee* and *Vielbig* decisions, not including a couple of procedural cases, reveals that in 30% of the cases there is simply no order for costs contained in the reported judgment; in 45% of the cases the costs orders were in line with *Lee* and *Vielbig*; leaving deviation in 25% of the cases. In *Moore v. Moore Estate*[29] the Court of Appeal left the successful appellant and the respondent to bear their own costs of the appeal because of fault it found on the part of both parties. In *Tweedale v. Tweedale Estate*[30] the Court reversed a dismissal and awarded the whole $18,000.00 estate to the widower explicitly making "no order as to costs"; it seems harsh not to have ordered the respondents' costs out of the estate for they had been successful at trial.

---

25 *Ibid.* at 345–49.

26 (1995), 1 B.C.L.R. (3d) 76 (B.C. C.A.) at 88–89. In *Kelly v. Baker* (1996), 15 E.T.R. (2d) 219 (B.C. C.A.) at paragraph 61, the court confirmed *Vielbig*.

27 (1993), 87 B.C.L.R. (2d) 271 (B.C. C.A.). Similarly, *Hutton v. Podgurski* (1989), 58 D.L.R. (4th) 637 (B.C. C.A.) at 641.

28 *Ibid.* at 272.

29 (1994), 93 B.C.L.R. (2d) 64 (B.C. C.A.).

30 (1995), 1 B.C.L.R. (3d) 167 (B.C. C.A.).

Holland v. Holland Estate[31] was a run-of-the-mill successful application in which inexplicably the parties were left to bear their own costs. *Howard v. Howard Estate*[32] is remarkable not so much for the trial judge's order that the unsuccessful widow's costs be paid out of the estate, because "her application certainly warranted consideration in light of the line of authorities as outlined by" her counsel, but for her costs to be paid on a solicitor and client basis. In dismissing her appeal the Court said:

> The matter of costs is discretionary, but an award of special costs (which I take the award of costs on a solicitor/client basis to mean) is reserved for cases of unusual complexity and/or public importance. This case was neither complex nor of importance to anyone other than the parties. Nor was this a "necessary" lawsuit in the sense of having been occasioned by some ambiguity in the testator's will. I would not interfere with the trial judge's exercise of his discretion to award Mrs. Howard costs in the court below, but those should have been costs on the usual scale. To that extent I would allow the cross-appeal.
>
> The estate should have its costs of the appeal to this Court.

McRae v. Royal Trust Corp. of Canada,[33] a successful action, is remarkable in two respects; first the court indicated its inclination to order the costs of *both* parties to be paid out of the estate on a *solicitor and client* basis and second the court's reason was that the action "was made necessary by the failure of [the testator] to leave a portion of his estate to [the plaintiff]", which, contrary to *Lee*, groups dependants' relief litigation with other estate litigation.

Finally, on another matter, *Ewasew v. Ewasew*[34] illustrates the point that where an executor is also a beneficiary or heir and thus is a defendant or respondent in two capacities, the court might decide to order the costs of the executor, but not the other respondent(s), to be paid out of the estate; this will require a nice apportionment of the costs as between the two capacities. On the other hand, the court might decide that such an apportionment is not worthwhile and so order the executor beneficiary simply to be paid his or her costs out of the estate.

2. INTERIM COSTS ORDER

There is authority for such an order against the estate to enable a dependant to pursue an application.[35]

---

31 (1995), 9 E.T.R. (2d) 119 (B.C. S.C.).

32 (1997), 32 B.C.L.R. (3d) 1 (B.C.C.A.) at 6–7.

33 (1997), 16 E.T.R. (2d) 223 (B.C. S.C. [In Chambers]) at 240.

34 (1996), 11 E.T.R. (2d) 309 (B.C. S.C.[In Chambers]).

35 *Re Mowchenko* (1925), [1926] 1 W.W.R. 139 (Sask. K.B.).

8

Appeal

The British Columbia, Ontario, New Brunswick, Nova Scotia, Prince Edward Island, Newfoundland, Northwest Territories, and Yukon Acts[1] contain a simple appeal section, such as s.18 of the New Brunswick Act:

> **18.** An appeal lies to the Court of Appeal from any order made under this Act.

The Newfoundland Act also provides:

> **19.** (2) Where the party or person having a right of appeal does not appeal from the order or decision, a person beneficially interested in the estate, by leave of a judge, may appeal from the order.
>
> (3) A person beneficially interested in the estate may, by leave of a judge, appear and be heard upon an appeal.

By comparison to the simple appeal sections, such as s. 18 of the New Brunswick Act, the sections in the Alberta and Saskatchewan Acts[2] provide:

Alberta:

> **21.** (1) An appeal lies to the Court of Appeal from any order made under this Act.
>
> (2) The Court of Appeal may affirm, annul or vary the order appealed from in any manner that in its discretion it considers proper.

---

1 British Columbia *Wills Variation Act*, R.S.B.C. 1996, c. 490 [hereinafter British Columbia Act]; Ontario *Succession Law Reform Act*, R.S.O. 1990, c. S.26, Part V [hereinafter Ontario Act]; New Brunswick *Provision for Dependants Act*, R.S.N.B. 1973, c. P-22.3 [hereinafter New Brunswick Act]; Nova Scotia *Testators' Family Maintenance Act*, R.S.N.S. 1989, c. 465 [hereinafter Nova Scotia Act]; Prince Edward Island *Dependants of a Deceased Person Relief Act*, R.S.P.E.I. 1988, c. D-7 [hereinafter Prince Edwad Island Act]; Newfoundland *Family Relief Act*, R.S.N. 1990, c. F-2 [hereinafter Newfoundland Act]; Northwest Territories *Dependants Relief Act*, R.S.N.W.T. 1988, c. D-4 [hereinafter Northwest Territories Act]; Yukon Territory *Dependants Relief Act*, R.S.Y.T. 1990, c. 44 [hereinafter Yukon Act].

2 Alberta *Family Relief Act*, R.S.A. 1980, c. F-2 [hereinafter Alberta Act]; Saskatchewan *Dependants' Relief Act, 1996*, S.S. 1996, c. D-25.01 [hereinafter Saskatchewan Act].

Saskatchewan:

> **22.** (1) An appeal lies to the Court of Appeal from an order, other than an order as to costs.
>
> (2) On an appeal, the Court of Appeal may:
>
> > (a) affirm or annul the order;
> >
> > (b) reduce or increase the amount or value of any maintenance fixed by the order; or
> >
> > (c) where the order dismissed the application, reverse the dismissal and fix the amount or value of the maintenance.

The Manitoba Act,[3] which formerly contained a simple appeal section, currently contains no appeal section, relying on the appeal section contained in the *Court of Queen's Bench Act*[4]:

> **Appeal to Court of Appeal**
>
> **89.** Unless otherwise provided by statute,
>
> > (a) an order made by the court may be set aside in whole or in part or varied; . . .
>
> on appeal to the Court of Appeal.

Essentially, there is no difference between s. 22 of the Saskatchewan Act, s. 89 of the *Court of Queen's Bench Act* of Manitoba, and the appellate jurisdiction that exists in the provinces with simple appeal sections. Do the words in s. 21(2) of the Alberta Act, "in any manner that in its discretion it considers proper" create a larger appellate jurisdiction? In *Re Edwards Estate*[5] Chief Justice Smith, writing for himself and Justice Kane, wrote:

> In *Re Anderson*, [1934] 2 D.L.R. 484, a case decided under the provisions of the *Widows Relief Act*, R.S.A. 1922, c.145, McGillivray, J.A., delivering the judgment of Harvey, C.J.A., Mitchell, J.A., and himself, said at p. 492:
>
> > As to the submission of counsel for the widow that this Court is not entitled to interfere with the discretion of the trial Judge exercised in favour of the widow, unless it first be shown that he acted upon a wrong principle or misconceived the facts, it is enough to say that in my opinion it is not only the right but the duty of this Court to consider the undisputed facts of this case and to come to its own conclusion as to what is just and equitable in all the circumstances.

---

3 Manitoba *Dependants Relief Act*, S.M. 1989-90, c. 42; C.C.S.M., c. D37 [hereinafter Manitoba Act].

4 S.M. 1988-89, c. 4; C.C.S.M., c. C280, s. 89(a).

5 (1961), 31 D.L.R. (2d) 308 (Alta. C.A.) at 310–11.

In 1934 there was in the *Widows Relief Act* no section such as s. 22 of the *Family Relief Act*, R.S.A. 1955, c.109, which reads as follows:

> **22.** (1) An appeal lies to the Appellate Division of the Supreme Court of Alberta from any order made under this Act.
>
> (2) The Appellate Division upon such appeal may affirm, annul or vary the order in such manner as in its discretion it deems proper.

In view of the provisions of that section, I am quite satisfied that on an appeal under the latter Act the Appellate Division is entitled to interfere with the discretion of the trial Judge without it being shown that he acted on a wrong principle or misconceived the facts and that it is not only the right but the duty of the Court to consider the facts of the case and to come to its conclusion as to what is just and equitable in the circumstances.

Again in *Re Randle*[6] the Alberta Court of Appeal reiterated the point of view expressed in *Anderson* and *Edwards*.

Chief Justice Smith's view was echoed in *Pope v. Stevens* regarding the simple appeal section in the then *Testator's Family Maintenance Act* of Manitoba.[7] Justice Montague spoke for his colleagues on this point:

> Counsel for the respondents, however, submitted that this court should not interfere with an award made in his discretion by the trial judge. With this I cannot agree.
>
> In *Walker v. McDermott* [1931] SCR 94 (reversing [1930] 1 WWR 332, 42 BCR 184) Rinfret, J., though dissenting from the judgment of the other members of the court, delivered by Duff, J. and which did not deal with the point now being considered by me, said at p. 99:
>
> > "It need not be said, however, that such discretion, although perhaps elastic, must be exercised judicially and according to legal rules. The 'opinion of the judge before whom the application is made' is not in every respect to be held final and conclusive. There are cases when a court of appeal may and should intervene. Failure on the part of the judge of first instance to take the proper view of the scope and application of the Act would be one of those cases."
>
> In *In re Anderson Estate* [1934] 1 WWR 430, where the same point was raised, McGillivray, J.A. said, at p.439:
>
> > ". . . it is enough to say that in my opinion it is not only the right but the duty of this Court to consider the undisputed facts of this case and come to its own conclusion as to what is just and equitable in all the circumstances."

---

6 (1976), 1 Alta. L.R. (2d) 52 (Alta. C.A.) at 58.

7 (1954), 63 Man. R. 162 (Man. C.A.) at 170–71.

> This should be a general rule in appeals from awards made under the Act in question. Here, where there are no reasons for the trial judge's decision, it is particularly applicable.
>
> The question this court has to decide is whether, taking into consideration all the circumstances of the case, adequate provision out of the testator's estate for the proper maintenance and support of his widow has been made by the order of the trial judge.
>
> The onus upon this appeal is, of course, upon the appellant as it was when her application was before the court below. . . . Likewise it is the duty of this court, as it was of the trial judge, to (*a*) first inquire as to the need of maintenance and support; (*b*) consider all relevant circumstances; . . .

Similarly, thus spoke Justice Martland for the Supreme Court of Canada in *Swain v. Dennison*[8] in regard to the simple appeal section in the then *Testator's Family Maintenance Act* of British Columbia:

> In my opinion, in view of the special nature of the provisions of the Act in question and the specific right of appeal which it confers, it is not proper to impose any fetters on the powers of the Court of Appeal in considering appeals under this Act. The entire jurisdiction of the trial judge under this statute is discretionary in character. The relief which may be granted under it is completely dependent on his opinion, first, as to whether adequate provision for proper maintenance and support has been provided for the spouse and children under the will, and second, if adequate provision is not thought to be made, as to what provision should be made. Notwithstanding this, the Act, by s. 14, gives to any party deeming himself to be prejudicially affected, a right to appeal. I construe s. 14 as meaning that any person who considers himself prejudicially affected by the discretion exercised by the trial judge has a right to appeal, and, in consequence, the Act must contemplate a review of that discretion by the Court of Appeal. This being so, that Court has the power and the duty to review the circumstances and reach its own conclusion as to the discretion properly to be exercised.[9]

---

8 (1966), [1967] S.C.R. 7 (S.C.C.) at 12–13.

9 See also, *Barker v. Westminster Trust Co.* (1941), 57 B.C.R. 21 (B.C. C.A.) at 44; *Barr v. Barr* (1971), 25 D.L.R. (3d) 401 (Man. C.A.) at 408; *Garrett v. Zwicker* (1976), 15 N.S.R. (2d) 118 (N.S. C.A.) at paragraph 12; *Bennett v. Morrison* (1976), 16 N.S.R. (2d) 476 (N.S. C.A.) at paragraph 5; *Nelson v. Nelson* (1977), 17 N.B.R. (2d) 457 (N.B. C.A.) at paragraph 12; *Coolen v. Coolen* (1980), 43 N.S.R. (2d) 67 (N.S. C.A.) at paragraph 7; *Morris v. Morris* (1982), 41 B.C.L.R. 239 (B.C. C.A.) at 253, leave to appeal refused (1983), 48 N.R. 79n (S.C.C.); *Lynds v. Lynds* (1986), 73 N.B.R. (2d) 296 (N.B. C.A.) at paragraph 20; *Cook v. Hrychuk* (1989), 71 Sask. R. 303 (Sask. C.A.) at paragraph 8; *Plut v. Plut Estate* (1991), 41 E.T.R. 49 (B.C. C.A.) at paragraph 12; *Currie v. Currie Estate* (1995), 166 N.B.R. (2d) 144 (N.B. C.A.) at paragraph 10; *Hutton v. Lapka Estate* (1991), 62 B.C.L.R. (2d) 371 (B.C. C.A.) at paragraph 34, leave to appeal refused (1992), 68 B.C.L.R. (2d) xxxi (S.C.C.).

And, most recently, Justice McLachlin in *Tataryn v. Tataryn Estate*[10] said:

> For the purposes of [the Wills Variation Act] an appellate tribunal is in the same position as the trial judge; deference to the findings of the trial judge is not required except on matters based on oral testimony: *Swain v. Dennison* . . .

Cautionary statements have been made on several occasions. In *Edwards Estate*,[11] above, Justice Johnson, who dissented, said:

> At the trial the appellant sought to prove that she had been compelled to leave her husband because of his cruelty. No doubt this evidence was much the same as she gave when trying to obtain a judicial separation from the husband. The fact that it did not impress the Judge on that occasion is, of course, immaterial. It does, however, point up the fact that it was open to the learned trial Judge who saw and heard her give this evidence in the present case, to reject her evidence in whole or in part. I think it is implicit in the dismissal of her claim that he did not accept her evidence in full. The learned trial Judge had the advantage of seeing and hearing the appellant give her evidence, and while it may be that under s. 22(2) quoted in the judgment of the Chief Justice, this Court is given wider powers than exercised by it on other appeals, the obvious advantage of seeing and hearing the witness (where credibility is so important and the testator cannot be present to give his version) should make an appeal Court very reluctant to disturb an order which has been made and I would not do so in this case.

In *Stadnyk v. Bulycz*[12] Justice Culliton for the Saskatchewan Court of Appeal said:

> The order made by the learned chamber judge was one in which he was entitled, and in fact he was bound, to exercise his own discretion, and having done so, that discretion should not be interfered with except on proper grounds. The principles by which that discretion may be disturbed, were, in my opinion, clearly stated by Robertson, C.J.O. in *Re Blackwell* [1948], 3 D.L.R. 621, at p. 624 when he said:

---

10 [1994] 2 S.C.R. 807 (S.C.C.) at 813, reconsideration refused (1994), 95 B.C.L.R. (2d) xxxiii (S.C.C.), noted in *Chernecki v. Vangolen* (1996), 28 B.C.L.R. (3d) 33 (B.C. C.A.) at paragraph 46 and *Crerar v. Crerar Estate* (1997), 40 B.C.L.R. (3d) 274 (B.C. S.C.) at paragraph 26, varied (1998), 111 B.C.A.C. 194 (B.C. C.A.). In *Moore v. Moore Estate* (1994), 93 B.C.L.R. (2d) 64 (B.C. C.A.) at paragraph 13, the Court accepted the *Swain* statement of the law, but wondered in paragraph 14 whether it reflected the current view of the Supreme Court of Canada. The subsequent *Tataryn* statement obviously indicated that the Court has not changed its mind.

11 *Supra* note 5 at 318.

12 (1961), 36 W.W.R. 680 (Sask. C.A.) at 682.

> "We should interfere only where he has taken into consideration matters that, under the statute, should not be considered, or has taken an improper view of the purpose, scope or application of the Act, or is otherwise plainly wrong."

A somewhat similar view was adopted by the British Columbia court of appeal in *In Re Dupaul* 56 BCR 532.[13]

Similarly, in *Sloane v. Bartley*[14] Justice Huband in dissent said:

> 25 Under what circumstances ought this court to intervene?
>
> 26 Obviously, where the Chambers judge misconceives the principles of law involved, or acts upon a wrong principle, or misapplies a principal relative to the particular facts of the case, then an appellate court's intervention is invited. In my view, however, none of these circumstances exist in the present case. The learned Chambers judge was familiar with the broad concepts of law in relation to *Testators Family Maintenance Act* applications.
>
> 29 The learned Chambers judge was fully acquainted with the legal authorities, and expressly stated that he could do no more than ". . . attempt to carry out the direction of the Privy Council in the *Bosch* case . . .". In the pursuit of that objective he awarded the applicant, Edra Sloane, the sum of $15,000.00, leaving the balance of the estate to be divided between the applicant's two sisters, each of whom would receive approximately twice the amount awarded to the applicant.
>
> 30 The learned Chambers judge also reviewed a number of decision of the Manitoba courts, and from them extracted a set of guidelines which the courts attempt to follow in resolving applications under the *Testator's Family Maintenance Act*. The learned Chambers judge enumerated those guidelines. . . .
>
> 31 No one has quarrelled with the delineation of guidelines by the learned Chambers judge. This is not a case where the learned Chambers judge has misconceived the principles involved. Nor is it a case where the learned Chambers judge acted on a wrong principle.
>
> . . . . .
>
> 33 . . . I can only conclude that the learned Chambers judge did not misapply the principles of law in reaching the decision to intervene for the benefit of the applicant, under the particular circumstances of the present case.
>
> 34 Nor, in my opinion, does the question of onus enter into the matter. The applicant tendered evidence. That evidence, which was never challenged,

---

13 *Ibid.* at 682. See also, *Re Hull,* [1943] O.R. 778 (Ont. C.A.) at 785, *Chernoff v. Chernoff* (1962), 33 D.L.R. (2d) 742 (Sask. C.A.), and *Black v. Kronberger Estate* (1990), 83 Sask. R. 73 (Sask. C.A.); *Dunn v. Dunn Estate* (1993), 12 O.R. (3d) 601 (Ont. Div. Ct.) at 604.

14 (1980), 7 Man. R. (2d) 222 (Man. C.A.) at 229–34.

> demonstrated that the applicant was as loving and dutiful towards her mother as her two sisters, that her economic condition was comparable to the others, and that there was no valid reason known to the applicant why her mother should treat her differently. There was ample evidence before the learned Chambers judge to justify his decision to make an award, and the magnitude of that award.
>
> 35 Aside from an identifiable error in the application of law, an appellate court does have the right to substitute its discretion for that of the learned Chambers judge under certain circumstances. When the gloss is removed from the present case, it comes down to this; should this court substitute its discretionary decision for that of the learned Chambers judge? In my opinion, no such substitution should take place unless it is perfectly clear that the discretion exercised by the learned Chambers judge was wrongly exercised.
>
> . . . . .
>
> 39 In my opinion, the discretion of the learned chambers judge was properly exercised. Even if I thought differently, I could not conclude that it is "perfectly clear" that the discretion was exercised wrongly.

The situation in Ontario at the Divisional Court level is not crystal clear. Arguably, the statements made in *Re Blackwell*, quoted in *Stadnyk v. Bulycz*, above, and *Re Hull*[15] have been superceded by *Swain v. Dennison*, above. However, in *McMacken v. McMacken*,[16] the court said:

> The appeal must be allowed. *Normally this matter would be sent back for a new hearing*. However, we are conscious of the expenses of another hearing as this is not a large claim or a large estate. Furthermore, everything that was before the court below is before us and there is no issue of credibility. We are in as good a position as the court below to consider the evidence and draw the proper inferences.
>
> We will therefore address ourselves to the issue of dependency and attempt to bring this matter to an end. (Emphasis added)

In the Ontario Act the initial appeal is to the Divisional Court.[17] A Divisional Court decision can be appealed to the Court of Appeal "on a question that is not a question of fact alone, with leave".[18] This explains the disposition of the appeal in *Re Mannion*:[19]

> There being no error of law disclosed, this Court is without jurisdiction on an appeal from the Divisional Court to review the adequacy of the provision made

15 *Supra* note 12.
16 (1984), 47 O.R. (2d) 701 (Ont. Div. Ct.) at 703–04.
17 s. 76.
18 *Courts of Justice Act*, R.S.O. 1990, c. C.43, s. 6(1)(a).
19 (1984), 45 O.R. (2d) 339 (Ont. C.A.) at 343.

by the trial judge as varied by the Divisional Court, which remains a pure question of fact.

9

The Supreme Court of Canada: An Historical Note

There have been twelve dependants' relief appeals entertained by the Supreme Court of Canada. Although they are appropriately referenced in the preceding chapters, this brief note may be of some interest. Chronologically, the first case is obsolete. *McBratney v. McBratney*[1] had to do with the initial dependants' relief Act of Alberta, the *Married Women's Relief Act*,[2] which provided that a widow could apply for relief if her husband died leaving a will pursuant to which she would receive less than if he had died intestate. The Act provided that ". . . the Court may make such allowance . . . as may be just and equitable in the circumstances".[3] The Court decided, reversing the trial judge and the 2-2 divided Court of Appeal, that the Court's jurisdiction was limited to awarding the widow's intestate share.

The second case, *Walker v. McDermott*,[4] is the most significant dependants' relief decision ever made by the Supreme Court. *Inter alia*, the Court commented that the court's need-maintenance jurisdiction is not limited to providing dependants with "the bare necessities of existence" and that the court should provide a dependant with a standard of living to which the dependant was or could have been accustomed. The deceased husband-father's estate, which he left to his widow, was modest in size; the daughter applicant could fend for herself as a stenographer and the court detailed the financial security which she currently enjoyed from her husband's income and assets; she had no moral claim to her father's estate other than being his daughter. In this light the Court's ordering an award for her, reversing the Court of Appeal of British Columbia and restoring the trial judgment, established that there was, in addition to the need-maintenance aspect, a moral aspect. For some courts this was developed to take care of a moral claim a dependant might have, principally based upon a contribution to the

1 (1919), 59 S.C.R. 550 (S.C.C.).

2 S.A. 1910, c. 18 (2nd Sess.).

3 *Supra* note 1 at 551.

4 (1930), [1931] S.C.R. 94 (S.C.C.).

accumulation of the deceased's estate or to the welfare of the deceased. For some courts the moral aspect also involved an obligation on deceased spouses and parents to give a fair share of the estate to the surviving spouse and children simply on the basis of the spousal or parental relationship. *Walker v. McDermott* continues to be of fundamental importance.

The third case, *Re Shaw Estate*,[5] was a decision similar to *McBratney* in connection with the *Dependants Relief Act* of Saskatchewan. The Court gave the widow the opportunity to pursue her application in the trial court to prove that her husband in his will had not made reasonable provision for her. Eventually, this resulted in the fourth case, *Shaw v. Regina (City)*,[6] in which the Supreme Court affirmed the decision of the Court of Appeal. It is the Court of Appeal decision, *Shaw v. Regina (City)*,[7] which is the more significant decision; it is the leading pre-*Tataryn* decision for Saskatchewan.

The next decision, *Meyer v. Capital Trust Corp.*[8] has gone by the board. It had to do with whether the marital relationship of the deceased and the applicant came within s. 7 of the *Dependants' Relief Act, 1929*[9] of Ontario, which required judges to inquire into and consider a number of specified matters and "(*g*) generally any other matters which the judge deems should be fairly taken into account". The specificity of the current Ontario Act supercedes this decision.

Case number six was *Kerslake v. Gray.*[10] It decided that the proceeds of a life insurance policy do not form part of the estate insofar as a dependants' relief application is concerned.

McCarvill v. Jones,[11] the seventh appeal, is generally an unremarkable case, affirming the decision of the British Columbia Court of Appeal. Going by Amighetti's treatment of the case the more significant decisions were made in the lower courts.

Swain v. Dennison[12] is memorable for the Court's affirmation that the jurisdiction of a court of appeal in dependants' relief proceedings comprises "the power and the duty to review the circumstances and reach its own conclusion as to the discretion properly to be exercised".

Downton v. Royal Trust Co.[13] had to do with whether a wife, who had agreed to her husband obtaining a foreign divorce, which was not recog-

---

5 [1942] S.C.R. 513 (S.C.C.).
6 (1944), [1945] S.C.R. 42 (S.C.C.).
7 (1943), [1944] 1 W.W.R. 433 (Sask. C.A.).
8 [1948] S.C.R. 329 (S.C.C.) at 311.
9 S.O. 1929, c. 47.
10 [1957] S.C.R. 516 (S.C.C.).
11 [1962] S.C.R. 273 (S.C.C.).
12 (1966), [1967] S.C.R. 7 (S.C.C.) at 12–13.
13 (1972), [1973] S.C.R. 437 (S.C.C.).

nized in Newfoundland, was precluded by her agreement from asserting her status as the lawful wife of her deceased husband. The Court decided in favour of the wife.

The tenth appeal was *Gilles v. Althouse*,[14] which is the authority for the construction of limitation and distribution suspension sections of the various dependants' relief Acts to mean that the personal representative of a deceased cannot make a distribution within the limitation period, even before notice of an application is served.

The penultimate case to date is *Kiss v. Palachik*.[15] It was an appeal of a decision in favour of a widower based upon constructive trust and s. 62(1)(h) and (i) of the current Ontario Act. The Supreme Court of Canada dismissed the appeal, deciding the case entirely on the basis of constructive trust, while simply agreeing "that the award can also be fully justified under . . . [s. 62(1)(h) and (i)]".

The most recent case, *Tataryn v. Tataryn Estate*,[16] is the leading decision for the British Columbia *Wills Variation Act*. The Court clarified the primary jurisdiction. The extent to which *Tataryn* becomes a leading case in the rest of Canada remains to be seen.

---

14 (1975), [1976] 1 S.C.R. 353 (S.C.C.).

15 [1983] 1 S.C.R. 623 (S.C.C.) at 639.

16 [1994] 2 S.C.R. 807 (S.C.C.), reconsideration refused 95 B.C.L.R. (2d) xxxiii (S.C.C.).

Appendix

Comparison of Dependants' Relief Legislation in Canada

1. Dependants Entitled to Apply

Province or Territory	*Statute*	*Dependants Entitled to Apply*
ALBERTA	**Family Relief Act**, R.S.A. 1980, c.F-2	(i) spouse; (ii) child under 18; (iii) child 18 or older and unable by reason of mental or physical disability to earn a livelihood. (s. 1)
BRITISH COLUMBIA	**Wills Variation Act**, R.S.B.C. 1996, c.490	(i) wife, husband; (ii) children; (s. 2)
MANITOBA	**Dependants Relief Act**, S.M. 1989-90, c. 42; C.C.S.M. c. D37	(i) spouse; (ii) child, including *loco parentis*, but not foster, under 18 or older who by reason of illness, disability or other cause was at the time of deceased's death unable to withdraw from the charge of the deceased or to provide himself or herself with the necessaries of life or who was substantially dependant on the deceased; (iii) co-habitee in various specified circumstances; (iv) parent, grandparent, sibling grandchild, who was substantially dependant on the deceased. (s. 1)
NEW BRUNSWICK	**Provision for Dependants Act**, R.S.N.B. 1973, c. P-22.3	(i) wife, husband; (ii) child; (iii) any other dependant as defined by s. 111 of the *Family Services Act*, which includes co-habitees and parents in specified circumstances. (s. 1)

Province or Territory	*Statute*		*Dependants Entitled to Apply*
NEWFOUND-LAND	**Family Relief Act**, R.S.N. 1990, c. F-3	(i)	widow, widower;
		(ii)	child. (s. 2)
NORTHWEST TERRITORIES	**Dependants Relief Act**, R.S.N.W.T. 1988 c. D-4	(i)	spouse;
		(ii)	child, including stepchild, under 19 or older and unable by reason of physical or mental disability to earn a livelihood;
		(iii)	foster parent;
		(iv)	cohabitee in a couple of circumstances. (s. 1)
NOVA SCOTIA	**Testators' Family Maintenance Act**, R.S.N.S. 1989, c. 465	(i)	widow, widower;
		(ii)	child. (s. 2)
ONTARIO	**Succession Law Reform Act**, Part V, R.S.O. 1990, c. 488.	(i)	spouse;
		(ii)	child, including *loco parentis*, but not foster;
		(iii)	ex-spouse;
		(iv)	co-habitee in a couple of circumstances;
		(v)	parent, grandparent;
		(vi)	sibling;
		(vii)	grandchild; —all dependants required to be persons to whom the deceased was providing support or was under a legal obligation to provide support immediately
		(viii)	before death; (s. 57) various agencies providing a benefit under the *Family Benefits Act* or the *General Welfare Assistance Act*. (s. 58(3))

Province or Territory	*Statute*		*Dependants Entitled to Apply*
PRINCE EDWARD ISLAND	**Dependants of a Deceased Person Relief Act**, R.S. P.E.I. 1988, c. D-7	(i)	widow, widower;
		(ii)	child under 18 or older and unable by reason of mental or physical disability to earn a livelihood;
		(iii)	grandparent, parent, descendant, and who for at least 3 years before death was dependant for maintenance and support;
		(iv)	co-habitee in specified circumstances. (s. 1)
SASKAT-CHEWAN	**Dependants' Relief Act, 1996**, S.S. 1996, c. D-25.01	(i)	wife, husband;
		(ii)	child under 18 or older and unable by reason of physical or mental disability to earn a livelihood or by reason of need or other circumstances ought to receive a greater share;
		(iii)	co-habitee in a couple of circumstances. (s. 2)
YUKON TERRITORY	**Dependants Relief Act**, R.S.Y.T. 1990, C.44	(i)	widow, widower;
		(ii)	child under 16 or older and unable by reason of physical or mental disability to earn a livelihood;
		(iii)	divorced spouse, grandparent, parent, or descendant who for at least three years immediately prior to death was dependant for maintenance and support;
		(iv)	co-habitee in specified circumstances. (s. 1)

All of the Acts, except the Sask. Act, provide that an application by any dependant may be treated as an application by all the dependants: B.C. s. 4(1); Alta. s. 16(1)(b); Man. s. 4; Ont. s. 60(2); N.B. s. 15; N.S. s. 15; P.E.I. s. 2; Nfld. s. 15; N.W.T. s. 2; Y.T. s. 4.

2. Testate, Intestate; Primary Jurisdiction

Province or Territory	*Testate/Intestate*	*Primary Jurisdiction*
ALBERTA	both s.3	If a person . . . dies . . . without making . . . adequate provision for proper maintenance and support . . . the judge . . . may . . . order such provision as he considers adequate . . . for . . . proper maintenance and support . . .
BRITISH COLUMBIA	testate only s. 2	. . . if a testator dies leaving a will which does not make adequate provision for the proper maintenance and support . . . the court may . . . order . . . the provision . . . it thinks adequate, just and equitable . . . (s. 2(1))
MANITOBA	both s. 2(2)	If . . . a dependant is in financial need, the court . . . may order reasonable provision . . . (s. 2(1))
NEW BRUNSWICK	both s.2	Where a person dies . . . without making . . . adequate provision for . . . proper maintenance and support . . . the judge . . . may . . . order such provision as the judge considers adequate . . . for . . . proper maintenance and support . . . (s. 2(1))
NEWFOUND-LAND	both s.3	Where a person . . . dies . . . without having made . . . adequate provision for . . . proper maintenance and support . . . a judge . . . may . . . order . . . adequate provision . . . for . . . proper maintenance and support . . . (s. 3(1))
NORTHWEST TERRITORIES	both s.2	Where a person . . . dies . . . .without making . . . adequate provision for . . . proper maintenance and support . . . a judge . . . may . . . order . . . provision . . . the judge considers adequate . . . for . . . proper maintenance and support . . . (s. 2(1))

Province or Territory	*Testate/Intestate*	*Primary Jurisdiction*
NOVA SCOTIA	testate only s.2	Where a testator dies without having made adequate provision . . . for . . . proper maintenance and support . . . a judge . . . has power . . . to order . . . whatever provision the judge deems adequate . . . for proper maintenance and support . . . (s. 3(1))
ONTARIO	both s. 58	Where a deceased . . . has not made adequate provision for . . . proper support . . . the court . . . may order . . . such provision as it considers adequate . . . for . . . proper support . . . (s. 58(1))
PRINCE EDWARD ISLAND	both s.1(b)	Where a deceased has not made adequate provision for . . . proper maintenance and support . . . a court . . . may order . . . such provision . . . it considers adequate . . . for . . . proper maintenance and support (s. 2)
SASKAT-CHEWAN	both s. 2(3)	. . . if . . . reasonable provision has not been made for . . . maintenance . . . the court may order . . . maintenance . . . that the court considers reasonable (s. 6(1))
YUKON TERRITORY	both s. 1	Where a deceased has not made adequate provision for . . . proper maintenance and support . . . the . . . Court . . . may order . . . such provision . . . it considers adequate . . . for proper maintenance and support (s. 2)

3. Limitation Period; Stay of Distribution

Province or Territory	*Limitation Period*	*Stay of Distribution*
ALBERTA	6 mos. s. 15(1)	ss. 17-18
BRITISH COLUMBIA	6 mos. s. 10	s. 11
MANITOBA	6 mos. s. 6(1)	s. 7

Province or Territory	*Testate/Intestate*	*Primary Jurisdiction*
NEW BRUNSWICK	4 mos. 2. 14(1)	s. 8
NEWFOUNDLAND	6 mos. s. 14	s. 9
NORTHWEST TERRITORIES	6 mos. s. 13	s. 8
NOVA SCOTIA	6 mos. s. 14(1)	s. 9
ONTARIO	6 mos. s. 61(1)	s. 67
PRINCE EDWARD ISLAND	6 mos. s. 13(1)	s. 9
SASKATCHEWAN	6 mos. s. 4(1)	ss. 17-18
YUKON TERRITORY	6 mos. s. 14(1)	s. 9

All of the Acts, except the B.C. Act, provide for late applications if the estate has not been fully administered: Alta. s. 15(2); Sask. s. 4(2); Man. s. 6(3); Ont. s. 61(2); N.B. s. 14(2); N.S. s. 14(2); P.E.I. s. 13(2); Nfld. s. 14(2); N.W.T. s. 13(2); Y.T. s. 14(2).

The Acts of B.C. s. 4(1); Man. s. 4; Ont. s. 61(2); N.B. s. 15; P.E.I. s. 4(2); Nfld. s. 15; and Y.T., s. 4 provide that an application made in time by any dependant includes all dependants.

4. Reasonable Advances; Interim Distribution

(i) The Acts of Alta. s. 17; Sask. s. 17; Man. s. 7; Ont. s. 67; N.S. s. 9; P.E.I. s. 9; N.W.T. s. 8; and Y.T. s. 9 allow a personal representative to make reasonable advances to dependants who are beneficiaries.

(ii) The Alta., Sask., Man., Ont., N.S., P.E.I., and Y.T. sections enable interim distribution either with the consent of all parties entitled to apply for a relief order or by court order. The N.W.T. section enables an interim distribution only by court order. The B.C. Act, s. 12, enables interim distribution either with the consent of all parties entitled to apply for a relief order or by court order; but, it is silent respecting advances.

(iii) The N.B. and Nfld. Acts are silent on advances and interim distribution.

5. Assets Available for Relief Orders

(i) All of the Acts in the primary jurisdiction section provide for a relief order to be made "out of the estate", meaning the net estate available for distribution to the heirs or beneficiaries. Only the Sask. Act defines "estate".

(ii) The Acts of Ont. s. 72; P.E.I. ss. 19-20; N.W.T. s. 19; and Y.T. s. 20 provide for various other non-estate transactions to be taken into account for the purposes of valuing the estate and being available to be charged for payment of a relief order.

(iii) All of the Acts, except those of B.C. and Man., contain a section exempting property devised or bequeathed to fulfill a contract, to the extent that the value of the property does not exceed the consideration therefor: Alta. s. 12; Sask. s. 10; Ont. s. 71; N.B. s. 16; N.S. s. 16; P.E.I. s. 14; Nfld. s. 16; N.W.T. s. 14; Y.T. s. 15.

6. Type of Relief Orders

(i) All of the Acts provide for lump sum or periodic payment orders and all but the B.C. Act provide for orders transferring specified property: B.C. s. 7; Alta. s. 5(3), (4); Sask. s. 7; Man. s. 9(2), (3); Ont. s. 63(2), (3); N.B. s. 5(3), (4); N.S. s. 6(2), (3); P.E.I. s. 6(2), (3); Nfld. s. 6(3), (4); N.W.T. s. 5(3), (4); Y.T. s. 6(2), (3). Maybe "or other payment" in s. 7 of the B.C. Act includes a specified property transfer order.

(ii) The Sask. Act, s. 9, contains a unique section providing for the creation of a trust fund for children 18 years of age or older to enhance their quality of life without effecting their entitlement to public assistance.

7. Conditions and Restrictions; Incidence

All of the Acts empower the court to impose conditions and restrictions on a relief order and to determine whether the incidence of a relief order is to fall on only specified assets as opposed to ratably on the whole estate: B.C. ss. 6, 8-10; Alta. ss. 5(1) and (2), 8-9; Sask. ss. 61(2), (3), 11-13; Man. ss. 9(1), 10, 12; Ont. ss. 63(1), 66, 68, 69; N.B. ss. 4, 5(1), (2), 7, 10, 12; N.S. ss. 6(1), (2), 8, 10; P.E.I. ss. 6(1), 8, 10, 11; Nfld. ss. 6(1), (2), 8, 10; N.W.T. ss. 5(1), (2), 7, 9, 10; Y.T. ss. 6(1), 10, 12.

8. Suspensory, Interim Relief and Variation Orders

Suspensory

All of the Acts, except the B.C. and Sask. Acts, provide for suspensory orders: Alta. s. 3(4); Man. s. 3; Ont. s. 59; N.B. s. 2(2); N.S. s. 3(2); P.E.I. s. 3; Nfld. s. 3(2); N.W.T. s. 2(2); Y.T. s. 3.

Interim Relief Orders

Only the Acts of Man. s. 11 and Ont. s. 64, empower interim relief orders, not to be confused with reasonable advances and interim distribution (orders).

Variation

All of the Acts provide for discharge, variation, or suspension of relief orders: B.C. s. 14; Alta. s. 6(6); Sask. s. 20; Man. ss. 14-15; Ont. s. 65; N.B. s. 6; N.S. s. 7; P.E.I. s. 7; Nfld. s. 7; N.W.T. s. 6; Y.T. s. 7.

9. Invalidity of Mortgaging, Assigning an Anticipated Relief Order

All of the Acts, except the Nova Scotia Act, contain a section declaring void a mortgage, charge or assignment of an anticipated relief provision: B.C. s. 13; Alta. s. 10; Sask. 19; Man. 17; Ont. s. 73; N.B. s. 17; P.E.I. s. 15; Nfld. s. 17; N.W.T. s. 15; Y.T. s. 16.

10. Filing

All of the Acts, except those of B.C. and Man., contain a section requiring a certified copy of any order to be filed with either the clerk or registrar of the Supreme Court or of the court from which letters probate or of administration are issued: Alta. s. 20; Sask. s. 16; Ont. s. 70; N.B. s. 13; N.S. s. 13; P.E.I. s. 12; Nfld. s. 13; N.W.T. s. 12; Y.T. s. 13.

The B.C. Act, s. 11, requires an order to be registered as a charge against any land affected.

11. Enforcement

All of the Acts, except the B.C. Act, contain a common section providing for enforcement of orders "in the same way and by the same means" as any other judgment of the court: Alta. s. 19; Sask. s. 23(1); Man. s. 16(1); Ont. s. 77(1); N.B. s. 19; N.S. s. 18; P.E.I. s. 18(1); Nfld. s. 18(1); N.W.T. s. 18; Y.T. s. 19(1).

12. Appeal

All of the Acts, except the Manitoba Act, contain an appeal section: B.C. s. 15; Alta. s. 21; Sask. s. 22; Ont. s. 76; N.B. s. 18; N.S. s. 19; P.E.I. s. 17; Nfld. s. 19; N.W.T. s. 16; Y.T. s. 18. For Manitoba an appeal is available by s. 89 of the *Queen's Bench Act*.

13. Miscellaneous Provisions

(i) The Alta. Act, s. 2, contains a presumption of death section which provides that, if the spouse of a presumed dead spouse re-marries, has more children, and the presumed dead spouse is alive, the remarried spouse and their children have "the same rights under this Act" as they would have had had the presumed dead spouse actually been dead. The Sask. Act, s. 2(2) contains a similar section.

(ii) The Acts of Ont. s. 63(4); N.S. s. 16(2); P.E.I. s. 16; and Y.T. s. 17 void *waivers* of the Act; by common law waivers do not bar applications in the other provinces. But, by common law in all provinces a waiver is a relevant circumstance.

(iii) The Acts generally provide for a court to consider all the circumstances. The Acts of Sask. s. 8; Man. s. 8; Ont. s. 62; N.S. s. 5; and Nfld. s. 5 provide more specificity in varying degrees of detail. All of the Acts, except the Man. Act, provide for disqualifying character or conduct of a dependant to be considered: B.C. s. 6(6); Alta. s. 3(5); Sask. s. 8(6); Ont. s. 62(1)(r); N.B. s. 2(3); N.S. s. 5(1)(a); P.E.I. s. 5(1)(d); Nfld. s. 5(1)(a); N.W.T. s. 4(1)(d); and Y.T. s. 5(1)(d).

(iv) The Acts of Man. s. 2(3) and Ont. s. 58(4) stipulate the date of the hearing as the date for the assessment of the circumstances of an application. By common law in the other provinces the assessment date is either the date of the deceased's death or the date of the hearing.

(v) The Man. Act, s. 13, contains a conflict of laws section, which restricts the court to dealing with applications respecting immovables situated in the province and movables if the deceased died domiciled in the province. In other provinces courts on their own have similarly restricted their jurisdiction.

(vi) The Acts of B.C. s. 11; Alta. s. 11(1); Sask. s. 15; Nfld. s. 11; and N.W.T. s. 11 stipulate the effect of a relief order on a will, namely that the will is to be read as if it contained the relief order. Surely, this goes without saying everywhere.

Bibliography

MONOGRAPHS

Amighetti, L., *The Law of Dependants' Relief in British Columbia* (Toronto: Carswell, 1991).

Feeney, T., *The Canadian Law of Wills, Probate,* Ch. 9 "Support of Dependants: Dependants' Relief (Family Maintenance) Legislation", 3rd ed. (Toronto and Vancouver: Butterworths, 1987).

Holland W., and Stalbecker-Pountney, B., *Cohabitation: The Law in Canada*, Ch. 4 "Death" (Toronto: Carswell, 1990).

Hull, R. and Hull, I., eds., *Macdonell, Sheard and Hull on Probate Practice*, Ch. 6 "Support of Dependants", 4th ed. (Toronto: Carswell, 1996).

Hull, R., *Support of Dependants under The Succession Law Reform Act of Ontario* (Toronto: Carswell, 1978).

Mellows, *Law of Succession*, 5th ed. by C. Margrave-Jones, Ch. 14 "Restrictions on Testamentary Freedom" (London: Butterworths, 1993).

Oosterhoff, A., *Oosterhoff on Wills and Succession*, Ch. 17 "Support of Dependants", 4th ed. 1995.

Oosterhoff, A., *Succession Law Reform in Ontario* (Toronto: Carswell, 1979) pp. 89-122.

ANNOTATIONS, ARTICLES, COMMENTS

Amighetti, L., "Tataryn v. Tataryn" (1995) 14 E.T.J. 277.

Bale, G., "Bates v. Bates, Testators Family Maintenance Legislation and Actuarial Evidence in Determining an Award" (1981) 9 E.T.R. 236.

Bale, G., "Annual Survey" (1968) 3 Ott. L.R. 654.

Bale, G., "Annual Survey" (1971) 5 Ott. L.R. 568.

Bale, G., "Limitation on Testamentary Dispositions in Canada" (1964) 42 C.B.R. 367.

Bale, G., "Maldaver v. Canada Permanent Trust Co., Power to Vary Orders Under Testator's Family Maintenance Legislation and the Relevant Date to Determine Adequacy on an Initial Application" (1982-83) 12 E.T.R. 231.

Bale, G., "Morris v. Morris, Duty Owed to Able-Bodied Adult Children under Testator's Family Maintenance Legislation and Need to Adopt an Objective Approach" (1983-84) 14 E.T.R. 35.

Bale, G., "Palm Tree Justice and Testator's Family Maintenance—The Continuing Saga of Confusion and Uncertainty in the B.C. Courts" (1987) 26 E.T.R. 295.

Bale, G., "Re Dentinger, Dependants' Relief Legislation and the Changed Emphasis Effected by Part V of The Succession Law Reform Act (Ontario)" (1982) 10 E.T.R. 7.

Bale, G., "Re Osland, Testator's Family Maintenance in British Columbia—Fair Share of Estate or Equitable Maintenance and the Dilemma Still Confronting the Courts by the Supreme Court of Canada Decision in Walker v. McDermott" (1977-78) 1 E.T.R. 129.

Brown, M., "Dependants' Relief Acts" (1940) 18 C.B.R. 261.

Freedman, R., and Berardino, E., "Tataryn v. Tataryn" (1995) 15 E.T.J. 6; also (1994) 52 The Advocate 897.

Goodman, W., "Dependants' Relief—Property Passing Outside of Administered Estate Considered "Estate" for Purposes of Legislation" (1983) 6 E.T.Q. 226.

Gray, V., "Dependants' Relief Legislation" (1939) 17 C.B.R. 233.

Harvey, C., "Checklist for Dependants Relief Proceedings (Manitoba)" (1983) 6 E.T.Q. 254.

Harvey, C., "The Dependants Relief Act, Manitoba" (1990) 19 Man. L.J. 633.

Harvey, C., "Re Bartel" (1982) 6 E.T.Q. 165.

Harvey, C., "The Continuing Relevance for Manitoba of Testators Family Maintenance Act Cases" (1998) 25 Man. L. J. 467.

Henderson, M., "Adequate Provision: Dividing the Family Pie" (1996) 21 L. Now No. 2, 17.

Hoffstein, M., "Support of Dependants—Part V of The Succession Law Reform Act" (1986) 21 E.T.R. 23.

Hull, R., "Support of Dependants Under The Succession Law Reform Act" (1977-78) 1 E.T.R. 145.

Hull, R., and Cullity, M., "The Succession Law Reform Act, 1977: An Overview" (1978) 4 E.T.Q. 366, 376.

Hull, R., "Contracts to Make Wills and Dependants' Relief Legislation" (1974) 1 E.T.Q. 240.

Hunt, J., "Testator's Family Maintenance Act" (1964) Pit. Lects. 38.

Jayne, A., "Re Ducherer, The 'Comparatively Small' Problem of the Dependants' Relief Act and the 'Small Estate'" (1978) 2 E.T.R. 146.

Litman, M., "Maladaver v. Canada Permanent Trust Co., Relevant Date for Determining Adequacy of Provision Made by Testator for Purposes of Dependant Relief Legislation" (1977-78) 1 E.T.R. 41.

Litman, M., "Re Cameron, Limitations on the Use of Future Contingencies in Calculating Awards made Under Dependants Relief Legislation" (1979) 4 E.T.R. 257.

Litman, M., "Survivors of "Marriages of Convenience": Their Status Under Dependant's Relief Legislation" (1979) 4 E.T.R. 17..

McMurtry, H., "Group Life Insurance and the SLRA" (1997) 16 E.T.J. 193.

McRae, D., "Applications under the Dependants' Relief Act of the Province of Ontario" (1971) 19 Chitty's L.J. 332.

McRae, D., "Contracts to Leave Property by Will and Dependants' Relief" (1972) 20 Chitty's L.J. 298.

Norwood, D., "Re Urquhart, Succession Law Reform Act—Group Life Insurance Proceeds—Designated Beneficiary—Conflict of Laws—Domicile" (1993) 12 E.T.J. 3.

Oosterhoff, A., "Re Mannion, Dependants' Support—New Principle Under the Succession Law Reform Act" (1982) 6 E.T.Q. 1.

Oosterhoff, A., "Sloane v. Bartley, Support of Adult Capacitated Dependants" (1980-81) 7 E.T.R. 166.

Oosterhoff, A., "Some Aspects of Support of Dependants" (1982-83) 12 E.T.R. 197.

Oosterhoff, A., "The Effect of Death on Familial Obligations" (1981) 23 R.F.L. (2d) 272.

Schnurr B. and Woodley, S., "Dependant Support Proceedings" (1995) 14 E.T.J. 159.

Simmonds, D., "Succession Law Reform in Ontario: An Old Cat Needs a New Kick" (1991) 10 E.T.J. 297 at 308-310..

Youdan, T., "The Status of a Dependant Under Part V of the Ontario Succession Law Reform Act" (1986) 21 E.T.R. 303.

Index